LINQ in Action

LINQ in Action

FABRICE MARGUERIE
STEVE EICHERT
JIM WOOLEY

MANNING

Greenwich
(74° w. long.)

For online information and ordering of this and other Manning books, please visit
www.manning.com. The publisher offers discounts on this book when ordered in quantity.
For more information, please contact:

> Special Sales Department
> Manning Publications Co.
> Sound View Court 3B   fax: (609) 877-8256
> Greenwich, CT 06830   email: orders@manning.com

Manning Publications Co.   Copyeditor: Benjamin Berg
Sound View Court 3B   Typesetter: Gordan Salinovic
Greenwich, CT 06830   Cover designer: Leslie Haimes

ISBN 1-933988-16-9
Printed in the United States of America
1 2 3 4 5 6 7 8 9 10 – MAL – 13 12 11 10 09 08

brief contents

PART 1 GETTING STARTED 1

    1 ■ Introducing LINQ   3

    2 ■ C# and VB.NET language enhancements   44

    3 ■ LINQ building blocks   82

PART 2 QUERYING OBJECTS IN MEMORY 113

    4 ■ Getting familiar with LINQ to Objects   115

    5 ■ Beyond basic in-memory queries   160

PART 3 QUERYING RELATIONAL DATA 203

    6 ■ Getting started with LINQ to SQL   205

    7 ■ Peeking under the covers of LINQ to SQL   237

    8 ■ Advanced LINQ to SQL features   267

PART 4 MANIPULATING XML 311

    9 ■ Introducing LINQ to XML   313

    10 ■ Query and transform XML with LINQ to XML   350

    11 ■ Common LINQ to XML scenarios   385

PART 5   LINQING IT ALL TOGETHER 435

12 ▪ Extending LINQ   437
13 ▪ LINQ in every layer   482

contents

foreword   xv
preface   xvii
acknowledgments   xix
about this book   xxii

PART 1   GETTING STARTED 1

1   *Introducing LINQ   3*

1.1   What is LINQ?   4

*Overview   5   ▪   LINQ as a toolset   6   ▪   LINQ as language
extensions   7*

1.2   Why do we need LINQ?   9

*Common problems   10   ▪   Addressing a paradigm mismatch   12
LINQ to the rescue   18*

1.3   Design goals and origins of LINQ   19

The goals of the LINQ project   20   ▪   A bit of history   21

1.4   First steps with LINQ to Objects: Querying collections
in memory   23

What you need to get started   23   ▪   Hello LINQ to Objects   25

1.5 First steps with LINQ to XML: Querying XML
documents   29

    Why we need LINQ to XML   30 ▪ *Hello LINQ to XML   32*

1.6 First steps with LINQ to SQL: Querying relational
databases   37

    Overview of LINQ to SQL's features   37 ▪ *Hello LINQ to
SQL   38* ▪ *A closer look at LINQ to SQL   42*

1.7 Summary   42

2 **C# and VB.NET language enhancements   44**

2.1 Discovering the new language enhancements   45

    Generating a list of running processes   46 ▪ *Grouping results
into a class   47*

2.2 Implicitly typed local variables   49

    Syntax   49 ▪ *Improving our example using implicitly
typed local variables   50*

2.3 Object and collection initializers   52

    The need for object initializers   52 ▪ *Collection initializers   53
Improving our example using an object initializer   54*

2.4 Lambda expressions   55

    A refresher on delegates   56 ▪ *Anonymous
methods   58* ▪ *Introducing lambda expressions   58*

2.5 Extension methods   64

    Creating a sample extension method   64 ▪ *More
examples using LINQ's standard query operators   68
Extension methods in action in our example   70
Warnings   71*

2.6 Anonymous types   73

    *Using anonymous types to group data into an object   74
Types without names, but types nonetheless   74
Improving our example using anonymous
types   76* ▪ *Limitations   76*

2.7 Summary   79

3   *LINQ building blocks   82*

3.1   How LINQ extends .NET   83

Refresher on the language extensions   83 ▪ The key elements of the LINQ foundation   85

3.2   Introducing sequences   85

IEnumerable<T>   86 ▪ Refresher on iterators   87 Deferred query execution   89

3.3   Introducing query operators   93

What makes a query operator?   93 ▪ The standard query operators   96

3.4   Introducing query expressions   97

What is a query expression?   98 ▪ Writing query expressions   98 ▪ How the standard query operators relate to query expressions   100 ▪ Limitations   102

3.5   Introducing expression trees   104

Return of the lambda expressions   105 ▪ What are expression trees?   105 ▪ IQueryable, deferred query execution redux   108

3.6   LINQ DLLs and namespaces   109

3.7   Summary   111

PART 2   QUERYING OBJECTS IN MEMORY.................. 113

4   *Getting familiar with LINQ to Objects   115*

4.1   Introducing our running example   116

Goals   116 ▪ Features   117 ▪ The business entities   117 Database schema   118 ▪ Sample data   118

4.2   Using LINQ with in-memory collections   121

What can we query?   121 ▪ Supported operations   126

4.3   Using LINQ with ASP.NET and Windows Forms   126

Data binding for web applications   127 ▪ Data binding for Windows Forms applications   133

4.4   Focus on major standard query operators   137

Where, the restriction operator   138 ▪ *Using projection operators   139* ▪ *Using Distinct   142* ▪ *Using conversion operators   143* ▪ *Using aggregate operators   145*

4.5   Creating views on an object graph in memory   146

Sorting   146 ▪ *Nested queries   147* ▪ *Grouping   150 Using joins   151* ▪ *Partitioning   155*

4.6   Summary   159

5   Beyond basic in-memory queries   160

5.1   Common scenarios   161

Querying nongeneric collections   162 ▪ *Grouping by multiple criteria   164* ▪ *Dynamic queries   167* ▪ *LINQ to Text Files   178*

5.2   Design patterns   180

The Functional Construction pattern   181 ▪ *The ForEach pattern   184*

5.3   Performance considerations   186

Favor a streaming approach   187 ▪ *Be careful about immediate execution   189* ▪ *Will LINQ to Objects hurt the performance of my code?   191* ▪ *Getting an idea about the overhead of LINQ to Objects   195* ▪ *Performance versus conciseness: A cruel dilemma?   198*

5.4   Summary   200

PART 3   QUERYING RELATIONAL DATA 203

6   Getting started with LINQ to SQL   205

6.1   Jump into LINQ to SQL   207

Setting up the object mapping   209 ▪ *Setting up the DataContext   212*

6.2   Reading data with LINQ to SQL   212

6.3   Refining our queries   217

Filtering   217 ▪ *Sorting and grouping   219 Aggregation   221* ▪ *Joining   222*

6.4 Working with object trees 226

6.5 When is my data loaded and why does it matter? 229

    Lazy loading 229 ▪ *Loading details immediately* 231

6.6 Updating data 233

6.7 Summary 236

7 Peeking under the covers of LINQ to SQL 237

7.1 Mapping objects to relational data 238

    Using inline attributes 239 ▪ *Mapping with external XML files* 245 ▪ *Using the SqlMetal tool* 247 ▪ *The LINQ to SQL Designer* 249

7.2 Translating query expressions to SQL 252

    IQueryable 252 ▪ *Expression trees* 254

7.3 The entity life cycle 257

    Tracking changes 259 ▪ *Submitting changes* 260 *Working with disconnected data* 263

7.4 Summary 266

8 Advanced LINQ to SQL features 267

8.1 Handling simultaneous changes 268

    Pessimistic concurrency 268 ▪ *Optimistic concurrency* 269 *Handling concurrency exceptions* 272 ▪ *Resolving conflicts using transactions* 276

8.2 Advanced database capabilities 278

    SQL pass-through: Returning objects from SQL queries 278 *Working with stored procedures* 280 ▪ *User-defined functions* 290

8.3 Improving the business tier 294

    Compiled queries 294 ▪ *Partial classes for custom business logic* 296 ▪ *Taking advantage of partial methods* 299 *Using object inheritance* 301

8.4 A brief diversion into LINQ to Entities 306

8.5 Summary 309

PART 4 MANIPULATING XML 311

9 Introducing LINQ to XML   313

9.1   What is an XML API?   314

9.2   Why do we need another XML programming API?   316

9.3   LINQ to XML design principles   317

Key concept: functional construction   319 ▪ *Key concept: context-free XML creation   320* ▪ *Key concept: simplified names   320*

9.4   LINQ to XML class hierarchy   323

9.5   Working with XML using LINQ   326

Loading XML   327 ▪ *Parsing XML   329* ▪ *Creating XML   330* ▪ *Creating XML with Visual Basic XML literals   335 Creating XML documents   338* ▪ *Adding content to XML   341 Removing content from XML   343* ▪ *Updating XML content   344* ▪ *Working with attributes   347* ▪ *Saving XML   348*

9.6   Summary   349

10 Query and transform XML with LINQ to XML   350

10.1   LINQ to XML axis methods   352

Element   354 ▪ *Attribute   355* ▪ *Elements   356* ▪ *Descendants 357* ▪ *Ancestors   360* ▪ *ElementsAfterSelf, NodesAfterSelf, ElementsBeforeSelf, and NodesBeforeSelf   362* ▪ *Visual Basic XML axis properties   363*

10.2   Standard query operators   366

Projecting with Select   369 ▪ *Filtering with Where   370 Ordering and grouping   372*

10.3   Querying LINQ to XML objects with XPath   376

10.4   Transforming XML   378

LINQ to XML transformations   378 ▪ *Transforming LINQ to XML objects with XSLT   382*

10.5   Summary   383

11 **Common LINQ to XML scenarios 385**

11.1 Building objects from XML 386

Goal 387 ▪ Implementation 389

11.2 Creating XML from object graphs 392

Goal 392 ▪ Implementation 393

11.3 Creating XML with data from a database 398

Goal 399 ▪ Implementation 401

11.4 Filtering and mixing data from a database with XML data 406

Goal 406 ▪ Implementation 407

11.5 Reading XML and updating a database 411

Goal 412 ▪ Implementation 413

11.6 Transforming text files into XML 428

Goal 428 ▪ Implementation 429

11.7 Summary 432

PART 5 LINQING IT ALL TOGETHER 435

12 **Extending LINQ 437**

12.1 Discovering LINQ's extension mechanisms 438

*How the LINQ flavors are LINQ implementations 439
What can be done with custom LINQ extensions 441*

12.2 Creating custom query operators 442

*Improving the standard query operators 443 ▪ Utility or
domain-specific query operators 446*

12.3 Custom implementations of the basic query operators 451

*Refresh on the query translation mechanism 452 ▪ Query
expression pattern specification 453 ▪ Example 1: tracing
standard query operators' execution 455 ▪ Limitation: query
expression collision 457 ▪ Example 2: nongeneric, domain-specific
operators 459 ▪ Example 3: non-sequence operator 461*

12.4   Querying a web service: LINQ to Amazon   463

Introducing LINQ to Amazon   463 ▪ *Requirements   465*
Implementation   467

12.5   IQueryable and IQueryProvider: LINQ to Amazon
advanced edition   474

The IQueryable and IQueryProvider interfaces   474
Implementation   479 ▪ *What happens exactly   480*

12.6   Summary   481

13   *LINQ in every layer*   482

13.1   Overview of the LinqBooks application   483

Features   483 ▪ *Overview of the UI   484* ▪ *The data model   486*

13.2   LINQ to SQL and the data access layer   486

Refresher on the traditional three-tier architecture   487 ▪ *Do we
need a separate data access layer or is LINQ to SQL enough?   488*
Sample uses of LINQ to SQL in LinqBooks   495

13.3   Use of LINQ to XML   502

Importing data from Amazon   502 ▪ *Generating RSS feeds   504*

13.4   Use of LINQ to DataSet   505

13.5   Using LINQ to Objects   509

13.6   Extensibility   509

Custom query operators   509 ▪ *Creating and using a custom LINQ
provider   510*

13.7   A look into the future   511

Custom LINQ flavors   511 ▪ *LINQ to XSD, the typed LINQ to
XML   513* ▪ *PLINQ: LINQ meets parallel computing   513*
*LINQ to Entities, a LINQ interface for the ADO.NET Entity
Framework   514*

13.8   Summary   515

appendix: The standard query operators   517
resources   523
index   527

bonus chapter: Working with LINQ and DataSets
available online only from www.manning.com/LINQinAction

foreword

It's difficult for me to write this foreword, not because the road to LINQ was long and arduous or that I'm teary-eyed, wrought with emotion, or finding it difficult to compose just the right the words for a send-off worthy of a product that I've poured my very soul into. It's difficult because I know that this is going to be a well-respected book and I'm finding it tricky to work in a punch line.

For me the LINQ project started years before anything official, back when I was involved in plotting and scheming over a new managed ADO. Back then, a few very smart developers had the audacity to suggest shucking off the chains of traditional data access APIs and designing around the ubiquity of objects and metadata that were fundamental to the new runtime—the Java runtime. Unfortunately, none of that happened. The traditionalists won, and at the time I was one of them. Yet what I gained from that experience was a perspective that data belongs *at the heart* of any programming system, not bolted on as an afterthought. It made sense that in a system based on objects, data should be objects too. But getting there was going to take overcoming a lot of challenges.

As an engineer, I was at the center of the advancements happening inside Microsoft, designing new APIs and influencing language features that would move us forward. Many of these never made it all the way to shipping products, yet each attempt was a step in the right direction. LINQ is a culmination of these endeavors, of battles fought and lessons learned. It is born out of an accretion of insights from a group of my peers, draws upon existing theories and techniques from computer science at large, and would never have come together without the clear-cut wisdom and attention to detail that is Anders Hejlsberg.

Of course, there were all of you too. LINQ was shaped significantly by the community of developers discussing it on forums and blogs. The ability to receive such immediate feedback was like turning on the lights in a darkened room. It was also energizing to watch as the spark caught fire in so many of you, how you became experts and evangelists, gave talks, wrote articles, and inspired each other.

That's why this book is so important. Fabrice, Jim, and Steve were a large part of that community and have captured its essence within the pages of their book. *LINQ in Action* is a book from the people to the people. It's as if they had decided to throw a party for LINQ and everyone who's anyone showed up.

So read on, enjoy, and don't waste time waiting in line for the punch.

MATT WARREN
PRINCIPAL ARCHITECT
MICROSOFT

preface

I chose software development as the way to make a living mainly because it's a technology that is constantly evolving. There's always something new to learn. No chance of getting bored in this line of work! In addition to learning, I also enjoy teaching software development. Writing *LINQ in Action* was a good opportunity to both learn and teach at the same time.

When we started writing this book, LINQ was still an early prototype. We followed its evolution as it was taking shape. There was a lot to discover and a lot to understand. This is part of a software developer's everyday job. We have to stay up-to-date with the technologies we use and learn new ones as they come out. The software development environment is evolving at an increasingly fast pace, and I don't see any signs that that's going to change.

.NET is a fast-moving environment. Over the last couple of years, we've seen two major releases of the .NET Framework, and several companion technologies have appeared: Windows Presentation Foundation, Windows Communication Foundation, Windows Workflow Foundation, ASP.NET AJAX, Silverlight, and LINQ have joined our developer toolbox. Another trend in .NET is the multiplication of programming languages. F#, which will receive the same support as C# or VB.NET in Visual Studio, introduces functional programming in .NET. Dynamic languages, such as Python and Ruby, are going to be supported by the .NET Dynamic Language Runtime.

In coming years, we'll have to deal with more programming languages than the ones we currently master. An advantage of C#, Visual Basic, and the other .NET languages is that they are constantly adapting. C# and VB.NET have been improved in their latest versions to offer support for language-integrated querying through LINQ.

In addition to offering novel approaches to deal with data, LINQ represents a shift toward declarative and functional programming. When people ask me for reasons to learn LINQ, I tell them that they should learn it in order to be able to use it with XML, relational data, or in-memory collections, but above all to be able to start using declarative programming, deferred execution, and lambda expressions.

Start learning LINQ now! When you do, you'll not only learn how to use this new technology, but you'll also discover where programming is heading. One of our main goals with *LINQ in Action* was to help you fully comprehend the new approaches associated with LINQ.

FABRICE MARGUERIE

acknowledgments

Writing this book was a long process. It gave us the opportunity to have informative discussions with a lot of interesting people, as well as to learn and get input from some very smart individuals. We received help from many different sources—this book would not have been possible without them. Not only that: They also brought out the best in us. The people who contributed to the book in ways both large and small kept pushing us to raise the quality of our work higher and higher. We forgive them now for being so demanding. It was all for a good cause.

First, we'd like to express our gratitude to everyone at Manning. We appreciate the trust they placed in us and their involvement in asking us for our best in this project. A sincere thank-you to our publisher Marjan Bace for his vote of confidence in offering us the opportunity to write this book and to our editor Michael Stephens for being there throughout the process and helping make this project a reality.

Thanks to the editorial team at Manning who worked with us on turning this book into the end product you are now holding in your hands: Cynthia Kane, Mary Piergies, Karen Tegtmeyer, Ron Tomich, Lianna Wlasiuk, Megan Yockey, Benjamin Berg, Gordan Salinovic, Dottie Marsico, Elizabeth Martin, and Tiffany Taylor all guided us and kept us moving in the right direction.

We would also thank the many reviewers of the manuscript, who looked at it in various stages of development and whose thoughtful feedback made this a much better book: Dave Corun, Marius Bancila, Keith Farmer, Curt Christianson, Mark

Monster, Darren Neimke, Jon Skeet, Tomas Restrepo, Javier G. Lozano, Oliver Sturm, Mohammad Azam, Eric Swanson, Keith Hill, Rama Krishna Vavilala, and Bruno Boucard.

Our technical proofreader was Keith Farmer and he did a great job checking the code and making sure it all ran properly shortly before the book went to press. Thanks, Keith.

We'd also like to thank the people from Microsoft with whom we've been in touch: Keith Farmer, Dinesh Kulkarni, Amanda Silver, Erick Thompson, Matt Warren, and Eric White. Their hints and assistance were precious when we were lost in the mysteries of the early LINQ machinery. Special thanks to Matt Warren for agreeing to write the foreword to our book.

We can't forget the subscribers to the Manning Early Access Program (MEAP) who reported errors either through the book's forum or directly in emails, helping us weed out a lot of early mistakes. Michael Vandemore is one such vigilant reader we'd like to acknowledge here.

Thanks again to all of you listed above and below—as well as to any others we may have forgotten to mention: You made it possible!

FABRICE MARGUERIE
When Michael Stephens first contacted me, I knew that writing a book wasn't an easy task, but I also knew that I was ready to take on the challenge. Only now, more than 20 months later, as I'm writing these acknowledgments, do I realize how big the challenge was and how much work was ahead of us.

I'd like to thank Jon Skeet, Troy Magennis, and Eric White for kindly allowing me to use parts of their work in my chapters.

I'm grateful to my co-workers and friends who were kind enough to review portions of the manuscript and provided many useful comments. They include Bruno Boucard, Pierrick Gourlain, Pierre Kovacs, Christophe Menet, and Patrick Smacchia.

Special thanks go to my wife for her patience during this long project. Who else could forgive me for all the extra time I spent in front of my computer during these last months?

Finally, I'd like to extend my thanks to Steve and Jim for their invaluable contributions to the book. They have been excellent partners. Steve and Jim, thank you for joining the project and bringing your talents to it.

STEVE EICHERT

I would like to thank my beautiful wife Christin, and three wonderful children, McKayla, Steven John, and Keegan. Your patience, encouragement, and love are what got me through this project. You continue to inspire me in ways that I never thought possible. Thank you!

JIM WOOLEY

I would like to thank Microsoft for their openness through blogs, forums, and access to tech previews. Without access to these, books like ours would not be possible. I am also appreciative of the support we have received from members of the product teams, particularly Keith Farmer, Matt Warren, and Amanda Silver, as well as the evangelists like Doug Turnure and Joe Healy who support us out in the field and encourage us to do crazy things like write books.

Saving the best for last, I want to thank my family, particularly my wife Sindee, son Daniel, and my parents, who supported me even when it meant sacrificing holidays and weekends to meet publication deadlines. I couldn't have done it without your patience and encouragement.

about this book

Welcome to *LINQ in Action*. This book is an introduction to the Microsoft .NET LINQ technology and the rich toolset that comes with it.

LINQ stands for *Language INtegrated Query*. In a nutshell, it makes query operations like SQL statements into first-class citizens in .NET languages like C# and VB. LINQ offers built-in support for querying in-memory collections such as arrays or lists, XML, DataSets, and relational databases. But LINQ is extensible and can be used to query various data sources.

Our goal with this book is to help developers who have an existing knowledge of the .NET Framework and the C# or VB.NET language to discover the concepts introduced by LINQ and gain a complete understanding of how the technology works, as well as how to make the best of it in their projects.

LINQ in Action covers the entire LINQ spectrum. From Hello World code samples and the new C# 3.0 and VB.NET 9.0 features to LINQ's extensibility and a tour of all the LINQ providers, this book has everything you need to get up to speed with LINQ and to be able to create applications that take advantage of it.

We believe this book provides the right mix of theory and examples. We made sure to keep the focus on the practical side of things, because we think that nothing's better than a hands-on exploration of the technology. Several additions have been made to the C# and VB.NET languages, as well as to the .NET class library. But fear not: These language innovations aren't difficult to grasp when you have the right code sample in front of you.

We'll guide you along as you make your way through this new world where beasts like *lambda expressions*, *query operators*, and *expression trees* live. You'll discover all the basics of LINQ that'll help you form a clear understanding of the complete LINQ toolset. We'll also provide a presentation of the common use cases for all the flavors of LINQ. Whether you want to use LINQ to query objects, XML documents, or relational databases, you'll find all the information you'll need. But we won't stop at the basic code. We'll also show you how LINQ can be used for advanced data processing. This includes coverage of LINQ's extensibility, which allows us to query more data sources than those supported by default.

In order to base our code samples on concrete business classes, we'll use a running example. This example, LinqBooks, is a personal book-cataloging system. This means that the LINQ queries you'll see throughout the book will deal with objects such as `Book`, `Publisher`, and `Author`. The running example we've chosen is broad enough to involve all aspects of LINQ. We'll progressively build the sample application throughout the chapters, finishing with a complete application in the last chapter.

Who should read this book

This book targets the .NET developer audience. Whether you don't know much about LINQ yet or you already have a good knowledge of it, this book is for you.

In order to fully appreciate this book, you should already know C# or VB.NET, ideally C# 2.0 or VB.NET 8.0.

How the book is organized

This book has been written so that you can choose what you want to read and how you want to read it. It has 5 parts, 13 chapters, an appendix, a list of resources, and a bonus chapter.

Part 1 introduces *LINQ and its toolset*. It also helps you to write your first LINQ queries. If LINQ is new to you or if you want to make sure that you have all the background information required to correctly understand LINQ code, the first part of this book is for you. If you're already familiar with LINQ and have a firm grasp on the *new* features of C# 3.0 and VB.NET 9.0, feel free to skip the first chapters and jump directly to other parts of the book that are related to specific uses of LINQ. If you want to understand where LINQ comes from, before you dive in, you may be interested in reading the bit of history we propose in chapter 1.

Part 2 is dedicated to *LINQ to Objects* and querying in-memory collections. This part also contains information about common LINQ use cases and best practices that'll be useful when working with any LINQ flavor.

Part 3 focuses on *LINQ to SQL*. It addresses the persistence of objects into relational databases. It will also help you discover how to query SQL Server databases with LINQ. Advanced LINQ to SQL features are also presented, such as inheritance, transactions, stored procedures, and more.

Part 4 covers *LINQ to XML*. It demonstrates how to use LINQ for creating and processing XML documents. In this part, you'll see what LINQ to XML has to offer compared to the other XML APIs. A comprehensive set of examples covers the most common LINQ to XML use cases.

Part 5 covers extensibility and shows how the LINQ flavors fit in a complete application. The extensibility chapter demonstrates various ways to enrich the LINQ toolset. The last chapter analyzes the use of LINQ in our running example and discusses choices you can make when you use LINQ.

The appendix contains a reference of the standard query operators, a key constituent of LINQ queries. *Resources* provides pointers to resources that will help you to learn more about LINQ, such as Microsoft's official web sites, articles, weblogs or forums.

An *online bonus chapter* available as a download at http://www.manning.com/LINQinAction and at http://LinqInAction.net introduces *LINQ to DataSet*. It demonstrates how LINQ can be used to query DataSets and DataTables.

It's up to you to decide whether you want to read the book from start to finish or jump right into one precise chapter. Wherever you are in the book, we tried to make it easy for you to navigate between chapters.

Tools used

The LINQ technology is included in .NET 3.5. It is supported by Visual Studio 2008, C# 3.0, and VB.NET 9.0. All the content of this book and the code samples it contains are based on Visual Studio 2008 and .NET 3.5 RTM,[1] the final products. You can refer to section 1.4.1 to find a detailed list of software requirements for working with LINQ and this book's samples.

Source code

This book contains extensive source code examples in C# and VB.NET. All code examples can be found as a downloadable archive at the book's web site at

---

[1] Release To Manufacturing.

http://www.manning.com/LINQinAction and at http://LinqInAction.net. Not all the examples are provided in both C# and VB.NET at the same time in the book, but they're all available in both languages in the companion source code.

Conventions

When we write "LINQ," we're referring to the LINQ technology or the complete LINQ framework. When we write "LINQ toolset," we mean the set of tools LINQ offers: LINQ to Objects, LINQ to XML, LINQ to SQL, and the others. We'll explicitly use *LINQ to Objects*, *LINQ to XML*, or *LINQ to SQL* to refer to specific parts of the LINQ toolset.

Typographical conventions

This book uses a `special code font` whenever certain code terms such as classes, objects, or operator names appear in the main text.

Particular bits of code that we want to draw attention to appear in **bold**. Furthermore, all code results and console output appears in *italics*.

Code annotations accompany many of the listings, highlighting important concepts. In some cases, numbered bullets ❶ link to explanations that follow the listing.

Icons like this differentiate between code in C# and VB.NET:

Author Online

Purchase of *LINQ in Action* includes free access to a private web forum run by Manning Publications where you can make comments about the book, ask technical questions, and receive help from the authors and from other users. To access the forum and subscribe to it, point your web browser to http://www.manning.com/LINQinAction. This page provides information on how to get on the forum once you are registered, what kind of help is available, and the rules of conduct on the forum.

Manning's commitment to our readers is to provide a venue where a meaningful dialogue between individual readers and between readers and the authors can take place. It is not a commitment to any specific amount of participation on the part of the authors, whose contribution to the book's forum remains voluntary (and unpaid). We suggest you try asking the authors some challenging questions, lest their interest stray!

The Author Online forum and the archives of previous discussions will be accessible from the publisher's website as long as the book is in print.

About the authors

FABRICE MARGUERIE is a software architect and developer with more than 13 years of experience in the software industry. He has diverse experience, ranging from consulting services and training to starting his own business. Fabrice has been awarded the C# MVP title by Microsoft in recognition for his involvement in the .NET community. His activities include speaking at conferences, writing technical articles in English and French, writing a weblog about .NET, and running websites such as sharptoolbox.com and proagora.com. Fabrice is based in Paris, France.

STEVE EICHERT is an architect and technical lead at Algorithmics, Inc. He also runs his own consulting company where he specializes in delivering solutions to clients utilizing the latest Microsoft .NET technologies. Steve can be found online at http://iqueryable.com. He is married and has three beautiful children. Steve is based in Philadelphia.

JIM WOOLEY has been working with .NET since PDC 2000 and has been actively evangelizing LINQ since its announcement in 2005. He leads the Atlanta VB Study Group and serves as INETA Membership Manager for the Georgia region.

About the title

By combining introductions, overviews, and how-to examples, the *In Action* books are designed to help learning *and* remembering. According to research in cognitive science, the things people remember are things they discover during self-motivated exploration.

Although no one at Manning is a cognitive scientist, we are convinced that for learning to become permanent it must pass through stages of exploration, play, and, interestingly, re-telling of what is being learned. People understand and remember new things, which is to say they master them, only after actively exploring them. Humans learn *in action*. An essential part of an *In Action* book is that it is example-driven. It encourages the reader to try things out, to play with new code, and explore new ideas.

There is another, more mundane, reason for the title of this book: our readers are busy. They use books to do a job or solve a problem. They need books that allow them to jump in and jump out easily and learn just what they want just when they want it. They need books that aid them *in action.* The books in this series are designed for such readers.

About the cover illustration

The caption for the figure on the cover of *LINQ in Action* reads "La Champenoise" or "The Champagne One." The drawing is of a young woman from the historic province of Champagne in the northeast of France, best known for the production of the sparkling white wine that bears the region's name. The illustration is taken from a French travel book, *Encyclopedie des Voyages* by J. G. St. Saveur, published in 1796. Travel for pleasure was a relatively new phenomenon at the time and travel guides such as this one were popular, introducing both the tourist as well as the armchair traveler to the inhabitants of other regions of the world, as well as to the and regional costumes and uniforms of French soldiers, civil servants, tradesmen, merchants, and peasants.

The diversity of the drawings in the *Encyclopedie des Voyages* speaks vividly of the uniqueness and individuality of the world's towns and provinces just 200 years ago. This was a time when the dress codes of two regions separated by a few dozen miles identified people uniquely as belonging to one or the other. The travel guide brings to life a sense of isolation and distance of that period and of every other historic period except our own hyperkinetic present.

Dress codes have changed since then and the diversity by region, so rich at the time, has faded away. It is now often hard to tell the inhabitant of one continent from another. Perhaps, trying to view it optimistically, we have traded a cultural and visual diversity for a more varied personal life. Or a more varied and interesting intellectual and technical life.

We at Manning celebrate the inventiveness, the initiative, and the fun of the computer business with book covers based on the rich diversity of regional life two centuries ago brought back to life by the pictures from this travel guide.

Part 1

Getting started

This part of the book introduces the LINQ technology and the C# and VB language enhancements.

Chapter 1 presents LINQ, its history, the reasons to use it, and quick "hello world" examples with objects, XML, and SQL. Chapter 2 introduces all the new languages features provided by the latest versions of C# and VB.NET to enable LINQ. Chapter 3 covers LINQ's technical fundamentals and shows how they fit together.

Introducing LINQ

1

This chapter covers

- LINQ's origins
- LINQ's design goals
- First steps with LINQ to Objects, LINQ to XML, and LINQ to SQL

Software is simple. It boils down to two things: code and data. Writing software is not so simple, and one of the major activities it involves is writing code that deals with data.

To write code, we can choose from a variety of programming languages. The selected language for an application may depend on the business context, on developer preferences, on the development team's skills, on the operating system, or on company policy.

Whatever language you end up with, at some point you will have to deal with data. This data can be in files on a disk, tables in a database, or XML documents coming from the Web, or often you have to deal with a combination of all of these. Ultimately, managing data is a requirement for every software project you'll work on.

Given that dealing with data is such a common task for developers, we would expect rich software development platforms like the .NET Framework to provide an easy way to do it. .NET *does* provide wide support for working with data. You will see, however, that something had yet to be achieved: deeper language and data integration. This is where LINQ to Objects, LINQ to XML, and LINQ to SQL fit in.

The technologies we present in this book have been designed as a new way to write code. This book has been written by developers for developers, so don't be afraid: You won't have to wait too long before you are able to write your first lines of LINQ code! In this chapter, we will quickly introduce "hello world" pieces of code to give you hints on what you will discover in the rest of the book. The aim is that, by the end of the book, you will be able to tackle real-world projects while being convinced that LINQ is a joy to work with.

The intent of this first chapter is to give you an overview of LINQ and to help you identify the reasons to use it. We will start by providing an overview of LINQ and the LINQ toolset, which includes LINQ to Objects, LINQ to XML, and LINQ to SQL. We will then review some background information to clearly understand why we need LINQ and where it comes from. The second half of this chapter will guide you while you make your first steps with LINQ code.

1.1   What is LINQ?

Suppose you are writing an application using .NET. Chances are high that at some point you'll need to persist objects to a database, query the database, and load the results back into objects. The problem is that in most cases, at least with relational databases, there is a gap between your programming language and the database. Good attempts have been made to provide object-oriented databases, which would be closer to object-oriented platforms and imperative programming languages such as C# and VB.NET. However, after all these years, relational databases are still pervasive, and you still have to struggle with data access and persistence in all of your programs.

The original motivation behind LINQ was to address the conceptual and technical difficulties encountered when using databases with .NET programming languages. With LINQ, Microsoft's intention was to provide a solution for the problem of object-relational mapping, as well as to simplify the interaction between objects and data sources. LINQ eventually evolved into a general-purpose language-integrated querying toolset. This toolset can be used to access data coming from in-memory objects (LINQ to Objects), databases (LINQ to SQL), XML documents (LINQ to XML), a file-system, or any other source.

We will first give you an overview of what LINQ is, before looking at the tools it offers. We will also introduce how LINQ extends programming languages.

1.1.1 Overview

LINQ could be the missing link—whether this pun is intended is yet to be discovered—between the data world and the world of general-purpose programming languages. LINQ unifies data access, whatever the source of data, and allows mixing data from different kind of sources. It allows for query and set operations, similar to what SQL statements offer for databases. LINQ, though, integrates queries directly within .NET languages such as C# and Visual Basic through a set of extensions to these languages: LINQ means *Language-INtegrated Query*.

Before LINQ, we had to juggle different languages like SQL, XML, or XPath along with various technologies and APIs like ADO.NET or System.Xml in every application written using general-purpose languages such as C# or VB.NET. It goes without saying that this approach had several drawbacks.[1] LINQ glues several worlds together. It helps us avoid the bumps we would usually find on the road from one world to another: using XML with objects, objects with relational data, and relational data with XML are some of the tasks that LINQ will simplify.

One of the key aspects of LINQ is that it was designed to be used against any type of object or data source and to provide a consistent programming model for doing so. The syntax and concepts are the same across all of its uses: Once you

---

[1] "It was like you had to order your dinner in one language and drinks in another," said Jason McConnell, product manager for Visual Studio at Microsoft. "The direct benefit is programmers are more productive because they have this unified approach to querying and updating data from within their language."

learn how to use LINQ against an array or a collection, you also know most of the concepts needed to take advantage of LINQ with a database or an XML file.

Another important aspect of LINQ is that when you use it, you work in a strongly typed world. The benefits include compile-time checking for your queries as well as nice hints from Visual Studio's IntelliSense feature.

LINQ will significantly change some aspects of how you handle and manipulate data with your applications and components. You will discover how LINQ is a step toward a more declarative programming model. Maybe you will wonder in the not-so-distant future why you used to write so many lines of code.

There is duality in LINQ. You can conceive of LINQ as consisting of two complementary parts: a set of tools that work with data, and a set of programming language extensions.

You'll first see how LINQ is a toolset that can be used to work with objects, XML documents, relational databases, or other kinds of data. You'll then see how LINQ is also an extension to programming languages like C# and VB.NET.

1.1.2 *LINQ as a toolset*

LINQ offers numerous possibilities. It will significantly change some aspects of how you handle and manipulate data with your applications and components. In this book, we'll detail the use of three major flavors of LINQ, or LINQ *providers*—LINQ to Objects, LINQ to SQL, and LINQ to XML, respectively—in parts 2, 3, and 4. These three LINQ providers form a family of tools that can be used separately for particular needs or combined for powerful solutions.

We will focus on LINQ to Objects, LINQ to SQL, and LINQ to XML in this book, but LINQ is open to new data sources. The three main LINQ providers discussed in this book are built on top of a common LINQ foundation. This foundation consists of a set of building blocks including *query operators*, *query expressions*, and *expression trees*, which allow the LINQ toolset to be extensible.

Other variants of LINQ can be created to provide access to diverse kinds of data sources. Implementations of LINQ will be released by software vendors, and you can also create your own implementations, as you'll see in chapter 12, which covers LINQ's extensibility. You can plug a wide array of data sources into LINQ, including the file system, Active Directory, WMI, the Windows Event Log, or any other data source or API. This is excellent because you can benefit from LINQ's features with a lot of the data sources you deal with every day. In fact, Microsoft already offers more LINQ providers than just LINQ to Objects, LINQ to SQL, and LINQ to XML. Two of them are LINQ to DataSet and LINQ to Entities (to work

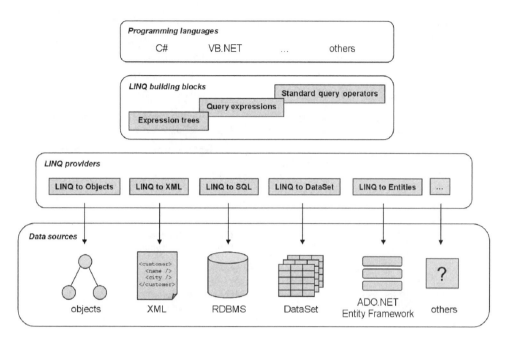

Figure 1.1   LINQ building blocks, LINQ providers, and data sources that can be queried using LINQ

with the new ADO.NET Entity Framework). We will present these tools in the second and third parts of this book. For now, let's keep the focus on the big picture.

Figure 1.1 shows how we can represent the LINQ building blocks and toolset in a diagram.

The LINQ providers presented in figure 1.1 are not standalone tools. They can be used directly in your programming languages. This is possible because the LINQ framework comes as a set of language extensions. This is the second aspect of LINQ, which is detailed in the next section.

1.1.3   LINQ as language extensions

LINQ allows you to access information by writing queries against various data sources. Rather than being simply *syntactic sugar*[2] that would allow you to easily

---

[2] Syntactic sugar is a term coined by Peter J. Landin for additions to the syntax of a computer language that do not affect its expressiveness but make it "sweeter" for humans to use. Syntactic sugar gives the programmer an alternative way of coding that is more practical, either by being more succinct or more like some familiar notation.

include database queries right into your C# code, LINQ provides the same type of expressive capabilities that SQL offers, but in the programming language of your choice. This is great because a declarative approach like the one LINQ offers allows you to write code that is shorter and to the point.

Listing 1.1 shows sample C# code you can write with LINQ.

Listing 1.1 Sample code that uses LINQ to query a database and create an XML document

```
var contacts =                    ◁──────── Retrieve customers from database
  from customer in db.Customers
  where customer.Name.StartsWith("A") && customer.Orders.Count > 0
  orderby customer.Name
  select new { customer.Name, customer.Phone };

var xml =                        ◁─────┐  Generate XML data
  new XElement("contacts",              │  from list of customers
    from contact in contacts
    select new XElement("contact",
      new XAttribute("name", contact.Name),
      new XAttribute("phone", contact.Phone)
    )
  );
```

The listing demonstrates all you need to write in order to extract data from a database and create an XML document from it. Imagine how you would do the same without LINQ, and you'll realize how things are easier and more natural with LINQ. You will soon see more LINQ queries, but let's keep focused on the language aspects for the moment. With the `from`, `where`, `orderby`, and `select` keywords in the listing, it's obvious that C# has been extended to enable language-integrated queries.

We've just shown you code in C#, but LINQ provides a common querying architecture across programming languages. It works with C# 3.0 and VB.NET 9.0 (also known as VB 2008), and as such requires dedicated compilers, but it can be ported to other .NET languages. This is already the case for F#, a functional language for .NET from Microsoft Research, and you can expect to see LINQ support appear in more .NET languages in the future.

Figure 1.2 shows a typical language-integrated query that is used to talk to objects, XML, or data tables.

The query in the figure is expressed in C# and not in a new language. LINQ is not a new language. It is integrated into C# and VB.NET. In addition, LINQ can be used to avoid entangling your .NET programming language with SQL, XSL, or

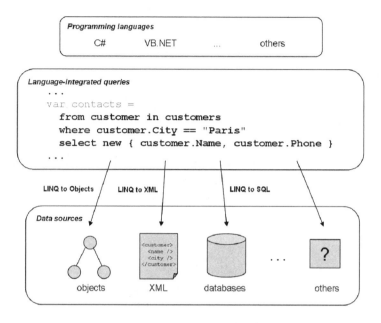

Figure 1.2   LINQ as language extensions and as a gateway to several data sources

other data-specific languages. The set of language extensions that come with LINQ enables queries over several kinds of data stores to be formulated right into programming languages. Think of LINQ as a universal remote control, if you wish. At times, you'll use it to query a database; at others, you'll query an XML document. But you'll do all this in your favorite language, without having to switch to another one like SQL or XQuery.

In chapter 2, we'll show you the details of how the programming languages have been extended to support LINQ. In chapter 3, you'll learn how to write LINQ queries. This is where you'll learn about query operators, query expressions, and expression trees. But you still have a few things to discover before getting there.

Now that we have given you an idea of what LINQ is, let's discuss the motivation behind it, and then we'll review its design goals and a bit of history.

1.2   Why do we need LINQ?

We have just provided you with an overview of LINQ. The big questions at this point are: Why do we want a tool like LINQ? What makes the previous tools inconvenient? Was LINQ created only to make working with programming languages, relational data, and XML at the same time more convenient?

At the origin of the LINQ project is a simple fact: The vast majority of applications that are developed access data or talk to a relational database. Consequently, in order to program applications, learning a language such as C# is not enough. You also have to learn another language such as SQL, and the APIs that tie it together with C# to form your full application.

We'll start by taking a look at a piece of data-access code that uses the standard .NET APIs. This will allow us to point out the common problems that are encountered in this kind of code. We will then extend our analysis by showing how these problems exist with other kinds of data such as XML. You'll see that LINQ addresses a general *impedance mismatch* between data sources and programming languages. Finally, a short code sample will give you a glimpse at how LINQ is a solution to the problem.

1.2.1 *Common problems*

The frequent use of databases in applications requires that the .NET Framework address the need for APIs that can access the data stored within. Of course, this has been the case since the first appearance of .NET. The .NET Framework Class Library (FCL) includes ADO.NET, which provides an API to access relational databases and to represent relational data in memory. This API consists of classes such as `SqlConnection`, `SqlCommand`, `SqlReader`, `DataSet`, and `DataTable`, to name a few. The problem with these classes is that they force the developer to work explicitly with tables, records, and columns, while modern languages such as C# and VB.NET use object-oriented paradigms.

Now that the object-oriented paradigm is the prevailing model in software development, developers incur a large amount of overhead in mapping it to other abstractions, specifically relational databases and XML. The result is that a lot of time is spent on writing plumbing code.[3] Removing this burden would increase productivity in data-intensive programming, which LINQ helps us do.

But it's not only about productivity! It also impacts quality. Writing tedious and fragile plumbing code can lead to insidious defects in software or degraded performance.

Listing 1.2 shows how we would typically access a database in a .NET program. By looking at the problems that exist with traditional code, you'll be able to see how LINQ comes to the rescue.

---

[3] It is estimated that dealing with the task of storing and retrieving objects to and from data stores accounts for between 30 and 40 percent of a development team's time.

Listing 1.2 Typical .NET data-access code

```
using (SqlConnection connection = new SqlConnection("..."))
{
  connection.Open();
  SqlCommand command = connection.CreateCommand();
  command.CommandText =
    @"SELECT Name, Country                          ❶ SQL query in
      FROM Customers                                   a string
      WHERE City = @City";
  command.Parameters.AddWithValue("@City", "Paris");  ⟵
  using (SqlDataReader reader = command.ExecuteReader())  ❷ Loosely bound
  {                                                      parameters
    while (reader.Read())
    {
      string name = reader.GetString(0);    ❸ Loosely typed
      string country = reader.GetString(1);    columns
      ...
    }
  }
}
```

Just by taking a quick look at this code, we can list several limitations of the model:

- Although we want to perform a simple task, several steps and verbose code are required.

- Queries are expressed as quoted strings ❶, which means they bypass all kinds of compile-time checks. What if the string does not contain a valid SQL query? What if a column has been renamed in the database?

- The same applies for the parameters ❷ and for the result sets ❸: they are loosely defined. Are the columns of the type we expect? Also, are we sure we're using the correct number of parameters? Are the names of the parameters in sync between the query and the parameter declarations?

- The classes we use are dedicated to SQL Server and cannot be used with another database server. Naturally, we could use DbConnection and its friends to avoid this issue, but that would solve only half of the problem. The real problem is that SQL has many vendor-specific dialects and data types. The SQL we write for a given DBMS is likely to fail on a different one.

Other solutions exist. We could use a code generator or one of the several object-relational mapping tools available. The problem is that these tools are not perfect either and have their own limitations. For instance, if they are designed for accessing databases, most of the time they don't deal with other data sources such as XML documents. Also, one thing that language vendors such as Microsoft can do that mapping tool vendors can't is integrate data-access and -querying features right into their languages. Mapping tools at best present a partial solution to the problem.

The motivation for LINQ is twofold: Microsoft did not have a data-mapping solution yet, and with LINQ it had the opportunity to integrate queries into its programming languages. This could remove most of the limitations we identified in listing 1.2.

The main idea is that by using LINQ you are able to gain access to any data source by writing queries like the one shown in listing 1.3, directly in the programming language that you master and use every day.

Listing 1.3   Simple query expression

```
from customer in customers
where customer.Name.StartsWith("A") && customer.Orders.Count > 0
orderby customer.Name
select new { customer.Name, customer.Orders }
```

In this query, the data could be in memory, in a database, in an XML document, or in another place; the syntax would remain similar if not exactly the same. As you saw in figure 1.2, this kind of query can be used with multiple types of data and different data sources, thanks to LINQ's extensibility features. For example, in the future we are likely to see an implementation of LINQ for querying a file system or for calling web services.

1.2.2   Addressing a paradigm mismatch

Let's continue looking at why we need LINQ. The fact that modern application developers have to simultaneously deal with general-purpose programming languages, relational data, SQL, XML documents, XPath, and so on means that we need two things:

- To be able to work with any of these technologies or languages individually
- To mix and match them to build a rich and coherent solution

The problem is that object-oriented programming (OOP), the relational database model, and XML—just to name a few—were not originally built to work together. They represent different paradigms that don't play well with each other.

What is this impedance mismatch everybody's talking about?

Data is generally manipulated by application software written using OOP languages such as C#, VB.NET, Java, Delphi, and C++. But translating an object graph into another representation, such as tuples of a relational database, often requires tedious code.

The general problem LINQ addresses has been stated by Microsoft like this: *"Data != Objects."* More specifically, for LINQ to SQL: *"Relational data != Objects."* The same could apply for LINQ to XML: *"XML data != Objects."* We should also add: *"XML data != Relational data."*

We've used the term *impedance mismatch*. It is commonly applied to incompatibility between systems and describes an inadequate ability of one system to accommodate input from another. Although the term originated in the field of electrical engineering, it has been generalized and used as a term of art in systems analysis, electronics, physics, computer science, and informatics.

Object-relational mapping

If we take the object-oriented paradigm and the relational paradigm, the mismatch exists at several levels. Let's name a few.

Relational databases and object-oriented languages don't share the same set of primitive data types. For example, strings usually have a delimited length in databases, which is not the case in C# or VB.NET. This can be a problem if you try to persist a 150-character string in a table field that accepts only 100 characters. Another simple example is that most databases don't have a Boolean type, whereas we frequently use true/false values in many programming languages.

OOP and relational theories come with different data models. For performance reasons and due to their intrinsic nature, relational databases are usually *normalized*. Normalization is a process that eliminates redundancy, organizes data efficiently, and reduces the potential for anomalies during data operations and improves data consistency. Normalization results in an organization of data that is specific to the relational data model. This prevents a direct mapping of tables and records to objects and collections. Relational databases are normalized in tables and relations, whereas objects use inheritance, composition, and complex reference graphs. A common problem exists because relational databases don't have concepts like inheritance: Mapping a class hierarchy to a relational database requires using "tricks."

Programming models. In SQL, we write queries, and so we have a higher-level, declarative way of expressing the set of data that we're interested in. With imperative programming languages such as C# or VB.NET, we have to write `for` loops and `if` statements and so forth.

Encapsulation. Objects are self-contained and include data as well as behavior. In databases, data records don't have behavior, per se. It's possible to act on database records only through the use of SQL queries or stored procedures. In relational databases, code and data are clearly separated.

The mismatch is a result of the differences between a relational database and a typical object-oriented class hierarchy. We might say relational databases are from Mars and objects are from Venus.

Let's take the simple example shown in figure 1.3. We have an object model we'd like to map to a relational model.

Concepts such as inheritance or composition are not directly supported by relational databases, which means that we cannot represent the data the same way in both models. You can see here that several objects and types of objects can be mapped to a single table.

Even if we wanted to persist an object model like the one we have here in a new relational database, we would not be able to use a direct mapping. For instance, for performance reasons and to avoid duplication, it's much better in this case to create only one table in the database. A consequence of doing so, however, is that data coming from the database table cannot be easily used to repopulate an object graph in memory. When we win on one side, we lose on the other.

We may be able to design a database schema or an object model to reduce the mismatch between both worlds, but we'll never be able to remove it because of

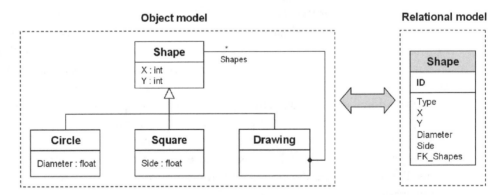

Figure 1.3   How simple objects can be mapped to a database model. The mapping is not trivial due to the differences between the object-oriented and the relational paradigms.

the intrinsic differences between the two paradigms. We don't even always have the choice. Often, the database schema is already defined, and in other cases we have to work with objects defined by someone else.

The complex problem of integrating data sources with programs involves more than simply reading from and writing to a data source. When programming using an object-oriented language, we normally want our applications to use an object model that is a conceptual representation of the business domain, instead of being tied directly to the relational structure. The problem is that at some point we need to make the object model and the relational model work together. This is not an easy task because object-oriented programming languages and .NET involve entity classes, business rules, complex relationships, and inheritance, whereas a relational data source involves tables, rows, columns, and primary and foreign keys.

A typical solution for bridging object-oriented languages and relational databases is *object-relational mapping*. This refers to the process of mapping our relational data model to our object model, usually back and forth. Mapping can be defined as the act of determining how objects and their relationships are persisted in permanent data storage, in this case relational databases.

Databases[4] do not map naturally to object models. Object-relational mappers are automated solutions to address the impedance mismatch. To make a long story short: We provide an object-relational mapper with our classes, database, and mapping configuration, and the mapper takes care of the rest. It generates the SQL queries, fills our objects with data from the database, persists them in the database, and so on.

As you can guess, no solution is perfect, and object-relational mappers could be improved. Some of their main limitations include the following:

- A good knowledge of the tools is required before being able to use them efficiently and avoid performance issues.

- Optimal use still requires knowledge of how to work with a relational database.

- Mapping tools are not always as efficient as handwritten data-access code.

- Not all the tools come with support for compile-time validation.

---

[4] We are talking only about relational databases here because this is what is used in the vast majority of business applications. Object-oriented databases offer a different approach that allows persisting objects more easily. Whether object-oriented databases are better than relational databases is another debate, which we are not going to address in this book.

Multiple object-relational mapping tools are available for .NET. There is a choice of open source, free, or commercial products. As an example, listing 1.4 shows a mapping configuration file for NHibernate, one of the open source mappers. Fields, relationships, and inheritance are defined using XML.

Listing 1.4   NHibernate mapping file used to map a `Cat` class to a `CATS` table in a relational database

```xml
<?xml version="1.0" ?>
<hibernate-mapping xmlns="urn:nhibernate-mapping-2.0"
    namespace="Eg" assembly="Eg">
  <class name="Cat" table="CATS" discriminator-value="C">
    <id name="Id" column="uid" type="Int64">
      <generator class="hilo"/>
    </id>
    <discriminator column="subclass" type="Char"/>
    <property name="Birthdate" type="Date"/>
    <property name="Color" not-null="true"/>
    <property name="Sex" not-null="true" update="false"/>
    <property name="Weight"/>
    <many-to-one name="Mate" column="mate_id"/>
    <set name="Kittens">
      <key column="mother_id"/>
      <one-to-many class="Cat"/>
    </set>
    <subclass name="DomesticCat" discriminator-value="D">
      <property name="Name" type="String"/>
    </subclass>
  </class>

  <class name="Dog">
    <!-- mapping for Dog could go here -->
  </class>
</hibernate-mapping>
```

In part 3 of this book, you'll see how LINQ to SQL is an object-relational mapping solution and how it addresses some of these issues. But for now, we are going to look at another problem LINQ can solve.

Object-XML mapping

Analogous to the object-relational impedance mismatch, a similar mismatch also exists between objects and XML. For example, the type system described in the W3C XML Schema specification has no one-to-one relationship with the type system of the .NET Framework. However, using XML in a .NET application is not much of a problem because we already have APIs that deal with this under the `System.Xml` namespace as well as the built-in support for serializing and deserializing objects.

Still, a lot of tedious code is required most of the time for doing even simple things on XML documents.

Given that XML has become so pervasive in the modern software world, something had to be done to reduce the work required to deal with XML in programming languages.

When you look at these domains, it is remarkable how different they are. The main source of contention relates to the following facts:

- Relational databases are based on relational algebra and are all about tables, rows, columns, and SQL.

- XML is all about documents, elements, attributes, hierarchical structures, and XPath.

- Object-oriented general-purpose programming languages and .NET live in a world of classes, methods, properties, inheritance, and loops.

Many concepts are specific to each domain and have no direct mapping to another domain. Figure 1.4 gives an overview of the concepts used in .NET and object-oriented programming, in comparison to the concepts used in data sources such as XML documents or relational databases.

Too often, programmers have to do a lot of plumbing work to tie together the different domains. Different APIs for each data type cause developers to spend an inordinate amount of time learning how to write, debug, and rewrite brittle code. The usual culprits that break the pipes are bad SQL query strings or XML tags, or content that doesn't get checked until runtime. .NET languages such as C# and

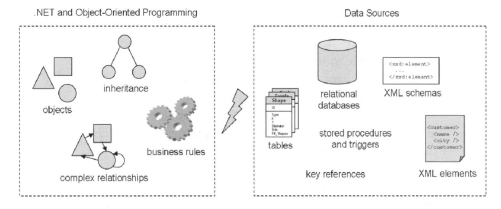

Figure 1.4   .NET applications and data sources are different worlds. The concepts used in object-oriented programming are different from the concepts used with relational databases and XML.

VB.NET assist developers and provide such things as IntelliSense, strongly typed code, and compile-time checks. Still, this can become broken if we start to include malformed SQL queries or XML fragments in our code, none of which are validated by the compiler.

A successful solution requires bridging the different technologies and solving the object-persistence impedance mismatch—a challenging and resource-intensive problem. To solve this problem, we must resolve the following issues between .NET and data source elements:

- Fundamentally different technologies
- Different skill sets
- Different staff and ownership for each of the technologies
- Different modelling and design principles

Some efforts have been made to reduce the impedance mismatch by bringing some pieces of one world into another. For example: SQLXML 4.0 ties SQL to XSD; System.Xml spans XML/XML DOM/XSL/XPath and CLR; the ADO.NET API bridges SQL and CLR data types; and SQL Server 2005 includes CLR integration. All these efforts are proof that data integration is essential; however, they represent distinct moves without a common foundation, which makes them difficult to use together. LINQ, in contrast, offers a common infrastructure to address the impedance mismatches.

1.2.3 *LINQ to the rescue*

To succeed in using objects and relational databases together, you need to understand both paradigms, along with their differences, and then make intelligent tradeoffs based on that knowledge. The main goal of LINQ and LINQ to SQL is to get rid of, or at least reduce, the need to worry about these limits.

An impedance mismatch forces you to choose one side or the other as the "primary" side. With LINQ, Microsoft chose the programming language side, because it's easier to adapt the C# and VB.NET languages than to change SQL or XML. With LINQ, the aim is toward deeply integrating the capabilities of data query and manipulation languages into programming languages.

LINQ removes many of the barriers among objects, databases, and XML. It enables us to work with each of these paradigms using the same language-integrated facilities. For example, we are able to work with XML data and data coming from a relational database within the same query.

Because code is worth a thousand words, let's take a look at a quick code sample using the power of LINQ to retrieve data from a database and create an XML document in a single query. Listing 1.5 creates an RSS feed based on relational data.

Listing 1.5   Working with relational data and XML in the same query

```
var database = new RssDB("server=.; initial catalog=RssDB");

XElement rss = new XElement("rss",
  new XAttribute("version", "2.0"),
  new XElement("channel",
    new XElement("title", "LINQ in Action RSS Feed"),
    new XElement("link", "http://LinqInAction.net"),
    new XElement("description", "The RSS feed for this book"),
    from post in database.Posts
    orderby post.CreationDate descending
    select new XElement("item",
      new XElement("title", post.Title),
      new XElement("link", "posts.aspx?id="+post.ID),
      new XElement("description", post.Description),
      from category in post.Categories
      select new XElement("category", category.Description)
    )
  )
);
```

Creating XML

Querying database

We will not detail here how this code works. You will see documented examples like this one in parts 3 and 4 of the book. What is important to note at this point is how LINQ makes it easy to work with relational data and XML in the same piece of code. If you have already done this kind of work before, it should be obvious that this code is very concise and readable in comparison to the solutions at your disposal before LINQ appeared.

Before seeing more code samples and helping you write your own LINQ code, we'll now quickly review where LINQ comes from.

1.3   Design goals and origins of LINQ

It's important to know clearly what Microsoft set out to achieve with LINQ. This is why we'll start this section by reviewing the design goals of the LINQ project. It's also interesting to know where LINQ takes its roots from and understand the links with other projects you may have heard of. We'll spend some time looking at the history of the LINQ project to know how it was born.

LINQ is not a recent project from Microsoft in the sense that it inherits a lot of features from research and development work done over the last several years.

We'll discuss the relationships LINQ has with other Microsoft projects so you know if LINQ replaces projects like Cω, ObjectSpaces, WinFS, or support for XQuery in the .NET Framework.

1.3.1   The goals of the LINQ project

Table 1.1 reviews the design goals Microsoft set for the LINQ project in order to give you a clear understanding of what LINQ offers.

The number-one LINQ feature presented in table 1.1 is the ability to deal with several data types and sources. LINQ ships with implementations that support

Table 1.1   LINQ's design goals and the motivations behind them

Goal	Motivation
Integrate objects, relational data, and XML	Unified query syntax across data sources to avoid different languages for different data sources. Single model for processing all types of data regardless of source or in-memory representation.
SQL and XQuery-like power in C# and VB	Integrate querying abilities right into the programming languages.
Extensibility model for languages	Enable implementation for other programming languages.
Extensibility model for multiple data sources	Be able to access other data sources than relational databases or XML documents. Allow other frameworks to enable LINQ support for their own needs.
Type safety	Compile-time type checking to avoid problems that were previously discovered at run-time only. The compiler will catch errors in your queries.
Extensive IntelliSense support (enabled by strong-typing)	Assist developers when writing queries to improve productivity and to help them get up to speed with the new syntax. The editor will guide you when writing queries.
Debugger support	Allow developers to debug LINQ queries step by step and with rich debugging information.
Build on the foundations laid in C# 1.0 and 2.0, VB.NET 7.0 and 8.0	Reuse the rich features that have been implemented in the previous versions of the languages.
Run on the .NET 2.0 CLR	Avoid requiring a new runtime and creating unnecessary deployment hassles.
Remain 100% backward compatible	Be able to use standard and generic collections, data binding, existing web and Windows Forms controls, and so on.

querying against regular object collections, databases, entities, and XML sources. Because LINQ supports rich extensibility, developers can also easily integrate it with other data sources and providers.

Another essential feature of LINQ is that it is strongly typed. This means the following:

- We get compile-time checking for all queries. Unlike SQL statements today, where we typically only find out at runtime if something is wrong, this means we can check during development that our code is correct. The direct benefit is a reduction of the number of problems discovered late in production. Most of the time, issues come from human factors. Strongly typed queries allow us to detect early typos and other mistakes made by the developer in charge of the keyboard.

- We get IntelliSense within Visual Studio when writing LINQ queries. This not only makes typing faster, but also makes it much easier to work against both simple and complex collection and data source object models.

This is all well and good, but where does LINQ come from? Before delving into LINQ and starting to use it, let's see how it was born.

1.3.2 A bit of history

LINQ is the result of a long-term research process inside Microsoft. Several projects involving evolutions of programming languages and data-access methods can be considered to be the parents of LINQ to Objects, LINQ to XML (formerly known as XLinq), and LINQ to SQL (formerly known as DLinq).

Cω (or the C-Omega language)

Cω (pronounced "c-omega") was a project from Microsoft Research that extended the C# language in several areas, notably the following:

- A control flow extension for asynchronous wide-area concurrency (formerly known as Polyphonic C#)

- A data type extension for XML and database manipulation (formerly known as Xen and as X#)

Cω covered more than what comes with LINQ, but a good deal of what is now included as part of the LINQ technologies was already present in Cω. The Cω project was conceived to experiment with integrated queries, mixing C# and SQL, C# and XQuery, and so on. This was carried out by researchers such as Erik

Meijer, Wolfram Schulte, and Gavin Bierman, who published multiple papers on the subject.

Cω was released as a preview in 2004. A lot has been learned from that prototype, and a few months later, Anders Hejlsberg, chief designer of the C# language, announced that Microsoft would be working on applying a lot of that knowledge in C# and other programming languages. Anders said at that time that his particular interest for the past couple of years had been to think deeply about the big impedance mismatch between programming languages—C# in particular—and the data world. This includes database and SQL, but also XML and XQuery, for example.

Cω's extensions to the .NET type system and to the C# language were the first steps to a unified system that treated SQL-style queries, query result sets, and XML content as full-fledged members of the language. Cω introduced the stream type, which is analogous to the .NET Framework 2.0 type `System.Collections.Generic.IEnumerable<T>`. Cω also defined constructors for typed tuples (called *anonymous structs*), which are similar to the anonymous types we get in C# 3.0 and VB.NET 9.0. Another thing Cω supported is embedded XML, something we are able to see in VB.NET 9.0 (but not in C# 3.0).

ObjectSpaces

LINQ to SQL is not Microsoft's first attempt at object-relational mapping. Another project with a strong relationship to LINQ was ObjectSpaces.

The first preview of the ObjectSpaces project appeared in a PDC 2001 ADO.NET presentation. ObjectSpaces was a set of data access APIs. It allowed data to be treated as objects, independent of the underlying data store. ObjectSpaces also introduced OPath, a proprietary object query language. In 2004, Microsoft announced that ObjectSpaces depended on the WinFS[5] project, and as such would be postponed to the Orcas timeframe (the next releases after .NET 2.0 and Visual Studio 2005). No new releases happened after that. Everybody realized that ObjectSpaces would never see the light of day when Microsoft announced that WinFS wouldn't make it into the first release of Windows Vista.

XQuery implementation

Similar to what happened with ObjectSpaces and about the same time, Microsoft had started working on an XQuery processor. A preview was included in the first beta release of the .NET Framework version 2.0, but eventually it was decided not

---

[5] WinFS was a project for a relational file system Microsoft had been developing for Windows. It was canceled in 2006.

to ship a client-side[6] XQuery implementation in the final version. One problem with XQuery is that it was an additional language we would have to learn specifically to deal with XML.

Why all these steps back? Why did Microsoft apparently stop working on these technologies? Well, the cat came out of the bag at PDC 2005, when the LINQ project was announced.

LINQ has been designed by Anders Hejlsberg and others at Microsoft to address this impedance mismatch from within programming languages like C# and VB.NET. With LINQ, we can query pretty much anything. This is why Microsoft favored LINQ instead of continuing to invest in separate projects like ObjectSpaces or support for XQuery on the client-side.

As you've seen, LINQ has a rich history behind it and has benefited from all the research and development work done on prior, now-defunct projects. Before we go further and show you how it works, how to use it, and its different flavors, what about writing your first lines of LINQ code?

The next three sections provide simple code that demonstrates LINQ to Objects, LINQ to XML, and LINQ to SQL. This will give you an overview of what LINQ code looks like and show you how it can help you work with object collections, XML, and relational data.

1.4 First steps with LINQ to Objects: Querying collections in memory

After this introduction, you're probably eager to look at some code and to make your first steps with LINQ. We think that you'll get a better understanding of the features LINQ provides if you spend some time on a piece of code. Programming is what this book is about, anyway!

1.4.1 What you need to get started

Before looking at code, let's spend some time reviewing all you need to be able to test this code.

---

[6] A server-side implementation of XQuery is included with SQL Server 2005, and now that the XQuery standard has been finalized, Microsoft is once again considering whether to add support for XQuery in .NET.

Compiler and .NET Framework support and required software

LINQ is delivered as part of the *Orcas* wave, which includes Visual Studio 2008 and the .NET Framework 3.5. This version of the framework comes with additional and updated libraries, as well as new compilers for the C# and VB.NET languages, but it stays compatible with the .NET Framework 2.0.

LINQ features are a matter of compiler and libraries, not runtime. It is important to understand that although the C# and VB.NET languages have been enriched and a few new libraries have been added to the .NET Framework, the .NET runtime (the CLR) did not need to evolve. New compilers are required for C# 3.0 and VB.NET 9.0, but the required runtime is still an unmodified version 2.0. This means that the applications you'll build using LINQ can run in a .NET 2.0 runtime.[7]

At the time of this writing, LINQ and LINQ to XML, or at least subsets of them, are supported by the current releases of the Silverlight runtime. They are available through the `System.Linq` and `System.Xml.Linq` namespaces.

All the content of this book and the code samples it contains are based on the final products, Visual Studio 2008 and .NET 3.5 RTM,[8] which were released on November 19, 2007.

To set up your machine and be able to run our code samples as you read, you only need to install the following:

At least one of these versions of Visual Studio:

- Visual C# 2008 Express Edition
- Visual Basic 2008 Express Edition
- Visual Web Developer 2008 Express Edition
- Visual Studio 2008 Standard Edition or higher

If you want to run the LINQ to SQL samples, one of the following is required:

- SQL Server 2005 Express Edition or SQL Server 2005 Compact Edition (included with most versions of Visual Studio)
- SQL Server 2005
- SQL Server 2000a
- A later version of SQL Server[9]

---

[7] Nevertheless, .NET 2.0 Service Pack 1 is required for LINQ to SQL.

[8] Release To Manufacturing.

[9] The new data types provided by SQL Server 2008 are not supported by the first release of LINQ to SQL.

That's all for the required software. Let's now review the programming languages we'll use in this book.

Language considerations

In this book, we assume you know the syntax of the C# programming language and occasionally a bit of VB.NET. For the sake of simplicity, we'll be light on the explanations while we introduce our first few code samples. Don't worry: In chapters 2 and 3, we'll take the time to present in detail the syntax evolutions provided by C# 2.0, C# 3.0, VB.NET 9.0, and LINQ. You will then be able to fully understand LINQ queries.

> **NOTE** Most of the examples contained in this book are in C#, but they can easily be ported to VB.NET, because the syntax is similar between the two languages.
>
> Code examples are in VB.NET when we examine the features specific to this language or simply when it makes sense. All the code samples are available both in C# and VB.NET as a companion source code download, so you can find them in your language of choice.

All right, enough preliminaries! Let's dive into a simple example that will show you how to query a collection in memory using LINQ to Objects. Follow the guide, and be receptive to the magic of all these new features you'll be using soon in your own applications.

1.4.2 Hello LINQ to Objects

You may have had little contact with these new concepts and syntactic constructs. Fear not! Our ultimate goal is for you to master these technologies, but don't force yourself to understand everything at once. We'll take the time we need to come back to every detail of LINQ and the new language extensions as we progress through the book.

Listing 1.6 shows our first LINQ example in C#.

C#   **Listing 1.6   Hello LINQ in C# (HelloLinq.csproj)**

```
using System;
using System.Linq;

static class HelloWorld
{
  static void Main()
  {
```

```
string[] words =
  { "hello", "wonderful", "linq", "beautiful", "world" };

var shortWords =        ◁           Get only
  from word in words                short words
  where word.Length <= 5
  select word;

foreach (var word in shortWords)    ◁    Print each
  Console.WriteLine(word);                 word out
}
}
```

Listing 1.7 shows the same example in VB.NET.

VB.NET   **Listing 1.7   Hello LINQ in VB.NET**
              (HelloLinq.vbproj)

```
Module HelloWorld
  Sub Main()
    Dim words As String() = _
      { "hello", "wonderful", "linq", "beautiful", "world" }

    Dim shortWords = _       ◁           Get only
      From word In words _               short words
      Where word.Length <= 5 _
      Select word

    For Each word In shortWords    ◁    Print each
      Console.WriteLine(word)             word out
    Next
  End Sub
End Module
```

NOTE   Most of the code examples contained in this book can be copied and
           pasted without modification into a console application for testing.

If you were to compile and run these codes, here is the output you'd see:

```
hello
linq
world
```

As is evident from the results, we have filtered a list of words to select only the
ones whose length is less than or equal to five characters.

We could argue that the same result could be achieved without LINQ using the
code in listing 1.8.

**Listing 1.8 Old-school version of Hello LINQ
          (OldSchoolHello.csproj)**

```csharp
using System;

static class HelloWorld
{
  static void Main()
  {
    string[] words = new string[] {
      "hello", "wonderful", "linq", "beautiful", "world" };

    foreach (string word in words)
    {
      if (word.Length <= 5)
        Console.WriteLine(word);
    }
  }
}
```

Notice how this "old-fashioned" code is much shorter than the LINQ version and very easy to read. Well, don't give up yet. There is much more to LINQ than what we show in this first simple program! If you read on, we will help you discover all the power of LINQ to Objects, LINQ to SQL, and LINQ to XML.

To give you some motivation to pursue reading, let's try to improve our simple example with grouping and sorting. This should give you an idea of why LINQ is useful and powerful.

In order to get this result

```
Words of length 9
  beautiful
  wonderful
Words of length 5
  hello
  world
Words of length 4
  linq
```

we can use the C# code shown in listing 1.9.

**Listing 1.9 Hello LINQ in C# improved with grouping and sorting
          (HelloLinqWithGroupingAndSorting.csproj)**

```csharp
using System;
using System.Linq;

static class HelloWorld
```

```
{
  static void Main()
  {
    string[] words =
      { "hello", "wonderful", "linq", "beautiful", "world" };

    var groups =                    ◁──────┐  Group words
      from word in words                   │  by length
      orderby word ascending
      group word by word.Length into lengthGroups
      orderby lengthGroups.Key descending
      select new {Length=lengthGroups.Key, Words=lengthGroups};

    foreach (var group in groups)     ◁─── Print each group out
    {
      Console.WriteLine("Words of length " + group.Length);
      foreach (string word in group.Words)
        Console.WriteLine("  " + word);
    }
  }
}
```

Listing 1.10 shows the equivalent VB.NET code.

VB.NET   **Listing 1.10   Hello LINQ in VB improved with grouping and sorting**
              (HelloLinqWithGroupingAndSorting.vbproj)

```
Module HelloWorld
  Sub Main()
    Dim words as String() = _
      {"hello", "wonderful", "linq", "beautiful", "world"}

    Dim groups = _                   ◁──────┐  Group words
      From word In words _                  │  by length
      Order By word Ascending _
      Group By word.Length Into TheWords = Group _
      Order By Length Descending          ┐  Print each
    For Each group In groups     ◁────────┘  group out
      Console.WriteLine("Words of length " + _
        group.Length.ToString())
      For Each word In group.TheWords
        Console.WriteLine("  " + Word)
      Next
    Next
  End Sub
End Module
```

In the preceding examples, we have expressed in one query (or two nested queries more precisely) what could be formulated in English as "Sort words from a list alphabetically and group them by their length in descending order."

We'll leave doing the same without LINQ as an exercise for you. If you take the time to do it, you'll notice that it takes more code and requires dealing a lot with collections. One of the first advantages of LINQ that stands out with this example is the expressiveness it enables: We can express declaratively what we want to achieve using queries instead of writing convoluted pieces of code.

We won't take the time right now to get into the details of the code you've just seen. If you are familiar with SQL, you probably already have a good idea of what the code is doing. In addition to all the nice SQL-like querying, LINQ also provides a number of other functions such as Sum, Min, Max, Average, and much more. They let us perform a rich set of operations.

For example, here we sum the amount of each order in a list of orders to compute a total amount:

```
decimal totalAmount = orders.Sum(order => order.Amount);
```

If you haven't dealt with C# 3.0 yet, you may find the syntax confusing. "What's this strange arrow?" you may wonder. We'll explain this type of code in greater detail later in the book so you can fully understand it. However, before we continue, you may wish to test our "Hello LINQ" example and start playing with the code. Feel free to do so to get an idea of how easy to use LINQ really is.

Once you are ready, let's move on to LINQ to XML and LINQ to SQL. We'll spend some time with these two other flavors of LINQ so you can get an idea of what they taste like. We will get back to LINQ to Objects in detail in part 2 of this book.

1.5 First steps with LINQ to XML: Querying XML documents

As we said in the first half of this chapter, the extensibility of the LINQ query architecture is used to provide implementations that work over both XML and SQL data. We will now help you to make your first steps with LINQ to XML.

LINQ to XML takes advantage of the LINQ framework to offer XML query and transform capabilities integrated into host .NET programming languages. You can also think of LINQ to XML as a full-featured XML API comparable to a modernized, redesigned .NET 2.0 System.Xml plus a few key features from XPath and XSLT. LINQ to XML provides facilities to edit XML documents and element trees in-memory, as well as streaming facilities. This means that you'll be able to use LINQ to XML to more easily perform many of the XML-processing tasks that you have been performing with the traditional XML APIs from the `System.Xml` namespace.

We will first examine why we need an XML API like LINQ to XML by comparing it to some alternatives. You'll then make your first steps with some code using LINQ to XML in an obligatory "Hello World" example.

1.5.1 Why we need LINQ to XML

XML is ubiquitous nowadays, and is used extensively in applications written using general-purpose languages such as C# or VB.NET. It is used to exchange data between applications, store configuration information, persist temporary data, generate web pages or reports, and perform many other things. It is everywhere!

Until now, XML hasn't been natively supported by most programming languages, which therefore required the use of APIs to deal with XML data. These APIs include `XmlDocument`, `XmlReader`, `XPathNavigator`, `XslTransform` for XSLT, and SAX and XQuery implementations. The problem is that these APIs are not well integrated with programming languages, often requiring several lines of unnecessarily convoluted code to achieve a simple result. You'll see an example of this in the next section (see listing 1.13). But for the moment, let's see what LINQ to XML has to offer.

LINQ to XML extends the language-integrated query features offered by LINQ to add support for XML. It offers the expressive power of XPath and XQuery but in our programming language of choice and with type safety and IntelliSense.

If you've worked on XML documents with .NET, you probably used the XML DOM (Document Object Model) available through the `System.Xml` namespace. LINQ to XML leverages experience with the DOM to improve the developer toolset and avoid the limitations of the DOM.

Table 1.2 compares the characteristics of LINQ to XML with those of the XML DOM.

Table 1.2   Comparing LINQ to XML with the XML DOM to show how LINQ to XML is a better value proposition

LINQ to XML characteristic	XML DOM characteristic
Element-centric	Document-centric
Declarative model	Imperative model
LINQ to XML code presents a layout close to the hierarchical structure of an XML document	No resemblance between code and document structure
Language-integrated queries	No integrated queries

Table 1.2 Comparing LINQ to XML with the XML DOM to show how LINQ to XML is a better value proposition *(continued)*

LINQ to XML characteristic	XML DOM characteristic
Creating elements and attributes can be done in one instruction; text nodes are just strings	Basic things require a lot of code
Simplified XML namespace support	Requires dealing with prefixes and "namespace managers"
Faster and smaller	Heavyweight and memory intensive
Streaming capabilities	Everything is loaded in memory
Symmetry in element and attribute APIs	Different ways to work with the various bits of XML documents

Whereas the DOM is low-level and requires a lot of code to precisely formulate what we want to achieve, LINQ to XML provides a higher-level syntax that allows us to do simple things simply.

LINQ to XML also enables an *element-centric* approach in comparison to the *document-centric* approach of the DOM. This means that we can easily work with XML fragments (elements and attributes) without having to create a complete XML document.

Two classes that the .NET Framework offers are `XmlReader` and `XmlWriter`. These classes provide support for working on XML text in its raw form and are lower-level than LINQ to XML. LINQ to XML uses the `XmlReader` and `XmlWriter` classes underneath and is not a completely new XML API. One advantage of this is that it allows LINQ to XML to remain compatible with `XmlReader` and `XmlWriter`.

LINQ to XML makes creating documents more direct, but it also makes it easier to query XML documents. Expressing queries against XML documents feels more natural than having to write of lot of code with several loop instructions. Also, being part of the LINQ family of technologies, it is a good choice when we need to join diverse data sources.

With LINQ to XML, Microsoft is aiming at 80 percent of the use cases. These cases involve straightforward XML formats and common processing. For the other cases, developers will continue to use the other APIs. Also, although LINQ to XML takes inspiration from XSLT, XPath, and XQuery, these technologies have benefits of their own and are designed for specific use cases, and within those scopes LINQ to XML is in no way able to compete with them. LINQ to XML is not enough for some specific cases, but its compatibility with the other XML APIs allows us to use it in combination with these APIs. We'll keep these kinds of advanced scenarios for part 4 of this book.

For the moment, let's discover how LINQ to XML makes a difference by looking at some code.

1.5.2 Hello LINQ to XML

The running example application we'll use in this book deals, appropriately enough, with books. We'll detail this example in chapter 4. For the moment, we'll stick to a simple Book class because it is enough for your first contact with LINQ to XML.

In our first example, we want to filter and save a set of Book objects as XML. Here is how the Book class could be defined in C#:[10]

C#
```csharp
class Book
{
  public string Publisher;
  public string Title;
  public int    Year;

  public Book(string title, string publisher, int year)
  {
    Title = title;
    Publisher = publisher;
    Year = year;
  }
}
```

And here it is in VB.NET:

VB.NET
```vbnet
Public Class Book
    Public Publisher As String
    Public Title As String
    Public Year As Integer

    Public Sub New( _
        ByVal title As String, _
        ByVal publisher As String, _
        ByVal year As Integer)
      Me.Title = title
      Me.Publisher = publisher
      Me.Year = year
    End Sub
End Class
```

---

[10] Here we use public fields in the Book class for the sake of simplicity, but properties and private fields would be better. Another option is to use *auto-implemented properties*, which is a new feature of C# 3.0. You'll see auto-implemented properties in action in chapters 2, 7, and 13.

Let's say we have the following collection of books:

```
Book[] books = new Book[] {
  new Book("Ajax in Action", "Manning", 2005),
  new Book("Windows Forms in Action", "Manning", 2006),
  new Book("RSS and Atom in Action", "Manning", 2006)
};
```

Here is the result we would like to get if we ask for the books published in 2006:

```
<books>
  <book title="Windows Forms in Action">
    <publisher>Manning</publisher>
  </book>
  <book title="RSS and Atom in Action">
    <publisher>Manning</publisher>
  </book>
</books>
```

Using LINQ to XML, this can be done with the code shown in listing 1.11.

C#

**Listing 1.11 Hello LINQ to XML in C#
(HelloLinqToXml.csproj)**

```
using System;
using System.Linq;
using System.Xml;
using System.Xml.Linq;

class Book
{
  public string Publisher;
  public string Title;
  public int     Year;

  public Book(string title, string publisher, int year)
  {
    Title = title;
    Publisher = publisher;
    Year = year;
  }
}

static class HelloLinqToXml
{
  static void Main()
  {
    Book[] books = new Book[] {                    ◁── Book
      new Book("Ajax in Action", "Manning", 2005),      collection
      new Book("Windows Forms in Action", "Manning", 2006),
      new Book("RSS and Atom in Action", "Manning", 2006)
    };
```

```
XElement xml = new XElement("books",
  from book in books
  where book.Year == 2006
  select new XElement("book",
    new XAttribute("title", book.Title),
    new XElement("publisher", book.Publisher)
  )
);
```
◁── **Build XML fragment based on collection**

```
Console.WriteLine(xml);
  }
}
```
◁── **Dump XML to console**

Listing 1.12 shows the same code in VB.NET.

VB.NET

> **Listing 1.12   Hello LINQ to XML in VB.NET (HelloLinqToXml.vbproj)**

```
Module HelloLinqToXml

  Public Class Book
    Public Publisher As String
    Public Title As String
    Public Year As Integer

    Public Sub New( _
        ByVal title As String, _
        ByVal publisher As String, _
        ByVal year As Integer)
      Me.Title = title
      Me.Publisher = publisher
      Me.Year = year
    End Sub
  End Class

  Sub Main()
    Dim books As Book() = { _
      New Book("Ajax in Action", "Manning", 2005), _
      New Book("Windows Forms in Action", "Manning", 2006), _
      New Book("RSS and Atom in Action", "Manning", 2006) _
    }

    Dim xml As XElement = New XElement("books", _
      From book In books _
      Where book.Year = 2006 _
      Select New XElement("book", _
        New XAttribute("title", book.Title), _
        New XElement("publisher", book.Publisher) _
```
◁── **Book collection**

◁── **Build XML fragment based on collection**

```
      ) _
    )

      Console.WriteLine(xml)
    End Sub

  End Module
```
Dump XML
to console

In contrast, listing 1.13 shows how we would build the same document without LINQ to XML, using the XML DOM.

 Listing 1.13   Old-school version of Hello LINQ to XML (OldSchoolXml.csproj)

```csharp
using System;
using System.Xml;

class Book
{
  public string Title;
  public string Publisher;
  public int    Year;

  public Book(string title, string publisher, int year)
  {
    Title = title;
    Publisher = publisher;
    Year = year;
  }
}

static class HelloLinqToXml
{
  static void Main()
  {
    Book[] books = new Book[] {              Book collection
      new Book("Ajax in Action", "Manning", 2005),
      new Book("Windows Forms in Action", "Manning", 2006),
      new Book("RSS and Atom in Action", "Manning", 2006)
    };

    XmlDocument doc = new XmlDocument();              Build XML fragment
    XmlElement root = doc.CreateElement("books");     based on collection
    foreach (Book book in books)
    {
      if (book.Year == 2006)
      {
```

```
        XmlElement element = doc.CreateElement("book");
        element.SetAttribute("title", book.Title);

        XmlElement publisher = doc.CreateElement("publisher");
        publisher.InnerText = book.Publisher;
        element.AppendChild(publisher);

        root.AppendChild(element);
      }
    }
    doc.AppendChild(root);

    doc.Save(Console.Out);        ◁────  Display
  }                                      result XML
}
```

As you can see, LINQ to XML is more visual than the DOM. The structure of the code to get our XML fragment is close to the document we want to produce itself. We could say that it's *WYSIWYM* code: What You See Is What You Mean.

Microsoft names this approach the *Functional Construction* pattern. It allows us to structure code in such a way that it reflects the shape of the XML document (or fragment) that we're constructing.

In VB.NET, the code can be even closer to the resulting XML, as shown in listing 1.14.

VB.NET

**Listing 1.14   Hello LINQ to XML VB.NET using XML literals
                (HelloLinqWithLiterals.vbproj)**

```
Module XmlLiterals

  Sub Main()                                         Book
    Dim books as Book() = { _          ◁────         collection
      New Book("Ajax in Action", "Manning", 2005), _
      New Book("Windows Forms in Action", "Manning", 2006), _
      New Book("RSS and Atom in Action", "Manning", 2006) _
    }

    Dim xml As XElement = _   ◁──  Build XML fragment
      <books>                      using XML literals
        <%= From book In books _
            Where book.Year = 2006 _
            Select _
              <book title=<%= book.Title %>>
                <publisher><%= book.Publisher %></publisher>
              </book> _
        %>
      </books>
```

```
        Console.WriteLine(xml)        Display
    End Sub                           result XML

End Module
```

The listing uses a new syntax named *XML literals,* which is highlighted in bold. Literal means something that is output as part of the result. Here, the books, book, and publisher XML elements will be part of the generated XML. XML literals allow us to use a template of the XML we'd like to get, with a syntax comparable to ASP.

The XML literals feature is not provided by C# 3.0. It exists only in VB.NET 9.0. You will discover that VB.NET comes with more language-integrated features than C# to work with XML.

You'll get the details about XML literals and everything else you need to know to make the best of LINQ to XML in part 4 of the book. For the moment, we still have one major piece of the LINQ trilogy to introduce: LINQ to SQL.

1.6   First steps with LINQ to SQL: Querying relational databases

LINQ's ambition is to make queries a natural part of the programming language. LINQ to SQL, which made its first appearance as DLinq, applies this concept to allow developers to query relational database using the same syntax that you have seen with LINQ to Objects and LINQ to XML.

After summing up how LINQ to SQL will help us, we'll show you how to write your first LINQ to SQL code.

1.6.1   Overview of LINQ to SQL's features

LINQ to SQL provides language-integrated data access by using LINQ's extension mechanism. It builds on ADO.NET to map tables and rows to classes and objects.

LINQ to SQL uses mapping information encoded in .NET custom attributes or contained in an XML document. This information is used to automatically handle the persistence of objects in relational databases. A table can be mapped to a class and the table's columns to properties of the class, and relationships between tables can be represented by additional properties.

LINQ to SQL automatically keeps track of changes to objects and updates the database accordingly through dynamic SQL queries or stored procedures. This is why we don't have to provide the SQL queries by ourself most of the time. But all this will be developed in part 3 of this book. For the moment, let's make our first steps with LINQ to SQL code.

1.6.2 *Hello LINQ to SQL*

The time has come to look at some code using LINQ to SQL. As you saw in our Hello LINQ example, we are able to write queries against a collection of objects. The following C# code snippet filters an in-memory collection of contacts based on their city:

```
from contact in contacts
where contact.City == "Paris"
select contact;
```

The good news is that thanks to LINQ to SQL, doing the same on data from a relational database is direct:

```
from contact in db.GetTable<Contact>()
where contact.City == "Paris"
select contact;
```

This query works on a list of contacts from a database. Notice how subtle the difference is between the two queries. Only the object on which we are working is different; the query syntax is exactly the same. This shows how we'll be able to work the same way with multiple types of data. This is what is so great about LINQ!

As an astute reader, you know that the language a relational database understands is SQL, and you suspect that our LINQ query must be translated into a SQL query at some point. This is the heart of the technology: In the first example, the collection is iterated in memory, whereas in the second code snippet, the query is used to generate a SQL query that is sent to a database server. In the case of LINQ to SQL queries, the real processing happens on the database server. What's appealing about these queries is that we have a nice strongly typed query API, in contrast with SQL, where queries are expressed in strings and not validated at compile-time.

We will dissect the inner workings of LINQ to SQL in the third part of this book, but let's first walk through a simple complete example. To begin with, you're probably wondering what `db.GetTable<Contact>()` means in our LINQ to SQL query.

Entity classes

The first step in building a LINQ to SQL application is declaring the classes we'll use to represent your application data: our entities.

In our simple example, we'll define a class named `Contact` and associate it with the `Contacts` table of the Northwind sample database provided by Microsoft with the LINQ code samples.[11] To do this, we need only to apply a custom attribute to the class:

```
[Table(Name="Contacts")]
class Contact
{
  public int ContactID;
  public string Name;
  public string City;
}
```

The `Table` attribute is provided by LINQ to SQL in the `System.Data.Linq.Mapping` namespace. It has a `Name` property that is used to specify the name of the database table.

In addition to associating entity classes with tables, we need to denote each field or property we intend to associate with a column of the table. This is done with the `Column` attribute:

```
[Table(Name="Contacts")]
class Contact
{
  [Column(IsPrimaryKey=true)]
  public int ContactID { get; set; }
  [Column(Name="ContactName")]
  public string Name { get; set; }
  [Column]
  public string City { get; set; }
}
```

The `Column` attribute is also part of the `System.Data.Linq.Mapping` namespace. It has a variety of properties we can use to customize the exact mapping between our fields or properties and the database's columns. You can see that we use the `IsPrimaryKey` property to tell LINQ to SQL that the table column named `ContactID` is part of the table's primary key. Notice how we indicate that the `ContactName` column is to be mapped to the `Name` field. We don't specify the names of the other columns or the types of the columns: In our case, LINQ to SQL will deduce them from the fields of the class.

The DataContext

The next thing we need to prepare before being able to use language-integrated queries is a `System.Data.Linq.DataContext` object. The purpose of `DataContext`

---

[11] See the CSharpSamples.zip and VBSamples.zip files in the Samples subfolder of your Visual Studio 2008 installation folder.

is to translate requests for objects into SQL queries made against the database and then assemble objects out of the results.

We will use the Northwnd.mdf database provided with the code samples accompanying this book. This database is in the Data directory, so the creation of the `DataContext` object looks like this:

```
string path = Path.GetFullPath(@"..\..\..\..\Data\northwnd.mdf");
DataContext db = new DataContext(path);
```

The constructor of the `DataContext` class takes a connection string as a parameter. Because we are using SQL Server 2005 Express Edition, a path to the database file is sufficient.

The `DataContext` provides access to the tables in the database. Here is how to get access to the `Contacts` table mapped to our `Contact` class:

```
Table<Contact> contacts = db.GetTable<Contact>();
```

`DataContext.GetTable` is a generic method, which allows us to work with strongly typed objects. This is what will allow us to use a LINQ query.

We are now able to write a complete code sample, as seen in listing 1.15.

Listing 1.15   Hello LINQ to SQL complete source code (HelloLinqToSql.csproj)

```
using System;
using System.Linq;
using System.Data.Linq;
using System.Data.Linq.Mapping;

static class HelloLinqToSql
{
  [Table(Name="Contacts")]
  class Contact
  {
    [Column(IsPrimaryKey=true)]
    public int ContactID { get; set; }
    [Column(Name="ContactName")]
    public string Name { get; set; }
    [Column]
    public string City { get; set; }
  }

  static void Main()                    Get access
  {                                     to database
    string path =        ⟵
      System.IO.Path.GetFullPath(@"..\..\..\..\Data\northwnd.mdf");
    DataContext db = new DataContext(path);
```

```
    var contacts =                              ◁────┐  Query for contacts
      from contact in db.GetTable<Contact>()         │  from Paris
      where contact.City == "Paris"
      select contact;

    foreach (var contact in contacts)          ◁────┐  Display list of
      Console.WriteLine("Bonjour "+contact.Name);    │  matching contacts
  }
}
```

Executing this code gives the following result:

```
Bonjour Marie Bertrand
Bonjour Dominique Perrier
Bonjour Guylène Nodier
```

Here is the SQL query that was sent to the server transparently:

```
SELECT [t0].[ContactID], [t0].[ContactName] AS [Name], [t0].[City]
FROM [Contacts] AS [t0]
WHERE [t0].[City] = @p0
```

Notice how easy it is to get strongly typed access to a database thanks to LINQ. This is a simplistic example, but it gives you a good idea of what LINQ to SQL has to offer and how it could change the way you work with databases.

Let's sum up what has been done automatically for us by LINQ to SQL:

- Opening a connection to the database
- Generating the SQL query
- Executing the SQL query against the database
- Creating and filling our objects out of the tabular results

As an exercise, you can try to do the same without LINQ to SQL. For example, you can try to use a `DataReader`. You'll notice the following things in the old-school code when comparing it with our LINQ to SQL code:

- Queries explicitly written SQL in quotes
- No compile-time checks
- Loosely bound parameters
- Loosely typed result sets
- More code required
- More knowledge required

Writing standard data-access code hinders productivity for simple cases. In contrast, LINQ to SQL allows us to write data-access code that doesn't get in the way.

Before concluding our introduction to LINQ to SQL, let's review some of its features.

1.6.3 *A closer look at LINQ to SQL*

You have seen that LINQ to SQL is able to generate dynamic SQL queries based on language-integrated queries. This may not be adapted to every situation, and so LINQ to SQL also supports custom SQL queries and stored procedures so that we can use our own handwritten SQL code and still benefit from the LINQ to SQL infrastructure.

In our example, we provided the mapping information using custom attributes on our classes; but if you prefer not to have this kind of information hard-coded in your binaries, you are free to use an external XML mapping file to do the same.

To get a better understanding of how LINQ to SQL works, we created our entity classes and provided the mapping information. In practice, typically this code would be generated by tools that come with LINQ to SQL or using the graphical LINQ to SQL Designer.

The list of LINQ to SQL's features is much longer than this and includes things such as support for data binding, interoperability with ADO.NET, concurrency management, support for inheritance, and help for debugging. Let's keep that for later; we promise that all this and more will be covered in detail in part 3 of the book.[12]

1.7 *Summary*

This first chapter presented the motivation behind the LINQ technologies. You also took your first steps with LINQ to Objects, LINQ to XML, and LINQ to SQL code.

Although we have just scratched the surface of the possibilities offered by LINQ, we hope you now have an idea of the potential power these technologies provide. As you've seen, LINQ is not about taking SQL or XML and slapping

---

[12] It should be noted that while LINQ to SQL includes a lot of functionality, its narrow focus means it doesn't include some of the features found in other object-relational mapper products available today on the market. In 2008, Microsoft will be providing an even broader object-relational mapping solution: the ADO.NET Entity Framework. We will include a quick introduction to it after discussing LINQ to SQL later in this book.

them into C# or VB.NET code. It's much more than that, as you'll see soon in the next chapters.

LINQ unlocks a whole new way to access data from within your applications. However, LINQ would not be possible without the addition of a number of features to programming languages. We will start the next chapter by reviewing the enhancements that have been made to the C# and VB.NET languages to enable language-integrated queries.

C# and VB.NET
language enhancements

2

This chapter covers:

- Key C# 3.0 and VB.NET 9.0 languages features for LINQ
- Implicitly typed local variables
- Object initializers
- Lambda expressions
- Extension methods
- Anonymous types

In chapter 1, we reviewed the motivation behind LINQ and introduced some code to give you an idea of what to expect. In this chapter, we'll present the language extensions that make LINQ possible and allow queries to blend into programming languages.

LINQ extends C# and VB.NET with new constructs. We find it important that you discover these language features before we get back to LINQ content. This chapter is a stepping stone that explains how the C# and VB.NET languages have been enriched to make LINQ possible. Please note that the full-fledged features we present here can be used in contexts other than just LINQ.

We won't go into advanced details about each feature, because we don't want to lose our focus on LINQ for too long. You'll be able to see all these features in action throughout this book, so you should grow accustomed to them as you read.

In chapter 3, we'll focus on LINQ-specific concepts such as expression trees and query operators. You'll then see how the features presented in this chapter are used by LINQ.

2.1 Discovering the new language enhancements

.NET 2.0 laid the groundwork for a lot of what LINQ needs to work. Indeed, it introduced a number of important language and framework enhancements. For example, .NET now supports generic types, and in order to achieve the deep data integration that LINQ targets, you need types that can be parameterized—otherwise the type system isn't rich enough.

C# 2.0 also added anonymous methods and iterators. These features serve as cornerstones for the new level of integration between data and programming languages.

We expect readers of this book to know the basics about the features offered by .NET 2.0. We'll provide you with a refresher on anonymous methods in section 2.4 when we present lambda expressions, and we'll review iterators in chapter 3.

More features were required, though, for LINQ to expose query syntaxes natively to languages such as C# and VB.NET. C# 3.0 and VB.NET 9.0 (also known as VB 2008) build on generics, anonymous methods, and iterators as key components of the LINQ facility.

These features include

- *Implicitly typed local variables*, which permit the types of local variables to be inferred from the expressions used to initialize them.
- *Object initializers*, which ease construction and initialization of objects.

- *Lambda expressions,* an evolution of anonymous methods that provides improved type inference and conversion to both delegate types and expression trees, which we'll discuss in the next chapter.

- *Extension methods,* which make it possible to extend existing types and constructed types with additional methods. With extension methods, types aren't extended but look as if they were.

- *Anonymous types,* which are types automatically inferred and created from object initializers.

Instead of merely listing these new language features and detailing them one by one, let's discover them in the context of an ongoing example. This will help us clearly see how they can help us in our everyday coding.

We'll start with the simplest code possible, using only .NET 2.0 constructs, and then we'll improve it by progressively introducing the new language features. Each refactoring step will address one specific problem or syntax feature. First, let's get acquainted with our simple example: an application that outputs a list of running processes.

2.1.1   *Generating a list of running processes*

Let's say we want to get a list of the processes running on our computer. This can be done easily thanks to the `System.Diagnostics.Process.GetProcesses` API.

> **NOTE**   We use the `GetProcesses` method in this example because it returns a generic list of results that are likely to be different each time the method is called. This makes our example more realistic than one that would be based on a static list of items.

Listing 2.1 shows sample C# 2.0 code that achieves our simple goal.

Listing 2.1   Sample .NET 2.0 code for listing processes (DotNet2.csproj)

```
using System;
using System.Collections.Generic;
using System.Diagnostics;

static class LanguageFeatures
{
  static void DisplayProcesses()                          Prepare list  ❶
  {                                                        of strings
    List<String> processes = new List<String>();   ◁──────
    foreach (Process process in Process.GetProcesses())         ❷  Build list of
      processes.Add(process.ProcessName);                          processes
```

```
      ObjectDumper.Write(processes);              Print to
    }                                         ❸  console

  static void Main()
  {
    DisplayProcesses();
  }
}
```

Our processes variable points to a list of strings ❶. The type we use is based on the generic type List<T>. *Generics* are a major addition to .NET that first appeared in .NET 2.0. They allow us to maximize code reuse, type safety, and performance. The most common use of generics is to create strongly typed collection classes, just like we're doing here. As you'll notice, LINQ makes extensive use of generics.

In the listing, we use a class named ObjectDumper to display the results ❸. ObjectDumper is a utility class provided by Microsoft as part of the LINQ code samples. We'll reuse ObjectDumper in many code samples throughout this book. (The complete source code for the samples is available for download at http://LinqInAction.net.) ObjectDumper can be used to dump an object graph in memory to the console. It's particularly useful for debugging purposes; we'll use it here to display the result of our processing.

This first version of the code is nothing more than a foreach loop that adds process names to a list ❷, so a call to Console.WriteLine on each item would be enough. However, in the coming examples, we'll have more complex results to display. ObjectDumper will then save us some code by doing the display work for us.

Here is some sample output produced by listing 2.1:

```
firefox
Skype
WINWORD
devenv
winamp
Reflector
```

This example is very simple. Soon, we'll want to be able to filter this list, sort it, or perform other operations, such as grouping or projections.

Let's improve our example a bit. For a start, what if we'd like more information about the process than just its name?

2.1.2 Grouping results into a class

Let's say we'd like the list to contain the ID, name, and memory consumption of each process. For instance:

```
Id=2300        Name=firefox     Memory=78512128
Id=2636        Name=Skype       Memory=23478272
Id=2884        Name=WINWORD     Memory=78442496
Id=2616        Name=devenv      Memory=54296576
Id=1824        Name=winamp      Memory=29188096
Id=2940        Name=Reflector   Memory=83857408
```

This requires creating a class or structure to group the information we'd like to retain about a process. Listing 2.2 shows the code with a new class shown in bold named ProcessData.

NOTE   Here we use public fields in the ProcessData class for the sake of simplicity, but properties and private fields would be better. Read on and in a few pages you'll discover how to easily use properties instead thanks to C# 3.0.

Listing 2.2   Improved .NET 2.0 code for listing processes (DotNet2Improved.csproj)

```csharp
using System;
using System.Collections.Generic;
using System.Diagnostics;

static class LanguageFeatures
{
  class ProcessData
  {
    public Int32  Id;
    public Int64  Memory;
    public String Name;
  }

  static void DisplayProcesses()
  {

    List<ProcessData> processes = new List<ProcessData>();
    foreach (Process process in Process.GetProcesses())
    {
      ProcessData data = new ProcessData();
      data.Id = process.Id;
      data.Name = process.ProcessName;
      data.Memory = process.WorkingSet64;
      processes.Add(data);
    }


    ObjectDumper.Write(processes);
  }
```

Prepare list of ProcessData objects ❶

Build list of running processes

Print out list to console

```
static void Main()
{
  DisplayProcesses();
}
}
```

Although our code produces the output we want, it has some duplicate information in it. The type of our objects is specified twice ❶: once for the declaration of the variables and once more for calling the constructor:

```
List<ProcessData> processes = new List<ProcessData>();
...
ProcessData data = new ProcessData();
```

New keywords will allow us to make our code shorter and avoid duplication, as you'll see next.

2.2 *Implicitly typed local variables*

```
var i = 5;
```

C# 3.0 offers a new keyword that allows us to declare a local variable without having to specify its type explicitly: var. When the var keyword is used to declare a local variable, the compiler infers the type of this variable from the expression used to initialize it.

Let's review the syntax proposed by this new keyword, and then we'll revise our example with it.

2.2.1 *Syntax*

The var keyword is easy to use. It should be followed by the name of the local variable and then by an initializer expression. For example, the following two code snippets are equivalent. They produce the exact same Intermediate Language (IL) code once compiled.

Let's compare some code with implicitly typed variables and some code without. Here is some code with implicitly typed variables:

```
var i = 12;
var s = "Hello";
var d = 1.0;
var numbers = new[] {1, 2, 3};
var process = new ProcessData();
var processes =
  new Dictionary<int, ProcessData>();
```

And here is equivalent code with the traditional syntax:

```
int i = 12;
string s = "Hello";
double d = 1.0;
int[] numbers = new int[] {1, 2, 3};
ProcessData process = new ProcessData();
Dictionary<int, ProcessData> processes =
  new Dictionary<int, ProcessData>();
```

Implicitly typed local variables can also be used in VB.NET, thanks to the `Dim` keyword. For example, here is the `Dim` keyword with implicitly typed variables:

```
Dim processes =
  New List(Of ProcessData)()
```

And here it is with the traditional syntax:

```
Dim processes As List(Of ProcessData) =
  New List(Of ProcessData)()
```

This looks like variants in VB, but the new syntax and variants aren't the same. Implicitly typed local variables are strongly typed. For example, the following VB.NET code isn't valid and will return an error stating that conversion from type `String` to type `Integer` isn't valid:

```
Dim someVariable = 12
someVariable = "Some string"
```

In the first line, `someVariable` is an Integer. The second line throws the error.

In comparison, the following code that uses a variant is valid:

```
Dim someVariable as Variant = 12
someVariable = "Some String"
```

2.2.2 *Improving our example using implicitly typed local variables*

Listing 2.3 shows how we could improve our `DisplayProcesses` method thanks to the var keyword. New code is shown in bold.

Listing 2.3 Our `DisplayProcesses` method using the `var` keyword (UsingVar.csproj)

```
using System;
using System.Collections.Generic;
using System.Diagnostics;

static class LanguageFeatures
{
  class ProcessData
  {
```

```
      public Int32   Id { get; set; }
      public Int64   Memory { get; set; }      ❶
      public String  Name { get; set; }
   }

   static void DisplayProcesses()
   {
     var processes = new List<ProcessData>();
     foreach (var process in Process.GetProcesses())   ←❸   ❷
     {
       var data = new ProcessData();
       data.Id = process.Id;
       data.Name = process.ProcessName;
       data.Memory = process.WorkingSet64;
       processes.Add(data);
     }

     ObjectDumper.Write(processes);
   }

   static void Main()
   {
     DisplayProcesses();
   }
}
```

NOTE   This time, we use *auto-implemented properties* to define the ProcessData
class ❶. This is a new feature of the C# 3.0 compiler that creates anonymous private variables to contain each of the values that the individual
property will be using. Using this new syntax, we can eliminate the need
for explicitly stating the private variables and repetitive property accessors.

Listing 2.3 does exactly the same thing as listing 2.2. It may not look like it at first,
but the processes, process, and data variables are still strongly typed!

With implicitly typed local variables ❷, we no longer have to write the types of
local variables twice. The compiler infers the types automatically. This means that
even though we use a simplified syntax, we still get all the benefits of strong types,
such as compile-time validation and IntelliSense.

Notice that we can use the same var keyword in foreach ❸ to avoid writing
the type of the iteration variable.

As you can see, the var and Dim keywords can be used extensively to write shorter
code. In some cases, they're required to use LINQ features. However, if you like to
have the local variable declarations grouped at the top of method bodies instead of
scattered all over the code statements, you'll use var and Dim thoughtfully.

Let's improve our example a bit more. Initializing a new ProcessData object
requires lengthy code. It's time to introduce a new improvement to fix this.

2.3 Object and collection initializers

```
new Point {X = 1, Y = 2}
```

As we continue to make progress in our journey through the new C# and VB.NET features, the features we introduce in this section will be useful when you start to write query expressions in the next chapter.

We'll start this section with an introduction to object and collection initializers. We'll then update our running example to use an object initializer.

2.3.1 The need for object initializers

Object initializers allow us to specify values for one or more fields or properties of an object in one statement. They allow declarative initializations for all kinds of objects.

> **NOTE** This is possible only for accessible fields and properties. The expression after the equals sign is processed the same way as an assignment to the field or property.

Until now, we have been able to initialize objects of primitive or array types, as follows:

```
int i = 12;
string s = "abc"
string[] names = new string[] {"LINQ", "In", "Action"}
```

It wasn't possible to use a simple instruction to initialize other objects, though. We had to use code like this:

```
ProcessData data = new ProcessData();
data.Id = 123;
data.Name = "MyProcess";
data.Memory = 123456;
```

Starting with C# 3.0 and VB.NET 9.0, we can initialize all objects using an initializer approach.

In C#
```
var data = new ProcessData {Id = 123, Name = "MyProcess",
                            Memory = 123456};
```

In VB.NET
```
Dim data = New ProcessData With {.Id = 123, .Name = "MyProcess", _
                                 .Memory = 123456}
```

The pieces of code with and without object initializers produce the same IL code. Object initializers simply offer a shortcut.

In cases where a constructor is required or useful, it's still possible to use object initializers. In the following example, we use a constructor in combination with an object initializer:

```
throw new Exception("message") { Source = "LINQ in Action" };
```

Here, we initialize two properties in one line of code: `Message` (through the constructor) and `Source` (through an object initializer). Without the new syntax, we would have to declare a temporary variable like this:

```
var exception = new Exception("message");
exception.Source = "LINQ in Action";
throw exception;
```

2.3.2 Collection initializers

Another kind of initializer has been added: the *collection initializer*. This new syntax allows us to initialize different types of collections, provided they implement `System.Collections.IEnumerable` and provide suitable `Add` methods.

Here's an example:

```
var digits = new List<int> {0, 1, 2, 3, 4, 5, 6, 7, 8, 9};
```

This line of code is equivalent to the following code, which is generated by the compiler transparently:

```
List<int> digits = new List<int>();
digits.Add(0);
digits.Add(1);
digits.Add(2);
...
digits.Add(9);
```

Object and collection initializers are particularly useful when used together in the same piece of code. The following two equivalent code blocks show how initializers allow us to write shorter code. Let's compare some code with object and collection initializers to code without. Here is the code with object and collection initializers:

```
var processes = new List<ProcessData> {
  new ProcessData {Id=123, Name="devenv"},
  new ProcessData {Id=456, Name="firefox"}
}
```

Here is the same code without initializers. Note that it's much longer:

```
ProcessData tmp;
var processes = new List<ProcessData>();
tmp = new ProcessData();
tmp.Id = 123;
tmp.Name = "devenv";
```

```
processes.Add(tmp);
tmp = new ProcessData();
tmp.Id = 456;
tmp.Name = "firefox";
processes.Add(tmp);
```

We can initialize collections represented by a class that implements the IEnumerable interface and provides an Add method. We can use syntax of the form {x, y, z} to describe arguments that match the Add method's signature if there is more than one argument. This enables us to initialize many preexisting collection classes in the framework and third-party libraries.

This generalization allows us to initialize a dictionary with the following syntax, for example:

```
new Dictionary<int, string> {{1, "one"}, {2, "two"}, {3, "three"}}
```

2.3.3 *Improving our example using an object initializer*

As you can see in the following code snippet, we have to write several lines of code and use a temporary variable in order to create a ProcessData object:

```
ProcessData data = new ProcessData();
data.Id = process.Id;
data.Name = process.ProcessName;
data.Memory = process.WorkingSet64;
processes.Add(data);
```

We could add a constructor to our ProcessData class to be able to initialize an object of this type in just one statement. This would allow us to write listing 2.4.

Listing 2.4 `DisplayProcesses` method using a constructor for `ProcessData`

```
static void DisplayProcesses()
{
  var processes = new List<ProcessData>();
  foreach (var process in Process.GetProcesses())
  {
    processes.Add( new ProcessData(process.Id,
      process.ProcessName, process.WorkingSet64) );
  }

  ObjectDumper.Write(processes);
}
```

Adding a constructor requires adding code to the ProcessData type. In addition, the constructor we add may not be suitable for every future use of this class. An alternative solution is to adapt our code to use the new *object initializer* syntax, as in listing 2.5.

Listing 2.5 `DisplayProcesses` method using an object initializer
(ObjectInitializer.csproj)

```
static void DisplayProcesses()
{
  var processes = new List<ProcessData>();
  foreach (var process in Process.GetProcesses())
  {
    processes.Add( new ProcessData { Id=process.Id,
      Name=process.ProcessName, Memory=process.WorkingSet64 } );
  }

  ObjectDumper.Write(processes);
}
```

Although the two syntaxes are similar, the latter doesn't require us to add a constructor!

We can see several advantages to the object initializer notation:

- We can initialize an object within just one instruction.
- We don't need to provide a constructor to be able to initialize simple objects.
- We don't need several constructors to initialize different properties of objects.

This doesn't mean that object initializers are an alternative to writing good constructors. Object initializers and constructors are language features that complement each other. You should still define the appropriate set of constructors for your types. Constructors help prevent the creation of objects that aren't completely initialized and define the correct initialization order for an object's members.

After these syntactic improvements, let's add new functionality to our example. We'll do this with the help of lambda expressions.

2.4 *Lambda expressions*

```
address => address.City == "Paris"
```

As a part of our tour of the new language features that are enablers for LINQ, we'll now introduce *lambda expressions*, which come from the world of the lambda calculus. Many functional programming languages such as Lisp use lambda notations to define functions. In addition to allowing the expression of LINQ queries, the introduction of lambda expressions into C# and VB.NET can be seen as a step toward functional languages.

Lambda calculus

In mathematical logic and computer science, the lambda calculus (λ-calculus) is a formal system designed to investigate function definition, function application, and recursion. It was introduced by Alonzo Church in the 1930s. Lambda calculus has greatly influenced functional programming languages, such as Lisp, ML, and Haskell. (Source: Wikipedia.)

Let's get back to our example. Suppose we want to improve it by adding filtering capabilities. In order to do this, we can use delegates, which allow us to pass one method as a parameter to another, for example.

We'll start with a refresher on delegates and anonymous methods before using lambda expressions.

2.4.1 *A refresher on delegates*

Let's build on the code of our `DisplayProcesses` method as we left it in listing 2.5. Here, we've added a hard-coded filtering condition, as you can see in listing 2.6.

Listing 2.6 `DisplayProcesses` method with a hard-coded filtering condition

```
static void DisplayProcesses()
{
  var processes = new List<ProcessData>();          ◁——  Build list of processes
  foreach (var process in Process.GetProcesses())          matching criterion
  {
    if (process.WorkingSet64 >= 20*1024*1024)
    {
      processes.Add(new ProcessData { Id=process.Id,
        Name=process.ProcessName, Memory=process.WorkingSet64 });
    }
  }

  ObjectDumper.Write(processes);
}
```

`WorkingSet64` is the amount of physical memory allocated for the associated process. Here we search for processes with more than 20 megabytes of allocated memory.

In order to make our code more generic, we'll try to provide the filter information as a parameter of our method instead of keeping it hard-coded. In C# 2.0 and earlier, this was possible thanks to delegates. A *delegate* is a type that can store a pointer to a method.

Our filtering method should take a `Process` object as an argument and return a `Boolean` value to indicate whether a process matches some criteria. Here is how to declare such a delegate:

```
delegate Boolean FilterDelegate(Process process);
```

Instead of creating our own delegate type, we can also use what .NET 2.0 provides: the `Predicate<T>` type. Here is how this type is defined:

```
delegate Boolean Predicate<T>(T obj);
```

The `Predicate<T>` delegate type represents a method that returns true or false, based on its input. This type is generic, so we need to specify that it will work on `Process` objects. The exact delegate type we'll use is `Predicate<Process>`.

Listing 2.7 shows our `DisplayProcesses` method adapted to take a predicate as a parameter.

Listing 2.7 `DisplayProcesses` **method that uses a delegate for filtering**

```
static void DisplayProcesses(Predicate<Process> match)
{
  var processes = new List<ProcessData>();
  foreach (var process in Process.GetProcesses())
  {
    if (match(process))
    {
      processes.Add(new ProcessData { Id=process.Id,
        Name=process.ProcessName, Memory=process.WorkingSet64 });
    }
  }

  ObjectDumper.Write(processes);
}
```

With the `DisplayProcesses` method updated as in the listing, it's now possible to pass any "filter" to it. In our case, the filtering method contains our condition and returns true if the criterion is matched:

```
static Boolean Filter(Process process)
{
  return process.WorkingSet64 >= 20*1024*1024;
}
```

To use this method, we provide it as an argument to the `DisplayProcesses` method, as in listing 2.8.

Listing 2.8 Calling the `DisplayProcesses` method using a standard delegate

```
DisplayProcesses(Filter);
```

2.4.2 Anonymous methods

Delegates existed in C# 1.0, but C# 2.0 was improved to allow working with delegates through anonymous methods. Anonymous methods allow you to write shorter code and avoid the need for explicitly named methods.

Thanks to anonymous methods, we don't need to declare a method like `Filter`. We can directly pass the code to `DisplayProcesses`, as in listing 2.9.

Listing 2.9 Calling the `DisplayProcesses` method using an anonymous method

```
DisplayProcesses( delegate (Process process)
  { return process.WorkingSet64 >= 20*1024*1024; } );
```

NOTE   VB.NET doesn't offer support for anonymous methods.

Those who have dealt with C++'s Standard Template Library (STL) may compare anonymous methods to functors. Similarly to functors, anonymous methods can be used to elegantly tweak a collection with a single line of code.

.NET 2.0 introduced a set of methods in `System.Collections.Generic.List<T>` and `System.Array` that are designed especially to be used with anonymous methods. These methods include `ForEach`, `Find`, and `FindAll`. They can operate on a list or an array with relatively little code.

For example, here is how the `Find` method can be used with an anonymous method to find a specific process:

```
var visualStudio = processes.Find(delegate (Process process)
  { return process.ProcessName == "devenv"; } );
```

2.4.3 Introducing lambda expressions

Instead of using an anonymous method, like in listing 2.9, starting with C# 3.0 we can use a lambda expression.

Listing 2.10 is strictly equivalent to the previous piece of code.

**Listing 2.10 Calling the `DisplayProcesses` method using a lambda expression
(LambdaExpressions.csproj)**

```
DisplayProcesses(process => process.WorkingSet64 >= 20*1024*1024);
```

Notice how the code is simplified when using a lambda expression. This lambda expression reads like this: "Given a process, return true if the process consumes 20 megabytes of memory or more."

As you can see, in the case of lambda expressions, we don't need to provide the type of the parameter. Again, this was duplicated information in the previous code: The new C# compiler is able to deduce the type of the parameters from the method signature.

Comparing lambda expressions with anonymous methods

C# 2.0 introduced anonymous methods, which allow code blocks to be written "inline" where delegate values are expected. The anonymous method syntax is verbose and imperative in nature. In contrast, lambda expressions provide a more concise syntax, providing much of the expressive power of functional programming languages.

Lambda expressions can be considered as a functional superset of anonymous methods, providing the following additional functionality:

- Lambda expressions can infer parameter types, allowing you to omit them.
- Lambda expressions can use both statement blocks and expressions as bodies, allowing for a terser syntax than anonymous methods, whose bodies can only be statement blocks.
- Lambda expressions can participate in type argument inference and method overload resolution when passed in as arguments. Note: anonymous methods can also participate in type argument inference (inferred return types).
- Lambda expressions with an expression body can be converted into expression trees. (We'll introduce expression trees in the next chapter.)

Lambda expressions introduce new syntaxes in C# and VB.NET. In the next section, we'll look at the structure of lambda expressions and review some samples so you can grow accustomed to them.

How to express lambda expressions

In C#, a lambda expression is written as a parameter list, followed by the => token, followed by an expression or a statement block, as shown in figure 2.1.

```
process    =>    process.WorkingSet64 >= 20*1024*1024
```
input parameters lambda operator expression or statement block

Figure 2.1
Structure of a lambda expression in C#

> **NOTE** The => token always follows the parameter list. It should not be confused with comparison operators such as <= and >=.

The lambda operator can be read as "goes to." The left side of the operator specifies the input parameters (if any), and the right side holds the expression or statement block to be evaluated.

There are two kinds of lambda expressions. A lambda expression with an expression on the right side is called an *expression lambda*. The second kind is a *statement lambda*, which looks similar to an expression lambda except that its right part consists of any number of statements enclosed in curly braces.

To give you a better idea of what lambda expressions look like in C#, see listing 2.11 for some examples.

Listing 2.11 Sample lambda expressions in C#

```
x => x + 1         1
x => { return x + 1; }     2
(int x) => x + 1       3
(int x) => { return x + 1; }     4
(x, y) => x * y      5
() => 1     6
() => Console.WriteLine()      7
customer => customer.Name
person => person.City == "Paris"
(person, minAge) => person.Age >= minAge
```

1. Implicitly typed, expression body
2. Implicitly typed, statement body
3. Explicitly typed, expression body
4. Explicitly typed, statement body
5. Multiple parameters
6. No parameters, expression body
7. No parameters, statement body

> **NOTE** The parameters of a lambda expression can be explicitly or implicitly typed.

In VB.NET, lambda expressions are written differently. They start with the Function keyword, as shown in figure 2.2:

**Figure 2.2
Structure of a lambda
expression in VB.NET**

NOTE VB.NET 9.0 doesn't support statement lambdas.

Listing 2.12 shows the sample expressions we provided for C#, but in VB.NET this time.

VB.NET

Listing 2.12   Sample lambda expressions in VB.NET

```
Function(x) x + 1        ❶
Function(x As Integer) x + 1       ❷
Function(x, y) x * y       ❸
Function() 1     ❹
Function(customer) customer.Name
Function(person) person.City = "Paris"
Function(person, minAge) person.Age >= minAge
```

❶ Implicitly typed

❷ Explicitly typed

❸ Multiple parameters

❹ No parameters

As you saw in the example, lambda expressions are compatible with delegates. To give you a feel for lambda expressions as delegates, we'll use some delegate types.

The System.Action<T>, System.Converter<TInput, TOutput>, and System.Predicate<T> generic delegate types were introduced by .NET 2.0:

```
delegate void Action<T>(T obj);
delegate TOutput Converter<TInput, TOutput>(TInput input);
delegate Boolean Predicate<T>(T obj);
```

Another interesting delegate type from previous versions of .NET is MethodInvoker. This type represents any method that takes no parameters and returns no results:

```
delegate void MethodInvoker();
```

We regret that MethodInvoker has been declared in the System.Windows.Forms namespace even though it can be useful outside Windows Forms applications. This has been addressed in .NET 3.5. A new version of the Action delegate type that takes no parameter is added to the `System` namespace by the new `System.Core.dll` assembly:

```
delegate void Action();
```

NOTE   The `System.Core.dll` assembly comes with .NET 3.5. We'll describe its content and the content of the other LINQ assemblies in chapter 3.

A whole set of additional delegate types is added to the `System` namespace by the `System.Core.dll` assembly:

```
delegate void Action<T1, T2>(T1 arg1, T2 arg2);
delegate void Action<T1, T2, T3>(T1 arg1, T2 arg2);
delegate void Action<T1, T2, T3, T4>(T1 arg1, T2 arg2,
  T3 arg3, T4 arg4);
delegate TResult Func<TResult>();
delegate TResult Func<T, TResult>(T arg);
delegate TResult Func<T1, T2, TResult>(T1 arg1, T2 arg2);
delegate TResult Func<T1, T2, T3, TResult>(T1 arg1, T2 arg2);
delegate TResult Func<T1, T2, T3, T4, TResult>(T1 arg1, T2 arg2,
  T3 arg3, T4 arg4);
```

A lambda expression is compatible with a delegate if the following rules are respected:

- The lambda must contain the same number of parameters as the delegate type.
- Each input parameter in the lambda must be implicitly convertible to its corresponding delegate parameter.
- The return value of the lambda (if any) must be implicitly convertible to the delegate's return type.

To give you a good overview of the various possible combinations, we have prepared a set of sample lambda expressions declared as delegates. These samples demonstrate the compatibility between the delegate types we have just introduced and some lambda expressions. Listings 2.13 and 2.14 contain the samples, which include lambda expressions and delegates with and without parameters, both with and without result, as well as expression lambdas and statement lambdas.

Listing 2.13 Sample lambda expressions declared as delegates in C# (LambdaExpressions.csproj)

```
Func<DateTime> getDateTime = () => DateTime.Now;              ❶

Action<string> printImplicit = s => Console.WriteLine(s);     ❷

Action<string> printExplicit = (string s) => Console.WriteLine(s);  ❸
```

```
Func<int, int, int> sumInts = (x, y) => x + y;      ④

Predicate<int> equalsOne1 = x => x == 1;       ⑤
Func<int, bool> equalsOne2 = x => x == 1;

Func<int, int> incInt = x => x + 1;            ⑥
Func<int, double> incIntAsDouble = x => x + 1;

Func<int, int, int> comparer = (int x, int y) =>   ⑦
  {
    if (x > y) return 1;
    if (x < y) return -1;
    return 0;
  };
```

❶ No parameter

❷ Implicitly typed string parameter

❸ Explicitly typed string parameter

❹ Two implicitly typed parameters

❺ Equivalent but not compatible

❻ Same lambda expression but different delegate types

❼ Statement body and explicitly typed parameters

Listing 2.14 shows similar lambda expressions declared as delegates in VB.

VB.NET   **Listing 2.14   Sample lambda expressions declared as delegates in VB.NET (LambdaExpressions.vbproj)**

```
Dim getDateTime As Func(Of DateTime) = Function() DateTime.Now   ❶

Dim upperImplicit As Func(Of String, String) = _    ❷
  Function(s) s.ToUpper()

Dim upperExplicit As Func(Of String, String) = _    ❸
  Function(s As String) s.ToUpper()

Dim sumInts As Func(of Integer, Integer, Integer) = _   ❹
  Function(x, y) x + y

Dim equalsOne1 As Predicate(of Integer) = Function(x) x = 1   ❺
Dim equalsOne2 As Func(Of Integer, Boolean) = Function(x) x = 1

Dim incInt As Func(Of Integer, Integer) = Function(x) x + 1   ❻
Dim incIntAsDouble As Func(Of Integer, Double) = Function(x) x + 1
```

❶ No parameter

❷ Implicitly typed string parameter

❸ Explicitly typed string parameter

❹ Two implicitly typed parameters

❺ Equivalent but not compatible

❻ Same lambda expression but different delegate types

The statement lambda isn't reproduced in VB in the listing because VB.NET doesn't support this kind of lambda expression. Furthermore, we use `Func(Of String, String)` ❷❸ instead of `Action(Of String)` because it would require a statement lambda.

Let's continue improving our example. This time, we'll work on the list of processes.

2.5   Extension methods

```
static void Dump(this object o);
```

The next topic we'd like to cover is *extension methods*. You'll see how this new language feature allows you to add methods to a type after it has been defined. You'll also see how extension methods compare to static methods and instance methods.

We'll start by creating a sample extension method, before going through more examples and using some predefined extension methods. Before jumping onto the next subject, we'll give you some warnings and show you the limitations of extension methods.

2.5.1   Creating a sample extension method

In our continuing effort to improve our example that displays information about the running processes, let's say we want to compute the total memory used by a list of processes. We could define a standard static method that accepts an enumeration of `ProcessData` objects as a parameter. This method would loop on the processes and sum the memory used by each process.

For an example, see listing 2.15.

Listing 2.15   The `TotalMemory` helper method coded as standard static method

```
static Int64 TotalMemory(IEnumerable<ProcessData> processes)
{
    Int64 result = 0;

    foreach (var process in processes)
```

```
    result += process.Memory;

  return result;
}
```

We could then use this method this way:

```
Console.WriteLine("Total memory: {0} MB",
  TotalMemory(processes)/1024/1024);
```

One thing we can do to improve our code is convert our static method into an extension method. This new language feature makes it possible to treat existing types as if they were extended with additional methods.

Declaring extension methods in C#

In order to transform our method into an extension method, all we have to do is add the `this` keyword to the first parameter, as shown in listing 2.16.

> **Listing 2.16** The `TotalMemory` helper method declared as an extension method
> (ExtensionMethods.csproj)

```
static Int64 TotalMemory(this IEnumerable<ProcessData> processes)    ❶
{
  Int64 result = 0;

  foreach (var process in processes)
    result += process.Memory;

  return result;
}
```

If we examine this new version of the method, it still looks more or less exactly like any run-of-the-mill helper routine, with the notable exception of the first parameter being decorated with the `this` keyword ❶.

The `this` keyword instructs the compiler to treat the method as an extension method. It indicates that this is a method that extends objects of type `IEnumerable<ProcessData>`.

> **NOTE** In C#, extension methods must be declared on a non-generic static class. In addition, an extension method can take any number of parameters, but the first parameter must be of the type that is extended and preceded by the keyword `this`.

We can now use the `TotalMemory` method as if it were an instance method defined on the type of our `processes` object. Here is the syntax it allows:

```
Console.WriteLine("Total memory: {0} MB",
  processes.TotalMemory()/1024/1024);
```

See how we have extended, in appearance at least, the `IEnumerable<ProcessData>` type with a new method. The type remains unchanged. The compiler converts the code to a static method call, comparable to what we used in listing 2.15.

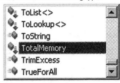

It may not appear that using an extension method makes a big difference, but it helps when writing code because our `TotalMemory` method is now listed by IntelliSense for the types supported by this method, as shown in figure 2.3.

Figure 2.3 IntelliSense displays extension methods with a specific icon in addition to instance methods.

Notice how a specific icon with a blue arrow is used for extension methods. The figure shows the `ToList` and `ToLookup` standard query operators (more on these in section 2.5.2), as well as our `TotalMemory` extension method. Now, when writing code, we clearly see that we can get a total of the memory used by the processes contained in an enumeration of `ProcessData` objects. Extension methods are more easily discoverable through IntelliSense than classic static helper methods are.

Another advantage of extension methods is that they make it much easier to chain operations together. Let's consider that we want to do the following:

1 Filter out some processes from a collection of `ProcessData` objects using a helper method.

2 Compute the total memory consumption of the processes using `TotalMemory`.

3 Convert the memory consumption into megabytes using another helper method.

We would end up writing code that looks like this with classical helper methods:

```
BytesToMegaBytes(TotalMemory(FilterOutSomeProcesses(processes)));
```

One problem with this kind of code is that the operations are specified in the opposite of the order in which they are executed. This makes the code both harder to write and more difficult to understand.

In comparison, if the three fictitious helper methods were defined as extension methods, we could write:

```
processes
    .FilterOutSomeProcesses()
    .TotalMemory()
    .BytesToMegaBytes();
```

In this latter version, the operations are specified in the same order they execute in. This is much easier to read, don't you think?

> **NOTE** Notice in the code sample that we insert line breaks and whitespace between method calls. We'll do this often in our code samples in order to improve code readability. This isn't a new feature offered by C# 3.0, because it's supported by all versions of C#.

You'll see more examples of chaining constructs in the next sections. As you'll see in the next chapter, this is a key feature for writing LINQ queries. For the moment, let's see how to declare extension methods in VB.NET.

Declaring extension methods in VB.NET

In VB.NET, extension methods are shared methods decorated with a custom attribute (`System.Runtime.CompilerServices.ExtensionAttribute`) that allow them to be invoked with instance-method syntax. (An extension method can be a Sub procedure or a Function procedure.) This attribute is provided by the new `System.Core.dll` assembly.

> **NOTE** In VB.NET, extension methods should be declared in a module.

The first parameter in a VB.NET extension method definition specifies which data type the method extends. When the method is run, the first parameter is bound to the instance of the data type against which the method is applied.

Listing 2.17 shows how we would declare our `TotalMemory` extension method in VB.NET.

VB.NET

Listing 2.17 Sample extension method in VB.NET (ExtensionMethods.vbproj)

```
<System.Runtime.CompilerServices.Extension()> _
Public Function TotalMemory( _
  ByVal processes As IEnumerable(Of ProcessData)) _
  As Int64
```

```
    Dim result As Int64 = 0
    For Each process In processes
      result += process.Memory
    Next
    Return Result
  End Function
```

> **NOTE** Extension members of other kinds, such as properties, events, and operators, are being considered by Microsoft for the future but are currently not supported in C# 3.0 and VB.NET 9.0.

To give you a better idea of what can be done with extension methods and why they are useful, we'll now use some standard extension methods provided with LINQ.

2.5.2 *More examples using LINQ's standard query operators*

LINQ comes with a set of extension methods you can use like any other extension method. We'll use some of them to show you more extension methods in action and give you a preview of the standard query operators, which we'll cover in the next chapter.

OrderByDescending

Let's say that we'd like to sort the list of processes by their memory consumption, memory hogs first. We can use the OrderByDescending extension method defined in the System.Linq.Enumerable class. Extension methods are imported through using namespace directives. For example, to use the extension methods defined in the Enumerable class, we need to add the following line of code to the top of our code file if it's not already there:

```
using System.Linq;
```

> **NOTE** Your project also needs a reference to System.Core.dll, but this is added by default for new projects.

We're now able to call OrderByDescending as follows to sort our processes:

```
ObjectDumper.Write(
  processes.OrderByDescending(process => process.Memory));
```

You can see that we provide the extension method with a lambda expression to decide how the sort operation will be performed. Here we indicate that we want to compare the processes based on their memory consumption.

It's important to note that type inference is used automatically to simplify the code. Although OrderByDescending is defined as a generic method, we don't need to explicitly indicate the types we're dealing with. The C# compiler deduces from the method call that `OrderByDescending` works here on `Process` objects and returns an enumeration of `Int64` objects.

When a generic method is called without specifying type arguments, a type inference process attempts to infer type arguments for the call. The presence of type inference allows a more convenient syntax to be used for calling a generic method, and allows the programmer to avoid specifying redundant type information.

Here is how `OrderByDescending` is defined:

```
public static IOrderedSequence<TSource>
  OrderByDescending<TSource, TKey>(
    this IEnumerable<TSource> source,
    Func<TSource, TKey> keySelector)
```

Here is how we would have to use it if type inference weren't occurring:

```
processes.OrderByDescending<Process, Int64>(
  (Process process) => process.Memory));
```

The code would be more difficult to read without type inference because we'd have to specify types everywhere in LINQ queries.

Let's now look at other query operators.

Take

If we're interested only in the two processes that consume the most memory, we can use the `Take` extension method:

```
ObjectDumper.Write(
  processes
    .OrderByDescending(process => process.Memory)
    .Take(2));
```

The `Take` method returns the first *n* elements in an enumeration. Here we want two elements.

Sum

If we want to sum the amount of memory used by the two processes, we can use another standard extension method: `Sum`. The `Sum` method can be used in place of the extension method we created, `TotalMemory`. Here is how to use it:

```
ObjectDumper.Write(
  processes
    .OrderByDescending(process => process.Memory)
    .Take(2)
    .Sum(process => process.Memory)/1024/1024);
```

2.5.3 Extension methods in action in our example

Listing 2.18 shows what our `DisplayProcess` method looks like after all the additions we made.

Listing 2.18 The `DisplayProcesses` methods with extension methods (ExtensionMethods.csproj)

```
static void DisplayProcesses(Func<Process, Boolean> match)
{
  var processes = new List<ProcessData>();
  foreach (var process in Process.GetProcesses())
  {
    if (match(process))
    {
      processes.Add(new ProcessData { Id=process.Id,
        Name=process.ProcessName, Memory=process.WorkingSet64 });
    }
  }

  Console.WriteLine("Total memory: {0} MB",
    processes.TotalMemory()/1024/1024);

  var top2Memory =
    processes
      .OrderByDescending(process => process.Memory)
      .Take(2)
      .Sum(process => process.Memory)/1024/1024;
  Console.WriteLine(
    "Memory consumed by the two most hungry processes: {0} MB",
    top2Memory);

  ObjectDumper.Write(processes);
}
```

You can see how extension methods are especially useful when you combine them. Without extension methods, we would have to write code that is more difficult to comprehend. For example, compare the following code snippets that use the same methods.

Note these methods used as classic static methods:

```
var top2Memory =
  Enumerable.Sum(
    Enumerable.Take(
      Enumerable.OrderByDescending(processes,
        process => process.Memory),
      2),
    process => process.Memory)/1024/1024;
```

Compare that to these methods used as extension methods:

```
var top2Memory =
  processes
    .OrderByDescending(process => process.Memory)
    .Take(2)
    .Sum(process => process.Memory)/1024/1024;
```

As you can see, extension methods facilitate a chaining pattern because they can be strung together using dot notation. This looks like a pipeline and could be compared to Unix pipes. This is important for working with query operators, which we'll cover in chapter 3.

> **Pipelines**
>
> In Unix-like computer operating systems, a pipeline is a set of processes chained by their standard streams, so that the output of each process (stdout) feeds directly as input (stdin) of the next one. Example: `who | grep "joe" | sort`.

Notice how much easier it is to follow the latter code. The processing steps are clearly expressed: We want to order the processes by memory, then keep the first two, and then sum their memory consumption. With the first code, it's not that obvious, because what happens first is nested in method calls.

2.5.4 Warnings

Let's review some limitations of extension methods before returning to our example application.

An important question arises when encountering extension methods: What if an extension method conflicts with an instance method? It's important to understand how the resolution of extension methods works.

Extension methods are less "discoverable" than instance methods, which means that they are always lower priority. An extension method can't hide an instance method.

Let's consider listing 2.19.

Listing 2.19 Sample code for demonstrating extension methods' discoverability

```
using System;

class Class1
{
}

class Class2
```

```
{
  public void Method1(string s)
  {
    Console.WriteLine("Class2.Method1");
  }
}

class Class3
{
  public void Method1(object o)
  {
    Console.WriteLine("Class3.Method1");
  }
}

class Class4
{
  public void Method1(int i)
  {
    Console.WriteLine("Class4.Method1");
  }
}

static class Extensions
{
  static public void Method1(this object o, int i)
  {
    Console.WriteLine("Extensions.Method1");
  }

  static void Main()
  {
    new Class1().Method1(12);      ◁──┐  Extensions.Method1 called
    new Class2().Method1(12);      ◁──┘  Extensions.Method1 called
    new Class3().Method1(12);      ◁───  Class3.Method1 called
    new Class4().Method1(12);      ◁───  Class4.Method1 called
  }
}
```

This code produces the following results:

```
Extensions.Method1
Extensions.Method1
Class3.Method1
Class4.Method1
```

You can see that as soon as an instance method exists with matching parameter types, it gets executed. The extension method is called only when no method with the same signature exists.

Warning

In VB.NET, the behavior is a bit different. With code similar to listing 2.19, the results are as follows if `Option Strict` is `Off`:

```
Extensions.Method1
Class2.Method1
Class3.Method1
Class4.Method1
```

As you can see, the VB.NET compiler gives higher priority to instance methods by converting parameters if needed. Here, the integer we pass to `Method1` is converted automatically to a string in order to call the method of `Class2`.

If `Option Strict` is `On`, the following compilation error happens: `"Option Strict On disallows implicit conversions from 'Integer' to 'String'"`. In such a case, a classic shared method call can be used, such as `Method1(New Class2(), 12)`.

See the sample `ExtensionMethodsDiscoverability.vbproj` project to experiment with this.

Extension methods are more limited in functionality than instance methods. They can't access non-public members, for example. Also, using extension methods intensively can negatively affect the readability of your code if it's not clear that an extension method is used. For those reasons, we recommend you use extension methods sparingly and only in situations where instance methods aren't feasible. We'll use and create extension methods in combination with LINQ, but that's a story for later.

With all these new features, we have greatly improved our code. But wait a minute: We can do better than that! Don't you think it would be a big improvement if we could get rid of the `ProcessData` class? As it stands, it's a temporary class with no real value, and it accounts for several lines of code. Getting rid of all the extra code would be perfect. This is just what *anonymous types* will allow us to do!

2.6   *Anonymous types*

```
var contact = new { Name = "Bob", Age = 8 }
```

We're approaching the end of this chapter. But we still have one language enhancement to introduce before we can focus again on LINQ in the next chapter, in which you'll be able to employ everything you learned in this chapter.

Using a syntax similar to that of object initializers, we can create anonymous types. They are usually used to group data into an object without first declaring a new class.

We'll start this section by demonstrating how to use anonymous types in our example. We'll then show you how anonymous types are real types, and point out some of their limitations.

2.6.1 Using anonymous types to group data into an object

Let's say we want to collect the results of our processing together. We want to group information into an object. Having to declare a specific type just for this would be a pain.

Here is how we can use an anonymous type in C#:

```
var results = new {
    TotalMemory = processes.TotalMemory()/1024/1024,
    Top2Memory = top2Memory,
    Processes = processes };
```

> **NOTE** To output content of the Processes property, which is created as part of our new object, we should instruct ObjectDumper to process the data one level deeper. In order to do this, call ObjectDumper.Write(results, 1) instead of ObjectDumper.Write(results).

The syntax for anonymous types in VB.NET is similar:

VB.NET

```
Dim results = New With { _
    .TotalMemory = processes.TotalMemory()/1024/1024, _
    .Top2Memory = top2Memory, _
    .Processes = processes }
```

> **NOTE** Objects declared using an anonymous type can be used only with the var or Dim keywords. This is because an anonymous type doesn't have a name we could use in our code!

2.6.2 Types without names, but types nonetheless

Anonymous types are types without names,[1] but types anyway. This means that a real type is created by the compiler. Our results variable points to an instance of a class that is created automatically based on our code. This class has three properties: TotalMemory, Top2Memory, and Processes. The types of the properties are deduced from the initializers.

Figure 2.4 shows what the anonymous type that is created for us looks like in the produced assembly.

---

[1] Without names we can use, at least.

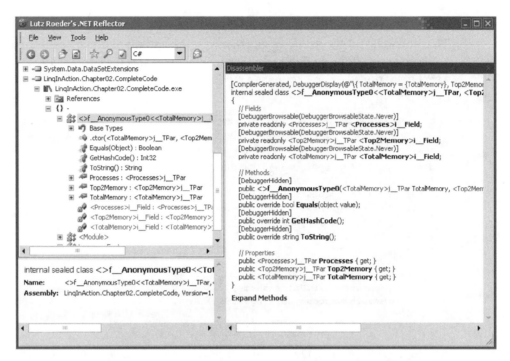

Figure 2.4 Sample anonymous type produced by the compiler, as displayed by .NET Reflector

The figure is a screenshot of .NET Reflector displaying the decompiled code of an anonymous type generated for the code we wrote in the previous section. (.NET Reflector is a free tool we highly recommend, available at http://aisto.com/roeder/dotnet.)

Be aware that compilers consider two anonymous types that are specified within the same program with properties of the same names and types in the same order to be the same type. For example, if we write the following two lines of code, only one type is created by the compiler:

```
var v1 = new { Person = "Suzie", Age = 32, CanCode = true }
var v2 = new { Person = "Barney", Age = 29, CanCode = false }
```

After this code snippet is executed, the two variables v1 and v2 contain two different instances of the same class.

If we add a third line like the following one, a different type is created for v3 because the order of the properties is different:

```
var v3 = new { Age = 17, Person = "Bill", CanCode = false }
```

2.6.3 *Improving our example using anonymous types*

That's all well and good, but we said that we could get rid of the `ProcessData` object, and we haven't done so. Let's get back to what we wanted to do. Listing 2.20 shows a version of our `DisplayProcesses` method that uses an anonymous type instead of the `ProcessData` class:

Listing 2.20 The `DisplayProcesses` method with an anonymous type (AnonymousTypes.csproj)

```
static void DisplayProcesses(Func<Process, Boolean> match)
{
  var processes = new List<Object>();
  foreach (var process in Process.GetProcesses())
  {
    if (match(process))
    {
      processes.Add( new {
        process.Id,        ❶
        Name=process.ProcessName,
        Memory=process.WorkingSet64 } );
    }
  }

  ObjectDumper.Write(processes);
}
```

NOTE If a name isn't specified for a property, and the expression is a simple name or a member access, the result property takes the name of the original member. Here we don't provide a name for the first member ❶, so it will be named `Id`.

For the sake of clarity, you may consider explicitly naming the members even if it isn't required.

The great advantage of using such code is that we don't need to declare our `ProcessData` class. This makes anonymous types a great tool for quick and simple temporary results. We don't have to declare classes to hold temporary results anymore—thanks to anonymous types.

Still, anonymous types suffer from a number of limitations.

2.6.4 *Limitations*

A problem with our new code is that now that we have removed the `ProcessData` class, we can't use our `TotalMemory` method any longer because it's defined to work with `ProcessData` objects. As soon as we use anonymous types, we lose the ability to work with your objects in a strongly typed manner outside of the method where they are defined. This means that we can pass an instance of an anonymous type to a method only if the method expects an `Object` as parameter, but not if it expects a more precise type. Reflection is the only way to work with an anonymous type outside of the method where it's created.

Likewise, anonymous types can't be used as method results, unless the method's return type is `Object`. This is why anonymous types should be used only for temporary data and can't be used like normal types in method signatures.

Well, that's not entirely true. We can use anonymous types as method results from generic methods. Let's consider the following method:

```
public static TResult ReturnAGeneric<TResult>(
  Func<TResult> creator)
{
  return creator();
}
```

The return type of the `ReturnAGeneric` method is generic. If we call it without explicitly specifying a type for the `TResult` type argument, it's inferred automatically from the signature of the `creator` parameter. Now, let's consider the following line of code that invokes `ReturnAGeneric`:

```
var obj = ReturnAGeneric(
  () => new {Time = DateTime.Now, AString = "abc"});
```

Because the creator function provided as an argument returns an instance of an anonymous type, `ReturnAGeneric` returns that instance. However, `ReturnAGeneric` isn't defined to return an `Object`, but a generic type. This is why the `obj` variable is strongly typed. This means it has a `Time` property of type `DateTime` and an `AString` property of type `String`.

Our `ReturnAGeneric` method is pretty much useless. But as you'll be able to see with the standard query operators, LINQ uses this extensively in a more useful way.

There is one more thing to keep in mind about anonymous types. In C#, instances of anonymous types are *immutable*. This means that once you create an anonymous type instance, its field and property values are fixed forever. If you look at the sample anonymous type the compiler creates in figure 2.4, you can see that properties have getters but no setters. The only way to assign values to the properties and their underlying fields is through the constructor of the class. When you use the syntax to initialize an instance of an anonymous type, the constructor of that type is invoked automatically and the values are set once and for all.

Because they are immutable, instances of anonymous types have stable hash codes. If an object can't be altered, then its hash code will never change either (unless the hash code of one of its fields isn't stable). This is useful for hash tables and data-binding scenarios, for example.

You may wonder why anonymous types in C# are designed to be immutable. What may appear to be a limitation is in fact a feature. It enables value-based programming, which is used in functional languages to avoid side effects. Objects that never change allow concurrent access to work much better. This will be useful to enable PLINQ (Parallel LINQ), a project Microsoft has started to introduce concurrency in LINQ queries. You'll learn more about PLINQ in chapter 13. Immutable anonymous types take .NET one step closer to a more functional programming world where we can use snapshots of state and side-effect-free code.

Keyed anonymous types

We wrote that anonymous types are immutable in C#. The behavior is different in VB.NET. By default, instances of anonymous types are mutable in VB.NET. But we can specify a `Key` modifier on the properties of an anonymous type, as shown in listing 2.21.

Listing 2.21   Testing keyed anonymous types (AnonymousTypes.csproj)

```
Dim v1 = New With {Key .Id = 123, .Name = "Fabrice"}
Dim v2 = New With {Key .Id = 123, .Name = "Céline"}
Dim v3 = New With {Key .Id = 456, .Name = "Fabrice"}
Console.WriteLine(v1.Equals(v2))
Console.WriteLine(v1.Equals(v3))
```

The `Key` modifier does two things: It makes the property on which it's applied read-only (keys have to be stable), and it causes the `GetHashCode` method to be overridden by the anonymous type so it calls `GetHashCode` on the key properties. You can have as many key properties as you like.

A consequence of using `Key` is that it affects the comparison of objects. For example, in the listing, `v1.Equals(v2)` returns `True` because the keys of `v1` and `v2` are equal. In contrast, `v1.Equals(v3)` returns `False`.

2.7   *Summary*

In this chapter, we have covered several language extensions provided by C# 3.0 and VB.NET 9.0:

- Implicitly typed local variables
- Object and collection initializers
- Lambda expressions
- Extension methods
- Anonymous types

All these new features are cornerstones for LINQ, but they are integral parts of the C# and VB.NET languages and can be used separately. They represent a move by Microsoft to bring some of the benefits that exist with dynamic and functional languages to .NET developers.

Feature notes

We also used auto-implemented properties in this chapter, but this new feature exists only for C# and isn't required for LINQ to exist. If you want to learn more about the new C# features and C# in general, we suggest you read another book from Manning: *C# in Depth*.

VB.NET 9.0 introduces more language features, but they aren't related to LINQ, and we won't cover them in this book. This includes `If` as a ternary operator similar to C#'s `?:` operator and as a replacement for `IIf`. Other VB improvements include *relaxed delegates* and *improved generic type inferencing*.

It's interesting to note that Visual Studio 2008 lets us write code that uses C# 3.0 or VB.NET 9.0 features but target .NET 2.0. In other words, we can run code that uses what we introduced in this chapter on .NET 2.0 without needing .NET 3.0 or 3.5 installed on the client or host machine, because all the features are provided by the compiler and don't require runtime or library support. One notable exception is extension methods, which require the `System.Runtime.CompilerServices.ExtensionAttribute` class; but we can introduce it ourselves or deliver the `System.Core` assembly that contains it with our .NET 2.0 program.

To sum up what we have introduced in this chapter, listing 2.22 shows the complete source code of the example we built. You can see all the new language features in action, as highlighted in the annotations.

**Listing 2.22   Complete code demonstrating the new language features
                (CompleteCode.csproj)**

```csharp
using System;
using System.Collections.Generic;
using System.Diagnostics;
using System.Linq;

static class LanguageFeatures
{
  class ProcessData
  {
    public Int32  Id { get; set; }
    public Int64  Memory { get; set; }
    public String Name { get; set; }
  }

  static void DisplayProcesses(Func<Process, Boolean> match)
  {
    var processes = new List<ProcessData>();              Implicitly typed
    foreach (var process in Process.GetProcesses())       local variables
    {
      if (match(process))                                            Object
      {                                                           initializers
        processes.Add(new ProcessData { Id=process.Id,
          Name=process.ProcessName, Memory=process.WorkingSet64 });
      }
    }

    Console.WriteLine("Total memory: {0} MB",
      processes.TotalMemory()/1024/1024);
    var top2Memory =                                          Extension
      processes                                               methods
        .OrderByDescending(process => process.Memory)
        .Take(2)
        .Sum(process => process.Memory)/1024/1024;
    Console.WriteLine(
      "Memory consumed by the two most hungry processes: {0} MB",
      top2Memory);

    var results = new {
      TotalMemory = processes.TotalMemory()/1024/1024,      Anonymous
      Top2Memory = top2Memory,                              types
      Processes = processes };
    ObjectDumper.Write(results, 1);

    ObjectDumper.Write(processes);
  }
```

```
static Int64 TotalMemory(this IEnumerable<ProcessData> processes)
{
  Int64 result = 0;

  foreach (var process in processes)                          Extension
    result += process.Memory;                                 methods

  return result;
}

static void Main()
{
  DisplayProcesses(                                           Lambda
    process => process.WorkingSet64 >= 20*1024*1024);   ⊲——┘  expressions
}
}
```

After this necessary digression, in the next chapter you'll see how all the language enhancements you have just discovered are used by LINQ to integrate queries into C# and VB.NET.

LINQ building blocks

This chapter covers:

- An introduction to the key elements of the LINQ foundation
- Sequences
- Deferred query execution
- Query operators
- Query expressions
- Expression trees
- LINQ DLLs and namespaces

In chapter 2, we reviewed the language additions made to C# and VB.NET: the basic elements and language innovations that make LINQ possible.

In this chapter, you'll discover new concepts unique to LINQ. Each of these concepts builds on the new language features we presented in chapter 2. You'll now begin to see how everything adds up when used by LINQ.

We'll start with a rundown of the language features we've already covered. We'll then present new features that form the key elements of the LINQ foundation. In particular, we'll detail the language extensions and key concepts. This includes sequences, the standard query operators, query expressions, and expression trees. We'll finish this chapter by taking a look at how LINQ extends the .NET Framework with new assemblies and namespaces.

At the end of this chapter, you should have a good overview of all the fundamental building blocks on which LINQ relies and how they fit together. With this foundation, you'll be ready to work on LINQ code.

3.1 How LINQ extends .NET

This section gives a refresher on the features we introduced in chapter 2 and puts them into the big picture so you can get a clear idea of how they all work together when used with LINQ. We'll also enumerate the elements LINQ brings to the party, which we'll detail in the rest of this chapter.

3.1.1 Refresher on the language extensions

As a refresher, let's sum up the significant additions to the languages that you discovered in chapter 2:

- Implicitly typed local variables
- Object initializers
- Lambda expressions
- Extension methods
- Anonymous types

These additions are what we call *language extensions*, the set of new language features and syntactic constructs added to C# and VB.NET to support LINQ. All of these extensions require new versions of the C# and VB.NET compilers, but no new IL instructions or changes of the .NET runtime.

These language extensions are full-fledged features that can be used in code that has nothing to do with LINQ. They are however required for LINQ to work, and you'll use them a lot when writing language-integrated queries.

In order to introduce LINQ concepts and understand why they are important, we'll dissect a code sample throughout this chapter. We'll keep the same subject as in chapter 2: filtering and sorting a list of running processes.

Here is the code sample we'll use:

```
static void DisplayProcesses()
{
  var processes =
    Process.GetProcesses()
      .Where(process => process.WorkingSet64 > 20*1024*1024)
      .OrderByDescending(process => process.WorkingSet64)
      .Select(process => new { process.Id,
                               Name=process.ProcessName });

  ObjectDumper.Write(processes);
}
```

The portion of code in bold is a LINQ query. If you take a close look at it, you can see all the language enhancements we introduced in the previous chapter, as shown in figure 3.1.

In the figure, you should clearly see how everything dovetails to form a complete solution. You can now understand why we called the language enhancements "key components" for LINQ.

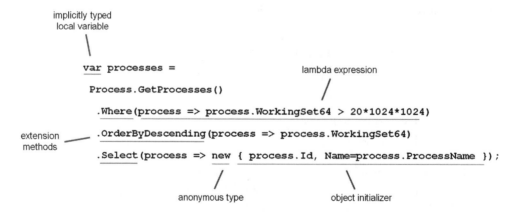

Figure 3.1 The language extensions all in one picture

3.1.2 *The key elements of the LINQ foundation*

More features and concepts are required for LINQ to work than those we've just listed. Several concepts specifically related to queries are also required:

- We'll start by explaining what *sequences* are and how they are used in LINQ queries.
- You'll also encounter *query expressions*. This is the name for the from...where...select syntax you've already seen.
- We'll explore *query operators*, which represent the basic operations you can perform in a LINQ query.
- We'll also explain what *deferred query execution* means, and why it is important.
- In order to enable deferred query execution, LINQ uses *expression trees*. We'll see what expression trees are and how LINQ uses them.

You need to understand these features in order to be able to read and write LINQ code, as we'll do in the next chapters.

3.2 *Introducing sequences*

The first LINQ concept we'll present in this chapter is the sequence.

In order to introduce sequences and understand why they are important, let's dissect listing 3.1.

Listing 3.1 Querying a list of processes using extension methods

```
var processes =
  Process.GetProcesses()                              ①
    .Where(process => process.WorkingSet64 > 20*1024*1024)        ②
    .OrderByDescending(process => process.WorkingSet64)      ③
    .Select(process => new { process.Id,
                             Name=process.ProcessName });    ④
```

① Get a list of running processes
② Filter the list
③ Sort the list
④ Keep only the IDs and names

To precisely understand what happens under the covers, let's analyze this code step by step, in the order the processing happens.

We'll start by looking at IEnumerable<T>, a key interface you'll find everywhere when working with LINQ. We'll also provide a small refresher on *iterators* and then stress how iterators allow *deferred query execution*.

3.2.1 IEnumerable<T>

The first thing you need to understand in listing 3.1 is what the call to Process.GetProcesses ❶ returns and how it is used. The GetProcesses method of the System.Diagnostics.Process class returns an array of Process objects. This is not surprising and probably wouldn't be interesting, except that arrays implement the generic IEnumerable<T> interface. This interface, which appeared with .NET 2.0, is key to LINQ. In our particular case, an array of Process objects implements IEnumerable<Process>.

The IEnumerable<T> interface is important because Where ❷, OrderByDescending ❸, Select ❹, and other standard query operators used in LINQ queries expect an object of this type as a parameter.

Listing 3.2 shows how the Where method is defined, for instance.

Listing 3.2 The Where method that is used in our sample query

```
public static IEnumerable<TSource> Where<TSource>(
  this IEnumerable<TSource> source,            ❶
  Func<TSource, Boolean> predicate)
{
  foreach (TSource element in source)
  {
    if (predicate(element))
      yield return element;                    ❷
  }
}
```

But where does this Where method come from? Is it a method of the IEnumerable<T> interface? Well, no. As you may have guessed if you remember chapter 2, it's an *extension method*. This can be detected by the presence of the this keyword on the first parameter of the method ❶.

The extension methods we see here (Where, OrderByDescending, and Select) are provided by the System.Linq.Enumerable class. The name of this class comes from the fact that the extension methods it contains work on IEnumerable<T> objects.

NOTE   In LINQ, the term *sequence* designates everything that implements IEnu-
merable<T>.

Let's take another look at the Where method. Note that it uses the yield return ❷
statement added in C# 2.0. This and the IEnumerable<TSource> return type in the
signature make it an iterator.

   We'll now take some time to review background information on iterators
before getting back to our example.

3.2.2   *Refresher on iterators*

An *iterator* is an object that allows you to traverse through a collection's elements.
What is named an iterator in .NET is also known as a *generator* in other languages
such as Python, or sometimes a *cursor*, especially within the context of a database.

   You may not know what an iterator is, but you surely have used several of them
before! Each time you use a foreach loop (For Each in VB.NET), an iterator is
involved. (This isn't true for arrays because the C# and VB.NET compilers optimize foreach and For Each loops over arrays to replace the use of iterators by a
simple loop, as if a for loop were used.) Every .NET collection (List<T>, Dictio-
nary<T>, and ArrayList for example) has a method named GetEnumerator that
returns an object used to iterate over its contents. That's what foreach uses
behind the scenes to iterate on the items contained in a collection.

   If you're interested in design patterns, you can study the classical Iterator pattern. This is the design iterators rely on in .NET.

   An iterator is similar, in its result, to a traditional method that returns a collection, because it generates a sequence of values. For example, we could create the
following method to return an enumeration of integers:

```
int[] OneTwoThree()
{
  return new [] {1, 2, 3};
}
```

However, the behavior of an iterator in C# 2.0 or 3.0 is very specific. Instead of
building a collection containing all the values and returning them all at once, an
iterator returns the values one at a time. This requires less memory and allows the
caller to start processing the first few values immediately, without having the complete collection ready.

   Let's look at a sample iterator to understand how it works. An iterator is easy to
create: it's simply a method that returns an enumeration and uses yield return
to provide the values.

Listing 3,3 shows an iterator named OneTwoThree that returns an enumeration containing the integer values 1, 2, and 3:

Listing 3.3   Sample iterator (Iterator.csproj)

```
using System;
using System.Collections.Generic;

static class Iterator
{
  static IEnumerable<int> OneTwoThree()
  {
    Console.WriteLine("Returning 1");
    yield return 1;
    Console.WriteLine("Returning 2");
    yield return 2;
    Console.WriteLine("Returning 3");
    yield return 3;
  }

  static void Main()
  {
    foreach (var number in OneTwoThree())
    {
      Console.WriteLine(number);
    }
  }
}
```

Here are the results of this code sample's execution:

```
Returning 1
1
Returning 2
2
Returning 3
3
```

As you can see, the OneTwoThree method does not exit until we reach its last statement. Each time we reach a yield return statement, the control is yielded back to the caller method. In our case, the foreach loop does its work, and then control is returned to the iterator method where it left so it can provide the next item.

It looks like two methods, or *routines,* are running at the same time. This is why .NET iterators could be presented as a kind of lightweight coroutine. A traditional method starts its execution at the beginning of its body each time it is called. This kind of method is named a *subroutine.* In comparison, a *coroutine* is a method that resumes its execution at the point it stopped the last time it was called, as if nothing had happened between invocations. All C# methods are sub-routines except methods that contain a `yield return` instruction, which can be considered to be coroutines.[1]

One thing you may find strange is that although we implement a method that returns an `IEnumerable<int>` in listing 3.3, in appearance we don't return an object of that type. We use `yield return`. The compiler does the work for us, and a class implementing `IEnumerable<int>` is created *automagically* for us. The `yield return` keyword is a time-saver that instructs the compiler to create a state engine in IL so you can create methods that retain their state without having to go through the pain of maintaining state in your own code.

We won't go into more details on this subject in this book, because it's not required to understand LINQ, and anyway, this is a standard C# 2.0 feature. However, if you want to investigate this, .NET Reflector is your friend.[2]

NOTE VB.NET has no instruction equivalent to `yield return`. Without this shortcut, VB.NET developers have to implement the `IEnumerable(Of T)` interface by hand to create enumerators. We provide a sample implementation in the companion source code download. See the `Iterator.vbproj` project.

The simple example provided in listing 3.3 shows that iterators are based on lazy evaluation. We'd like to stress that this big characteristic of iterators is essential for LINQ, as you'll see next.

3.2.3 *Deferred query execution*

LINQ queries rely heavily on lazy evaluation. In LINQ vocabulary, we'll refer to this as *deferred query execution*, also called *deferred query evaluation*. This is one of the most important concepts in LINQ. Without this facility, LINQ would perform very poorly.

Let's take a simple example to demonstrate how a query execution behaves.

---

[1] See Patrick Smacchia's book *Practical .NET2 and C#2* (Paradoxal Press) if you want to learn more about iterators.

[2] If you want to look into the low-level machinery of how state engines are built to make iterators work in .NET, you can download .NET Reflector at http://aisto.com/roeder/dotnet.

Demonstrating deferred query execution

In listing 3.4, we'll query an array of integers and perform an operation on all the items it contains.

Listing 3.4   Deferred query execution demonstration (DeferredQueryExecution.csproj)

```
using System;
using System.Linq;

static class DeferredQueryExecution
{
  static double Square(double n)
  {
    Console.WriteLine("Computing Square("+n+")...");
    return Math.Pow(n, 2);
  }

  public static void Main()
  {
    int[] numbers = {1, 2, 3};

    var query =
      from n in numbers
      select Square(n);

    foreach (var n in query)
      Console.WriteLine(n);
  }
}
```

The results of this program clearly show that the query does not execute at once. Instead, the query evaluates as we iterate on it:

```
Computing Square(1)...
1
Computing Square(2)...
4
Computing Square(3)...
9
```

As you'll see soon in section 3.4, queries such as the following one are translated into method calls at compile-time:

```
var query =
  from n in numbers
  select Square(n);
```

Once compiled, this query becomes

```
IEnumerable<double> query =
  Enumerable.Select<int, double>(numbers, n => Square(n));
```

The fact that the `Enumerable.Select` method is an iterator explains why we get delayed execution.

It is important to realize that our query variable represents not the result of a query, but merely the *potential* to execute a query. The query is not executed when it is assigned to a variable. It executes afterward, step by step.

One advantage of deferred query evaluation is that it conserves resources. The gist of lazy evaluation is that the data source on which a query operates is not iterated until you iterate over the query's results. Let's suppose a query returns thousands of elements. If we decide after looking at the first element that we don't want to further process the results, these results won't be loaded in memory. This is because the results are provided as a sequence. If the results were contained in an array or list as is often the case in classical programming, they would all be loaded in memory, even if we didn't consume them.

Deferred query evaluation is also important because it allows us to define a query at one point and use it later, exactly when we want to, several times if needed.

Reusing a query to get different results
An important thing to understand is that if you iterate on the same query a second time, it can produce different results. An example of this behavior can be seen in listing 3.5. New code is shown in bold.

Listing 3.5 Same query producing different results between two executions

```
using System;
using System.Linq;

static class QueryReuse
{
  static double Square(double n)
  {
    Console.WriteLine("Computing Square("+n+")...");
    return Math.Pow(n, 2);
  }

  public static void Main()
  {
    int[] numbers = {1, 2, 3};
```

```
var query =
  from n in numbers
  select Square(n);

foreach (var n in query)
  Console.WriteLine(n);

for (int i = 0; i < numbers.Length; i++)
  numbers[i] = numbers[i]+10;

Console.WriteLine("- Collection updated -");

foreach (var n in query)
  Console.WriteLine(n);
}
}
```

Here we reuse the query object after changing the underlying collection. We add 10 to each number in the array before iterating again on the query.

As expected, the results are not the same for the second iteration:

```
Computing Square(1)...
1
Computing Square(2)...
4
Computing Square(3)...
9
- Collection updated -
Computing Square(11)...
121
Computing Square(12)...
144
Computing Square(13)...
169
```

The second iteration executes the query again, producing new results.

Forcing immediate query execution

As you've seen, deferred execution is the default behavior. Queries are executed only when we request data from them. If you want immediate execution, you have to request it explicitly.

Let's say that we want the query to be executed completely, before we begin to process its results. This would imply that all the calls to the Square method happen before the results are used.

Here is how the output should look without deferred execution:

```
Computing Square(1)...
Computing Square(2)...
Computing Square(3)...
1
4
9
```

We can achieve this by adding a call to `ToList`—another extension method from the `System.Linq.Enumerable` class—to our code sample:

```
foreach (var n in query.ToList())
  Console.WriteLine(n);
```

With this simple modification, our code's behavior changes radically.

`ToList` iterates on the query and creates an instance of `List<double>` initialized with all the results of the query. The `foreach` loop now iterates on a prefilled collection, and the `Square` method is not invoked during the iteration.

Let's go back to our `DisplayProcesses` example and continue analyzing the query.

The `Where`, `OrderByDescending`, and `Select` methods used in listing 3.1 are iterators. This means for example that the enumeration of the source sequence provided as the first parameter of a call to the `Where` method won't happen before we start enumerating the results. This is what allows delayed execution.

You'll now learn more about the extension methods provided by the `System.Linq.Enumerable` class.

3.3   *Introducing query operators*

We've used extension methods from the `System.Linq.Enumerable` class several times in our code samples. We'll now spend some time describing them more precisely. You'll learn how such methods, called query operators, are at the heart of the LINQ foundation. You should pay close attention to query operators, because you'll use them the most when writing LINQ queries.

We'll first define what a query operator is, before introducing the standard query operators.

3.3.1   *What makes a query operator?*

Query operators are not a language extension per se, but an extension to the .NET Framework Class Library. Query operators are a set of extension methods that perform operations in the context of LINQ queries. They are the real elements that make LINQ possible.

Before spending some time on iterators, we were looking at the `Where` method that is used in the following code sample:

```
var processes =
  Process.GetProcesses()
    .Where(process => process.WorkingSet64 > 20*1024*1024)        Call to
    .OrderByDescending(process => process.WorkingSet64)        ① Where
    .Select(process => new { process.Id,
                             Name=process.ProcessName });
```

Let's take a deeper look at the `Where` method and analyze how it works. This method is provided by the `System.Linq.Enumerable` class. Here again is how it's implemented, as we showed in listing 3.2:

```
public static IEnumerable<TSource> Where<TSource>(
  this IEnumerable<TSource> source,
  Func<TSource, Boolean> predicate)
{                                                    ② foreach
  foreach (TSource element in source)                  loop
  {
    if (predicate(element))            ③ Filter source
      yield return element;
  }                                    Return
}                                    ④ elements
}
```

Note that the `Where` method takes an `IEnumerable<T>` as an argument. This is not surprising, because it's an extension method that gets applied to the result of the call to `Process.GetProcesses`, which returns an `IEnumerable<Process>` as we've seen before. What is particularly interesting at this point is that the `Where` method also returns an `IEnumerable<T>`, or more precisely an `IEnumerable<Process>` in this context.

Here is how the `Where` method works:

① It is called with the list of processes returned by `Process.GetProcesses`.

② It loops on the list of processes it receives.

③ It filters this list of processes.

④ It returns the filtered list element by element.

Although we present the processing as four steps, you already know that the processes are handled one by one thanks to the use of `yield return` and iterators.

If we tell you that `OrderByDescending` and `Select` also take `IEnumerable<T>` and return `IEnumerable<T>`, you should start to see a pattern. `Where`, `OrderBy-Descending`, and `Select` are used in turn to refine the processing on the original enumeration. These methods operate on enumerations and generate enumerations. This looks like a Pipeline pattern, don't you think?

Do you remember how we said in chapter 2 that extension methods are basically static methods that can facilitate a chaining or pipelining pattern? If we remove the dot notation from this code snippet

```
var processes =
  Process.GetProcesses()
    .Where(process => process.WorkingSet64 > 20*1024*1024)
    .OrderByDescending(process => process.WorkingSet64)
    .Select(process => new { process.Id,
                             Name=process.ProcessName });
```

and transform it to use standard static method calls, it becomes listing 3.6.

Listing 3.6   A query expressed as static method calls

```
var processes =
  Enumerable.Select(
    Enumerable.OrderByDescending(
      Enumerable.Where(
        Process.GetProcesses(),
        process => process.WorkingSet64 > 20*1024*1024),
      process => process.WorkingSet64),
    process => new { process.Id, Name=process.ProcessName });
```

Again, you can see how extension methods make this kind of code much easier to read! If you look at the code sample that doesn't use extension methods, you can see how difficult it is to understand that we start the processing with a list of processes. It's also hard to follow how the method calls are chained to refine the results. It is in cases like this one that extension methods show all their power.

Until now in this chapter, we've stressed several characteristics of extension methods such as `Where`, `OrderByDescending`, and `Select`:

- They work on enumerations.
- They allow pipelined data processing.
- They rely on delayed execution.

All these features make these methods useful to write queries. This explains why these methods are called query operators.

Here is an interesting analogy. If we consider a query to be a factory, the query operators would be machines or engines, and sequences would be the material the query operators work on (see figure 3.2):

1 A sequence is provided at the start of the processing.

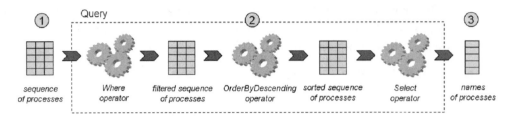

Figure 3.2   A LINQ query represented as a factory where query operators are machines and sequences are the material.

2   Several operators are applied on the sequence to refine it.

3   The final sequence is the product of the query.

NOTE   Don't be misled by figure 3.2. Each element in the sequence is processed only when it is requested. This is how delayed execution works. The elements in sequences are not processed in batch, and maybe even not all processed if not requested.

As we'll highlight in chapter 5, some intermediate operations (such as sorting and grouping) require the entire source be iterated over. Our `OrderByDescending` call is an example of this.

If we look at listing 3.6, we could say that queries are just made of a combination of query operators. Query operators are the key to LINQ, even more than language constructs like query expressions.

3.3.2   *The standard query operators*

Query operators can be combined to perform complex operations and queries on enumerations. Several query operators are predefined and cover a wide range of operations. These operators are called the *standard query operators*.

Table 3.1 classifies the standard query operators according to the type of operation they perform.

Table 3.1   The standard query operators grouped in families

Family	Query operators
Filtering	`OfType, Where`
Projection	`Select, SelectMany`
Partitioning	`Skip, SkipWhile, Take, TakeWhile`
Join	`GroupJoin, Join`

Table 3.1   The standard query operators grouped in families *(continued)*

Family	Query operators
Concatenation	`Concat`
Ordering	`OrderBy, OrderByDescending, Reverse, ThenBy, ThenByDescending`
Grouping	`GroupBy, ToLookup`
Set	`Distinct, Except, Intersect, Union`
Conversion	`AsEnumerable, AsQueryable, Cast, ToArray, ToDictionary, ToList`
Equality	`SequenceEqual`
Element	`ElementAt, ElementAtOrDefault, First, FirstOrDefault, Last, LastOrDefault, Single, SingleOrDefault`
Generation	`DefaultIfEmpty, Empty, Range, Repeat`
Quantifiers	`All, Any, Contains`
Aggregation	`Aggregate, Average, Count, LongCount, Max, Min, Sum`

As you can see, many operators are predefined. For reference, you can find this list augmented with a description of each operator in the appendix. You'll also learn more about the standard query operators in chapter 4, where we'll provide several examples using them. We'll then demonstrate how they can be used to do projections, aggregation, sorting, or grouping.

Thanks to the fact that query operators are mainly extension methods working with `IEnumerable<T>` objects, you can easily create your own query operators. We'll see how to create and use domain-specific query operators in chapter 12, which covers extensibility.

3.4   Introducing query expressions

Another key concept of LINQ is a new language extension. C# and VB.NET propose syntactic sugar for writing simpler query code in most cases.

Until now, in this chapter, we've used a syntax based on method calls for our code samples. This is one way to express queries. But most of the time when you look at code based on LINQ, you'll notice a different syntax: *query expressions.*

We'll explain what query expressions are and then describe the relationship between query expressions and query operators.

3.4.1 What is a query expression?

Query operators are static methods that allow the expression of queries. But instead of using the following syntax

```
var processes =
  Process.GetProcesses()
    .Where(process => process.WorkingSet64 > 20*1024*1024)
    .OrderByDescending(process => process.WorkingSet64)
    .Select(process => new { process.Id,
                             Name=process.ProcessName });
```

you can use another syntax that makes LINQ queries resemble SQL queries (see QueryExpression.csproj):

```
var processes =
  from process in Process.GetProcesses()
  where process.WorkingSet64 > 20*1024*1024
  orderby process.WorkingSet64 descending
  select new { process.Id, Name=process.ProcessName };
```

This is called a query expression or query syntax.

The two code pieces are semantically identical. A query expression is convenient declarative shorthand for code you could write manually. Query expressions allow us to use the power of query operators, but with a query-oriented syntax.

Query expressions provide a language-integrated syntax for queries that is similar to relational and hierarchical query languages such as SQL and XQuery. A query expression operates on one or more information sources by applying one or more query operators from either the standard query operators or domain-specific operators. In our code sample, the query expression uses three of the standard query operators: `Where`, `OrderByDescending`, and `Select`.

When you use a query expression, the compiler automagically translates it into calls to standard query operators.

Because query expressions compile down to method calls, they are not necessary: We could work directly with the query operators. The big advantage of query expressions is that they allow for greater readability and simplicity.

3.4.2 Writing query expressions

Let's detail what query expressions look like in C# and in VB.NET.

C# syntax

Figure 3.3 shows the exhaustive syntax for a query expression.

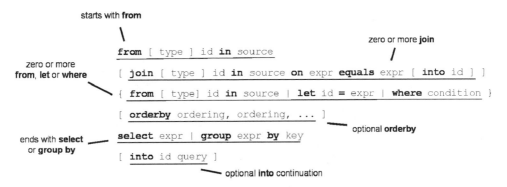

Figure 3.3 C# query expression syntax

Let's review how this syntax is presented in the C# 3.0 language specification. A query expression begins with a from clause and ends with either a select or group clause. The initial from clause can be followed by zero or more from, let, where, join, or orderby clauses.

Each from clause is a generator introducing a variable that ranges over the elements of a sequence. Each let clause introduces a range variable representing a value computed by means of previous range variables. Each where clause is a filter that excludes items from the result.

Each join clause compares specified keys of the source sequence with keys of another sequence, yielding matching pairs. Each orderby clause reorders items according to specified criteria. The final select or group clause specifies the shape of the result in terms of the range variables.

Finally, an into clause can be used to splice queries by treating the results of one query as a generator in a subsequent query.

This syntax should not be unfamiliar if you know SQL.

VB.NET syntax

Figure 3.4 depicts the syntax of a query expression in VB.NET.

Notice how the VB.NET query expression syntax is richer compared to C#. More of the standard query operators are supported in VB, such as Distinct, Skip, Take, and the aggregation operators.

We'll use query expressions extensively in the rest of the book. We believe it's easier to discover the syntax through code samples instead of analyzing and exposing the exact syntax at this point. You'll see query expressions in action in chapter 4, for instance, where we'll use all kinds of queries. This will help you to

starts with **From**

```
From id [As type] In source [, id2 [As type2] In source2 […]]
{
    Aggregate id [As type] In source _
        [, id2 [As type2] In source2 […]]
        [clause]
        Into [alias =] aggregationExpression
            [, [alias =] aggregationExpression […]]
    Distinct
    From id [As type] In source [, id2 [As type2] In source2 […]]
    Group [column [, column2 […]]] _
        By keyExpr [, keyExpr2 […] _
        Into groupAlias = Group [, aggregations]
    Group Join id [As type] In source _
        On keyA Equals keyB [And keyA2 Equals keyB2 […]] _
        Into expressionList
    Join id In source [joinClause] [groupJoinClause … ] _
        On keyA Equals keyB [And keyA2 Equals keyB2 […]]
    Let id = expression [, id2 = expression2 […]]
    Order By orderExpr [Ascending | Descending] _
        [, orderExpr2 [Ascending | Descending] […]]
    Select [alias =] columnExpr [, [alias2 =] columnExpr2 […]]
    Skip count
    Skip While condition
    Take count
    Take While condition
    Where condition
}
```

zero or more
of any clause

Figure 3.4   VB.NET query expression syntax

learn everything you need to use query expressions. In addition, Visual Studio's IntelliSense will help you to write query expressions and discover their syntax as you type them.

3.4.3   *How the standard query operators relate to query expressions*

You've seen that a translation happens when a query expression is compiled into calls to standard query operators.

For instance, consider our query expression:

```
from process in Process.GetProcesses()
where process.WorkingSet64 > 20*1024*1024
orderby process.WorkingSet64 descending
select new { process.Id, Name=process.ProcessName };
```

Here is the same query formulated with query operators:

```
Process.GetProcesses()
   .Where(process => process.WorkingSet64 > 20*1024*1024)
   .OrderByDescending(process => process.WorkingSet64)
   .Select(process => new { process.Id, Name=process.ProcessName });
```

Table 3.2 shows how the major standard query operators are mapped to the new C# and VB.NET query expression keywords.

Table 3.2   Mapping of standard query operators to query expression keywords by language

Query operator	C# syntax	VB.NET syntax
All	N/A	Aggregate … In … Into All(…)
Any	N/A	Aggregate … In … Into Any()
Average	N/A	Aggregate … In … Into Average()
Cast	Use an explicitly typed range variable, for example: from int i in numbers	From … As …
Count	N/A	Aggregate … In … Into Count()
Distinct	N/A	Distinct
GroupBy	group … by or group … by … into …	Group … By … Into …
GroupJoin	join … in … on … equals … into…	Group Join … In … On …
Join	join … in … on … equals …	From x In …, y In … Where x.a = b.a or Join … [As …] In … On …
LongCount	N/A	Aggregate … In … Into LongCount()
Max	N/A	Aggregate … In … Into Max()
Min	N/A	Aggregate … In … Into Min()
OrderBy	orderby	Order By
OrderByDescending	orderby … descending	Order By … Descending
Select	select	Select
SelectMany	Multiple from clauses	Multiple From clauses
Skip	N/A	Skip
SkipWhile	N/A	Skip While

Table 3.2   Mapping of standard query operators to query expression keywords by language *(continued)*

Query operator	C# syntax	VB.NET syntax
Sum	N/A	Aggregate … In … Into Sum()
Take	N/A	Take
TakeWhile	N/A	Take While
ThenBy	orderby …, …	Order By …, …
ThenByDescending	orderby …, … descending	Order By …, … Descending
Where	where	Where

As you can see, not all operators have equivalent keywords in C# and VB.NET. In your simplest queries, you'll be able to use the keywords proposed by your programming language; but for advanced queries, you'll have to call the query operators directly, as you'll see in chapter 4.

Also, writing a query using a query expression is only for comfort and readability; in the end, once compiled, it gets converted into calls to standard query operators. You could decide to write all your queries only with query operators and avoid the query expression syntax if you prefer.

3.4.4   Limitations

Throughout this book, we'll write queries either using the query operators directly or using query expressions. Even when using query expressions, we may have to explicitly use some of the query operators. Only a subset of the standard query operators is supported by the query expression syntax and keywords. It's often necessary to work with some of the query operators right in the context of a query expression.

The C# compiler translates query expressions into invocations of the following operators: Where, Select, SelectMany, Join, GroupJoin, OrderBy, OrderByDescending, ThenBy, ThenByDescending, GroupBy, and Cast, as shown in table 3.2. If you need to use other operators, you can do so in the context of a query expression.

For example, in listing 3.7, we use the Take and Distinct operators.

Listing 3.7 C# query expression that uses query operators (QueryExpressionWithOperators.csproj)

```
var authors =
  from distinctAuthor in (
    from book in SampleData.Books
    where book.Title.Contains("LINQ")
    from author in book.Authors.Take(1)
    select author)
    .Distinct()
  select new {distinctAuthor.FirstName, distinctAuthor.LastName};
```

NOTE   SampleData is a class we'll define when we introduce our running example in chapter 4. It provides some sample data on books, authors, and publishers.

We use Take and Distinct explicitly. Other operators are used implicitly in this query, namely Where, Select, and SelectMany, which correspond to the where, select, and from keywords.

In listing 3.7, the query selects a list of the names of the first author of each book that contains "LINQ" in its title, a given author being listed only once.

Listing 3.8 shows how the same query can be written with query operators only.

Listing 3.8 C# query that uses query operators only (QueryExpressionWithOperators.csproj)

```
var authors =
  SampleData.Books
    .Where(book => book.Title.Contains("LINQ"))
    .SelectMany(book => book.Authors.Take(1))
    .Distinct()
    .Select(author => new {author.FirstName, author.LastName});
```

It's up to you to decide what's more readable. In some cases, you'll prefer to use a combination of query operators because a query expression wouldn't make things clearer. Sometimes, query expressions can even make code more difficult to understand.

In listing 3.7, you can see that parentheses are required to use the Distinct operator. This gets in the middle of the query expression and makes it more difficult to read. In listing 3.8, where only query operators are used, it's easier to follow the pipelined processing. The query operators allow us to organize the operations sequentially. Note that in VB, the question is less important because the language offers more keywords mapped to query operators. This includes Take and Distinct. Consequently, the query we've just written in C# can be written completely in VB as a query expression without resorting to query operators.

If you're used to working with SQL, you may also like query expressions because they offer a similar syntax. Another reason for preferring query expression is that they offer a more compact syntax than query operators.

Let's take the following queries for example. First, here is a query with query operators:

```
SampleData.Books
  .Where(book => book.Title == "Funny Stories")
  .OrderBy(book => book.Title)
  .Select(book => new {book.Title, book.Price});
```

Here is the same query with a query expression:

```
from book in SampleData.Books
where book.Title == "Funny Stories"
orderby book.Title
select new {book.Title, book.Price};
```

The two queries are equivalent. But you might notice that the query formulated with query operators makes extensive use of lambda expressions. Lambda expressions are useful, but too many in a small block of code can be unattractive. Also, in the same query, notice how the book identifier is declared several times. In comparison, in the query expression, you can see that the book identifier only needs to be declared once.

Again, it's mainly a question of personal preference, so we do not intend to tell you that one way is better than the other.

After query expressions, we have one last LINQ concept to introduce.

3.5 *Introducing expression trees*

You might not use expression trees as often as the other concepts we've reviewed so far, but they are an important part of LINQ. They allow advanced extensibility and make LINQ to SQL possible, for instance.

We'll spend some time again with lambda expressions because they allow us to create expression trees. We'll then detail what an expression tree is, before stressing how expression trees offer another way to enable deferred query execution.

3.5.1 *Return of the lambda expressions*

When we introduced lambda expressions in chapter 2, we presented them mainly as a new way to express anonymous delegates. We then demonstrated how they could be assigned to delegate types. Here is one more example:

```
Func<int, bool> isOdd = i => (i & 1) == 1;
```

Here we use the Func<T, TResult> generic delegate type defined in the System namespace. This type is declared as follows in the System.Core.dll assembly that comes with .NET 3.5:

```
delegate TResult Func<T, TResult>(T arg);
```

Our isOdd delegate object represents a method that takes an integer as a parameter and returns a Boolean. This delegate variable can be used like any other delegate:

```
for (int i = 0; i < 10; i++)
{
  if (isOdd(i))
    Console.WriteLine(i + " is odd");
  else
    Console.WriteLine(i + " is even");
}
```

One thing we'd like to stress at this point is that a lambda expression can also be used as *data* instead of code. This is what expression trees are about.

3.5.2 *What are expression trees?*

Consider the following line of code that uses the Expression<TDelegate> type defined in the System.Linq.Expressions namespace:

C#
```
Expression<Func<int, bool>> isOdd = i => (i & 1) == 1;
```

Here is the equivalent line of code in VB.NET:

VB.NET
```
Dim isOdd As Expression(Of Func(Of Integer, Boolean)) = _
    Function(i) (i And 1) = 1
```

This time, we can't use isOdd as a delegate. This is because it's not a delegate, but an *expression tree.*

It turns out that the compiler knows about this Expression<TDelegate> type and behaves differently than with delegate types such as Func<T, TResult>. Rather than compiling the lambda expression into IL code that evaluates the expression, it generates IL that constructs a tree of objects representing the expression.

Note that only lambda expressions with an expression body can be used as expression trees. Lambda expressions with a statement body are not convertible to expression trees. In the following example, the first lambda expression can be used to declare an expression tree because it has an expression body, whereas the second can't be used to declare an expression tree because it has a statement body (see chapter 2 for more details on the two kinds of lambda expressions):

```
Expression<Func<Object, Object>> identity = o => o;
Expression<Func<Object, Object>> identity = o => { return o; };
```

When the compiler sees a lambda expression being assigned to a variable of an Expression<> type, it will compile the lambda into a series of factory method calls that will build the expression tree at runtime. Here is the code that is generated behind the scenes by the compiler for our expression:

C#
```
ParameterExpression i = Expression.Parameter(typeof(int), "i");
Expression<Func<int, bool>> isOdd =
  Expression.Lambda<Func<int, bool>>(
    Expression.Equal(
      Expression.And(
        i,
        Expression.Constant(1, typeof(int))),
      Expression.Constant(1, typeof(int))),
    new ParameterExpression[] { i });
```

Here is the VB syntax:

VB.NET
```
Dim i As ParameterExpression = _
  Expression.Parameter(GetType(Integer), "i")
Dim isOdd As Expression(Of Func(Of Integer, Boolean)) = _
  Expression.Lambda(Of Func(Of Integer, Boolean))( _
    Expression.Equal( _
      Expression.And( _
        i, _
        Expression.Constant(1, GetType(Integer))), _
      Expression.Constant(1, GetType(Integer))), _
    New ParameterExpression() {i})
```

> **NOTE** Expression trees are constructed at runtime when code like this executes, but once constructed they cannot be modified.

Note that you could write this code by yourself. It would be uninteresting for our example, but it could be useful for advanced scenarios. We'll keep that for chapter 5, where we use expression trees to create dynamic queries.

Apart from being grateful to the compiler for generating this for us, you can start to see why this is called an expression tree. Figure 3.5 is a graphical representation of this tree.

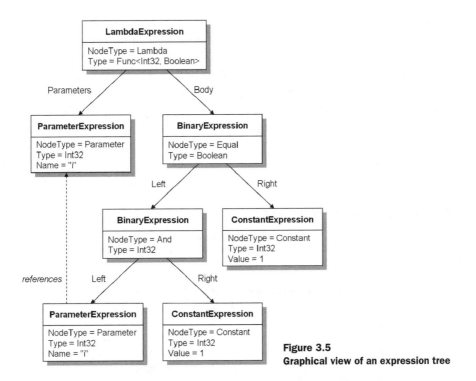

Figure 3.5
Graphical view of an expression tree

At this stage, you've learned that lambda expressions can be represented as code (delegates) or as data (expression trees). Assigned to a delegate, a lambda expression emits IL code; assigned to `Expression<TDelegate>`, it emits an expression tree, which is an in-memory data structure that represents the parsed lambda.

The best way to prove that an expression completely describes a lambda expression is to show how expression trees can be compiled down to delegates:

```
Func<int, bool> isOddDelegate = i => (i & 1) == 1;
Expression<Func<int, bool>> isOddExpression = i => (i & 1) == 1;
Func<int, bool> isOddCompiledExpression =
  isOddExpression.Compile();
```

In this code, `isOddDelegate` and `isOddCompiledExpression` are equivalent. Their IL code is the same.

The burning question at this point should be, "Why would we need expression trees?" Well, an expression is a kind of an *abstract syntax tree (AST)*. In computer science, an AST is a data structure that represents source code that has been parsed. An AST is often used as a compiler or interpreter's internal representation of a computer program while it is being optimized, from which code generation is performed. In our case, an expression tree is the result of the parsing operation the C# compiler does on a lambda expression. The goal here is that some code will analyze the expression tree to perform various operations.

Expression trees can be given to tools at runtime, which use them to guide their execution or translate them into something else, such as SQL in the case of LINQ to SQL. As you'll see in more detail in parts 4 and 5 of this book, LINQ to SQL uses information contained in expression trees to generate SQL and perform queries against a database.

For the moment, we'd like to point out that expression trees are another way to achieve deferred query execution.

3.5.3   *IQueryable, deferred query execution redux*

You've seen that one way to achieve deferred query execution is to rely on IEnumerable<T> and iterators. Expression trees are the basis for another way to out-of-process querying.

This is what is used in the case of LINQ to SQL. When we write code as follows, as we did in chapter 1, no SQL is executed before the foreach loop starts iterating on contacts:

```
string path =
   System.IO.Path.GetFullPath(@"..\..\..\..\Data\northwnd.mdf");
DataContext db = new DataContext(path);

var contacts =
  from contact in db.GetTable<Contact>()
  where contact.City == "Paris"
  select contact;

foreach (var contact in contacts)
  Console.WriteLine("Bonjour "+contact.Name);
```

This behavior is similar to what happens with IEnumerable<T>, but this time, the type of contacts is not IEnumerable<Contact>, like you could expect, but IQueryable<Contact>. What happens with IQueryable<T> is different than with sequences. An instance of IQueryable<T> receives an expression tree it can inspect to decide what processing it should perform.

In this case, as soon as we start enumerating the content of contacts, the expression tree it contains gets analyzed, SQL is generated and executed, and the results of the database query are returned as Contact objects.

We won't go into detail about how things work here, but IQueryable is more powerful than sequences based on IEnumerable because intelligent processing based on the analysis of expression trees can happen. By examining a complete query through its expression tree representation, a tool can take smart decisions and make powerful optimizations. `IQueryable` and expression trees are suitable for cases where `IEnumerable` and its pipelining pattern are not flexible enough.

Deferred query execution with expression trees allow LINQ to SQL to optimize a query containing multiple nested or complex queries into the fewest number of efficient SQL statements possible. If LINQ to SQL were to use a pipelining pattern like the one supported by `IEnumerable<T>`, it would only be able to execute several small queries in cascade against databases instead of a reduced number of optimized queries.

As you'll see later, expression trees and `IQueryable` can be used to extend LINQ and are not limited to LINQ to SQL. We'll demonstrate how we can take advantage of LINQ's extensibility in chapter 12.

Now that we've explored all the main elements of LINQ, let's see where to find the nuts and bolts you need to build your applications.

3.6 *LINQ DLLs and namespaces*

The classes and interfaces that you need to use LINQ in your applications come distributed in a set of assemblies (DLLs) provided with .NET 3.5. You need to know what assemblies to reference and what namespaces to import.

The main assembly you'll use is `System.Core.dll`. In order to write LINQ to Objects queries, you'll need to import the `System.Linq` namespace it contains. This is how the standard query operators provided by the `System.Linq.Enumerable` class become available to your code. Note that the `System.Core.dll` assembly is referenced by default when you create a new project with Visual Studio 2008.

If you need to work with expression trees or create your own `IQueryable` implementation, you'll also need to import the `System.Linq.Expressions` namespace, which is also provided by the `System.Core.dll` assembly.

In order to work with LINQ to SQL or LINQ to XML, you have to use dedicated assemblies: respectively `System.Data.Linq.dll` or `System.Xml.Linq.dll`. LINQ's features for the `DataSet` class are provided by the `System.Data.DataSetExtensions.dll` assembly.

The `System.Xml.Linq.dll` and `System.Data.DataSetExtensions.dll` assemblies are referenced by default when you create projects with Visual Studio 2008. `System.Data.Linq.dll` is not referenced by default. You need to reference it manually.

Table 3.3 is an overview of the LINQ assemblies and namespaces, and their content.

Table 3.3   Content of the assemblies provided by .NET 3.5 that are useful for LINQ

File name	Namespaces	Description and content
System.Core.dll		
	`System`	`Action` and `Func` delegate types

	`System.Linq`	`Enumerable` class (extension methods for `IEnumerable<T>`)
		`IQueryable` and `IQueryable<T>` interfaces
		`Queryable` class (extension methods for `IQueryable<T>`)
		`IQueryProvider` interface
		`QueryExpression` class
		Companion interfaces and classes for query operators:
		`Grouping<TKey, TElement>`
		`ILookup<TKey, TElement>`
		`IOrderedEnumerable<TElement>`
		`IOrderedQueryable`
		`IOrderedQueryable<T>`
		`Lookup<TKey, TElement>`

	`System.Linq.Expressions`	`Expression<TDelegate>` class and other classes that enable expression trees
System.Data.DataSetExtensions.dll		
	`System.Data`	Classes for LINQ to DataSet, such as `TypedTableBase<T>`, `DataRowComparer`, `DataTableExtensions`, and `DataRowExtensions`
System.Data.Linq.dll		
	`System.Data.Linq`	Classes for LINQ to SQL, such as `DataContext`, `Table<TEntity>`, and `EntitySet<TEntity>`
	`System.Data.Linq.Mapping`	Classes and attributes for LINQ to SQL, such as `ColumnAttribute`, `FunctionAttribute`, and `TableAttribute`
	`System.Data.Linq.SqlClient`	The `SqlMethods` and `SqlHelpers` classes

Table 3.3 Content of the assemblies provided by .NET 3.5 that are useful for LINQ *(continued)*

File name	Namespaces	Description and content
System.Xml.Linq.dll		
	`System.Xml.Linq`	Classes for LINQ to XML, such as `XObject`, `XNode`, `XElement`, `XAttribute`, `XText`, `XDocument`, and `XStreamingElement`
	`System.Xml.Schema`	`Extensions` class that provides extension methods to deal with XML schemas
	`System.Xml.XPath`	`Extensions` class that provides extension methods to deal with XPath expressions and to create XPathNavigator objects from XNode instances

3.7 *Summary*

In this chapter, we've explained how LINQ extends C# and VB.NET, as well as the .NET Framework. You should now have a better idea of what LINQ is.

We've walked through some important foundational LINQ material. You've learned some new terminology and concepts.

Here is a summary of what we've introduced in this chapter:

- Sequences, which are enumerations and iterators applied to LINQ
- Deferred query execution
- Query operators, extension methods that allow operations in the context of LINQ queries
- Query expressions, which allow the SQL-like from...where...select syntax
- Expression trees, which represent queries as data and allow advanced extensibility

You're now prepared to read and write LINQ code. We'll now get to action and start using LINQ for useful things. In part 2, we'll use LINQ to Objects to query objects in memory. In part 3, we'll address persistence to relational databases with LINQ to SQL. In part 4, we'll detail how to work on XML documents with LINQ to XML.

Part 2

Querying objects in memory

Now that we know what LINQ is all about, it's time to cover the major LINQ flavors. LINQ to Objects allows us to query collections of objects in memory. This part of the book will help us discover LINQ to Objects and also provide important knowledge we'll reuse with the other flavors of LINQ.

Chapter 4 introduces our running LinqBooks example, presents LINQ to Objects in the context of ASP.NET and Windows Forms applications, and goes through the major query operations we can perform with LINQ. Chapter 5 looks at ways of using LINQ queries in common scenarios and design patterns, and addresses performance considerations.

Getting familiar
with LINQ to Objects

4

This chapter covers:

- The LinqBooks running example
- Querying collections
- Using LINQ with ASP.NET and Windows Forms
- Major standard query operators

In chapter 1 we introduced LINQ, and in chapters 2 and 3 we described new language features and LINQ concepts. We'll now sample each LINQ flavor in turn. This part focuses on LINQ to Objects. We'll cover LINQ to SQL in part 3, and LINQ to XML in part 4.

The code samples you'll encounter in the rest of this book are based on a running example: a book cataloging system. This chapter starts with a description of this example application, its database schema, and its object model.

We'll use this sample application immediately as a base for discovering LINQ to Objects. We'll review what can be queried with LINQ to Objects and what operations can be performed.

Most of what we'll show you in this chapter applies to all LINQ flavors and not just LINQ to Objects. We'll focus on how to write language-integrated queries and how to use the major standard query operators. The goal of this chapter is that you become familiar with query expressions and query operators, as well as feel comfortable using LINQ features with in-memory object collections.

4.1   Introducing our running example

While we were introducing the new language features (chapter 2) and key LINQ concepts (chapter 3), we used simple code samples. We should now be able to tackle more useful and complex real-life examples. Starting at this point, the new code samples in this book will be based on an ongoing example: *LinqBooks*, a personal book-cataloging system.

We'll discuss the goals behind the example and review the features we expect it to implement. We'll then show you the object model and database schema we'll use throughout this book. We'll also introduce sample data we'll use to create our examples.

4.1.1   Goals

A running example will allow us to base our code samples on something solid. We've chosen to develop an example that is rich enough to offer opportunities to use the complete LINQ toolset.

Here are some of our requirements for this example:

- The object model should be rich enough to enable a variety of LINQ queries.
- It should deal with objects in memory, XML documents, and relational data, both independently and in combination.

- It should include ASP.NET web sites as well as Windows Forms applications.

- It should involve queries to local data stores as well as to external data sources, such as public web services.

Although we may provide a complete sample application after this book is published, our goal here is not to create a full-featured application. However, in chapter 13, we'll focus on using all the parts of our running example to see LINQ in action in a complete application.

Let's review the set of features we plan to implement.

4.1.2 Features

The main features LinqBooks should have include the ability to

- Track what books we have
- Store what we think about them
- Retrieve more information about our books
- Publish our list of books and our review information

The technical features we'll implement in this book include

- Querying/inserting/updating data in a local database
- Providing search capabilities over both the local catalog and third parties (such as Amazon or Google)
- Importing data about books from a web site
- Importing and persisting some data from/in XML documents
- Creating RSS feeds for the books you recommend

In order to implement these features, we'll use a set of business entities.

4.1.3 The business entities

The object model we'll use consists of the following classes: Book, Author, Publisher, Subject, Review, and User.

Figure 4.1 is a class diagram that shows how these objects are defined and how they relate to each other.

We'll first use these objects in memory with LINQ to Objects, but later on we'll have to persist this data in a database. Let's see the database model we'll use.

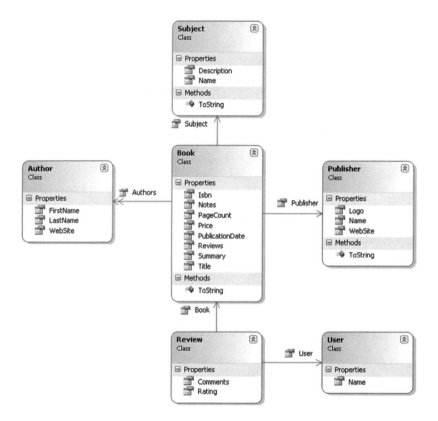

Figure 4.1   Object model for the running example

4.1.4   *Database schema*

In part 3 of this book, we'll demonstrate how to use LINQ to work with relational databases. Figure 4.2 shows the database schema we'll use.

We'll use this database to save and load the information the application handles. This schema was designed to involve several kinds of relations and data types. This will be useful to demonstrate the features LINQ to SQL offers for dealing with relational data.

4.1.5   *Sample data*

In this part of the book, we'll use a set of in-memory data for the purpose of demonstrating LINQ to Objects.

Listing 4.1 contains the `SampleData` class that contains the data we'll use.

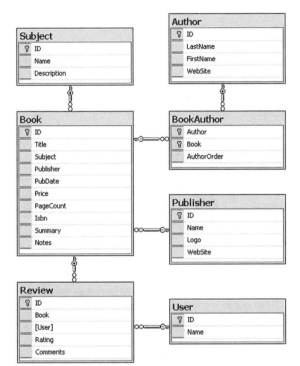

Figure 4.2
Database schema for the running example

Listing 4.1   The `SampleData` class provides sample data (LinqBooks.Common\SampleData.cs)

```
using System;
using System.Collections.Generic;
using System.Text;

namespace LinqInAction.LinqBooks.Common
{
  static public class SampleData
  {
    static public Publisher[] Publishers =
    {
      new Publisher {Name="FunBooks"},
      new Publisher {Name="Joe Publishing"},
      new Publisher {Name="I Publisher"}
    };

    static public Author[] Authors =
    {
      new Author {FirstName="Johnny", LastName="Good"},
      new Author {FirstName="Graziella", LastName="Simplegame"},
      new Author {FirstName="Octavio", LastName="Prince"},
```

```
        new Author {FirstName="Jeremy", LastName="Legrand"}
    };
    static public Book[] Books =
    {
      new Book {
        Title="Funny Stories",
        Publisher=Publishers[0],
        Authors=new[]{Authors[0], Authors[1]},
        PageCount=101,
        Price=25.55M,
        PublicationDate=new DateTime(2004, 11, 10),
        Isbn="0-000-77777-2"
      },
      new Book {
        Title="LINQ rules",
        Publisher=Publishers[1],
        Authors=new[]{Authors[2]},
        PageCount=300,
        Price=12M,
        PublicationDate=new DateTime(2007, 9, 2),
        Isbn="0-111-77777-2"
      },
      new Book {
        Title="C# on Rails",
        Publisher=Publishers[1],
        Authors=new[]{Authors[2]},
        PageCount=256,
        Price=35.5M,
        PublicationDate=new DateTime(2007, 4, 1),
        Isbn="0-222-77777-2"
      },
      new Book {
        Title="All your base are belong to us",
        Publisher=Publishers[1],
        Authors=new[]{Authors[3]},
        PageCount=1205,
        Price=35.5M,
        PublicationDate=new DateTime(2005, 5, 5),
        Isbn="0-333-77777-2"
      },
      new Book {
        Title="Bonjour mon Amour",
        Publisher=Publishers[0],
        Authors=new[]{Authors[1], Authors[0]},
        PageCount=50,
        Price=29M,
        PublicationDate=new DateTime(1973, 2, 18),
        Isbn="2-444-77777-2"
      }
    };
  }
}
```

Notice how we use object and collection initializers—introduced in chapter 2—to easily initialize our collections. This sample data and the classes it relies on are provided with the source code of this book in the `LinqBooks.Common` project.

When we address LINQ to XML and LINQ to SQL, we'll use a set of sample XML documents and sample records in a database. We'll show you this additional data when we use it.

Before using this sample data and actually working with our running example, we'll review some basic information about LINQ to Objects.

4.2 Using LINQ with in-memory collections

LINQ to Objects is the flavor of LINQ that works with in-memory collections of objects. What does this mean? What kinds of collections are supported by LINQ to Objects? What operations can we perform on these collections?

We'll start by reviewing the list of collections that are compatible with LINQ, and then we'll give you an overview of the supported operations.

4.2.1 What can we query?

As you might guess, not everything can be queried using LINQ to Objects. The first criterion for applying LINQ queries is that the objects need to be collections.

All that is required for a collection to be queryable through LINQ to Objects is that it implements the `IEnumerable<T>` interface. As a reminder, objects implementing the `IEnumerable<T>` interface are called *sequences* in LINQ vocabulary. The good news is that almost every generic collection provided by the .NET Framework implements `IEnumerable<T>`! This means that you'll be able to query the usual collections you were already working with in .NET 2.0.

Let's review the collections you'll be able to query using LINQ to Objects.

Arrays
Any kind of array is supported. It can be an untyped array of objects, like in listing 4.2.

> **Listing 4.2   Querying an untyped array with LINQ to Objects (UntypedArray.csproj)**

```
using System;
using System.Linq;

static class TestArray
{
  static void Main()
  {
    Object[] array = {"String", 12, true, 'a'};
```

```
    var types =
      array
        .Select(item => item.GetType().Name)
        .OrderBy(type => type);

    ObjectDumper.Write(types);
  }
}
```

NOTE   We already used the `ObjectDumper` class in chapter 2. It is a utility class useful for displaying results. It is provided by Microsoft as part of the LINQ code samples. You'll be able to find it in the downloadable source code accompanying this book.

This code displays the types of an array's elements, sorted by name. Here is the output of this example:

```
Boolean
Char
Int32
String
```

Of course, queries can be applied to arrays of custom objects. In listing 4.3, we query an array of `Book` objects.

Listing 4.3   Querying a typed array with LINQ to Objects (TypedArray.csproj)

```
using System;
using System.Collections.Generic;
using System.Linq;
using LinqInAction.LinqBooks.Common;

static class TestArray
{
  static void Main()
  {
    Book[] books = {
      new Book { Title="LINQ in Action" },
      new Book { Title="LINQ for Fun" },
      new Book { Title="Extreme LINQ" } };

    var titles =
      books
        .Where(book => book.Title.Contains("Action"))
        .Select(book => book.Title);

    ObjectDumper.Write(titles);
  }
}
```

In fact, LINQ to Objects queries can be used with an array of any data type!

Other important collections, such as generic lists and dictionaries, are also supported by LINQ to Objects. Let's see what other types you can use.

Generic lists

The most common collection you use in .NET 2.0 with arrays is without a doubt the generic List<T>. LINQ to Objects can operate on List<T>, as well as on the other generic lists.

Here is a list of the main generic list types:

- System.Collections.Generic.List<T>
- System.Collections.Generic.LinkedList<T>
- System.Collections.Generic.Queue<T>
- System.Collections.Generic.Stack<T>
- System.Collections.Generic.HashSet<T>
- System.Collections.ObjectModel.Collection<T>
- System.ComponentModel.BindingList<T>

Listing 4.4 shows how the previous example that worked with an array can be adapted to work with a generic list.

Listing 4.4 Querying a generic list with LINQ to Objects (GenericList.csproj)

```
using System;
using System.Collections.Generic;
using System.Linq;
using LinqInAction.LinqBooks.Common;

static class TestList
{
  static void Main()
  {
    List<Book> books = new List<Book>() {
      new Book { Title="LINQ in Action" },
      new Book { Title="LINQ for Fun" },
      new Book { Title="Extreme LINQ" } };

    var titles =
      books
        .Where(book => book.Title.Contains("Action"))
        .Select(book => book.Title);

    ObjectDumper.Write(titles);
  }
}
```

Note that the query remains unchanged, because both the array and the list implement the same interface used by the query: IEnumerable<Book>.

Although you'll most likely primarily query arrays and lists with LINQ, you may also write queries against generic dictionaries.

Generic dictionaries

As with generic lists, all generic dictionaries can be queried using LINQ to Objects:

- System.Collections.Generic.Dictionary<TKey,TValue>
- System.Collections.Generic.SortedDictionary<TKey, TValue>
- System.Collections.Generic.SortedList<TKey, TValue>

Generic dictionaries implement IEnumerable<KeyValuePair<TKey, TValue>>. The KeyValuePair structure holds the typed Key and Value properties.

Listing 4.5 shows how we can query a dictionary of strings indexed by integers.

Listing 4.5 Querying a generic dictionary with LINQ to Objects
(GenericDictionary.csproj)

```
using System;
using System.Collections.Generic;
using System.Linq;

static class TestDictionary
{
  static void Main()
  {
      Dictionary<int, string> frenchNumbers;
      frenchNumbers = new Dictionary<int, string>();
      frenchNumbers.Add(0, "zero");
      frenchNumbers.Add(1, "un");
      frenchNumbers.Add(2, "deux");
      frenchNumbers.Add(3, "trois");
      frenchNumbers.Add(4, "quatre");

      var evenFrenchNumbers =
        from entry in frenchNumbers
        where (entry.Key % 2) == 0
        select entry.Value;

    ObjectDumper.Write(evenFrenchNumbers);
  }
}
```

Here is the output of this sample's execution:

```
zero
deux
quatre
```

We've listed the most important collections you'll query. You can query other collections, as you'll see next.

String

Although `System.String` may not be perceived as a collection at first sight, it actually is one, because it implements `IEnumerable<Char>`. This means that string objects can be queried with LINQ to Objects, like any other collection.

> **NOTE** In C#, these extension methods will not be seen in IntelliSense. The extension methods for `System.String` are specifically excluded because it is seen as highly unusual to treat a string object as an `IEnumerable<char>`.

Let's take an example. The LINQ query in listing 4.6 works on the characters from a string.

Listing 4.6   Querying a string with LINQ to Objects (String.csproj)

```
var count =
  "Non-letter characters in this string: 8"
    .Where(c => !Char.IsLetter(c))
    .Count();
```

Needless to say, the result of this query is 8.

Other collections

We've listed only the collections provided by the .NET Framework. Of course, you can use LINQ to Objects with any other type that implements `IEnumerable<T>`. This means LINQ to Objects will work with your own collection types or collections from other frameworks.

A problem you may encounter is that not all .NET collections implement `IEnumerable<T>`. In fact, only strongly typed collections implement this interface. Arrays, generic lists, and generic dictionaries are strongly typed: you can work with an array of integers, a list of strings, or a dictionary of `Book` objects.

The nongeneric collections do not implement `IEnumerable<T>`, but implement `IEnumerable`. Does this mean that you won't be able to use LINQ with `DataSet` or `ArrayList` objects, for example?

Fortunately, solutions exist. In section 5.1.1, we'll demonstrate how you can query nongeneric collections thanks to the `Cast` and `OfType` query operators.

Let's now review what LINQ allows us to do with all these collections.

4.2.2 *Supported operations*

The operations that can be performed on the types we've just listed are those supported by the standard query operators. LINQ comes with a number of operators that provide useful ways of manipulating sequences and composing queries.

Here is an overview of the families of the standard query operators: Restriction, Projection, Partitioning, Join, Ordering, Grouping, Set, Conversion, Equality, Element, Generation, Quantifiers, and Aggregation. As you can see, a wide range of operations is supported. We won't detail all of them, but we'll focus on the most important of them in section 4.4.

Remember that the standard query operators are defined in the `System.Linq.Enumerable` class as extension methods for the `IEnumerable<T>` type, as we've seen in chapter 3.

These operators are called the standard query operators because we can provide our own custom query operators. Because query operators are merely extension methods for the `IEnumerable<T>` type, we're free to create all the query operators we wish. This allows us to enrich our queries with operations that the designers of LINQ overlooked and that aren't supported by the standard operators. We'll demonstrate this in chapter 12 when we cover extensibility.

We'll soon use several query operators and demonstrate how to perform the supported operations we've just presented. In order to be able to create our sample applications, we'll now take some time to create our first ASP.NET web sites and Windows Forms applications that work with LINQ.

4.3 *Using LINQ with ASP.NET and Windows Forms*

In previous chapters, we used LINQ code in console applications. That was okay for simple examples, but most real-life projects take the form of web sites or Windows applications, not console applications. We'll now make the jump and start creating ASP.NET or Windows Forms applications that use LINQ.

Support for LINQ is built into .NET 3.5 and Visual Studio 2008, so creating applications that use LINQ is not different than creating other applications. You simply need to use the standard project templates coming with Visual Studio. This is the case for both ASP.NET web sites and Windows Forms applications. We'll show you how to use these templates to create your first applications that query data using LINQ and display the results using standard .NET controls.

> **NOTE** If you used prerelease versions of LINQ, you may remember using specific project templates. The standard templates that come with Visual Studio 2008 now support LINQ. The project templates create the required references to the LINQ assemblies. Of course, this is true only if you select .NET Framework 3.5 as the target for your project, the default value.

4.3.1 Data binding for web applications

ASP.NET controls support data binding to any `IEnumerable` collection. This makes it easy to display the result of language-integrated queries using controls like `GridView`, `DataList`, and `Repeater`.

Let's create a sample web site and improve it step by step.

Step 0: Creating an ASP.NET web site

To create a new ASP.NET web site, choose File > New > Web Site in Visual Studio, and select the ASP.NET Web Site template, as shown in figure 4.3.

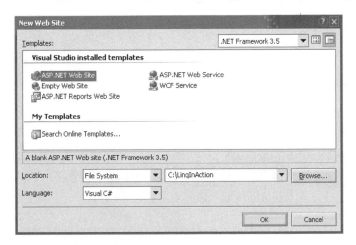

**Figure 4.3
Creating a new ASP.NET
web site**

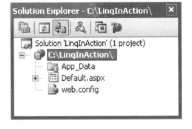

This creates a web site project that looks like figure 4.4.

We'll add a new page to this project to display some data.

**Figure 4.4   Default content for a
web site**

Step 1: Creating our first ASP.NET page using LINQ

Create a new page called `Step1.aspx` and add a `GridView` control to it so it looks like listing 4.7.

Listing 4.7 Markup for the first ASP.NET page (Step1.aspx)

```
<%@ Page Language="C#" AutoEventWireup="true"
  CodeFile="Step1.aspx.cs" Inherits=" Step1" %>

<!DOCTYPE html PUBLIC "-//W3C//DTD XHTML 1.0 Transitional//EN"
  "http://www.w3.org/TR/xhtml1/DTD/xhtml1-transitional.dtd">

<html xmlns="http://www.w3.org/1999/xhtml" >
<head runat="server">
    <title>Step 1</title>
</head>
<body>
    <form id="form1" runat="server">
    <div>
      <asp:GridView ID="GridView1" runat="server">
      </asp:GridView>
    </div>
    </form>
</body>
</html>
```

Listing 4.8 contains the code you should write in the code-behind file to bind a query to the `GridView`.

Listing 4.8 Code-behind for the first ASP.NET page (Step1.aspx.cs)

```csharp
using System;
using System.Linq;

using LinqInAction.LinqBooks.Common;

public partial class Step1 : System.Web.UI.Page
{
  protected void Page_Load(object sender, EventArgs e)
  {
    String[] books = { "Funny Stories",
      "All your base are belong to us", "LINQ rules",
      "C# on Rails", "Bonjour mon Amour" };

    GridView1.DataSource =
```

```
    from book in books
    where book.Length > 10
    orderby book
    select book.ToUpper();
  GridView1.DataBind();
}
}
```

Make sure you have a using System.Linq statement at the top of the file to ensure we can use
LINQ querying features.

Here, we use a query expression, a syntax we
introduced in chapter 3. The query selects all the
books with names longer than 10 characters, sorts
the result in alphabetical order, then returns the
names converted into uppercase.

LINQ queries return results of type IEnumera-
ble<T>, where T is determined by the object type
of the select clause. In this sample, book is a
string, so the result of the query is a generics-
based collection of type IEnumerable<String>.

Figure 4.5 ASP.NET step 1 result

Because ASP.NET controls support data binding to any IEnumerable collection,
we can easily assign this LINQ query to the GridView control. Calling the Data-
Bind method on the GridView generates the display.

The result page looks like figure 4.5 when the application is run.

> **NOTE** Instead of using the GridView control, you can use as easily a Repeater,
> DataList, DropDownList, or any other ASP.NET list control. This
> includes the new ListView control that comes with .NET 3.5.
>
> You could also use the new LinqDataSource control to enable richer
> data binding. You'll be able to see it in action in the last chapter of this
> book, when we create the LinqBooks web application.

That's it! We've created our first ASP.NET web site that uses LINQ. Not terribly difficult, right? Let's improve our example a bit, because everything is so easy.

Step 2: Using richer collections
Searching an array of strings is not extremely interesting (although sometimes useful). To make our application more realistic, let's add the ability to search and work
against richer collections. The good news is that LINQ makes this easy.

Let's use the types and sample data from our running example. For instance, we could query our collection of books filtered and ordered on prices. We'd like to achieve something like figure 4.6.

Notice that this time we're also displaying the price. `Title` and `Price` are two properties of our `Book` object. A `Book` object has more than these two properties, as you can see in figure 4.7.

Figure 4.6 Result of using richer collections in ASP.NET

Figure 4.7
The `Book` **class**

We can use two methods to display only the properties we want: either declare specific columns at the grid level, or explicitly select only the `Title` and `Price` properties in the query.

Let's try the former method first.

In order to use the `Book` class and the sample data provided with this book, start by adding a reference to the `LinqBooks.Common` project. Then, create a new page named `Step2a.aspx` with a `GridView` control that defines two columns, as in listing 4.9.

**Listing 4.9 Markup for a richer collection
(Step2a.aspx)**

```
<%@ Page Language="C#" AutoEventWireup="true"
  CodeFile="Step2a.aspx.cs" Inherits="Step2a" %>

<!DOCTYPE html PUBLIC "-//W3C//DTD XHTML 1.0 Transitional//EN"
  "http://www.w3.org/TR/xhtml1/DTD/xhtml1-transitional.dtd">

<html xmlns="http://www.w3.org/1999/xhtml" >
<head runat="server">
    <title>Step 2 - Grid columns</title>
</head>
<body>
    <form id="form1" runat="server">
    <div>
```

```
      <asp:GridView ID="GridView1" runat="server"
        AutoGenerateColumns="false">
        <Columns>
          <asp:BoundField HeaderText="Book" DataField="Title" />
          <asp:BoundField HeaderText="Price" DataField="Price" />
        </Columns>
      </asp:GridView>
    </div>
    </form>
</body>
</html>
```

Listing 4.10 shows the new query that works on our sample data and returns Book objects.

Listing 4.10   Code-behind for a richer collection (Step2a.aspx.cs)

```
protected void Page_Load(object sender, EventArgs e)
{
  GridView1.DataSource =
    from book in SampleData.Books
    where book.Title.Length > 10
    orderby book.Price
    select book;
  GridView1.DataBind();
}
```

Make sure there is a using System.Linq statement at the top of the file.

The GridView displays only the two properties specified as columns because we've specified that we don't want it to generate columns automatically based on the properties of the objects.

As we said, another way to specify the columns displayed in the grid is to select only the properties we want in the query. This is what we do in listing 4.11.

Listing 4.11   Code-behind for a richer collection using an anonymous type (Step2b.aspx.cs)

```
using System;
using System.Linq;

using LinqInAction.LinqBooks.Common;

public partial class Step2b : System.Web.UI.Page
{
  protected void Page_Load(object sender, EventArgs e)
  {
    GridView1.DataSource =
      from book in SampleData.Books
```

```
        where book.Title.Length > 10
        orderby book.Price
        select new { book.Title, book.Price };
    GridView1.DataBind();
  }
}
```

As you can see, this is done using an anonymous type, a language extension we introduced in chapter 2. Anonymous types allow you to easily create and use type structures inline, without having to formally declare their object model before-hand. A type is automatically inferred by the compiler based on the initialization data for the object.

Instead of returning a `Book` object from our select clause like before, we're now creating a new anonymous type that has two properties—`Title` and `Price`. The types of these properties are automatically calculated based on the value of their initial assignment (in this case a `String` and a `Decimal`).

This time, thanks to the anonymous type, we don't need to specify the columns in the grid: See listing 4.12.

> **NOTE**   Keep in mind that the columns in the grid may not appear in the order you expect. The `GridView` control relies on reflection to get the properties of the objects it should display. This technique does not ensure that the properties are returned in the same order as they are declared in the bound object.

Listing 4.12   Markup for listing 4.11 (Step2b.aspx)

```
...
<body>
    <form id="form1" runat="server">
    <div>
      <asp:GridView ID="GridView1" runat="server"
        AutoGenerateColumns="true">
      </asp:GridView>
    </div>
    </form>
</body>
</html>
```

Both of the methods we've just presented to limit the number of columns are useful. The first method allows us to specify header text or other options for the columns. For instance, here we used "Book" as the header for the column that displays the title. The second method allows us to select only the data we need and not the complete objects. This will be useful especially when working with LINQ to SQL, as you'll see in part 3 of this book, to avoid retrieving too much data from the database server.

An even more important benefit of using anonymous types is that you can avoid having to create new types just for presenting data. In trivial situations, you can use an anonymous type to map your *domain model* to a *presentation model.* In the following query, creating an anonymous type allows a flat view of our domain model:

```
from book in SampleData.Books
where book.Title.Length > 10
orderby book.Price
select new { book.Title, book.Price
   Publisher=book.Publisher.Name, Authors=book.Authors.Count() };
```

Here we create a view on a graph of objects by projecting data from the object itself and data from the object's relations into an anonymous type.

After creating an ASP.NET site, let's see how to do the same with Windows Forms.

4.3.2 *Data binding for Windows Forms applications*

Using LINQ in a Windows Forms application isn't more difficult than with ASP.NET in a web application. We'll show you how to do the same kind of data-binding operations between LINQ query results and standard Windows Forms controls in a sample application.

We'll proceed the same way we did with ASP.NET. We'll build a sample application step by step, starting with the creation of a new project.

Step 0: Creating a Windows Forms application

To create a new Windows Application, choose File > New > Project, and select Windows Forms Application, as shown in figure 4.8.

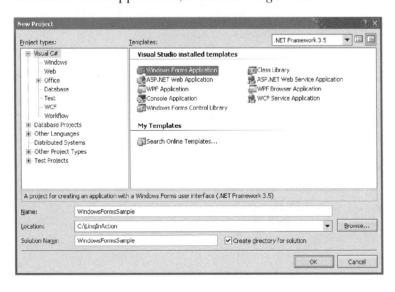

**Figure 4.8
Visual Studio
2008's new
project dialog box**

Figure 4.9 shows the default content created by this template.

Step 1: Creating our first form using LINQ

We'll start our sample by creating a new form for displaying books returned by a query. Create a form named `FormStrings`, and drop a `DataGridView` control on it, as shown in figure 4.10.

Add an event handler for the `Load` event of the page as in listing 4.13.

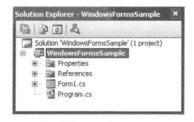

**Figure 4.9
Default content
for a new Windows
Forms application**

**Figure 4.10
New form with a
`DataGridView`**

Listing 4.13   Code-behind for the first form (FormStrings.cs)

```
using System;
using System.Collections.Generic;
using System.Linq;
using System.Windows.Forms;

namespace LinqInAction.Chapter04.Win
{
  public partial class FormStrings : Form
  {
    public FormStrings()
    {
      InitializeComponent();
    }

    private void FormStrings_Load(object sender, EventArgs e)
    {
      String[] books = { "Funny Stories",
        "All your base are belong to us", "LINQ rules",
        "C# on Rails", "Bonjour mon Amour" };

      var query =
        from book in books
        where book.Length > 10
        orderby book
```

```
        select new { Book=book.ToUpper() };

    dataGridView1.DataSource = query.ToList();
    }
  }
}
```

Make sure you import the `System.Linq` namespace with a `using` clause.

You should notice two things in comparison to the code we used for the ASP.NET web application sample in section 4.3.1. First, we use an anonymous type to create objects containing a `Book` property. This is because the `DataGridView` control displays the properties of objects by default. If we returned strings instead of custom objects, all we would see displayed would be the title's `Length`, because that's the only property on strings. Second, we convert the result sequence into a list. This is required for the grid to perform data binding. Alternatively, we could use a `BindingSource` object.

Figure 4.11 shows the result of this code sample's execution.

This is not perfect, because the titles are not completely displayed. We'll improve this in the next step, while we display more information at the same time.

Figure 4.11 Result of the first Windows Forms step

Step 2: Using richer collections

As we did for ASP.NET, we'll now use richer objects and not just strings. We'll reuse the same sample data from our running example, so make sure you reference the `LinqBooks.Common` project.

Figure 4.12 shows the result we'd like to get with a query that filters and sorts our book collection.

To achieve this result, first create a new form named `FormBooks`. Add a `DataGridView` control to it, just like you did for the previous sample.

Figure 4.12 Result of the second Windows Forms step

This time, we'll specify the grid columns. Edit the columns using the grid's smart tags, as shown in figure 4.13.

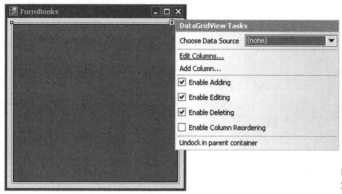

Figure 4.13
`DataGridView`'s **smart tags**

Add two columns, `Book` and `Price`, as shown in figure 4.14.

Note that we can also specify the width of each column. We could for example specify that we wish the columns to be automatically sized according to their content, using the `AutoSizeMode` setting.

That's all there is to it. We now have a rich collection mapped to a grid.

Because you now have some knowledge of data binding of LINQ queries in web and Windows applications, let's move on to building richer examples. We'll use the data binding techniques we just showed you to write advanced queries. You'll see how to use the query operators to perform several kinds of common operations, such as projections or aggregations.

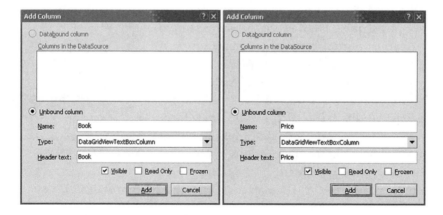

Figure 4.14   Adding two columns to the `DataGridView` control

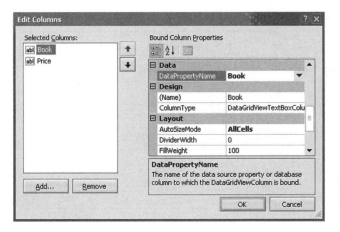

Figure 4.15
Mapping columns to properties and specifying column width

Make sure you map the columns to the result objects' properties using the Data-PropertyName setting, as shown in figure 4.15.

4.4 *Focus on major standard query operators*

Before using query expressions and query operators to start creating the sample application we introduced at the beginning of this chapter, we'll take a small detour to focus on some of the standard query operators. It's important to know the standard query operators because they are the elements that make queries. You need to get a good idea of the existing operators and what they can be used for.

We won't be able to cover all of the 51 standard query operators, but only a subset of them. We'll highlight the major operators like Where, Select, Select-Many, the conversion operators, and some aggregation operators. Don't worry—you'll see many of the other standard query operators in action throughout the code samples contained in this book.

As a reminder, table 4.1 lists all the standard query operators.

Table 4.1 The standard query operators grouped in families

Family	Query operators
Filtering	OfType, **Where**
Projection	**Select, SelectMany**
Partitioning	**Skip**, SkipWhile, **Take**, TakeWhile
Join	**GroupJoin, Join**
Concatenation	Concat

Table 4.1 The standard query operators grouped in families *(continued)*

Family	Query operators
Ordering	**OrderBy**, **OrderByDescending**, Reverse, **ThenBy**, **ThenByDescending**
Grouping	**GroupBy**, ToLookup
Set	**Distinct**, Except, Intersect, Union
Conversion	AsEnumerable, AsQueryable, Cast, **ToArray**, **ToDictionary**, **ToList**
Equality	SequenceEqual
Element	ElementAt, ElementAtOrDefault, First, FirstOrDefault, Last, LastOrDefault, Single, SingleOrDefault
Generation	**DefaultIfEmpty**, Empty, Range, Repeat
Quantifiers	All, Any, Contains
Aggregation	Aggregate, Average, **Count**, LongCount, **Max**, **Min**, **Sum**

The operators covered in this chapter are highlighted in bold text. We'll let you discover the others by yourself.[1] Once we've shown you about half of the operators in this chapter, it should be easier to learn new ones. You'll see most of them in action in the rest of this book, even if we don't provide full details about them.

Let's start our exploration of the query operators with `Where`.

4.4.1 Where, the restriction operator

Similar to a sieve, the `Where` operator filters a sequence of values based on some criteria. `Where` enumerates a source sequence yielding only those values that match the predicate you provide.

Here is how the `Where` operator is declared:

```
public static IEnumerable<T> Where<T>(
    this IEnumerable<T> source,
    Func<T, bool> predicate);
```

The first argument of the predicate function represents the element to test. This function returns a Boolean value indicating whether test conditions are satisfied.

The following example creates a sequence of the books that have a price greater than or equal to 15:

```
IEnumerable<Book> books =
    SampleData.Books.Where(book => book.Price >= 15);
```

---

[1] The complete list of the standard query operators with their descriptions is available in the appendix.

In a query expression, a `where` clause translates to an invocation of the `Where` operator. The previous example is equivalent to the translation of the following query expression:

```
var books =
   from book in SampleData.Books
   where book.Price >= 15
   select book;
```

An overload of the `Where` operator uses predicates that work with the index of elements in the source sequence:

```
public static IEnumerable<T> Where<T>(
   this IEnumerable<T> source,
   Func<T, int, bool> predicate);
```

The second argument of the predicate, if present, represents the zero-based index of the element within the source sequence.

The following code snippet uses this version of the operator to filter the collection of books and keep only those that have a price greater than or equal to 15 and are in odd positions (should you wish to do so for some strange reason):

```
IEnumerable<Book> books =
   SampleData.Books.Where(
      (book, index) => (book.Price >= 15) && ((index & 1) == 1));
```

`Where` is a restriction operator. It's simple, but you'll use it often to filter sequences.
Another operator you'll use often is `Select`.

4.4.2 *Using projection operators*

Let's review the two projection operators: `Select` and `SelectMany`.

Select

The `Select` operator is used to perform a projection over a sequence, based on the arguments passed to the operator. `Select` is declared as follows:

```
public static IEnumerable<S> Select<T, S>(
   this IEnumerable<T> source,
   Func<T, S> selector);
```

The `Select` operator allocates and yields an enumeration, based on the evaluation of the selector function applied to each element of the source enumeration. The following example creates a sequence of the titles of all books:

```
IEnumerable<String> titles =
   SampleData.Books.Select(book => book.Title);
```

In a query expression, a `select` clause translates to an invocation of `Select`. The following query expression translates to the preceding example:

```
var titles =
  from book in SampleData.Books
  select book.Title;
```

This query narrows a sequence of books to a sequence of string values. We could also select an object. Here is how we would select `Publisher` objects associated with books:

```
var publishers =
  from book in SampleData.Books
  select book.Publisher;
```

The resulting collection of using `Select` can also be a direct pass-through of the source objects, or any combination of fields in a new object. In the following sample, an anonymous type is used to project information into an object:

```
var books =
  from book in SampleData.Books
  select new { book.Title, book.Publisher.Name, book.Authors };
```

This kind of code creates a projection of data, hence the name of this operator's family. Let's take a look at the second projection operator.

SelectMany

The second operator in the projection family is `SelectMany`. Its declaration is similar to that of `Select`, except that its selector function returns a sequence:

```
public static IEnumerable<S> SelectMany<T, S>(
  this IEnumerable<T> source,
  Func<T, IEnumerable<S>> selector);
```

The `SelectMany` operator maps each element from the sequence returned by the selector function to a new sequence, and concatenates the results. To understand what `SelectMany` does, let's compare its behavior with `Select` in the following code samples.

Here is some code that uses the `Select` operator:

```
IEnumerable<IEnumerable<Author>> tmp =
  SampleData.Books
    .Select(book => book.Authors);
foreach (var authors in tmp)
{
  foreach (Author author in authors)
  {
    Console.WriteLine(author.LastName);
  }
}
```

And here's the equivalent code using `SelectMany`. As you can see, it is much shorter:

```
IEnumerable<Author> authors =
  SampleData.Books
    .SelectMany(book => book.Authors);
foreach (Author author in authors)
{
  Console.WriteLine(author.LastName);
}
```

Here we're trying to enumerate the authors of our books. The `Authors` property of the `Book` object is an array of `Author` objects. Therefore, the `Select` operator returns an enumeration of these arrays as is. In comparison, `SelectMany` spreads the elements of these arrays into a sequence of `Author` objects.

Here is the query expression we could use in place of the `SelectMany` invocation in our example:

```
from book in SampleData.Books
from author in book.Authors
select author.LastName
```

Notice how we chain two `from` clauses. In a query expression, a `SelectMany` projection is involved each time `from` clauses are chained. When we cover the join operators in section 4.5.4, we'll show you how this can be used to perform a *cross join*.

The `Select` and `SelectMany` operators also provide overloads that work with indices. Let's see what they can be used for.

Selecting indices

The `Select` and `SelectMany` operators can be used to retrieve the index of each element in a sequence. Let's say we want to display the index of each book in our collection before we sort them in alphabetical order:

```
index=3        Title=All your base are belong to us
index=4        Title=Bonjour mon Amour
index=2        Title=C# on Rails
index=0        Title=Funny Stories
index=1        Title=LINQ rules
```

Listing 4.14 shows how to use `Select` to achieve that.

Listing 4.14 Sample use of the `Select` query operator with indices (SelectIndex.csproj)

```
var books =
  SampleData.Books
    .Select((book, index) => new { index, book.Title })
    .OrderBy(book => book.Title);
ObjectDumper.Write(books);
```

This time we can't use the query expression syntax because the variant of the Select operator that provides the index has no equivalent in this syntax. Notice that this version of the Select method provides an index variable that we can use in our lambda expression. The compiler automatically determines which version of the Select operator we want just by looking at the presence or absence of the index parameter. Note also that we call Select before OrderBy. This is important to get the indices before the books are sorted, not after.

Let's now review another query operator: Distinct.

4.4.3   *Using Distinct*

Sometimes, information is duplicated in query results. For example, listing 4.15 returns the list of authors who have written books.

> **Listing 4.15   Retrieving a list of authors without using the Distinct query operator (Distinct.csproj)**

```
var authors =
  SampleData.Books
    .SelectMany(book => book.Authors)
    .Select(author => author.FirstName+" "+author.LastName);
ObjectDumper.Write(authors);
```

You can see that a given author may appear more than once in the results:

```
Johnny Good
Graziella Simplegame
Octavio Prince
Octavio Prince
Jeremy Legrand
Graziella Simplegame
Johnny Good
```

This is because an author can write several books. To remove duplication, we can use the Distinct operator. Distinct eliminates duplicate elements from a sequence. In order to compare the elements, the Distinct operator uses the elements' implementation of the IEquatable<T>.Equals method if the elements implement the IEquatable<T> interface. It uses their implementation of the Object.Equals method otherwise.

Listing 4.16 does not yield the same author twice.

Listing 4.16   Retrieving a list of authors using the `Distinct` query operator (Distinct.csproj)

```
var authors =
  SampleData.Books
    .SelectMany(book => book.Authors)
    .Distinct()
    .Select(author => author.FirstName+" "+author.LastName);
ObjectDumper.Write(authors);
```

The new result is:

```
Johnny Good
Graziella Simplegame
Octavio Prince
Jeremy Legrand
```

As with many query operators, there is no equivalent keyword for `Distinct` in the C# query expression syntax. In C#, `Distinct` can only be used as a method call. However, VB.NET offers support for the `Distinct` operator in query expressions. Listing 4.17 shows how the query from listing 4.16 can be written in VB.NET.

Listing 4.17   Retrieving a list of authors using the VB `Distinct` keyword (Distinct.vbproj)

```
Dim authors = _
  From book In SampleData.Books _
  From author In book.Authors _
  Select author.FirstName + " " + author.LastName _
  Distinct
```

The next family of operators that we're going to explore does not have equivalent keywords in query expressions, either in C# or in VB.NET. These operators can be used to convert sequences to standard collections.

4.4.4   Using conversion operators

LINQ comes with convenience operators designed to convert a sequence to other collections. The `ToArray` and `ToList` operators, for instance, convert a sequence to a typed array or list, respectively. These operators are useful for integrating queried data with existing code libraries. They allow you to call methods that expect arrays or list objects, for example.

By default, queries return sequences, collections implementing `IEnumerable<T>`:

```
IEnumerable<String> titles =
    SampleData.Books.Select(book => book.Title);
```

Here is how such a result can be converted to an array or a list:

```
String[] array = titles.ToArray();
List<String> list = titles.ToList();
```

`ToArray` and `ToList` are also useful when you want to request immediate execution of a query or cache the result of a query. When invoked, these operators completely enumerate the source sequence on which they are applied to build an image of the elements returned by this sequence.

Remember that, as we showed you in chapter 3, a query can return different results in successive executions. You'll use `ToArray` and `ToList` when you want to take an instant snapshot of a sequence. Because these operators copy all the result elements into a new array or list each time you call them, you should be careful and avoid abusing them on large sequences.

Let's consider a use case worth mentioning. If we're querying a disposable object created by a `using` block, and if we're yielding from inside that block, the object will be disposed of before we want it to. The workaround is to materialize the results with `ToList`, exit the `using` block, and then yield the results out.

Here is pseudocode that pictures this:

```
IEnumerable<Book> results;

using (var db = new LinqBooksDataContext())
{
    results = db.Books.Where(...).ToList();
}

foreach (var book in results)
{
    DoSomething(book);
    yield return book;
}
```

Another interesting conversion operator is `ToDictionary`. Instead of creating an array or list, this operator creates a dictionary, which organizes data by keys.

Let's see an example:

```
Dictionary<String, Book> isbnRef =
    SampleData.Books.ToDictionary(book => book.Isbn);
```

Here we create a dictionary of books that is indexed by each book's ISBN. A variable of this kind can be used to find a book based on its ISBN:

```
Book linqRules = isbnRef["0-111-77777-2"];
```

After these conversion operators,[2] let's see one last family: aggregate operators.

4.4.5 Using aggregate operators

Some standard query operators are available to apply math functions to data: the aggregate operators. These operators include the following:

- Count, which counts the number of elements in a sequence
- Sum, which computes the sum of a sequence of numeric values
- Min and Max, which find the minimum and the maximum of a sequence of numeric values, respectively

The following example demonstrates how these operators can be used:

```
var minPrice = SampleData.Books.Min(book => book.Price);
var maxPrice = SampleData.Books.Select(book => book.Price).Max();
var totalPrice = SampleData.Books.Sum(book => book.Price);
var nbCheapBooks =
  SampleData.Books.Where(book => book.Price < 30).Count();
```

You may have noticed that in this code sample, Min and Max are not invoked in the same way. The Min operator is invoked directly on the book collection, whereas the Max operator is chained after the Select operator. The effect is identical. In the former case, the aggregate function is applied just to the sequences that satisfy the expression; in the latter case it is applied to all the objects. All the aggregate operators can take a selector as a parameter. The choice of one overload or the other depends on whether you're working on a prerestricted sequence.

We've introduced some important query operators. You should now be more familiar with Where, Select, SelectMany, Distinct, ToArray, ToList, Count, Sum, Min, and Max. This is a good start! There are many more useful operators, as you'll see next.

---

[2] These conversion operators are demonstrated in ConversionOperators.csproj and ConversionOperators.vbproj.

4.5   *Creating views on an object graph in memory*

After focusing on the major operators in the previous section, we'll now use them to discover others in the context of our sample application. We'll see how to write queries and use the query operators to perform common operations such as sorting, dealing with nested data, and grouping.

Let's start with sorting.

4.5.1   *Sorting*

The objects in our sample data come in a specific order. This is an arbitrary order, and we may wish to view the data sorted by specific orderings. Query expressions allow us to use `orderby` clauses for this.

Let's return to our web example. Let's say we'd like to view our books sorted by publisher, then by descending price, and then by ascending title. The result would look like figure 4.16.

The query we'd use to achieve this result is shown in listing 4.18.

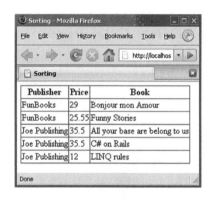

Figure 4.16   Sorting result

**Listing 4.18   Using an `orderby` clause to sort results
(Sorting.aspx.cs)**

```
from book in SampleData.Books
    orderby book.Publisher.Name, book.Price descending, book.Title
    select new { Publisher=book.Publisher.Name,
             book.Price,
             book.Title };
```

The `orderby` keyword can be used to specify several orderings. By default, items are sorted in ascending order. It's possible to use the `descending` keyword on a per-member basis, as we do here for the price.

A query expression's `orderby` clause translates to a composition of calls to the `OrderBy`, `ThenBy`, `OrderByDescending`, and `ThenByDescending` operators. Here is our example expressed with query operators:

```
SampleData.Books
    .OrderBy(book => book.Publisher.Name)
    .ThenByDescending(book => book.Price)
```

```
.ThenBy(book => book.Title)
.Select(book => new { Publisher=book.Publisher.Name,
                      book.Price,
                      book.Title });
```

In order to get the results displayed in a web page as in figure 4.16, we use a Grid-View control with the markup shown in listing 4.19.

Listing 4.19   Markup used to display the results of the sorting sample (Sorting.aspx)

```
<asp:GridView ID="GridView1" runat="server"
  AutoGenerateColumns="false">
  <Columns>
    <asp:BoundField HeaderText="Publisher" DataField="Publisher" />
    <asp:BoundField HeaderText="Price" DataField="Price" />
    <asp:BoundField HeaderText="Book" DataField="Title" />
  </Columns>
</asp:GridView>
```

That's all there is to sorting. It's not difficult. Let's jump to another type of operation we can use in queries.

4.5.2   Nested queries

In the previous example, the data is collected using a projection. All the information appears at the same level. We don't see the hierarchy between a publisher and its books. Also, there is some duplication we could avoid. For example, the name of each publisher appears several times because we've projected this information for each book.

We'll try to improve this by using nested queries.

Let's look at an example to show how we can avoid projections. Let's say we want to display publishers and their books in the same grid, as in figure 4.17.

We can start by writing a query for publishers:

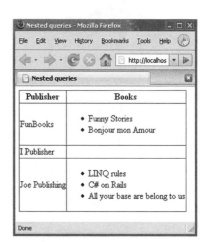

Figure 4.17   Books grouped by publisher using nested queries

```
from publisher in SampleData.Publishers
select publisher
```

We said that we want both the publisher's name and books, so instead of returning a `Publisher` object, we'll use an anonymous type to group this information into an object with two properties: `Publisher` and `Books`:

```
from publisher in SampleData.Publishers
select new { Publisher = publisher.Name, Books = ... }
```

You should be used to this by now. The interesting part is: how do we get a publisher's books? This is not a trick question.

In our sample data, books are attached to a publisher through their `Publisher` property. You may have noticed though that there is no backward link from a `Publisher` object to `Book` objects. Fortunately, LINQ helps us compensate for this. We can use a simple query expression, nested in the first one:

```
from publisher in SampleData.Publishers
select new {
  Publisher = publisher.Name,
  Books =
    from book in SampleData.Books
    where book.Publisher.Name == publisher.Name
    select book }
```

Listing 4.20 contains the complete source code to use in a web page.

Listing 4.20   Code-behind that demonstrates nested queries (Nested.aspx.cs)

```csharp
using System;
using System.Linq;

using LinqInAction.LinqBooks.Common;

public partial class Nested : System.Web.UI.Page
{
  protected void Page_Load(object sender, EventArgs e)
  {
    GridView1.DataSource =
      from publisher in SampleData.Publishers
      orderby publisher.Name
      select new {
        Publisher = publisher.Name,
        Books =
          from book in SampleData.Books
          where book.Publisher == publisher
          select book};
    GridView1.DataBind();
  }
}
```

To display the Books property's data, we'll use an interesting feature of ASP.NET data controls: they can be nested. In listing 4.21, we use this feature to display the books in a bulleted list.

Listing 4.21 Markup for the nested queries (Nested.aspx)

```
<%@ Page Language="C#" AutoEventWireup="true"
  CodeFile="Nested.aspx.cs" Inherits="Nested" %>

<!DOCTYPE html PUBLIC "-//W3C//DTD XHTML 1.0 Transitional//EN"
  "http://www.w3.org/TR/xhtml1/DTD/xhtml1-transitional.dtd">

<html xmlns="http://www.w3.org/1999/xhtml" >
<head runat="server">
    <title>Nested queries</title>
</head>
<body>
    <form id="form1" runat="server">
    <div>
      <asp:GridView ID="GridView1" runat="server"
        AutoGenerateColumns="false">
        <Columns>
          <asp:BoundField HeaderText="Publisher"
            DataField="Publisher" />
        <asp:TemplateField HeaderText="Books">
          <ItemTemplate>
            <asp:BulletedList ID="BulletedList1" runat="server"
                DataSource='<%# Eval("Books") %>'
                DataValueField="Title" />
          </ItemTemplate>
        </asp:TemplateField>
        </Columns>
      </asp:GridView>
    </div>
    </form>
</body>
</html>
```

In this markup, we use a TemplateField for the "Books" column. In this column, a BulletedList control is bound to the Books property of the anonymous type. As specified by DataValueField, it displays the Title property of each book.

In this sample, we've created a view on hierarchical data. This is just one kind of operation we can do with LINQ. We'll now show you more ways to work with object graphs.

4.5.3   *Grouping*

In the previous sample, we showed how to create a hierarchy of data by using nested queries. We'll now consider another way to achieve the same result using LINQ's grouping features.

Using grouping, we'll get the same result as with the previous sample except that we don't see the publishers without books this time. See figure 4.18.

We'll also reuse the same markup. Only the query is different. See listing 4.22.

Figure 4.18   Books grouped by publisher using grouping

Listing 4.22   Grouping books by publisher using a `group` clause (Grouping.aspx.cs)

```
protected void Page_Load(object sender, EventArgs e)
{
  GridView1.DataSource =
    from book in SampleData.Books
    group book by book.Publisher into publisherBooks
    select new { Publisher=publisherBooks.Key.Name,
                 Books=publisherBooks };
  GridView1.DataBind();
}
```

What happens here is that we ask for books grouped by publishers. All the books that belong to a specific publisher will be in the same group. In our query, such a group is named `publisherBooks`. The `publisherBooks` group is an instance of the `IGrouping<TKey, T>` interface. Here is how this interface is defined:

```
public interface IGrouping<TKey, T> : IEnumerable<T>
{
  TKey Key { get; }
}
```

You can see that an object that implements the `IGrouping` generic interface has a strongly typed key and is a strongly typed enumeration. In our case, the key is a `Publisher` object, and the enumeration is of type `IEnumerable<Book>`.

Our query returns a projection of the publisher's name (the group's key) and its books. This is exactly what was happening in the previous example using nested queries! This explains why we can reuse the same grid configuration for this sample.

Using the grouping operator instead of a nested query—like we did in the previous sample—offers at least two advantages. The first is that the query is shorter. The second is that we can name the group. This makes it easier to understand what the group consists of, and it allows us to reuse the group in several places within the query. For example, we could improve our query to show the books for each publisher, as well as the number of books in a separate column:

```
from book in SampleData.Books
group book by book.Publisher into publisherBooks
select new {
  Publisher=publisherBooks.Key.Name,
  Books=publisherBooks,
  publisherBooks.Count() };
```

Grouping is commonly used in SQL alongside aggregation operators. Notice how we use the `Count` operator in a similar way in the latest code snippet. You'll often use `Count` and the other aggregation operators like `Sum`, `Min`, and `Max` on groups.

Grouping is one way LINQ offers to deal with relationships between objects. Another is join operations.

4.5.4 Using joins

After seeing how to group data using nested queries or the grouping operator, we'll now discover yet another way to achieve about the same result. This time, we'll use join operators.

Join operators allow us to perform the same kind of operations as projections, nested queries, or grouping do, but their advantage is that they follow a syntax close to what SQL offers.

Group join

In order to introduce the join operators, let's consider a query expression that uses a *join* clause, shown in listing 4.23.

Listing 4.23 Using a `join..into` **clause to group books by publisher (Joins.aspx.cs)**

```
from publisher in SampleData.Publishers
join book in SampleData.Books
  on publisher equals book.Publisher into publisherBooks
select new { Publisher=publisher.Name, Books=publisherBooks };
```

This is a *group join*. It bundles each publisher's books as sequences named publisherBooks. This new query is equivalent to the one we wrote in section 4.5.3, which uses a group clause:

```
from book in SampleData.Books
group book by book.Publisher into publisherBooks
select new { Publisher=publisherBooks.Key.Name,
            Books=publisherBooks };
```

Look at figure 4.19 and note how the result is different than with a grouping operation. As with nested queries (see figure 4.17), publishers with no books appear in the results this time.

After group joins, we'll now take a look at *inner joins*, *left outer joins*, and *cross joins*.

Inner join

An inner join essentially finds the intersection between two sequences. With an inner join, the elements from two sequences that meet a matching condition are combined to form a single sequence.

The Join operator performs an inner join of two sequences based on matching keys extracted from the elements. For example, it can be used to display a flat view of publishers and books like the one in figure 4.20.

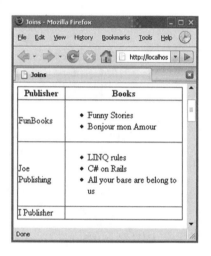

Figure 4.19   Group join result

The query to use to get this result looks like listing 4.24.

This query is similar to the one we used in the group join sample. The difference here is that we don't use the into keyword to group the elements. Instead, the books are projected on the publishers. As you can see in figure 4.20, the result sequence contains an element for each book. In our sample data, one publisher isn't associated with any book. Note that this publisher isn't part of the results. This is why

Figure 4.20   Inner join result

this kind of join operation is called an *inner* join. Only elements from the sequences that have at least one matching element in the other sequence are kept. We'll see in a minute how this compares with a *left outer* join.

Listing 4.24 Using a join clause to group books by publisher (Joins.aspx.cs)

```
from publisher in SampleData.Publishers
join book in SampleData.Books on publisher equals book.Publisher
select new { Publisher=publisher.Name, Book=book.Title };
```

Before going further, let's take a look at listing 4.25, which shows how our last query can be written using the `Join` query operator.

Listing 4.25 Using the `Join` operator to group books by publisher

```
SampleData.Publishers            Inner
   .Join(SampleData.Books,    ←  sequence    Outer key
      publisher => publisher,          ←     selector       Inner key
      book => book.Publisher,                        ←      selector
      (publisher, book) => new { Publisher=publisher.Name,   Result
                           Book=book.Title });              selector
```

This is a case where a query expression is clearly easier to read than code based on operators. The SQL-like syntax offered by query expressions can really help avoid the complexity of some query operators.

Let's now move on to *left outer joins*.

Left outer join

As we've just seen, with an inner join, only the combinations with elements in both joined sequences are kept. When we want to keep all elements from the outer sequence, independently of whether there is a matching element in the inner sequence, we need to perform a *left outer join*.

A left outer join is like an inner join, except that all the left-side elements get included at least once, even if they don't match any right-side elements.

Let's say for example that we want to include the publishers with no books in the results. Note

Figure 4.21 Left outer join result

in figure 4.21 how the last publisher shows up in the output even though it has no matching books.

A so-called outer join can be expressed with a group join. Listing 4.26 shows the query that produces these results.

**Listing 4.26   Query used to perform a left outer join
(Joins.aspx.cs)**

```
from publisher in SampleData.Publishers
join book in SampleData.Books
  on publisher equals book.Publisher into publisherBooks
from book in publisherBooks.DefaultIfEmpty()
select new {
  Publisher = publisher.Name,
  Book = book == default(Book) ? "(no books)" : book.Title
};
```

The `DefaultIfEmpty` operator supplies a default element for an empty sequence.
`DefaultIfEmpty` uses the `default` keyword of generics. It returns null for reference types and zero for numeric value types. For structs, it returns each member of the struct initialized to zero or null depending on whether they are value or reference types.

In our case, the default value is null, but we can test against `default(Book)` to decide what to display for books.

We've just seen group joins, inner joins, and left outer joins. There is one more kind of join operation we'd like to introduce: cross joins.

Cross join

A *cross join* computes the Cartesian product of all the elements from two sequences. The result is a sequence that contains a combination of each element from the first sequence with each element from the second sequence. As a consequence, the number of elements in the result sequence is the product of the number of elements in each sequence.

Before showing you how to perform a cross join, we'd like to point out that in LINQ, it is not done with the `Join` operator. In LINQ terms, a cross join is a projection. It can be achieved using the `SelectMany` operator or by chaining `from` clauses in a query expression, both of which we introduced in section 4.4.2.

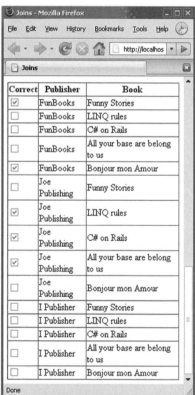

Figure 4.22   Cross join result

As an example, let's say we want to display all the publishers and the books projected together, regardless of whether there is a link between them. We can add a column to indicate the correct association, as in figure 4.22.

Listing 4.27 shows the query expression that yields this result.

Listing 4.27 Query used to perform a cross join (Joins.aspx.cs)

```
from publisher in SampleData.Publishers
from book in SampleData.Books
select new {
  Correct = (publisher == book.Publisher),
  Publisher = publisher.Name,
  Book = book.Title };
```

Here is how we would do the same without a query expression, using the `Select-Many` and `Select` operators:

```
SampleData.Publishers.SelectMany(
  publisher => SampleData.Books.Select(
    book => new {
      Correct = (publisher == book.Publisher),
      Publisher = publisher.Name,
      Book = book.Title }));
```

Again, this is a case where the syntactic sugar offered by query expressions makes things easier to write and read!

After joins, we'll discover one more way to create views on objects in memory. This time we'll partition sequences to keep only a range of their elements.

4.5.5 *Partitioning*

For the moment, we've been displaying all the results in a single page. This is not a problem, as we don't have long results. If we had more results to display, it could be interesting to enable some pagination mechanism.

Adding paging

Let's say we want to display a maximum of three books on a page. This can be done easily using the `GridView` control's paging features. A grid looks like with paging enabled looks like figure 4.23.

Figure 4.23 Grid with paging

The numbers at the bottom of the grid give access to the pages. Paging can be configured in the markup, as follows:

```
<asp:GridView ID="GridView1" runat="server"
  AllowPaging="true" PageSize="3"
  OnPageIndexChanging="GridView1_PageIndexChanging">
</asp:GridView>
```

The code-behind file in listing 4.28 shows how to handle paging.

Listing 4.28   Code-behind for paging in a `GridView` control (Paging.aspx.cs)

```
using System;
using System.Linq;
using System.Web.UI.WebControls;

using LinqInAction.LinqBooks.Common;

public partial class Paging : System.Web.UI.Page
{
  private void BindData()
  {
    GridView1.DataSource =
      SampleData.Books
        .Select(book => book.Title).ToList();
    GridView1.DataBind();
  }

  protected void Page_Load(object sender, EventArgs e)
  {
    if (!IsPostBack)
      BindData();
  }

  protected void GridView1_PageIndexChanging(object sender,
    GridViewPageEventArgs e)
  {
    GridView1.PageIndex = e.NewPageIndex;
    BindData();
  }
}
```

NOTE   Here we use `ToList` in order to enable paging because a sequence doesn't provide the necessary support for it.

Paging is useful and easy to activate with the `GridView` control, but this does not have a lot to do with LINQ. The grid handles it all by itself.

We can perform the same kind of operations programmatically in LINQ queries thanks to the Skip and Take operators.

Skip and Take

When you want to keep only a range of the data returned by a sequence, you can use the two partitioning query operators: Skip and Take.

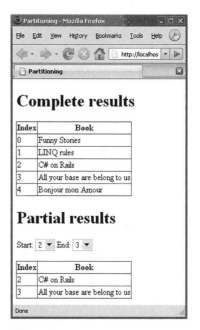

The Skip operator skips a given number of elements from a sequence and then yields the remainder of the sequence. The Take operator yields a given number of elements from a sequence and then skips the remainder of the sequence. The canonical expression for returning page index n, given pageSize is: sequence.Skip(n * pageSize).Take(pageSize).

Let's say we want to keep only a subset of the books. We can do this thanks to two combo boxes allowing us to select the start and end indices. Figure 4.24 shows the complete list of books, as well as the filtered list:

Listing 4.29 shows the code that yields these results.

Figure 4.24   Partitioning results

Listing 4.29   Code-behind for demonstrating partitioning
(Partitioning.aspx.cs)

```
using System;
using System.Linq;
using System.Web.UI.WebControls;

using LinqInAction.LinqBooks.Common;

public partial class Partitioning : System.Web.UI.Page
{
  protected void Page_Load(object sender, EventArgs e)
  {
    if (!IsPostBack)
    {
      GridViewComplete.DataSource = #1
      SampleData.Books #1
        .Select((book, index) => new { Index=index,
                                 Book=book.Title});         Display
      GridViewComplete.DataBind();                          complete list
```

```
int count = SampleData.Books.Count();
for (int i = 0; i < count; i++)
{
  ddlStart.Items.Add(i.ToString());          Prepare
  ddlEnd.Items.Add(i.ToString());            combo boxes
}
ddlStart.SelectedIndex = 2;
ddlEnd.SelectedIndex = 3;

DisplayPartialData();        ◁──┐ Display
                                │ filtered list
}
}

protected void ddlStart_SelectedIndexChanged(object sender,
  EventArgs e)
{
  DisplayPartialData();
}

private void DisplayPartialData()
{
  int startIndex = int.Parse(ddlStart.SelectedValue);   Retrieve start
  int endIndex = int.Parse(ddlEnd.SelectedValue);       and end indices

  GridViewPartial.DataSource =
    SampleData.Books
      .Select(                                            Display
        (book, index) => new { Index=index, Book=book.Title })  filtered
      .Skip(startIndex).Take(endIndex-startIndex+1);      list
  GridViewPartial.DataBind();
}
}
```

Here's the associated markup:

```
...
<body>
  <form id="form1" runat="server">
    <div>
      <h1>Complete results</h1>
      <asp:GridView ID="GridViewComplete" runat="server" />

      <h1>Partial results</h1>
      Start:
      <asp:DropDownList ID="ddlStart" runat="server"
        AutoPostBack="True" CausesValidation="True"
        OnSelectedIndexChanged="ddlStart_SelectedIndexChanged" />
      End:
      <asp:DropDownList ID="ddlEnd" runat="server"
```

```
          AutoPostBack="True" CausesValidation="True"
          OnSelectedIndexChanged="ddlStart_SelectedIndexChanged" />
        <asp:CompareValidator ID="CompareValidator1" runat="server"
          ControlToValidate="ddlStart" ControlToCompare="ddlEnd"
          ErrorMessage=
            "The second index must be higher than the first one"
          Operator="LessThanEqual" Type="Integer" /><br />
        <asp:GridView ID="GridViewPartial" runat="server" />
      </div>
    </form>
  </body>
</html>
```

Partitioning was the last LINQ operation we wanted to show you for now. You've seen several query operators as well as how they can be used in practice to create views on object collections in memory. You'll discover more operations and operators in the next chapters.

4.6   *Summary*

This chapter—the first on LINQ to Objects—demonstrated how to perform several kinds of operations on object collections in memory.

This chapter also introduced the LinqBooks running example. We'll continue using it for the code samples in subsequent chapters. You also created your first ASP.NET web site and your first Windows Forms application using LINQ. Most importantly, we reviewed major standard query operators and applied typical query operations such as filtering, grouping, and sorting.

What you've learned in this chapter is useful for working with LINQ to Objects, but it's important to remember that most of this knowledge also applies to all the other LINQ flavors. You'll see how this is the case with LINQ to XML and LINQ to SQL in parts 3 and 4 of this book.

When we cover LINQ's extensibility in chapter 12, we'll demonstrate how to enrich the standard set of query operators with your own operators.

After learning a lot about language features and LINQ flavors in four chapters, it's time to consider some common scenarios to help you write LINQ code. This is the subject of the next chapter, which will also cover performance considerations in order to help you avoid writing suboptimal queries.

Beyond basic
in-memory queries

This chapter covers:

- LINQ to Objects common scenarios
- Dynamic queries
- Design patterns
- Performance considerations

After learning the basics of LINQ in part 1 of this book and gaining knowledge of in-memory LINQ queries in part 2, it's time to have a break before discovering other LINQ variants. You've already learned a lot about LINQ queries and in particular about LINQ to Objects in chapter 4. You may think that this is enough to write efficient LINQ queries. Think again. LINQ is like an ocean where each variant is an island. We have taught you the rudiments of swimming, but you need to learn more before you can travel safely to all the islands. You know how to write a query, but do you know how to write an efficient query? In this chapter, we'll expand on some of our earlier ideas to improve your skills of LINQ. We're going to step back and look at how to make the most of what we've covered so far.

This chapter is important for anyone who plans on using LINQ. Most of what you'll learn in this chapter applies not only to LINQ to Objects, but to other in-memory LINQ variants as well, such as LINQ to XML. One of our goals is to help you identify common scenarios for in-memory LINQ queries and provide you with ready-to-use solutions. Other goals are to introduce LINQ design patterns, expose best practices, and advise you on what to do and what to avoid in your day-to-day LINQ coding. We also want to address concerns you may have about the performance of in-memory queries.

Once you've read this chapter, you'll be prepared to take the plunge into LINQ to SQL and LINQ to XML, which we'll cover in detail in parts 3 and 4.

5.1 *Common scenarios*

We're pretty sure that you're eager to start using LINQ for real development now that you have some knowledge about it and have practiced with several examples. When you write LINQ code on your own, you'll likely encounter some problems that weren't covered in the usual examples. The short code samples used in the official documentation, on the Internet, or even in the previous chapters of this book focus on small tasks. They help you to get a grip on the technology but do not address everyday LINQ programming and the potential difficulties that come with it.

In this section, we show you some common scenarios for LINQ to Objects and provide solutions to get you up-to-speed faster with LINQ application programming. We start by showing how to query nongeneric collections. We then demonstrate how to group by multiple criteria in queries. We also give you an introduction to dynamic and parameterized queries. Finally, we finish the section with a demonstration of a fictitious flavor of LINQ named LINQ to Text Files, which shows how LINQ to Objects is powerful enough to work with many data sources without needing a specific flavor for each kind of data source.

5.1.1   *Querying nongeneric collections*

If you've read the preceding chapters attentively, you should now be able to query in-memory collections with LINQ to Objects. There is one problem, though. You may think you know how to query collections, but in reality you only know how to query some collections. The problem comes from the fact that LINQ to Objects was designed to query generic collections that implement the `System.Collections.Generic.IEnumerable<T>` interface. Don't get us wrong: most collections implement `IEnumerable<T>` in the .NET Framework. This includes the major collections such as the `System.Collections.Generic.List<T>` class, arrays, dictionaries, and queues. The problem is that `IEnumerable<T>` is a generic interface, and not all classes are generic.

Generics have been available since .NET 2.0, but are still not adopted yet by everyone.[1] Moreover, even if you use generics in your own code, you may have to deal with legacy code that isn't based on generics. For example, the most commonly used collection in .NET before the arrival of generics was the `System.Collections.ArrayList` data structure. An `ArrayList` is a nongeneric collection that contains a list of untyped objects and does not implement `IEnumerable<T>`. Does this mean that you can't use LINQ with `ArrayList`s?

If you try to use the query in listing 5.1, you'll get a compile-time error because the type of the books ❶ variable is not supported:

> **Listing 5.1   Trying to query an `ArrayList` using LINQ to Objects directly fails**

```
ArrayList books = GetArrayList();

var query =
   from book in books        ❶ Source type not
   where book.PageCount > 150      supported
   select new { book.Title, book.Publisher.Name };
```

It would be too bad if we couldn't use LINQ with ArrayLists or other nongeneric collections. As you can guess, there is a solution. Nongeneric collections aren't a big problem with LINQ once you know the trick.

Suppose that you get results from a method that returns a nongeneric collection, such as an `ArrayList` object. What you need to query a collection with LINQ is something that implements `IEnumerable<T>`. The trick is to use the `Cast` operator, which

---

[1]   Those heathens!

gives you just that: Cast takes a nongeneric IEnumerable and gives you back a generic IEnumerable<T>. The Cast operator can be used each time you need to bridge between nongeneric collections and the standard query operators.

Listing 5.2 demonstrates how to use Cast to convert an ArrayList into a generic enumeration that can be queried using LINQ to Objects.

Listing 5.2   Querying an `ArrayList` is possible thanks to the `Cast` query operator

```
ArrayList books = GetArrayList();

var query =
  from book in books.Cast<Book>()
  where book.PageCount > 150
  select new { book.Title, book.Publisher.Name };

dataGridView.DataSource = query.ToList();
```

Notice how simply applying the Cast operator to an ArrayList allows us to integrate it in a LINQ query! The Cast operator casts the elements of a source sequence to a given type. Here is the signature of the Cast operator:

```
public static IEnumerable<T> Cast<T>(this IEnumerable source)
```

This operator works by allocating and returning an enumerable object that captures the source argument. When the object returned by Cast is enumerated, it iterates the source sequence and yields each element cast to type T. An Invalid-CastException is thrown if an element in the sequence cannot be cast to type T.

NOTE   In the case of value types, a null value in the sequence causes a NullReferenceException. In the case of reference types, a null value is cast without error as a null reference of the target type.

It's interesting to note that thanks to a feature of query expressions, the code of our last example can be simplified. We don't need to explicitly invoke the Cast operator! In a C# query expression, an explicitly typed iteration variable translates to an invocation of Cast. Our query can be formulated without Cast by explicitly declaring the book iteration variable as a Book. Listing 5.3 is equivalent to listing 5.2, but shorter.

**Listing 5.3   Querying an `ArrayList` is possible thanks to type declarations in
query expressions**

```
var query =
  from Book book in books
  where book.PageCount > 150
  select new { book.Title, book.Publisher.Name };
```

The same technique can be used to work with `DataSet` objects. For instance, here
is how you can query the rows of a `DataTable` using a query expression:

```
from DataRow row in myDataTable.Rows
where (String)row[0] == "LINQ"
select row
```

NOTE   You'll see in our bonus chapter how LINQ to DataSet offers an alternative
for querying `DataSets` and `DataTables`.

As an alternative to the `Cast` operator, you can also use the `OfType` operator. The
difference is that `OfType` only returns objects from a source collection that are of
a certain type. For example, if you have an `ArrayList` that contains `Book` and `Pub-
lisher` objects, calling `theArrayList.OfType<Book>()` returns only the instances
of `Book` from the `ArrayList`.

As time goes by, you're likely to encounter nongeneric collections less and less
because generic collections offer type checking and improved performance. But
until then, if you want to apply your LINQ expertise to all collections including
nongeneric ones, the `Cast` and `OfType` operators and explicitly typed `from` iteration variables are your friends!

Querying nongeneric collections was the first common scenario we wanted to
show you. We'll now introduce a completely different scenario that consists of
grouping query results by composite keys. Although grouping by multiple criteria
seems like a pretty simple task, the lack of a dedicated syntax for this in query
expressions does not make how to do it obvious.

5.1.2   *Grouping by multiple criteria*

When we introduced grouping in chapter 4, we grouped results by a single property, as in the following query:

```
var query =
  from book in SampleData.Books
  group book by book.Publisher;
```

Here we group books by publisher. But what if you need to group by multiple criteria? Let's say that you want to group by publisher and subject, for example. If you try to adapt the query to do this, you may be disappointed to find that the LINQ query expression syntax does not accept multiple criteria in a group clause, nor does it accept multiple group clauses in a query.

The following queries are not valid, for example:

```
var query1 =
   from book in SampleData.Books
   group book by book.Publisher, book.Subject;
var query2 =
   from book in SampleData.Books
   group book by book.Publisher
   group book by book.Subject;
```

This doesn't mean that it's impossible to perform grouping by multiple criteria in a query expression. The trick is to use an anonymous type to specify the members on which to perform the grouping. We know this may sound difficult and several options are possible, so we'll break it down into small examples.

Let's consider that you want to group by publisher and subject. This would produce the following results for our sample data:

```
Publisher=FunBooks        Subject=Software development
   Books: Title=Funny Stories      PublicationDate=10/11/2004...
Publisher=Joe Publishing        Subject=Software development
   Books: Title=LINQ rules         PublicationDate=02/09/2007...
   Books: Title=C# on Rails        PublicationDate=01/04/2007...
Publisher=Joe Publishing        Subject=Science fiction
   Books: Title=All your base are belong to us
➥PublicationDate=05/05/2006...
Publisher=FunBooks        Subject=Novel
   Books: Title=Bonjour mon Amour PublicationDate=18/02/1973...
```

To achieve this result, your group clause needs to contain an anonymous type that combines the Publisher and Subject properties of a Book object. In listing 5.4, we use a composite key instead of a simple key.

Listing 5.4 Grouping books by publisher and subject

```
var query =
   from book in SampleData.Books
   group book by new { book.Publisher, book.Subject };
```

This query results in a collection of groupings. Each grouping contains a key (an instance of the anonymous type) and an enumeration of books matching the key.

In order to produce a more meaningful result similar to the one we showed earlier, you can improve the query by adding a `select` clause, as in listing 5.5.

Listing 5.5   Using the `into` keyword in a `group by` clause

```
var query =
  from book in SampleData.Books
  group book by new { book.Publisher, book.Subject }    ❶ into
    into grouping                                           keyword
  select new {
    Publisher = grouping.Key.Publisher.Name,
    Subject = grouping.Key.Subject.Name,         Key  ❸    ❷ Select
    Books = grouping                                          clause
  };                                grouping     property
                                 ❹  variable
```

The `into` keyword ❶ is introduced to provide a variable we can use in `select` ❷ or other subsequent clauses. The `grouping` variable ❶ we declare after `into` contains the key of the grouping, which is accessible through its `Key` property ❸, as well as the elements in the grouping. The key represents the thing that we group on. The elements of each grouping can be retrieved by enumerating the `grouping` variable ❹, which implements `IEnumerable<T>`, where `T` is the type of what is specified immediately after the `group` keyword. Here, `grouping` is an enumeration of `Book` objects. Note that the `grouping` variable can be named differently if you prefer.

To display the results, you can use the `ObjectDumper` class again:

```
ObjectDumper.Write(query, 1);
```

REMINDER   `ObjectDumper` is a utility class we already used in several places, like in chapters 2 and 4. It's provided by Microsoft as part of the LINQ code samples. You'll be able to find it in the downloadable source code that comes with this book.

The result elements of a grouping do not need to be of the same type as the source's elements. For example, you may wish to retrieve only the title of each book instead of a complete `Book` object. In this case, you would adapt the query as in listing 5.6.

Listing 5.6   Query that groups book titles, and not book objects, by publisher and subject

```
var query =
  from book in SampleData.Books
  group book.Title by new { book.Publisher, book.Subject }
    into grouping
```

```
select new {
  Publisher = grouping.Key.Publisher.Name,
  Subject = grouping.Key.Subject.Name,
  Titles = grouping
};
```

To go further, you may use an anonymous type to specify the shape of the resulting elements. In the following query, we specify that we want to retrieve the title and publisher name for each book in grouping by subject:

```
var query =
  from book in SampleData.Books
  group new { book.Title, book.Publisher.Name } by book.Subject
    into grouping
  select new {Subject=grouping.Key.Name, Books=grouping };
```

In this query, we use only the subject as the key for the grouping for the sake of simplicity, but you could use an anonymous type as in the previous query if you wish.

> **NOTE**   Anonymous types can be used as composite keys in other query clauses, too, such as `join` and `orderby`.

Are you ready for another scenario? The next common scenario we'd like to address covers dynamic queries. You may wonder what we mean by this. This is something you'll want to use when queries depend on the user's input or other factors. We'll show you how to create dynamic queries by parameterizing and customizing them programmatically.

5.1.3 *Dynamic queries*

There is something that may be worrisome when you start working with LINQ. Your first queries, at least the examples you can see everywhere, seem very static.

Let's look at a typical query:

```
from book in books
where book.Title = "LINQ in Action"
select book.Publisher
```

This construct may give you the impression that a LINQ query can only be used for a specific search. In this section, we show you that the title used for the condition can be parameterized, and even further than that, the whole `where` clause can be specified or even omitted dynamically. We'll show you that a query is not static at all and can be parameterized, enriched, or customized in several ways.

Let's start by seeing how to change the value of a criterion in a LINQ to Objects query.

Parameterized query

If you remember what we demonstrated in chapter 3 when we introduced deferred query execution, you already know that a given query can be reused several times but produce different results each time. The trick we used in that chapter is changing the source sequence the query operates on between executions. It's like using a cookie recipe but substituting some of the ingredients. Do you want pecans or walnuts? Another solution to get different results from a query is to change the value of some criteria used in the query. After all, you have the right to add more chocolate chips to your cookies!

Let's consider a simple example. In the following query, a `where` clause is used to filter books by their number of pages:

```
int minPageCount = 200;

var books =
    from book in SampleData.Books
    where book.PageCount >= minPageCount
    select book;
```

The criterion used in the `where` clause of this query is based on a variable named `minPageCount`. Changing the value of the `minPageCount` variable affects the results of the query. Your small "My top 50 cookie recipes" book and its 100 pages won't appear in here.

In listing 5.7, when we change the value of `minPageCount` from 200 to 50 and execute the query a second time, the result sequence contains five books instead of three:

Listing 5.7   Using a local variable to make a query dynamic

```
                          Set minPageCount to 200
minPageCount = 200;    ◁──┘
Console.WriteLine("Books with at least {0} pages: {1}",    Query returns
    minPageCount, books.Count());    ◁──────────────         3 books
                          Change minPageCount
minPageCount = 50;    ◁──┘
Console.WriteLine("Books with at least {0} pages: {1}",    Query now
    minPageCount, books.Count());    ◁──────────────         returns 5 books
```

NOTE   Applying the `Count` operator to the query contained in the books variable executes the query immediately. `Count` completely enumerates the query it's invoked on in order to determine the number of elements.

This technique may not seem very advanced, but it's good to remember that it's possible and provide an example to demonstrate how to use it. Such small tricks are useful when using LINQ queries.

Let's consider a variant of this technique. Often you'll use queries in a method with parameters. If you use the method parameters in the query, they impact the results of the query.

The method in listing 5.8 reuses the same technique as in our last example, but this time a parameter is used to specify the minimum number of pages.

Listing 5.8 Using a method parameter to make a query dynamic

```
void ParameterizedQuery(int minPageCount)
{
  var books =
    from book in SampleData.Books
    where book.PageCount >= minPageCount
    select book;

  Console.WriteLine("Books with at least {0} pages: {1}",
    minPageCount, books.Count());
}
```

This technique is very common. It's the first solution you can use to introduce some dynamism in LINQ queries. Other techniques can be used also. For example, we'll now show you how to change the sort order used in a query.

Custom sort

Sorting the results of a query based on the user's preference is another common scenario where dynamic queries can help. In a query, the sort order can be specified using an `orderby` clause or with an explicit call to the `OrderBy` operator. Here is a query expression that sorts books by title:

```
from book in SampleData.Books
orderby book.Title
select book.Title;
```

Here is the equivalent query written using the method syntax:

```
SampleData.Books
  .Orderby(book => book.Title)
  .Select(book => book.Title);
```

The problem with these queries is that the sorting order is hard-coded: the results of such queries will always be ordered by titles. What if we wish to specify the order dynamically?

Suppose you're creating an application where you wish to let the user decide how books are sorted. The user interface may look like figure 5.1.

You can implement a method that accepts a sort key selector delegate as a parameter. This parameter can then be used in the call to the OrderBy operator. Here is the signature of the OrderBy operator:

Figure 5.1   A user interface that allows the user to choose the sort order he wants to see applied to a list of books

```
OrderedSequence<TElement> OrderBy<TElement, TKey>(
    this IEnumerable<TElement> source, Func<TElement, TKey> keySelector)
```

This shows that the type of the delegate you need to provide to OrderBy is Func<TElement, TKey>. In our case, the source is a sequence of Book objects, so TElement is the Book class. The key is selected dynamically and can be a string (for the Title property for example) or an integer (for the PageCount property). In order to support both kinds of keys, you can use a generic method, where TKey is a type parameter.

Listing 5.9 shows how you can write a method that takes a sort key selector as an argument.

Listing 5.9   Method that uses a parameter to enable custom sorting

```
void CustomSort<TKey>(Func<Book, TKey> selector)
{
  var books = SampleData.Books.OrderBy(selector);
  ObjectDumper.Write(books);
}
```

The method can also be written using a query expression, as in listing 5.10.

Listing 5.10   Method that uses a parameter in a query expression to enable custom sorting

```
void CustomSort<TKey>(Func<Book, TKey> selector)
{
  var books =
    from book in SampleData.Books
    orderby selector(book)
    select book;
  ObjectDumper.Write(books);
}
```

This method can be used as follows:

```
CustomSort(book => book.Title);
```

or

```
CustomSort(book => book.Publisher.Name);
```

One problem is that this code does not allow sorting in descending order. In order to support descending order, the `CustomSort` method needs to be adapted as shown in listing 5.11.

Listing 5.11 Method that uses a parameter to enable custom sorting in ascending or descending order

```
void CustomSort<TKey>(Func<Book, TKey> selector, Boolean ascending)
{
  IEnumerable<Book> books = SampleData.Books;
  books = ascending ? books.OrderBy(selector)
                    : books.OrderByDescending(selector);
  ObjectDumper.Write(books);
}
```

This time, the method can be written only using explicit calls to the operators. The query expression cannot include the test on the `ascending` parameter because it needs a static `orderby` clause.

The additional `ascending` parameter allows us to choose between the `OrderBy` and `OrderByDescending` operators. It then becomes possible to use the following call to sort using a descending order instead of the default ascending order:

```
CustomSort(book => book.Title, false);
```

Finally, we have a complete version of the `CustomSort` method that uses a dynamic query to allow you to address our common scenario. All you have to do is use a `switch` statement to take into account the user's choice for the sort order, as in listing 5.12.

Listing 5.12 Switch statement used to choose between several custom sorts

```
switch (cbxSortOrder.SelectedIndex)
{
  case 0:
    CustomSort(book => book.Title);
    break;
  case 1:
```

```
        CustomSort(book => book.Title, false);
        break;
    case 2:
        CustomSort(book => book.Publisher.Name);
        break;
    case 3:
        CustomSort(book => book.PageCount);
        break;
}
```

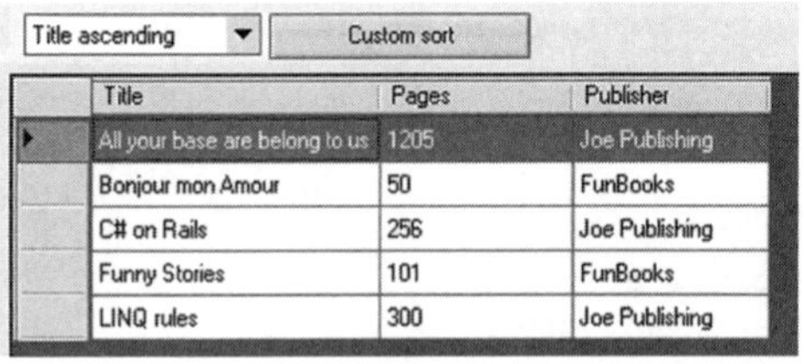

Figure 5.2   Books sorted by title in ascending order according to the user's choice of a sort order

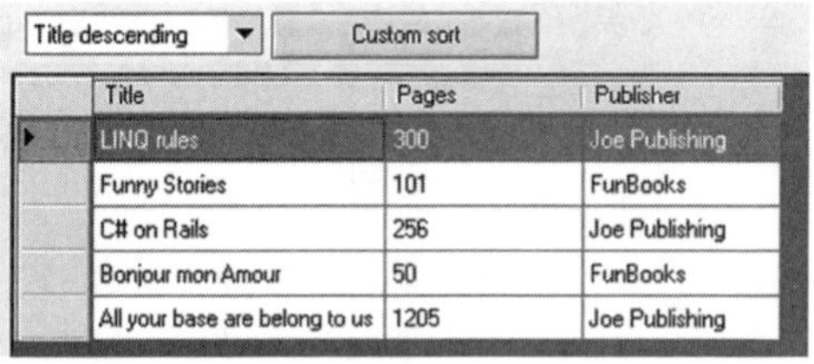

Figure 5.3   Books sorted by title in descending order according to the user's choice of a sort order

This produces the display shown in figure 5.2 for an ascending sort by title.

Figure 5.3 shows the display for a descending sort by title.

After showing you how to parameterize the condition of a query's where clause and use a dynamic sort order, we'd like to show you a more advanced scenario. This new example will demonstrate how to dynamically define a query, including or excluding clauses and operators depending on the context. This is something you'd want to achieve often, so queries can take into account the application's context, settings, or the user's input.

Conditionally building queries

The previous examples showed how to customize queries by changing the values they use as well as the sort order. A new example will show you how to add criteria and operators to a query dynamically. This technique allows us to shape queries based on user input, for example.

Let's consider a common scenario. In most applications, data isn't presented to the user directly as is. After being extracted from a database, an XML document, or another data source, the data is filtered, sorted, formatted, and so on. This is where LINQ is of great help. LINQ queries allow us to perform all these data manipulation operations with a nice declarative syntax. Most of the time, the data is filtered and dynamically shaped based on what the user specifies.

As an example, a typical search screen consists of an area where the user can input a set of criteria, combined with a grid or another list control that displays the results. Figure 5.4 shows such a screen.

This is the dialog window we'll use for our example. In order to take the user's criteria into account, we can write a simple query that looks like listing 5.13.

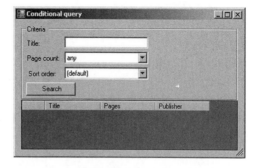

Figure 5.4   A typical search screen with a criteria area used to filter books by page count and title, and to specify the results' sort order

---

Listing 5.13   Building a conditional query based on user input

```
var query =                                      Prepare query according
  SampleData.Books                                       to user's criteria
    .Where(
       book => book.PageCount >= (int)cbxPageCount.SelectedValue)
    .Where(book => book.Title.Contains(txtTitleFilter.Text))

if (cbxSortOrder.SelectedIndex == 1)
  query = query.OrderBy(book => book.Title);              Call
else if (cbxSortOrder.SelectedIndex == 2)                OrderBy
  query = query.OrderBy(book => book.Publisher.Name);    if needed
else if (cbxSortOrder.SelectedIndex == 3)
  query = query.OrderBy(book => book.PageCount);

query = query.Select(
  book => new { book.Title,                    Call
                book.PageCount,                Select
                Publisher=book.Publisher.Name });

dataGridView1.DataSource = query.ToList();     ⟵  Bind results to DataGridView
```

For code reusability and clarity, it's better to refactor the code to move this query to a dedicated method, as in listing 5.14.

Listing 5.14   Dynamic query refactored into a method

```
void ConditionalQuery<TSortKey>(
  int minPageCount, String titleFilter,
  Func<Book, TSortKey> sortSelector)
{
  var query =
    SampleData.Books
```

```
        .Where(book => book.PageCount >= minPageCount.Value)
        .Where(book => book.Title.Contains(titleFilter))
        .OrderBy(sortSelector)
        .Select(
          book => new { book.Title,
                        book.PageCount,
                        Publisher=book.Publisher.Name });

  dataGridView1.DataSource = query.ToList();
}
```

Here we use the explicit method syntax instead of a query expression because it will make the transition to the next version of the code. This method can be called using the code in listing 5.15.

Listing 5.15   Invoking the `ConditionalQuery` method according to user input

```
int? minPageCount;
string titleFilter;

minPageCount = (int?)cbxPageCount.SelectedValue;
titleFilter = txtTitleFilter.Text;
if (cbxSortOrder2.SelectedIndex == 1)
{
  ConditionalQuery(minPageCount, titleFilter,
    book => book.Title);
}
else if (cbxSortOrder2.SelectedIndex == 2)
{
  ConditionalQuery(minPageCount, titleFilter,
    book => book.Publisher.Name);
}
else if (cbxSortOrder2.SelectedIndex == 3)
{
  ConditionalQuery(minPageCount, titleFilter,
    book => book.PageCount);
}
else
{
  ConditionalQuery<Object>(minPageCount, titleFilter, null);
}
```

This is all fine, but our example is not complete. We don't have the flexible query we promised! In fact, we have a small problem. What will happen if the user doesn't provide values for all the criteria? We won't get the correct results, because the method was not created to handle blank values.

We need to take this into account and test whether we have values for the criteria. When there is no value for a criterion, we simply exclude the corresponding clause from the query. In fact, if you look at the new version of our method in listing 5.16, you'll notice that we create the query on the fly by adding clauses one after another.

Listing 5.16 Complete version of the `ConditionalQuery` method that tests for the provided criteria

```
void ConditionalQuery<TSortKey>(
  int? minPageCount, String titleFilter,
  Func<Book, TSortKey> sortSelector)
{
  IEnumerable<Book> query;

  query = SampleData.Books;                         ❶ List of books
  if (minPageCount.HasValue)
    query =                                              ❷ Where operator call
      query.Where(book => book.PageCount >= minPageCount.Value);
  if (!String.IsNullOrEmpty(titleFilter))
    query = query.Where(book => book.Title.Contains(titleFilter));
  if (sortSelector != null)                         ❸ Second Where call
    query = query.OrderBy(sortSelector);

  var completeQuery = query.Select(                 ❹ OrderBy operator call
    book => new { book.Title,
                  book.PageCount,                   ❺ Select operator call
                  Publisher=book.Publisher.Name });

  dataGridView1.DataSource = completeQuery.ToList();
}
```

At the beginning, our query simply consists of the complete list of books ❶. If the user specifies a value for the minimum page count, then we add a call to the `Where` operator to the query ❷. If the user decides to filter the results based on the title of books, then we add another call to `Where` ❸. If a sort order is specified, we add the `OrderBy` operator to the mix ❹. Finally, we define the shape of the results by using the `Select` operator and an anonymous type ❺.

REMINDER   When we use something like `query = query.Where(…)`, we're actually chaining method calls and not creating a new query object. The fact that the query operators are extension methods (see chapters 2 and 3) allows us to use a temporary `query` variable to chain operations. We would not be able to write this kind of code without extension methods.

Armed with the technique we have just demonstrated, you should now be able to create rich dynamic queries. Yet, there is one more approach that can be used for advanced cases. We'll now take some time to introduce this technique, which uses expression trees.

Creating queries at run-time

In the previous examples, we showed you how to create dynamic queries. These queries are dynamic because some of the values they use or even the clauses that make them are not decided at compile-time, but at run-time. The information these queries are based on is not available when the code is written because it can depend on the user or on the context. In more advanced scenarios, you may have to completely create queries on the fly. Imagine that your application needs to query data based on a description coming from an XML file, a remote application, or the user. In these cases, it's possible to rely on expression trees.

Suppose the following XML fragment describes the criteria to apply to a collection of books in order to filter it:

```
<and>
  <notEqual property="Title" value="Funny Stories" />
  <greaterThan property="PageCount" value="100" />
</and>
```

This XML stipulates that the `Title` property of a book should be different from "Funny Stories" and its `PageCount` property should be greater than 100. If we were to write a query that matches these conditions, it would look like this:

```
var query =
  from book in SampleData.Books
  where (book.Title != "Funny Stories") && (book.PageCount > 100)
  select book;
```

This is a typical query completely defined at compile-time. However, if the XML is provided to our application at run-time, we cannot write the query this way because the application is already compiled. The solution is to use expression trees.

As you've seen in chapter 3, the simplest way to create an expression tree is to let the compiler convert a lambda expression declared with the `Expression<TDelegate>` class into a series of factory method calls that will build the expression tree at run-time. In order to create dynamic queries, you can take advantage of another way of working with expression trees. You can "roll your own" expression tree by calling the factory methods—they're static methods on the `Expression<TDelegate>` class—and compile the expression tree into a lambda expression at run-time.

Listing 5.17 dynamically creates a query at run-time that is equivalent to the preceding query expression.

Listing 5.17   Completely creating a query at run-time using an expression tree

```
var book = Expression.Parameter(typeof(Book), "book");        ◁──┐ Define book
                                                                  │ variable

var titleExpression = Expression.NotEqual(         ◁──┐ book.Title !=
  Expression.Property(book, "Title"),                 │ "Funny Stories"
  Expression.Constant("Funny Stories"));

var pageCountExpression = Expression.GreaterThan(   ◁──┐ book.PageCount
  Expression.Property(book, "PageCount"),               │ > 100
  Expression.Constant(100));

var andExpression = Expression.And(titleExpression,   ◁── and
                         pageCountExpression);

var predicate = Expression.Lambda(andExpression, book);   ◁──┐ Create the
var query = Enumerable.Where(SampleData.Books,               │ where clause
  (Func<Book, Boolean>)predicate.Compile());
```

The listing creates an expression tree that describes the filtering condition. Each statement augments the expression tree by adding new expressions to it. The last two statements convert the expression tree into code that forms an executable query. The query variable from the code can then be used like any other LINQ query.

Of course, the code from listing 5.17 uses hard-coded values such as "Title", "Funny Stories", "PageCount", and "100". In a real application, these values would come from our XML document or any other source of information that exists at run-time.

Expression trees represent an advanced topic. We won't describe further how to use them in the context of dynamic queries, but they're powerful once you master them. You can refer to the LINQ to Amazon example in chapter 13 to see another use of expression trees.

NOTE   Using dynamic queries with LINQ to SQL is another story because everything in the query needs to be translatable to SQL.

Tomas Petricek, a C# MVP, shows how to easily build dynamic LINQ to SQL queries at run-time in C# on his web site. See http://tomasp.net/blog/dynamic-linq-queries.aspx.

The last common scenario we'd like to cover in this chapter will show you how to write LINQ queries against text files. You know how to query collections in memory, but how can you query text files? The question is: do we need another variation of LINQ for this?

5.1.4 *LINQ to Text Files*

Varieties of LINQ exist to deal with several kinds of data and data structures. You already know the major "islands": We have LINQ to Objects, LINQ to DataSet, LINQ to XML, LINQ to SQL. What if you'd like to use LINQ queries with text files? Is there a small island somewhere we didn't let you know about yet? Should you create a new island, since LINQ's extensibility allows this? You could code a few query operators to deal with file streams and text lines... . Wait a second; don't jump straight to your keyboard to create LINQ to Text Files! We don't need it. Let's see how LINQ to Objects is enough for our scenario.

We'll develop an example inspired by Eric White, a Microsoft programming writer who works on the LINQ to XML documentation among other things. Eric's example[2] shows how to extract information from a CSV file.

NOTE   CSV stands for comma-separated values. In a CSV file, different field values are separated by commas.

The sample CSV file we'll use is shown in listing 5.18.

Listing 5.18   Sample CSV document containing information about books

```
#Books (format: ISBN, Title, Authors, Publisher, Date, Price)
0735621632,CLR via C#,Jeffrey Richter,Microsoft Press,02-22-2006,
59.99
0321127420,Patterns Of Enterprise Application Architecture,
Martin Fowler,Addison-Wesley, 11-05-2002,54.99
0321200683,Enterprise Integration Patterns,Gregor Hohpe,
Addison-Wesley,10-10-2003,54.99
0321125215,Domain-Driven Design,Eric Evans,
Addison-Wesley Professional,08-22-2003,54.99
1932394613,Ajax In Action,Dave Crane;Eric Pascarello;Darren James,
Manning Publications,10-01-2005,44.95
```

This CSV contains information about books. In order to read the CSV data, the first step is to open the text file and retrieve the lines it contains. One easy solution to

---

[2] See Eric White's blog at http://blogs.msdn.com/ericwhite/archive/2006/08/31/734383.aspx.

achieve this is to use the `File.ReadAllLines` method. `ReadAllLines` is a static method available on the `System.IO.File` class. This method reads all lines from a text file and returns them as a string array. The second step is to filter out comments. This can be done easily using a where clause.

Here is how to write the start of the query:

```
from line in File.ReadAllLines("books.csv")
where !line.StartsWith("#")
```

Here, we use the string array returned by `File.ReadAllLines` as the source sequence in our `from` clause, and we ignore the lines that start with #.

The next step is to split each line into parts. In order to do this, we can leverage the `Split` method available on string objects. `Split` returns a string array containing the substrings that are delimited by a character or a set of characters in a string instance. Here, we'll split the string based on commas.

We need to refer to each part of the line in the rest of the query, but it's important to perform the split operation only once. This is a typical situation in which the `let` clause is useful. A `let` clause computes a value and introduces an identifier representing that value. Here, we use the `let` clause to hold the parts contained in each line. Once we have a line split apart, we can wrap it into a new object using an anonymous type in a `select` clause.

Listing 5.19 shows is the complete query.

Listing 5.19 Querying information about books from a CSV file

```
from line in File.ReadAllLines("books.csv")
where !line.StartsWith("#")
let parts = line.Split(',')
select new { Isbn=parts[0], Title=parts[1], Publisher=parts[3] };
```

Here is the result you get if you use `ObjectDumper` with the query:

```
Isbn=0735621632   Title=CLR via C#   Publisher=Microsoft Press
Isbn=0321127420   Title=Patterns Of Enterprise Application Architecture
⇒Publisher=Addison-Wesley
Isbn=0321200683   Title=Enterprise Integration Patterns   Publisher=
⇒Addison-Wesley
Isbn=0321125215   Title=Domain-Driven Design   Publisher=Addison-Wesley
Isbn=1932394613   Title=Ajax In Action   Publisher=Manning Publications
```

That's all you need to do to read simple CSV files using LINQ. With four lines of code, you get a query that produces a sequence of objects that contain a title, a publisher name, and an ISBN! This demonstrates that LINQ to Objects is enough to deal with several data sources. We don't need a specific flavor of LINQ to query text files.

> **WARNING** This example shows a naïve approach to parsing CSV files. It doesn't deal with escaped commas or other advanced CSV features. You may want to strengthen the code or use another approach for dealing with CSV in your applications.
>
> In addition, this version of the code can have bad performance implications. We'll show you how it can be improved to solve this in section 5.3.1.

We have just seen common scenarios and how to deal with them. Without the kind of ready-to-use solutions we gave you, you'd have to search by yourself how to address each scenario. In order to optimize the development of common scenarios, design patterns are often created. The next section gives you an overview of design patterns that can be applied to LINQ. We'll get started with a design pattern that is widely used in LINQ queries: the Functional Construction pattern.

Since the LINQ to Text Files example is nice, we'll reuse it as the base for our introduction to this first pattern. We'll also use it again in section 5.3.1, where we'll discuss how to improve the query we wrote in the current section to save resources and increase performance.

5.2   *Design patterns*

Like with any other technology, with LINQ some designs are used again and again over time. These designs eventually become well documented as *design patterns* so they can be reused easily and efficiently. A design pattern is a general repeatable solution to a commonly occurring problem in software design. Design patterns gained popularity in computer science after the book *Design Patterns* from the Gang of Four (aka GoF) was published in 1994.[3] Design patterns were initially defined for object-oriented programming, but have since been used for domains as diverse as organization, process management, and software architecture.

The patterns we cover here apply to LINQ contexts: Functional Construction and ForEach.

---

[3] *Design Patterns: Elements of Reusable Object-Oriented Software.* By Erich Gamma, Richard Helm, Ralph Johnson, John Vlissides. Addison-Wesley; ISBN 0-201-63361-2

5.2.1   *The Functional Construction pattern*

The first design pattern we'll present uses collection initializers and query composition. This pattern is widely used in LINQ queries, especially with LINQ to XML as you'll see in part 4 of this book.

   This pattern is named Functional Construction because it's used to construct a tree or a graph of objects, with a code structure similar to what is used in functional programming languages such as Lisp.

   In order to introduce the Functional Construction pattern, let's reuse and extend the LINQ to Text Files example that we presented in the previous section. Here is the query we used:

```
from line in File.ReadAllLines("books.csv")
where !line.StartsWith("#")
let parts = line.Split(',')
select new { Isbn=parts[0], Title=parts[1], Publisher=parts[3] };
```

We conveniently left the authors out of the query since they require a little extra work. We'll now handle them to get the following kind of results:

```
Isbn=0735621632  Title=CLR via C#  Publisher=Microsoft Press
   Authors: FirstName=Jeffrey  LastName=Richter
Isbn=0321127420  Title=Patterns Of Enterprise Application Architecture
➥Publisher=Addison-Wesley
   Authors: FirstName=Martin  LastName=Fowler
Isbn=0321200683  Title=Enterprise Integration Patterns  Publisher=
➥Addison-Wesley
   Authors: FirstName=Gregor  LastName=Hohpe
Isbn=0321125215  Title=Domain-Driven Design  Publisher=Addison-Wesley
➥Professional
   Authors: FirstName=Eric  LastName=Evans
Isbn=1932394613  Title=Ajax In Action  Publisher=Manning Publications
   Authors: FirstName=Dave  LastName=Crane
   Authors: FirstName=Eric  LastName=Pascarello
   Authors: FirstName=Darren  LastName=James
```

Unlike the other fields in our text file, there can be more than one author specified for a single book. If we go back and review the sample text file from listing 5.18, we see that the authors are delimited by a semicolon:

```
Dave Crane;Eric Pascarello;Darren James
```

As we did with the entire line, we can split the string of authors into an array, with each author being an individual element in the array. To be sure we get our fill of Split, we use it one final time to break the full author name into first and last names. Finally, we place the statements for parsing out the authors into a subquery and wrap the results of our many splits into each book's `Author` property. Listing 5.20 shows the full query.

Listing 5.20   Declarative approach for parsing a CSV file, with anonymous types

```
var books =
  from line in File.ReadAllLines("books.csv")
  where !line.StartsWith("#")
  let parts = line.Split(',')
  select new {
    Isbn = parts[0],
    Title = parts[1],
    Publisher = parts[3],
    Authors =
      from authorFullName in parts[2].Split(';')
      let authorNameParts = authorFullName.Split(' ')
      select new {
        FirstName = authorNameParts[0],
        LastName = authorNameParts[1]
      }
  };

ObjectDumper.Write(books, 1);
```

In the query, we use anonymous types for the results, but we could use regular types instead. Listing 5.21 shows how to reuse our existing `Book`, `Publisher`, and `Author` types.

Listing 5.21   Declarative for parsing a CSV file, with existing types

```
var books =
  from line in File.ReadAllLines("books.csv")
  where !line.StartsWith("#")
  let parts = line.Split(',')
  select new Book {
    Isbn = parts[0],
    Title = parts[1],
    Publisher = new Publisher { Name = parts[3] },
    Authors =
      from authorFullName in parts[2].Split(';')
      let authorNameParts = authorFullName.Split(' ')
      select new Author {
        FirstName=authorNameParts[0],
        LastName=authorNameParts[1]
      }
  };
```

It's interesting to note how the Authors property is initialized with a nested query. This is possible thanks to query compositionality. LINQ queries are fully compositional, meaning that queries can be arbitrarily nested. The result of the subquery is automatically transformed into a collection of type IEnumerable<Author>.

The Functional Construction pattern is sometimes called *Transform pattern* because it's used to create a new object graph based on source objects graphs and sequences. It allows us to write code that is more declarative than imperative in nature. If you don't use this pattern then in a lot of cases you have to write a lot of contrived imperative code.

Listing 5.22 is imperative code that is equivalent to listing 5.21.

Listing 5.22 Imperative approach for parsing a CSV file

```
List<Book> books = new List<Book>();
foreach (String line in File.ReadAllLines("books.csv"))
{
  if (line.StartsWith("#"))
    continue;

  String[] parts = line.Split(',');
  Book book = new Book();
  book.Isbn = parts[0];
  book.Title = parts[1];
  Publisher publisher = new Publisher();
  publisher.Name = parts[3];
  book.Publisher = publisher;
  List<Author> authors = new List<Author>();
  foreach (String authorFullName in parts[2].Split(';'))
  {
    String[] authorNameParts = authorFullName.Split(' ');
    Author author = new Author();
    author.FirstName = authorNameParts[0];
    author.LastName = authorNameParts[1];
    authors.Add(author);
  }
  book.Authors = authors;

  books.Add(book);
}
```

As you can see, the Functional Construction pattern offers a more concise style. Of course, the difference could be reduced if the Book, Publisher, and Author classes had constructors or if you used initializers. In fact, the real difference is elsewhere. Comparing the two pieces of code allows you to see how the Functional

Construction pattern favors a declarative approach, in contrast to the imperative approach, which requires loops in our example. With a declarative approach, you describe what you want to achieve, but not necessarily how to achieve it.

One big advantage of the Functional Construction pattern is that the code often has the same shape as the result. We can clearly see the structure of the resulting object tree in listing 5.21 just by looking at the source code. This pattern is fundamental for LINQ to XML. In part 4, you'll be able to see how this pattern is heavily used for creating XML.

> **WARNING** If you plan to use a similar approach for querying text files, make sure you read section 5.3.1 to see how the call to `ReadAllLines` we use in the query should be replaced for better performance.

Let's now see a second design pattern that can be used to iterate over a sequence in a query.

5.2.2 *The ForEach pattern*

The design pattern we present in this section allows you to write shorter code when you have a query immediately followed by an iteration of this query. Typical LINQ code you've seen in this book until now looks like listing 5.23.

Listing 5.23 Standard code used to execute and enumerate a LINQ query

```
var query =
  from sourceItem in sequence
  where some condition
  select some projection

foreach (var item in query)
{
  // work with item
}
```

We don't know about you, but a question we had after seeing this pattern over and over is "Is there a way to perform the iteration within the query instead of in a separate `foreach` loop?" The short answer is that there is no query operator that comes with LINQ that can help you to do that. Our answer is that you can easily create one by yourself.

You can create the `ForEach` operator, which addresses this issue, with the code in listing 5.24.

Listing 5.24 `ForEach` query operator that executes a function over each element in a source sequence

```
public static void ForEach<T>(
  this IEnumerable<T> source,
  Action<T> func)
{
  foreach (var item in source)
    func(item);
}
```

ForEach is simply an extension method for IEnumerable<T>, similar to the one that already exists on List<T>, that loops on a sequence and executes the function it receives over each item in the sequence. The ForEach operator can be used in queries using the method syntax shown in listing 5.25.

Listing 5.25 Using the `ForEach` query operator using the method syntax

```
SampleData.Books
  .Where(book => book.PageCount > 150)
  .ForEach(book => Console.WriteLine(book.Title));
```

ForEach can also be used with the query syntax shown in listing 5.26.

Listing 5.26 Using the `ForEach` query operator with a query expression

```
(from book in SampleData.Books
 where book.PageCount > 150
 select book)
  .ForEach(book => Console.WriteLine(book.Title));
```

In these examples, we use only one statement in ForEach. Thanks to the support lambda expressions offer for statement bodies (see chapter 2), it's also possible to use multiple statements in a call to ForEach. Listing 5.27 is a small example in which we perform an update on the iterated object.

Listing 5.27 Using multiple statements in a `ForEach` call

```
SampleData.Books
  .Where(book => book.PageCount > 150)
  .ForEach(book => {
    book.Title += " (long)";
    Console.WriteLine(book.Title);
  });
```

Using a query operator this way, instead of foreach or for loops, offers a better integration with queries. It follows the same general orientation as LINQ. It takes inspiration from functional programming. In fact, Eric White suggested this operator in his functional programming tutorial.[4] We recommend you take a look at Eric's tutorial to get an introduction to how LINQ features relate to functional programming.

> **WARNING**   ForEach cannot be used in VB because it requires a statement lambda and VB.NET 9.0 does not offer support for statement lambdas.
>
> The samples we have in C# cannot be converted to VB. Calls to ForEach in VB produce the following error at compile-time: Expression does not produce a value.

Now that we've covered common scenarios and design patterns, it's time to focus on the second major topic of this chapter. So far, we have taught you how to use LINQ to Objects, first in simple queries and then in more advanced ones. But there's one thing you need to pay attention to if you want to write LINQ queries you can actually use in production: performance. At this point, you know how to write simple LINQ queries and rich LINQ queries, but you still need to make sure that you write efficient queries. In the next section, we'll give you an idea about performance overhead in LINQ to Objects and warn you about a number of pitfalls. All of which should help you write better LINQ applications.

5.3   *Performance considerations*

LINQ's main advantage is not that it allows you to do new things, but it allows you to do things in new, simpler, more concise ways. The usual trade-off to get these benefits is performance. LINQ is no exception. The goal of this section is to make sure you know the performance implications of LINQ queries. We'll show you how to get an idea of LINQ's overhead and provide some figures. We'll also highlight the main pitfalls. If you know where they are, you'll be in a better position to avoid them.

As always, we have several ways to perform one task with the .NET Framework. Sometimes, the choice is only a matter of taste, other times it's a matter of conciseness, but more often than not, making the right choice is critical and impacts the behavior of your program. Some methods are well adapted for LINQ queries and others should be avoided.

In this section, we'll test the performance of several ways to use LINQ. We'll also compare code written with LINQ and code written without LINQ. The goal is

---

[4] See http://blogs.msdn.com/ericwhite/pages/Programming-in-a-Functional-Style.aspx.

to compare the benefits for the developer in terms of productivity and code read-ability between the various options. We'll make sure you understand the impact of each option in terms of performance.

To get started, we'll get back to our LINQ to Text Files example one more time. It will be useful to demonstrate how it's important to choose the right methods for reading text from a file in LINQ queries.

5.3.1 *Favor a streaming approach*

Let's get back to our LINQ to Text Files example from sections 5.1.4 and 5.2.1. This example clearly demonstrates the ability of LINQ to Objects to query various data sources. As significant as this example is, we'd like to point out that it suffers from a potential problem: the use of ReadAllLines. This method returns an array populated with all the lines from the CSV file. This is fine for small files with few lines, but imagine a file with a lot of lines. The program can potentially allocate an enormous array in memory!

Moreover, the query somewhat defeats the standard deferred execution we expect with a LINQ query. Usually, the execution of a query is deferred, as we demonstrated in chapter 3. This means that the query doesn't execute before we start to iterate it, using a foreach loop for example. Here, ReadAllLines executes immediately and loads the complete file in memory, before any iteration happens. Of course, this consumes a lot of memory, but in addition, we load the complete file while we may not process it completely.

LINQ to Objects has been designed to make the most of deferred query execution. The streaming approach it uses also saves resources, like memory and CPU. It's important to walk down the same path whenever possible.

There are several ways to read text from a file using the .NET Framework. File.ReadAllLines is simply one. A better solution for our example is to use a streaming approach for loading the file. This can be done with a StreamReader object. It will allow us to save resources and give us a smoother execution. In order to integrate the StreamReader in the query, an elegant solution is to create a custom query operator, as Eric White suggests in his example.[5] See Listing 5.28.

> **Listing 5.28 Lines query operator that yields the text lines from a source StreamReader**

```
public static class StreamReaderEnumerable
{
  public static IEnumerable<String> Lines(this StreamReader source)
  {
```

---

[5] See Eric White's blog at http://blogs.msdn.com/ericwhite/archive/2006/08/31/734383.aspx.

```
    String line;

    if (source == null)
      throw new ArgumentNullException("source");

    while ((line = source.ReadLine()) != null)
      yield return line;
  }
}
```

The query operator is implemented as an extension method for the `StreamReader` class. (You can see more examples of custom query operators in chapter 13.) It enumerates the lines provided by the `StreamReader` one by one, but does not load a line in memory before it's actually needed. The integration of this technique into our query from listing 5.19 is easy; see listing 5.29.

> **Listing 5.29   Using the `Lines` query operator to use a streaming approach in CSV parsing**

```
using (StreamReader reader = new StreamReader("books.csv"))
{
  var books =
    from line in reader.Lines()
    where !line.StartsWith("#")
    let parts = line.Split(',')
    select new {Title=parts[1], Publisher=parts[3], Isbn=parts[0]}

  ObjectDumper.Write(books, 1);
}
```

The main point is that this technique allows you to work with huge files while maintaining a small memory usage profile. This is the kind of thing you should pay attention to in order to improve your queries. It's easy to write queries that are not optimal and consume a lot of memory.

Before moving on to another subject, let's review what happens with the last version of our LINQ to Text Files query. The key is lazy evaluation. Objects are created on the fly, as you loop through the results, and not all at the beginning.

Let's suppose we loop on the query's results using `foreach` as follows—this is similar to what `ObjectDumper.Write` does in the previous code snippet:

```
foreach (var book in books)
{
  ...      ◁—— Work with book object
}
```

The book object used in each iteration of the foreach loop exists only within that iteration. Not all objects are present in memory at the same time. Each iteration consists in reading a line from the file, splitting its content, and creating an object based on that information. Once we're done with this object, another line is read, and so on.

It's important that you try to take advantage of deferred execution so that fewer resources are consumed and less memory pressure happens. The next pitfall we'd like to highlight also has to do with deferred query execution or lack thereof.

5.3.2 *Be careful about immediate execution*

Most of the standard query operators are based on deferred execution through the use of iterators (see chapter 3). As we have seen in the previous section, this allows a lower resource burden. We'd like to draw your attention to the fact that some query operators defeat deferred execution. Indeed, some query operators iterate all the elements of the sequence they operate on as part of their behavior.

In general, the operators that do not return a sequence but a scalar value are executed immediately. This includes all the aggregation operators (Aggregate, Average, Count, LongCount, Max, Min, and Sum). This is not surprising because aggregation is the process of taking a collection and making a scalar. In order to compute their result, these operators need to iterate all the elements from the source sequence.

In addition, some other operators that return a sequence and not a scalar also iterate the source sequence completely before returning. Examples are OrderBy, OrderByDescending, and Reverse. These operators change the order of the elements from a source sequence. In order to know how to sort the elements in their result sequence, these operators need to completely iterate the source sequence.

Let's elaborate what the problem is. Again, we'll reuse our LINQ to Text Files example. We said in section 5.3.1 that it's better to use a streaming approach to avoid loading complete files in memory. The code we used is shown in listing 5.30.

Listing 5.30 Code used to parse a CSV document

```
using (StreamReader reader = new StreamReader("books.csv"))
{
  var books =
    from line in reader.Lines()
    where !line.StartsWith("#")
    let parts = line.Split(',')
    select new {Title=parts[1], Publisher=parts[3], Isbn=parts[0]}
```

```
foreach (var book in books)
{
   ...                              Work with
}                                   book objects
}
```

If you run this code, here is what happens:

1   A loop starts, using the `Lines` operator to read a line from the file.

   a. If there are no more lines to deal with, the process halts.

2   The `Where` operator executes on the line.

   a. If the line starts with #, it's a comment so the line is skipped. Execution resumes at step 1.

   b. If the line is not a comment, the process continues.

3   The line is split into parts.

4   An object is created by the `Select` operator.

5   Work is performed on the book object as specified in the body of the `foreach` statement.

6   The process continues at step 1.

NOTE   You can clearly see these steps execute if you do step-by-step debugging of the code under Visual Studio. We highly encourage you to do so to get used to the way LINQ queries execute.

If you decide to process the files in a different order by introducing an `orderby` clause or a call to the `Reverse` operator in the query, the process changes. Let's say you add a call to `Reverse` as follows:

```
...
from line in reader.Lines().Reverse()
...
```

This time, the query executes as follows:

1   The `Reverse` operator executes.

   a. `Reverse` loops on all lines, invoking the `Lines` operator immediately for each line.

2   A loop starts by retrieving a line returned by `Reverse`.

   a. If there are no more lines to deal with, the process halts.

3 The `Where` operator executes on the line.

    a. If the line starts with #, it's a comment so the line is skipped. Execution resumes at step 1.

    b. If the line is not a comment, the process continues.

4 The line is split into parts.

5 An object is created by the `Select` operator.

6 Work is performed on the book object as specified in the body of the `foreach` statement.

7 The process continues at step 2.

You can see that the `Reverse` operator breaks the nice pipeline flow we had in the original version because it loads all lines in memory at the beginning of the process. Make sure you absolutely need to call this kind of operator before using them in your queries. At least, you need to be aware of how they behave; otherwise you may have bad performance and memory surprises when dealing with large collections.

Keep in mind that some conversion operators also exhibit the same behavior. These operators are `ToArray`, `ToDictionary`, `ToList`, and `ToLookup`. They all return sequences, but create new collections that contain all the elements from the source sequence they're applied on, which requires immediately iterating the sequence.

Now that you've been warned about the behavior of some query operators, we'll take a look at a common scenario that will show that you need to use LINQ and the standard query operators carefully.

5.3.3 *Will LINQ to Objects hurt the performance of my code?*

Sometimes LINQ to Objects does not provide what you need right from the box. Let's consider a fairly common scenario that Jon Skeet, author of *C# in Depth* and a C# MVP, presents on his blog.[6] Imagine you have a collection of objects and you need to find the object that has the maximum value for a certain property. This is like having a box full of cookies and you want to find the one that has the most chocolate chips—not for you, but to offer it to your darling, of course. The box of cookies is the collection, and the number of chocolate chip's is the property.

At first, you might think that the `Max` operator, which is part of the standard query operators, is all you need. But the `Max` operator doesn't help in this case

---

[6] See http://msmvps.com/blogs/jon.skeet/archive/2005/10/02/68712.aspx.

because it returns the maximum value, not the object that has that value. Max can tell you the maximum number of chocolate chips on one cookie, but cannot tell you which cookie this is!

This is a typical scenario where we have the choice among several options, including using LINQ in one way or another or resorting to LINQ-free code and classical constructs. Like Jon Skeet, let's review possible ways to find a replacement for the inadequate Max.

Options

A first option is to use a simple foreach loop, as in listing 5.31.

Listing 5.31 Using a foreach statement to find the book with the highest number of pages in a collection

```
Book maxBook = null;
foreach (var book in books)
{
  if ((maxBook == null) || (book.PageCount > maxBook.PageCount))
    maxBook = book;
}
```

This solution is pretty straightforward. It keeps a reference to the "maximum element so far". It iterates through the list only once. It has a complexity of O(n), which is mathematically the best we can get without knowing something about the list.

A second option is to sort the collection and take the first element, as in listing 5.32.

Listing 5.32 Using sorting and First to find the book with the highest number of pages in a collection

```
var sortedList =
  from book in books
  orderby book.PageCount descending
  select book;
var maxBook = sortedList.First();
```

In this solution, we use a LINQ query to sort the books in descending number of pages, and then take the first book in the resulting list. The disadvantage with this approach is that all the books are sorted before we can get the result. This operation is likely to be O(n log n).

A third option is to use a use a subquery, as in listing 5.33.

Listing 5.33 Using a subquery to find the book with the highest number of pages in a collection

```
var maxList =
  from book in books
  where book.PageCount == books.Max(b => b.PageCount)
  select book;
var maxBook = maxList.First();
```

This goes through the list, finding every book whose number of pages is equal to the maximum, and then takes the first of those books. Unfortunately, the comparison calculates the maximum size on every iteration. This makes it an $O(n^2)$ operation.

A fourth option is to use two separate queries, like in listing 5.34.

Listing 5.34 Using two separate queries to find the book with the highest number of pages in a collection

```
var maxPageCount = books.Max(book => book.PageCount);
var maxList =
  from book in books
  where book.PageCount == maxPageCount
  select book;
var maxBook = maxList.First();
```

This is similar to the previous version, but solves the problem of the repeated calculation of the maximum number of pages by doing it before anything else. This makes the whole operation $O(n)$, but it's somewhat dissatisfying, as we have to iterate the list twice.

The last solution we'd recommend for its higher integration with LINQ is to create a custom query operator. Listing 5.35 shows how to code such an operator, which we'll call `MaxElement`.

Listing 5.35 Creating a custom operator named `MaxElement` to find the object with the maximum value

```
public static TElement MaxElement<TElement, TData>(
  this IEnumerable<TElement> source,
  Func<TElement, TData> selector)
  where TData : IComparable<TData>
{
```

```
    if (source == null)
      throw new ArgumentNullException("source");
    if (selector == null)
      throw new ArgumentNullException("selector");

    Boolean firstElement = true;
    TElement result = default(TElement);
    TData maxValue = default(TData);
    foreach (TElement element in source)
    {
      var candidate = selector(element);
      if (firstElement ||
          (candidate.CompareTo(maxValue) > 0))
      {
        firstElement = false;
        maxValue = candidate;
        result = element;
      }
    }
    return result;
}
```

This query operator is easy to use:

```
var maxBook = books.MaxElement(book => book.PageCount);
```

Table 5.1 shows how the different options behave if you run a benchmark with 20 runs.

These results[7] show that the performance can vary a lot between different solutions. It's important to use correct LINQ queries! In particular, it's definitely

Table 5.1   Time measured for each `MaxElement` option

Option	Average time (in ms)	Minimum time (in ms)	Maximum time (in ms)
foreach	37	35	42
OrderBy + First	1724	1704	1933
Sub-query	37482	37201	45233
Two queries	66	65	69
Custom operator	56	54	73

---

[7] Results measured with .NET 3.5 RTM on a machine with two Intel Xeon 2.4 GHz CPUs and 2 GB of RAM. The application was compiled with the Release configuration.

cheaper to iterate through the collection only once. The custom operator is not quite as fast as the non-LINQ way, but it's still much better than most of the other options. It's up to you to decide whether such a custom query operator can safely be used in place of the `foreach` solution. What we can say is that the custom query operator is an appealing solution for LINQ contexts, even if it comes with a performance cost.

> **NOTE**   You can easily experiment with other solutions by building on the complete example packaged with the code coming with this book.

Lessons learned

You need to think about the complexity of LINQ to Objects queries. Because we deal with lists and loops, it's particularly important to try to spare CPU cycles if possible. Keep in mind that you should avoid writing queries that iterate collections more than once; otherwise your queries may perform poorly. In other words, you don't want to waste your time counting chocolate chips again and again. Your goal is to find the cookie quickly, so you can attack the next one without delay.

You also need to take into account the context in which they will be executed. For example, the same scenario in the context of a LINQ to SQL query would be very different because LINQ to SQL interprets queries in its own way, which is dictated by what the SQL language supports.

The conclusion is that you should use LINQ to Objects wisely. LINQ to Objects is not the ultimate solution for all use cases. In some cases, it may be preferable to use traditional approaches, such as `for` and `foreach` loops. In other cases, you can stick to LINQ, but it's better to create your own query operators for optimal performance. There's a lesson from the Python philosophy: write everything in Python for simplicity, readability, and maintainability, and optimize what you need in C++. The analog here is: Write everything in LINQ, and optimize when you must using domain-specific operators.

In this section, we have mainly compared different solutions that use LINQ. In the next section, we'll focus on comparing LINQ solutions to traditional ones. The goal is to give you an idea of LINQ's overhead.

5.3.4   *Getting an idea about the overhead of LINQ to Objects*

LINQ to Objects is fantastic because it allows you to write code that is simpler to read and write. Coding some of the operations that LINQ to Objects allows on in-memory collections using classic constructs can be difficult. Often you'd have to use tedious code with a lot of nested loops and temporary variables. You're probably convinced that LINQ to Objects is really nice, so we won't to try to persuade you further. What we'll do instead is closer to the opposite! Of course, our goal is not to deter you from using LINQ, but you need to know how much LINQ costs performance-wise. We'll try to answer the question "Should I always use LINQ or are standard solutions better in some cases?"

Let's determine the level of overhead you can expect with LINQ. We don't want to provide you with figures straight off, first because performance can vary largely from one machine to another, and second because it's better if you can perform tests by yourself. This is why we propose to show you what tests we did, and you'll then be able to adapt and run them.

The simplest operation that a LINQ query can perform is a filter, such as in the one in listing 5.36.

Listing 5.36   Filtering a collection of books with a LINQ query

```
var results =
  from book in books
  where book.PageCount > 500
  select book;
```

Let's review how we can reproduce the same operation with alternative solutions. Listing 5.37 shows the equivalent code with a `foreach` statement.

Listing 5.37   Filtering a collection of books with a `foreach` loop

```
var results = new List<Book>()
foreach (var book in books)
{
  if (book.PageCount > 500)
    results.Add(book);
}
```

And listing 5.38 shows the same with a `for` statement.

Listing 5.38   Filtering a collection of books with a `for` loop

```
var results = new List<Book>()
for (int i = 0; i < books.Count; i ++)
{
  Book book = books[i];
  if (book.PageCount > 500)
    results.Add(book);
}
```

This can also be achieved using `List<T>.FindAll`, as in listing 5.39.

Listing 5.39   Filtering a collection of books with the `List<T>.FindAll` method

```
var results = books.FindAll(book => book.PageCount > 500);
```

There are other possibilities, but the goal here is not list them all. You'll be able to find the complete tests in the code accompanying this book, with other alternatives included.

To give you an idea of the performance of each option, we have run a benchmark with one million randomly initialized objects. Table 5.2 shows the results we got for 50 runs with a release build.

Table 5.2   Time measured for each search option executed 50 times using a condition on an int

Option	Average time (in ms)	Minimum time (in ms)	Maximum time (in ms)
foreach	68	47	384
for	59	42	383
List<T>.FindAll	62	51	278
LINQ	91	74	404

Surprised? Disappointed? LINQ to Objects seems to be almost 50 percent slower than the other options on average! But wait: don't decide to stop using LINQ immediately after reading these results. We all know that tests and results need to be taken carefully, so follow us a bit more.

First of all, these are the results for one query. What if we change the query a little? For example, let's change the condition in the where clause. Here we use a test on a string (`Title`) instead of an int (`PageCount`):

```
var results =
  from book in books
  where book.Title.StartsWith("1")
  select book;
```

If we adapt the queries for all options and run the test 50 times again, we get the results in table 5.3.

What do we notice with these new results? The LINQ option takes approximately four times what was needed for the previous test with the condition on

Table 5.3 Time measured for each search option executed 50 times using a condition on a string

Option	Average time (in ms)	Minimum time (in ms)	Maximum time (in ms)
foreach	327	323	361
for	292	288	329
List<T>.FindAll	325	321	355
LINQ	339	377	377

an `int`. This is because operations on strings are much more expensive than on integers/numbers. But the most interesting is that this time, the LINQ option is only around 10 percent slower than the fastest option. This clearly shows that the impact of LINQ does not always cause a big drop in performance.

Why do we see a difference between the two series of tests? When we changed the condition in the `where` clause from a test on an `int` to a test on a `string`, we increased the work to be performed each time the test executes. The additional time spent testing the condition affects each option, but LINQ's overhead remains more or less the same. If we look at this the other way around, we could say that the less work there is to do in the query, the higher the overhead appears.

There are no surprises. LINQ does not come for free. LINQ queries cause additional work, object creations, and pressure on the garbage collector. The additional cost of using LINQ can vary a lot depending on the query. It can be as low as 5 percent, but can sometimes be around 500 percent.

In conclusion, don't be afraid to use LINQ, but use it wisely. For simple operations that are executed extensively in your code, you may consider using the traditional alternatives. For simple filter or search operations, you can stick to the methods offered by `List<T>` and arrays, such as `FindAll`, `ForEach`, `Find`, `ConvertAll`, or `TrueForAll`. Of course, you can continue to use the classic `for` and `foreach` statements wherever LINQ would be overkill. For queries that are not executed several times per second, you can probably use LINQ to Objects safely. A query that is executed only once in a non–time-critical context won't make a big difference if it takes 60 milliseconds to execute instead of 10. Don't forget the benefits at the source code level in terms of clarity and maintainability.

Let's take another example to compare code with LINQ and code without.

5.3.5 *Performance versus conciseness: A cruel dilemma?*

We have just seen that LINQ seems to impose a trade-off on performance versus conciseness and code clarity. We propose to look at a new example to confirm or refute this theory. This time, we'll perform a grouping operation. Listing 5.40 shows a LINQ query that can be used for grouping books by publisher, with the resulting groups sorted alphabetically by publisher name.

Listing 5.40 Grouping with a LINQ query

```
var results =
   from book in SampleData.Books
   group book by book.Publisher.Name into publisherBooks
   orderby publisherBooks.Key
   select publisherBooks;
```

Listing 5.41 shows what would be required to perform the same grouping without LINQ.

Listing 5.41 Grouping without LINQ

```
var results = new SortedDictionary<String, IList<Book>>();

foreach (var book in SampleData.Books)
{
  IList<Book> publisherBooks;

  if (!results.TryGetValue(book.Publisher.Name,
                           out publisherBooks))
  {
    publisherBooks = new List<Book>();
    results[book.Publisher.Name] = publisherBooks;
  }
  publisherBooks.Add(book);
}
```

There's no doubt that the code without LINQ is longer and more complex. It remains accessible, but you can easily imagine that things can get more complicated with more complex queries. After all, we used a relatively simple LINQ query!

The main difference between the two code samples lies in the use of opposite approaches. The LINQ query follows a declarative approach, while the code without LINQ is imperative in nature. All the code written in C# or VB.NET before LINQ appeared is imperative because these languages were imperative. The code without LINQ completely indicates how the work is performed. The code that uses LINQ simply consists of a query that describes the results we want to get. Instead of describing in great detail how to deal with data, writing non-procedural code in LINQ is more akin to describing the results that you want. This is fundamental.

We already said that you're probably convinced about the benefits of LINQ. So, what's the point of this new example? If you run a performance benchmark of the two solutions, you'll find that the LINQ solution is faster this time! In fact, it takes less than half the time to execute compared to the non-LINQ solution. In this case, we get all the benefits with LINQ!

Of course, you may wonder why the second solution is slower. We'll let you investigate this on your own. Our point remains the same: if you want to achieve the same performance level without the LINQ query, you'll have to write even more complex code.

> **HINTS** SortedDictionary is an expensive data structure in terms of memory use and speed of insertion. In addition, we use TryGetValue during each loop iteration. The LINQ operators handle this scenario in a much more efficient way. The non-LINQ code can certainly be improved, but it will remain more complex in any case.

5.4   Summary

This chapter was an occasion to take a second look at in-memory LINQ queries.

We showed you how to handle common scenarios, such as querying nongeneric collections, grouping by multiple criteria, creating dynamic queries, or querying text files. We also introduced design patterns you can apply in your queries. The Functional Construction pattern, for example, is critical for LINQ to XML, as you'll see in part 4 of the book.

The second major topic we covered in this chapter is performance. We drew your attention to performance problems that can happen with LINQ queries. This should help you to avoid writing suboptimal queries. We also carried out some testing to compare the performance of LINQ code to other more traditional solutions. This allowed you to see LINQ's strengths and weaknesses.

In previous chapters, we introduced LINQ and showed you how to write queries quickly and easily. Like everything new, LINQ may have seemed delightful at first sight. In this chapter, we tried to disillusion you somewhat by looking beyond the shiny surface. Of course, our goal is not to draw you away from LINQ, but we wanted to make sure that you can handle advanced use cases and write efficient queries.

The conclusion is that life is not a fairy tale. Not everything is black or white. LINQ helps you greatly to query data in innovative ways. LINQ queries are also easier to read and maintain. However, performance-wise LINQ comes at a cost you have to bear in mind. In fact, in the future LINQ queries will help you to boost the performance of your code. Microsoft is working on PLINQ, which will allow you to implicitly use concurrency in LINQ to Objects-like queries. PLINQ hasn't been released at the same time as the other LINQ technologies, but it should follow some time in 2008.

And now for something completely different. Now that you know so much about in-memory queries, it's time to discover other LINQ flavors. In the next parts of this book, you'll learn about LINQ to SQL and LINQ to XML. Since we discussed performance in this chapter, it may be a good place to recommend you take a look at the blog of Microsoft's Rico Mariani.[8] You'll find there a series of posts on the performance of LINQ to SQL. But maybe you should learn about LINQ to SQL first, so let's jump right into this subject with the next chapter!

---

[8] Visit the following URL to find Rico Mariani's study about LINQ to SQL's performance: http://
blogs.msdn.com/ricom/archive/2007/06/22/dlinq-linq-to-sql-performance-part-1.aspx

Part 3

Querying relational data

When discussing querying techniques, we typically turn our attention to databases. In this part, we'll continue to build on the core LINQ infrastructure, this time focusing on relational data. With minor changes, we can eliminate repetitive data access code and work with the SQL Server family of databases using LINQ queries. By changing our underlying data source and leaving our queries intact, we can quickly utilize the power of LINQ directly against our database. In addition, LINQ to SQL moves beyond querying data to updating data and accessing some of SQL Server's more powerful stored procedures and user-defined functions.

Chapter 6 begins our journey into LINQ to SQL and shows the differences between a LINQ to Objects query and one using LINQ to SQL. Chapter 7 peeks under the covers to explore some of the underlying infrastructure that enables LINQ to SQL. Chapter 8 explores some of the more advanced capabilities that LINQ to SQL offers from the database and client perspectives.

Getting started
with LINQ to SQL

6

This chapter covers:

- Using LINQ to SQL to access data from SQL Server
- The advantages of LINQ to SQL for fetching relational data
- Updating data with LINQ to SQL

205

So far in this book, we've focused on working with data once it is already in memory. In order to query it, we need a group of items we can iterate over using the `IEnumerable<T>` interface. While the ability to work with data already in memory is a much-needed feature, it fails to address a large part of the picture—moving data to and from a persistence medium, typically a relational database system like SQL Server.

By this point, we should be able to handle a fairly complex LINQ to Objects query. In this chapter, we're going to take a look at converting a query and associated classes to use LINQ to SQL rather than custom ADO.NET. We'll start with a query that will return a listing of books that cost less than $30 and group them by their subject. This will require us to combine information from two collections: `Books` and `Subjects`. Listing 6.1 represents a possible solution to the problem at hand.

Listing 6.1   Querying `Subjects` and `Books` with LINQ to Objects

```
IEnumerable<Book> books = Book.GetBooks();
IEnumerable<Subject> subjects = Subject.GetSubjects();

var query = from subject in subjects
            join book in books
                on subject.SubjectId equals book.SubjectId
            where book.Price < 30
            orderby subject.Description, book.Title
            select new
            {
                subject.Description,
                book.Title,
                book.Price
            };
```

In this example, we fill collections of books and subjects and then query from the resulting collections. While this achieves our goal, it does not do so as efficiently as we'd like. Here are the resulting SQL queries that are passed to the database when running the code samples that accompany this chapter:

```
SELECT      ID, Isbn, Notes, PageCount, Price, PubDate,
            Publisher, Subject, Summary, Title
FROM        Book

SELECT      ID, Name, Description
FROM        Subject
```

Since the filtering, projecting, and sorting are being done on the client, we have to fetch all fields of all records before we start processing. As a result, we will fetch more records and fields than we need. Additionally, we cannot take advantage of the powerful indexes that the database has available. This means we're putting undue stress on our network and processing power. Worse yet, we have to manually write all of the data access code, which is repetitive and ripe with potential pitfalls.

Here, LINQ to SQL comes to our rescue to reduce the network stress, reduce the client processing, and utilize the database indexes. At the same time, we can eliminate most of the previously necessary plumbing code. When we're done, we will end up with the following database query:

```
SELECT     t0.Description, t1.Title, t1.Price
FROM       Subject AS t0 INNER JOIN
                         Book AS t1 ON t0.ID = t1.Subject
WHERE      (t1.Price < @p0)
ORDER BY   t0.Description, t1.Title
```

Amazingly, we can do all this by adding one line of code and changing two others. The corresponding changes in our business objects allow us to eliminate dozens of lines of ADO.NET code. Additionally, the same changes we make will allow us to eliminate specialized code needed to update records that we fetch.

Over the next three chapters we will dig into LINQ to SQL. In this chapter, we will show how to take advantage of LINQ to SQL with our starting query and identify how we can increase performance while reducing code. In chapter 7, we will peek under the covers and explore how the framework achieves this magic. We'll conclude our exploration of LINQ to SQL in chapter 8 by diving deeper into the framework to see some of the more advanced techniques LINQ to SQL offers.

6.1 Jump into LINQ to SQL

In our example for this chapter, we're exploring ways to query our books to see those that cost less than $30 and group them by subject. To do this, we can separate the process into several separate tasks: selecting the ordered subjects, selecting the corresponding books filtered on price, combining the subjects with the books, and projecting only the results that we need. Let's start by looking at the book-related tasks first and then deal with joining them to the subjects. Listing 6.2 restates the book portion of our starting query.

Listing 6.2 Selecting the book title and price for books less than $30

```
IEnumerable<Book> books = Book.GetBooks();
var query = from book in books
            where book.Price < 30
            orderby book.Title
```

```
select new
{
    book.Title,
    book.Price
};
```

At this point, we're still requesting everything from the database and filtering it on the client. To prove this, here is the SQL statement sent to the database:

```
SELECT      ID, Isbn, Notes, PageCount, Price, PubDate,
            Publisher, Subject, Summary, Title
FROM        Book
```

NOTE Throughout our discussion, the generated SQL we present is based on a prerelease version of Visual Studio 2008. Some of the query details may differ from the final release, but the basic concepts should still apply.

We're still retrieving all of the fields from the database even though we're only using two of them. Additionally, we're fetching all records from the database, not just the ones that meet our criteria. Also, we're not leveraging our indexes because we're ordering the results on the client. Ideally, we'd like to issue a statement to the database like the following:

```
SELECT      Title, Price
FROM        Book AS t0
WHERE       (Price < @p0)
ORDER BY    Title
```

How many changes does it take to our query to make this change? None! All we need to do is modify our Book class and change how we're accessing it. Let's start by revisiting the Book object and table (shown in figure 6.1) to see what changes we will need to make.

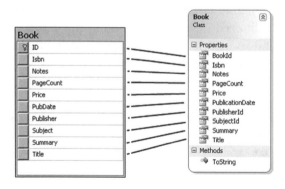

Figure 6.1
Comparing the Book table with the Book class

To begin, we're going to apply a 1-1 field mapping between the table and our destination object. Later in this chapter, we will take a look at joining this table with the corresponding subjects and see how we can handle the foreign key relationships in the database. For now, we will limit our focus to a single table. Let's start by looking at the code for the `Book` class, shown in listing 6.3.

Listing 6.3   Starting `Book` class definition

```
public class Book
{
  public Guid BookId { get; set; }
  public String Isbn { get; set; }
  public String Notes { get; set; }
  public Int32 PageCount { get; set; }
  public Decimal Price { get; set; }
  public DateTime PublicationDate { get; set; }
  public String Summary { get; set; }
  public String Title { get; set; }
  public Guid SubjectId { get; set; }
  public Guid PublisherId { get; set; }
}
```

For the sake of this discussion, we use the auto-implemented properties discussed in section 2.2.2. We're left with a clean class definition that includes only the public property declarations. At this point, we still need a way to fill our objects with data from the database. We do this by setting up a series of mappings to specify how our objects relate to the database tables and columns.

NOTE   Auto-implemented properties are not available in VB 9.0. With VB, you will need to explicitly include the private backing fields along with the get/set accessors.

6.1.1   *Setting up the object mapping*

Let's start our exploration of LINQ to SQL by enabling the `Book` class. To begin, add a reference to the `System.Data.Linq` assembly, which is part of the .NET 3.5 Framework, and add a `using` statement to the top of the class. The `Mapping` namespace contains attributes that enable us to declaratively establish the relationship between the database and objects.

```
using System.Data.Linq.Mapping;
```

For the sake of clarity, we will use attributes to declare our data mappings for this chapter. We'll only look at the basics at this point. In chapter 7, we will dive deeper into the mapping options, but for now we simply want to get it working.

In most cases, we need to identify two things in a class: what table it is related to, and what columns the values are mapped to. Mapping the book table with the object is perhaps the simplest mapping possible. In this case, our database has a table called Book. Our object structure also represents a book instance with a class called Book. Thus we have a one-to-one mapping between both objects, and they are named the same. To declare the mapping, we add an attribute to the class declaration called Table as follows:

```
[Table]
public class Book {…}
```

If we want to be more explicit, we can declare the name of the source table by using a named parameter, Name, as follows:

```
[Table(Name="dbo.Book")]
public class Book {…}
```

Now that we've mapped the class to the table, we need to indicate which properties are stored as columns in the table and how the columns map to the property information. We do this by adding a Column attribute to the properties we wish to map. For example, to map the Title property to the Title column of the book table, we add a Column attribute before the property declaration:

```
[Column]
public String Title { get; set; }
```

We're not limited to direct mappings. We can specify some translation between the table column name and the object's property name. For example, our Book table has a column called PubDate. To make the business object easier for the client application developer to work with, we may wish to use a more verbose naming convention and name the property PublicationDate. To do this, we specify the name of the source column as part of the attribute's parameters.

```
[Column(Name="PubDate")]
public DateTime PublicationDate { get; set; }
```

One thing we need to identify for each object is the primary key. In our case that will be the BookId property. Here, we combine the Name parameter with a new IsPrimaryKey parameter to declare the mapping. LINQ to SQL requires that at least one property from each object be specified as the primary key in order to manage object identity.

```
[Column(Name="ID", IsPrimaryKey=true)]
public Guid BookId { get; set; }
```

We use the same method to declare the mappings for all of the properties in our class. The resulting declaration is shown in listing 6.4.

Listing 6.4   The full Book class with basic mapping

```
using System.Data.Linq;

    [Table]        <————————————  Table
    public class Book                mapping
    {                                                      Identity
        [Column(Name="ID", IsPrimaryKey=true)]    <————  column
        public Guid BookId { get; set; }
        [Column]                    <——————————  Standard
        public String Isbn { get; set; }          column mapping
        [Column(CanBeNull=true)]
        public String Notes { get; set; }
        [Column]
        public Int32 PageCount { get; set; }
        [Column]
        public Decimal Price { get; set; }
        [Column(CanBeNull=true)]                    Specify the
        public String Summary { get; set; }    |   column name
        [Column(Name="PubDate")]        <————
        public DateTime PublicationDate { get; set; }
        [Column]
        public String Title { get; set; }
        [Column(Name="Subject")]
        public Guid SubjectId { get; set; }
        [Column(Name="Publisher")]
        public Guid PublisherId { get; set; }
    }
```

Although it may appear that we've doubled the number of lines of code in our Book class, the net result will be drastically reduced code, as we will not need to worry about creating separate methods for the Create, Read, Update, and Delete (CRUD) methods. Additionally, we won't need a customized implementation for specialized querying operations. We declare the mappings once and the framework takes care of the rest.

With the necessary changes made to our Book, you may be itching to see how to use LINQ to SQL to access our database. Although we've specified how to access the tables and columns, we can't do anything until we identify the database that the tables live in. We need to set up our connection to the database. We do this by using a new DataContext object located in the System.Data.Linq namespace. Once that is done, rest assured, we will jump right in to querying our data.

6.1.2   *Setting up the DataContext*

The DataContext, shown in figure 6.2, lies at the heart of LINQ to SQL and handles the majority of the work. First and foremost, it manages our connection to the database. We instruct the DataContext about the connection string. The DataContext will handle opening and closing the connection for us. As a result, we don't need to worry about abusing our expensive connection external resources.

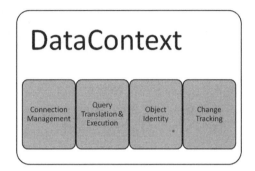

Figure 6.2   Services offered by the DataContext

To begin working with the DataContext, create an instance of a DataContext object passing it the connection string for our database.

```
DataContext dataContext = new DataContext(liaConnectionString);
```

The DataContext also handles managing our mappings and provides a vital resource—the ability to fill a collection of objects from the database. It fills the object into a specialized generic collection type called a Table<>. To get a table of books from the DataContext object, we call dataContext.GetTable<Book>():

```
DataContext dataContext = new DataContext(liaConnectionString);
Table<Book> books = dataContext.GetTable<Book>();
```

Without LINQ to SQL, when returning a list of objects, the return type could be a generic List<Book>. In this case, we're returning a new type—Table<Book>. By making this change, we don't bring back the raw data, but rather the means through which we can more dynamically access and manipulate our data. This will allow us to modify the query prior to actually issuing the request to the database. Now that we can access our data, let's see what we can do with LINQ to SQL beyond that.

6.2   *Reading data with LINQ to SQL*

The first thing we need to do is select values from the database. We've already seen one way to access data using the GetTable method. The generic Table class implements a new IQueryable<T> interface, which extends IEnumerable<T>. Because it extends IEnumerable<T>, we're free to use the standard query operators from LINQ to Objects. Let's start with a basic query fetching all of the books from our newly refactored Book object. See listing 6.5.

Listing 6.5   Fetch books using LINQ to SQL

```
DataContext dataContext = new DataContext(liaConnectionString);
IQueryable<Book> query = from book in dataContext.GetTable<Book>()
                         select book;
```

With this example, we've effectively eliminated any custom ADO.NET code that we'd have otherwise needed to write. However, we're fetching all of the fields regardless of whether we need to use them.

As we're learning the capabilities of LINQ to SQL, we may want to examine our code on the database. At times, the resulting query may be surprising. We have several options to see the query that is issued to the database. Using the SQL Server Profiler tool that comes with SQL Server, we can watch statements as they are being issued against the database. Alternatively, we can attach the DataContext's Log property to an output stream, like the one Console has:

```
dataContext.Log = Console.Out;
```

With this logging function enabled, any SQL statements issued to the database will be sent to an output stream. If we attach it to the console in a console application, the statements will appear in the console window. In a Windows Forms application, the results will be sent to the Output window. We will use the log frequently throughout these chapters to see what is happening behind the scenes.

As another alternative, Microsoft has a Query Visualizer tool that can be downloaded separately from Visual Studio 2008. The tool, along with the source code and installation instructions, is available at http://weblogs.asp.net/scottgu/archive/2007/07/31/linq-to-sql-debug-visualizer.aspx. Once this tool is installed, we can break into our code and hover over the instantiated query object to see a new magnifying glass as part of the debugging assistance, as shown in figure 6.3.

Click the magnifying glass, and the window shown in figure 6.4 opens, allowing access to the full SQL statement that will be issued. The visualizer also allows us to see the results in a data grid and optionally to hand edit the generated SQL.

```
IQueryable<Book> query = from book in dataContext.GetTable<Book>()
                         select book;

ObjectDumper.Write(query);
   query   Q ▾ {System.Data.Linq.DataQuery<LinqInAction.LinqBooks.Common.SampleClasses.Ch7.Book>}
```

Figure 6.3   Accessing the LINQ to SQL query visualizer while debugging

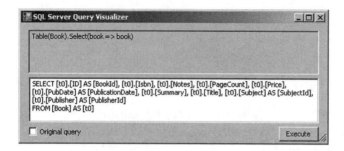

Figure 6.4
LINQ to SQL query visualizer in action

We can also programmatically access the query using the `DataContext`'s `GetCommand` method as follows:

```
Console.Writeline(dataContext.GetCommand(query).CommandText);
```

This command will not identify when the query is executed, but it will show the statement that will be issued. While you're getting used to LINQ to SQL, try each of these techniques out to see which ones work the best for you. Regardless of which you choose, make sure to watch the statements that are being issued. As you learn LINQ to SQL, you will find the need to alter queries to avoid unexpected results you may not notice otherwise.

Let's return our focus to our query. In the previous example, we showed how we could use the mappings to fetch values, but rather than fetching just the fields we need, we were fetching the entire book object. Since LINQ to SQL builds on the base query expressions, we can project the columns we want into our result set. Thus, if we only want to get a listing of the titles from our query, we could change our `select` clause as shown in listing 6.6.

Listing 6.6 Fetch the list of book titles

```
DataContext dataContext = new DataContext(liaConnectionString);
dataContext.Log = Console.Out;
IEnumerable<String> query =
    from book in dataContext.GetTable<Book>()
    select book.Title;
```

Because we used `dataContext.Log`, we can look at the output window and see the resulting query.

```
SELECT [t0].[Title]
FROM [Book] AS [t0]
```

Viewing this SQL statement, we see that we're no longer returning all of the book properties from our database. We're almost back to achieving our first task for this chapter: fetching the book titles and prices. To achieve this goal, we need to change our `select` clause to return an anonymous type with just the `Title` and `Price` values. See listing 6.7.

Listing 6.7   Project into an anonymous type

```
var query = from book in dataContext.GetTable<Book>()
            select new
            {
               book.Title,
               book.Price
            };
```

Notice that the generated SQL code only selects the fields asked for as part of the `Select` extension method, rather than filling the full book object.

```
SELECT [t0].[Title], [t0].[Price]
FROM [Book] AS [t0]
```

Try the sample again, but this time step through the code. Pay attention to the console window. Note that the SQL code is not inserted in the window when we call the `dataContext.GetTable<Book>()` method, nor is it displayed when we declare the `query` object. In fact, the SQL is not generated and submitted to the database until we first access the data. The `query` variable contains the definition of how we want to access the data, not the data itself. Execution of the query is deferred until it is first used. We will discuss this more in section 6.6.

Because we don't create the query until the results are first requested, we can continue to compose the query by adding more functionality. In listing 6.8, we add paging functions to the query after it is first defined using the `Skip` and `Take` extension methods. LINQ to SQL then pieces them together to create an optimized single statement.

Listing 6.8   Adding data paging using composition

```
DataContext dataContext = new DataContext(liaConnectionString);
dataContext.Log = Console.Out;

var books = dataContext.GetTable<Book>();

var query = from book in books          ⊲─┐  Define
            select new                     │  query
```

```
                {
                    book.Title,
                    book.Price
                };
        var pagedTitles = query.Skip(2);              Paging
        var titlesToShow = pagedTitles.Take(2);

        ObjectDumper.Write(titlesToShow);      ◁─── Evaluate
```

The same query in VB.NET can be performed as a single statement because VB.NET includes the `Skip` and `Take` methods as query expressions. Listing 6.9 shows the corresponding VB syntax.

VB.NET

Listing 6.9 VB syntax for paging data

```
Dim query = From book In books _
            Skip 2 _
            Take 2 _
            Select book.Title, book.Price
```

Regardless which option is used, the resulting SQL is as follows:

```
SELECT    TOP 2 [t1].[Title], [t1].[Price]     ◁─── Take next two
FROM      (SELECT    ROW_NUMBER()                          ◁─────
                     OVER (ORDER BY [t0].[Title], [t0].[Price])
                     AS [ROW_NUMBER],                        Use
                     [t0].[Title], [t0].[Price]         Row_Number
          FROM       [Book] AS [t0]) AS [t1]
WHERE     [t1].[ROW_NUMBER] > @p0             ◁─── Skip first two
```

Standard LINQ to Objects would have issued a single SELECT statement that fetched all of the books. Since LINQ to SQL was smart enough to detect the additional operations, it was able to optimize the query to be specific to our database (SQL Server 2005). If we were using SQL Server 2000, a different SQL syntax would have been used because the ROW_NUMBER() option is not available prior to SQL Server 2005.

We've seen a bit of the power that LINQ to SQL brings to the table. Instead of blanket fetching our records and relying on LINQ to Objects to do the heavy lifting, LINQ to SQL has the power to evaluate our requests and only return the requested results. If we want to perform additional selection operations including filtering and sorting, we use common LINQ query syntax. The declarative query expression is parsed and adjusted as necessary for the specific business needs at hand. Let's return our focus on extending our basic fetching queries by adding more functionality.

6.3 *Refining our queries*

So far, we've focused on retrieving results from a table. We've shown how LINQ to SQL is better than ADO.NET because we don't need to rewrite all of the repetitive plumbing code. LINQ to SQL is also able to reduce our network overhead by returning only the fields we need. If the framework were to stop here, it would have already offered a vast improvement over prior techniques.

Relational databases offer specialized capabilities to access and manipulate associated sets of data. By leveraging the indexing and query execution plans, the database can provide data access faster than we'd be able to do without indexes. Additionally, by processing the query on the server, we can often limit the amount of information that must be transmitted over the network. Reducing the network demands is important because the network pipe is typically one of the biggest bottlenecks of data-centric applications. Let's continue our look at LINQ by seeing how we can refine our queries using some of these additional server-side processes.

6.3.1 *Filtering*

LINQ to SQL supports a full range of filtering functionality. A filter can be as simple as finding a record with a specific value. In our example for this chapter, we want to see books that cost less than 30 dollars. We can accomplish this with the code from listing 6.10.

Listing 6.10 Filtering using a range

```
var books = dataContext.GetTable<Book>();
var query = from book in books
            where book.Price < 30
            select book;
```

If we look at the generated SQL, the results are just as we'd expect.

```
SELECT [t0].[Title]
FROM [dbo].[Book] AS [t0]
WHERE [t0].[Price] < @p0
```

The object-based query we started with fetched all rows from the database. When using LINQ to SQL, we're able to translate the filtering clause into a parameterized query that is executed on the server, limiting the results to rows that meet our criteria.

Additionally, by using parameterized queries, we solve a couple of common issues. First, one of the biggest security vulnerabilities is the ability to inject functionality into a query (like dropping a table).[1] One of the easiest ways to thwart this kind of vulnerability, called a *SQL injection attack*, is to use parameterized queries or stored procedures.

Another advantage of using parameterized queries is the fact that we can take advantage of SQL Server's query plan caching. By reusing queries where the only change is the input parameters, SQL Server can determine an appropriate execution plan and cache it for later use. On subsequent requests, the server will use the cached plan rather than reevaluating the expression. If we concatenated the request SQL, the server would need to parse the expression each time to determine the most efficient execution plan based on the indexes available.

Some SQL filtering options do not have a direct translation to keywords in the .NET Framework. In many cases, there is an alternative that performs the same or similar function. When it can, LINQ will translate the function call to the SQL equivalent.

Let's consider the SQL `LIKE` clause. `LIKE` finds records based on a pattern-matching scheme. Instead, the `String` type has three methods that serve the same function—`StartsWith`, `EndsWith`, and `Contains`. LINQ to SQL has been designed to map these functions to the `LIKE` expression using the `SqlMethods.Like` method and inserts the wildcard matching pattern as appropriate. Thus in order to find all books containing the string `"on"`, we use the LINQ expression shown in listing 6.11.

Listing 6.11   Using mapped CLR methods

```
var books = dataContext.GetTable<Book>();
var query = from book in books
            where book.Title.Contains("on")
            select book.Title;
```

The query using the `Contains` method translates to the following SQL expression:

```
SELECT [t0].[Title]
FROM [dbo].[Book] AS [t0]
WHERE [t0].[Title] LIKE @p0
-- @p0: Input NVarChar (Size = 4) NOT NULL [%on%]
```

---

[1] For a look at SQL injection in action, see the webcast at http://www.rockyh.net/AssemblyHijacking/AssemblyHijacking.html.

Note that the `Contains` method has been translated to `LIKE` and the parameter value now includes the `%` wildcard, which is specific to SQL Server.

Not all CLR functions can be translated to a database equivalent. Consider the following query:

```
var query =
    from book in books
    where book.PubDate >= DateTime.Parse("1/1/2007")   <──── Works
    select book.PubDate.Value.ToString("MM/dd/yyyy");   <──── Fails
```

In this example, the translation provider is able to convert the `DateTime.Parse` method and insert a database-specific representation of the date. It is not able to handle the `ToString` method for formatting the data in the `select` clause. Identifying all of the supported and unsupported expressions that are translated is impossible. Additionally, translation support is dependent on the provider. When you're unsure whether a method is supported, try it out and see if it works.

In many cases, filtering works as expected. In other cases, experimentation is necessary to find the proper method. We cannot cover all of the mappings here, but hopefully we have enough to get started. By allowing the filter to be applied on the server rather than the client, we can greatly reduce the amount of network bandwidth and take advantage of the database indexes.

So far, we've been able to rewrite our original query and objects to return only the desired fields and rows from our database while eliminating custom ADO.NET code. We're not quite back to the query that we started with, because we still need to utilize the server indexes for sorting our results. Let's continue to refine our query by adding sorting.

6.3.2 Sorting and grouping

If we needed to perform sorting functions manually, we'd need to write a lot of custom code. LINQ to Objects allows us to simplify the query, but to truly utilize our database's power, we need to use the indexes that the database has defined. The query expressions `orderby` and `orderby...descending` are designed to translate our sorting expression to the database. Consider the change we made to our running query by adding the sorting function, shown in listing 6.12.

Listing 6.12 Sorting with LINQ to SQL

```
var books = dataContext.GetTable<Book>();
var query = from book in books
            where book.Price < 30        ┐ Add
            orderby book.Title    <──────┘ sorting
            select book.Title;
```

As we indicated early on in this book, this query is truly an example of *WYSIWYW* (What You See Is What You Want). As seen in the resulting query string, we've now accomplished another part of our goal—leveraging the database's indexes to handle sorting rather than sorting on the client.

```
SELECT [t0].[Title]
FROM [Book] AS [t0]
WHERE [t0].[Price] < @p0
ORDER BY [t0].[Title]
```

If we wanted to order the results in descending order, we'd use the descending query expression as part of the clause. Also, if we wanted to sort on multiple columns, we'd include the list of fields separated by commas just as we would with a standard SQL expression.

Often, instead of just sorting the results, we need to group the results to combine like results. In listing 6.13, we group our listing of books by their subject. We project the results of the grouping operation into a temporary result which we can then reuse.

Listing 6.13 Grouping and sorting

```
var query =
    from book in dataContext.GetTable<Book>()
    group book by book.SubjectId into groupedBooks
    orderby groupedBooks.Key
    select new
    {
        SubjectId = groupedBooks.Key,
        Books = groupedBooks
    };

foreach (var groupedBook in query)
{
    Console.WriteLine("Subject: {0}", groupedBook.SubjectId);
    foreach (Book item in groupedBook.Books)
    {
        Console.WriteLine("Book: {0}", item.Title);
    }
}
```

The resulting object is an ordered collection of collections. To view the results, we need to iterate over both the grouped results and the contained collection of books for each grouping of subjects. This produces the following SQL:

```
SELECT [t1].[SubjectId] AS [Key]
FROM (
    SELECT [t0].[Subject] AS [SubjectId]
    FROM [dbo].[Book] AS [t0]
    GROUP BY [t0].[Subject]
    ) AS [t1]
ORDER BY [t1].[SubjectId]
```

Note that this query only selects the key values. As we iterate over the results, separate queries are issued for each grouping. The resulting collection is contained in the groupedBooks object. While we have our results grouped, it would be nice if we could perform some aggregation on the values so that we can see counts, averages, and totals by the groupings.

6.3.3 Aggregation

LINQ to SQL fully supports all of the standard aggregation methods that extend IEnumerable<T>. Thus, we can create a query to display the number of books that belong to each category. Listing 6.14 uses an anonymous type on our select clause to take our grouped book collections and return the count of the books by subject.

Listing 6.14   Including aggregates in the results

```
Table<Book> books = dataContext.GetTable<Book>();
var query = from book in books
            group book by book.SubjectId into groupedBooks
            select new
            {
                groupedBooks.Key,
                BookCount = groupedBooks.Count()
            };
```

Notice that in this example, we could return all of the books as we iterate over the result set and then count them on the client. LINQ to SQL offers the additional benefit of performing the count on the server and only returning that value rather than overloading the network with unnecessary data. Here is the corresponding SQL statement for this query:

```
SELECT COUNT(*) AS [BookCount], [t0].[Subject] AS [SubjectId]
FROM [Book] AS [t0]
GROUP BY [t0].[Subject]
```

We continue our tradition of only returning the results we want and not overloading our database or the network with needless data.

Using the other aggregate methods is just as easy. Listing 6.15 aggregates the total price, lowest price, highest price, and average price for the books grouped by each subject.

Listing 6.15 Using multiple aggregates

```
Table<Book> books = dataContext.GetTable<Book>();
var query =
    from book in books
    group book by book.SubjectId into groupedBooks
    select new
    {
        groupedBooks.Key,
        TotalPrice = groupedBooks.Sum(b => b.Price),
        LowPrice = groupedBooks.Min(b => b.Price),
        HighPrice = groupedBooks.Max(b => b.Price),
        AveragePrice = groupedBooks.Average(b => b.Price)
    };
```

Once again, the aggregation methods are translated into the appropriate SQL and the aggregation is performed in the database itself. The database only returns the results that we ask for, limiting the amount of data that needs to be returned.

Throughout our discussion so far, we've been limited to working only with values from a single table. It would be nice if we could join our Book table with the corresponding Subject table so that we could include the descriptive name of the subject rather than the cryptic unique identifier contained in the Book table. Naturally, LINQ to SQL offers several options for joining our results.

6.3.4 Joining

Combing data from multiple tables is the heart and soul of relational databases. If we didn't need to combine different pieces of data, we'd be happy writing our enterprise applications in Excel or flat text files. By being able to join related data, we're able to dig into information otherwise hidden in the individual records. LINQ to SQL offers several mechanisms for joining data between related sources. In our case, we're going to join the Books table with the Subject table. This way, we can display the name of the subject rather than just the foreign key.

LINQ to SQL supports two syntaxes for joins. One uses a comparison in the Where clause, which is similar to the ANSI-82 SQL syntax. To use this syntax, we can get a reference to the Book and Subject table objects. Notice we didn't say we're going to fetch the tables. With the reference to the table objects, the code in listing 6.16 shows how we can compose our query expression selecting from both of the tables where the `SubjectId` of the `Subject` object is the same as the `SubjectId` of the corresponding `Book` object.

Listing 6.16 Joining Books and Subjects

```
var subjects = dataContext.GetTable<Subject>();
var books = dataContext.GetTable<Book>();
var query = from subject in subjects
            from book in books
            where subject.SubjectId == book.SubjectId
            select new { subject.Name, book.Title, book.Price };
```

More than 15 years ago, the ANSI-92 standard replaced ANSI-82. Reverting to the older ANSI-82 syntax may appear unusual. Fortunately, LINQ also supports the join syntax reminiscent of the ANSI-92 SQL syntax. The previous query expression can be rewritten as shown in listing 6.17.

Listing 6.17 Joining with the `Join` keyword

```
var query = from subject in subjects join book in books
            on subject.SubjectId equals book.SubjectId
            select new { subject.Name, book.Title, book.Price };
```

Be aware that the order of the source and destination objects is important in LINQ `join` clauses. Unlike the forgiving nature of SQL interpreted by the database, LINQ is less forgiving. Because the query expressions are translated to methods, changing the order of the tables but not the fields will result in a compile time error. Here is the definition for the `System.Enumerable.Linq.Join` extension method:

```
public static IEnumerable<TResult> Join<TOuter, TInner, TKey, TResult>
   (this IEnumerable<TOuter> outer, IEnumerable<TInner> inner,
   Func<TOuter, TKey> outerKeySelector,
   Func<TInner, TKey> innerKeySelector,
   Func<TOuter, TInner, TResult> resultSelector)
```

Notice how the first and third parameters match up, as do the second and fourth. Figure 6.5 shows how the `Join` in our query maps to the parameters of the extension method. We can see how the `outer` and `outerKeySelector` parameters match up. If we were to transpose the `outer` and `inner` parameters or the corresponding `innerKeySelector` and `outerKeySelector`, we'd end up with a mismatch on our parameters when translating them to the underlying extension method.

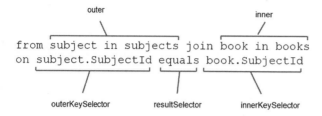

**Figure 6.5
Mapping the join to the
extension method parameters**

So far each of these joins has been a cross join (or *inner join*), where we only return the values that have similar results in both tables. But often, we want to return results from one table regardless of whether there are matching results in the other table. In standard SQL terms, this is typically referred to as an *outer join*. In the previous example, we may want to get a listing of all of the subjects regardless of whether any books are actually in our database for that subject. This would typically be expressed with the following ANSI-92 SQL expression:

```
SELECT      Subject.Name, Book.Title
FROM        Subject LEFT OUTER JOIN
                Book ON Subject.ID = Book.Subject
```

To accomplish the same thing with LINQ, we need to observe that we're looking for books where the subject exists or is null. The `DefaultIfEmpty()` extension method comes to our rescue, as shown in listing 6.18.

Listing 6.18   Approximating an outer join

```
var query =
    from subject in Subjects
    join book in books
        on subject.SubjectId equals book.SubjectId into joinedBooks
    from joinedBook in joinedBooks.DefaultIfEmpty()
    select new
    {
        subject.Name,
        joinedBook.Title,
        joinedBook.Price
    };
```

In this case, we tell LINQ that we want to join the books and subjects and place the results in a new temporary object called `joinedBooks`. Then we want to view the results from the `Subjects` and the joined `Books`, using the `DefaultIfEmpty` extension method to return a default value if the subject doesn't contain a book.

Now that we can combine our books and subjects, let's return to the original query we started at the beginning of the chapter to see how far we've come. Listing 6.19 shows the end result.

Listing 6.19 Rewriting the original example using LINQ to SQL

```
DataContext dataContext = new DataContext(liaConnectionString);

Table<Subject> subjects = dataContext.GetTable<Subject>();
Table<Book> books = dataContext.GetTable<Book>();

var query = from subject in subjects
            join book in books
                on subject.SubjectId equals book.SubjectId
            where book.Price < 30
            orderby subject.Name
            select new
            {
                subject.Name,
                joinedBook.Title,
                joinedBook.Price
            };
```

Comparing this query, we can see that the only real change in listing 6.1 is the source of the data. The LINQ query is identical. But a quick look at the generated SQL statement shows that we've now fetched only the rows and fields that we want. Additionally, we're performing the join, filter, and sort on the server. Here is the SQL that is generated from our LINQ to SQL query:

```
SELECT    t0.Name, t1.Title, t1.Price
FROM      Subject AS t0 INNER JOIN
                    Book AS t1 ON t0.ID = t1.Subject
WHERE     (t1.Price < @p0)
ORDER BY  t0.Name
```

The LINQ expression is more explicit than the corresponding SQL statement due to the fact that LINQ is designed to work not only with relational data, but other data sources as well, including objects and hierarchical sources. Since we've accomplished our goal, we could easily stop here, but LINQ to SQL offers more functionality that we need to look into before moving on.

Although there are times where forcing a relational construct into an object-oriented model is necessary, working with object hierarchies directly can often be more appropriate for application development.

6.4   *Working with object trees*

At the heart of the object/relational impedance mismatch is the clash between rows of data joined by identifying columns (relational) and memory constructs containing collections of objects (object-oriented). These objects can contain additional collections of objects. Thus where our database contains rows of books and subjects that we can join, it doesn't have an easy way to read a subject and then automatically show us the books associated with that subject. We need to explicitly tell the database to join the two tables to return the results.

In an object-oriented world, we typically obtain an instance of an object, like the Subject. From the Subject, we can drill in to identify the Books that belong to that Subject. We could potentially also drill in through the book to see the Authors, or any other property that we choose to expose. Luckily, LINQ to SQL offers an easy way to navigate these object hierarchies.

If we return to the definition of the Subject class, we may determine that we'd like a method that allows us to drill into the books that belong to that subject. Typically, we'd do that by lazy loading the books related to each subject as we called for them (see section 6.5.1 for more on lazy loading). Books would then be a property of a Subject object that we could drill into and work with as we wished. The mapping functionality in LINQ to SQL used in listing 6.20 shows how we can expose our collection of Book objects as a generic System.Data.Linq.Entity-Set<Book> object and call it Books. Again, we will use the auto-implemented property syntax for brevity.

Listing 6.20   Mapping the object associations

```
using System.Data.Linq.Mapping;
{
    [Table]
    public class Subject
    {
        [Column(IsPrimaryKey = true, Name = "ID")]
        public Guid SubjectId { get; set; }
        [Column]
        public String Description { get; set; }
        [Column]
        public String Name { get; set; }

        [Association(OtherKey="SubjectId")]
        public EntitySet<Book> Books { get; set; }
    }
}
```

Just like the table and columns, we need to tell the framework how the objects are related. We will do that using the `Association` attribute. In order for the association to work, we need to identify how our `Book` type is related to the `Subject`. We associate the two objects by specifying the property of the related object we will be joining with our current object. Our `Book` object contains a `SubjectId` property that we've already mapped to the `Subject` field of the `Book` table in the database. Thus, for the contained `Books` property of the `Subject` class, we specify the property of the `Book` class that represents the key to our record is called `SubjectId`. This key is the `OtherKey`, or the key property in the related object.

Now that we've specified the relationship between the two objects, we can fetch our `Subjects` using a standard LINQ to SQL expression, as in listing 6.21. Instead of explicitly joining the tables, we can directly drill into the books collection of each object. To display the results, we will iterate through the `Subjects`. As we loop through each subject, we will nest a loop to display the names of the books that are in that `Subject`.

Listing 6.21   Iterating over object trees

```
foreach (Subject subject in dataContext.GetTable<Subject>())
{
    Console.WriteLine(subject.Name);
    foreach (Book book in subject.Books)
    {
        Console.WriteLine("…{0}", book.Title);
    }
}
```

When we run the query, we may notice that by default, we achieve the same results as an outer join. From an object perspective, when we fetch the list of subjects, we don't know whether there are any associated books attached to each book. It is only when we iterate over the books for each subject that we find out if there are subjects with no associated books. Thus there may be cases where we display a subject that doesn't contain any books. Likewise, if we have a book that doesn't have a subject, it won't appear in the resulting list.

In order to filter our results a bit, we have at our disposal a couple of additional extension methods: `Any` and `All`. The `Any` method only returns results where related records exist in both result sets. Thus to refine our query to return only the subjects that also have related books (similar to an inner join), listing 6.22 uses the `Any` extension method.

Listing 6.22   Using `Any` to achieve an inner join on object trees

```
var query = from subject in Subjects
            where subject.Books.Any()
            select subject;
```

If we want, we can simply negate the where clause of the query to return any subjects where there aren't any related books, as follows:

```
var query = from subject in Subjects
            where !subject.Books.Any()
            select subject;
```

If we want to filter the results and see only subjects where the price of the book is less than 30 dollars, we call the `All` extension method as shown in listing 6.23.

Listing 6.23   Filtering child objects using `All`

```
var query = from subject in Subjects
            where subject.Books.All(b => b.Price < 30)
            select subject;
```

The ability to represent our data through more natural object hierarchies allows us to work with it in a more familiar programming manner. We establish the object dependencies based on the specific business needs and we can work with it as we would any set of objects. This allows us to maintain our business rules and integrity without having to focus on the relational nature of the underlying store. If we want, we can restate our running example using a hierarchical syntax as shown in listing 6.24.

Listing 6.24   Running query using object hierarchies

```
Table<Subject> subjects = dataContext.GetTable<Subject>();

var query = from subject in subjects          ❶
            orderby subject.Name
            select new
            {
                subject.Name,
                Books = from book in subject.Books          ❷
                        where book.Price < 30
                        select new { book.Title, book.Price }
            };
```

In this version, we not only implement the more natural object hierarchies ❶, but also nest the results as a similar set of hierarchical object structures ❷. Again, we let the database do what it's best at and only return the necessary portions of the underlying objects.

There are times where we will want to query otherwise unrelated items. In those cases, joining data is still required. Both options are available as the business needs demand. Regardless of which method works best for each situation, LINQ to SQL attempts to return just the values requested and only return them when needed. Usually, this is advantageous. Occasionally the lazy loading behavior results in more frequent interaction with the database than originally intended. Let's continue our exploration of LINQ to SQL by looking at times where the default behavior may result in more frequent database inquiries.

6.5 *When is my data loaded and why does it matter?*

When we fetch data from the database, LINQ to SQL utilizes a technique called *deferred execution*. With deferred execution, the results are only loaded into memory when they are requested. Stepping through our examples in this chapter and paying attention to when the SQL statements are being generated, we can see that they are not generated when we define the query. Instead, the database is not accessed until we actually request each record. Waiting to access the values until they are needed is called *lazy loading*.

6.5.1 *Lazy loading*

When displaying results, lazy loading offers the benefit of only retrieving the data when we request it, and only returning the data we request. In many cases, this provides performance benefits, but in other cases it can lead to some unexpected results. Consider the code from listing 6.25, which displays the list of subjects that may or may not have associated books. In this case, we will send the generated SQL commands to the console window to be displayed when the request is submitted to the database. When running this example, step through the code and watch the console window carefully to see exactly when each command is being issued.

Listing 6.25 Lazy loading child objects

```
DataContext dataContext = new DataContext(liaConnectionString);
dataContext.Log = Console.Out;
var subjects = dataContext.GetTable<Subject>();
ObjectDumper.Write(subjects);
```

Since we only want to list the subjects, we're not fetching the books. By only fetching the books if and when we really need them, we can optimize our network bandwidth, minimize memory consumption, and limit the amount of work the database needs to do.

We can extend this sample by instructing the `ObjectDumper` to not only display the `Subjects`, but also display its children by telling it we want to view one child level in addition to the base level. The `ObjectDumper.Write` method accepts an overload to indicate the level we want to view. Change the last line in listing 6.25 to request the first-level children as well as follows:

```
ObjectDumper.Write(Subjects, 1);
```

Note that the child records for each subject are fetched only when we want them. This lazy loading behavior is beneficial when we don't need to display all of the children for all parent objects, but only want to fetch them as the user requests the details. As we request the books for each subject, we will send a separate query to the database for each row of the `Subject` table. Listing 6.26 shows sample output from the changed version of the code.

Listing 6.26   Generated output when lazy loading the child elements

```
SELECT [t0].[ID], [t0].[Description], [t0].[Name]          ◄──┐  Selecting
FROM [Subject] AS [t0]                                         │  Subjects

SubjectId=a0e2a5d7-88c6-4dfe-a416-10eadb978b0b  Description=null
        Name=Software development        Books=...                  For first
SELECT [t0].[ID] AS [BookId], [t0].[Isbn], [t0].[Notes],    ◄─────  Subject
   [t0].[PageCount], [t0].[Price], [t0].[PubDate] AS [PublicationDate],
   [t0].[Summary], [t0].[Title], [t0].[Subject] AS [SubjectId],
   [t0].[Publisher] AS [PublisherId]
FROM [dbo].[Book] AS [t0]
WHERE [t0].[Subject] = @p0
-- @p0: Input UniqueIdentifier (Size = 0; Prec = 0; Scale = 0)
   NOT NULL [a0e2a5d7-88c6-4dfe-a416-10eadb978b0b]

  Books: BookId=b1c7670c-fdf5-45e5-8f06-3b7994b6a346 Isbn=0-222-77777-2
   Notes=null       PageCount=256       Price=35.5000
   PublicationDate=4/1/2007        Summary=null       Title=C# on Rails
   SubjectId=a0e2a5d7-88c6-4dfe-a416-10eadb978b0b        Subject={ }
   PublisherId=855cb02e-dc29-473d-9f40-6c3405043fa3
  Books: BookId=4f3b0ac1-3746-4067-a810-79a9ce02a7bf Isbn=0-000-77777-2
   Notes=null       PageCount=101    Price=25.5500
   PublicationDate=11/10/2004       Summary=null       Title=Funny Stories
   SubjectId=a0e2a5d7-88c6-4dfe-a416-10eadb978b0b  Subject={ }
   PublisherId=4ab0856e-51f3-4b67-9355-8b11510119ba
```

```
SELECT [t0].[ID] AS [BookId], [t0].[Isbn],     ◁────── For second Subject
   [t0].[Notes], [t0].[PageCount], [t0].[Price],
   [t0].[PubDate] AS [PublicationDate], [t0].[Summary], [t0].[Title],
   [t0].[Subject] AS [SubjectId], [t0].[Publisher] AS [PublisherId]
FROM [dbo].[Book] AS [t0]
WHERE [t0].[Subject] = @p0
-- @p0: Input UniqueIdentifier (Size = 0; Prec = 0; Scale = 0)
 NOT NULL [92f10ca6-7970-473d-9a25-1ff6cab8f682]

  Books: BookId=09017e35-ca66-40b8-80a4-ba5253716e33 Isbn=2-444-77777-2
   Notes=null      PageCount=50     Price=29.0000
   PublicationDate=2/18/1973      Summary=null  Title=Bonjour mon Amour
   SubjectId=92f10ca6-7970-473d-9a25-1ff6cab8f682  Subject={ }
   PublisherId=4ab0856e-51f3-4b67-9355-8b11510119ba
```

In the generated code, we fetch the list of subjects, then as we iterate through each item, we issue a separate query for each book, passing in the id column of the subject for each row. This means that instead of issuing one statement, we send separate statements for each child record. Before improving the situation, let's make it worse. In this case, copy the last line and paste it twice so that we call `ObjectDumper.Write` twice. Step through the code and pay attention to the SQL that is generated.

We will spare you from having to read the gory results again here. In this case, all of the queries were sent to the database twice, once for each `Write` method. We've now turned a very good thing (lazy loading) into a potentially bad thing (too much network traffic to the database). What can we do to improve the situation?

6.5.2   *Loading details immediately*

If all we want to do is fetch the results more than once, we can prefetch them and store them in an array or list using the `ToList`, `ToDictionary`, `ToLookup`, or `ToArray` extension methods. Thus, we could change our earlier implementation to indicate that we want to load all of the customers once and then continue to use the results as long as our `subjects` variable is in scope.

```
var subjects = dataContext.GetTable<Subject>().ToList<Subject>();
```

By explicitly stating that we want to retrieve the results, we force LINQ to SQL to immediately fetch the results and populate a new generic `List` with the resulting `Subject` objects. This has the advantage of not requiring round trips to the database each time we want to fetch our list. Additionally, we can use the LINQ to Objects query mechanisms to continue to manipulate our results and perform grouping, joining, aggregating, or sorting as necessary.

Unfortunately, by converting our results into a List or Array, we lose some of the benefits of LINQ to SQL, specifically the ability to optimize the data we retrieve from the database by leveraging the server-side functionality and limiting the amount of data we have to put into memory. Any query expressions applied to the resulting Subjects list will be processed by LINQ to Objects rather than LINQ to SQL.

Simply casting the results ToList still doesn't help eliminate the separate queries to fetch each of the lazy loaded child collections. Fortunately, LINQ to SQL supports a mechanism to instruct the DataContext which optimizations to make. By using a DataLoadOptions type as shown in listing 6.27, we can shape (but not fetch) the result sets ahead of time. As soon as a record of the declared object type is fetched, it will also retrieve the associated child records.

Listing 6.27   Using DataLoadOptions to optimize object loading

```
DataLoadOptions options = new DataLoadOptions();          ❶
options.LoadWith<Subject>(subject => subject.Books);       ❷
dataContext.LoadOptions = options;        ❸
```

In this example, we create a new DataLoadOptions object called options ❶. The main function of DataLoadOptions is to indicate which child objects load with a given object type. Since we want to make sure we load our books whenever we load the subjects, we tell the options to LoadWith<Subject> and pass it a function in the form of an expression ❷. We could pass an actual delegate, but since we have lambda expressions at our disposal, we can tell it, "given a subject, load the Books EntitySet." All that remains is to attach our options to our data context ❸.

With the new options in place, run the example again. Here is the SQL that LINQ generates:

```
SELECT [t0].[ID], [t0].[Description], [t0].[Name],
  [t1].[ID] AS [BookId], [t1].[Isbn], [t1].[Notes], [t1].[PageCount],
  [t1].[Price], [t1].[PubDate] AS [PublicationDate], [t1].[Summary],
  [t1].[Title], [t1].[Subject] AS [SubjectId],
  [t1].[Publisher] AS [PublisherId], (
    SELECT COUNT(*)
    FROM [dbo].[Book] AS [t2]
    WHERE [t2].[Subject] = [t0].[ID]
    ) AS [count]
FROM [Subject] AS [t0]
LEFT OUTER JOIN [dbo].[Book] AS [t1] ON [t1].[Subject] = [t0].[ID]
ORDER BY [t0].[ID], [t1].[ID]
```

By specifying the `DataLoadOptions` of the data that we want to access, we eliminate the multiple subqueries that were necessary with the previous lazy loaded implementation. This should provide much-improved interaction between our client application and the database. Of course, if we know we won't need the books, we shouldn't fetch them, but if we know we will need to work with the books for each category, we can load them up-front and provide a more responsive application.

Be aware that the load options can be set only once on an instance of a context. Once set, they cannot be changed for that instance. Using the `DataLoad-Options` offers powerful control over the desired results, but take more care when using it.

Simply by specifying the `DataLoadOptions`, we do not eliminate the multiple fetches if we try to iterate over our results twice. In order to finish our optimization, we can combine the `DataLoadOptions` with the `ToList` method. Using both of these together, we can make sure that we access our database once and ensure that the subjects and books are joined properly.

Using joins gives LINQ to SQL a powerful ability to drill into data. Whether we choose to work in an object-oriented manner or mimic relational interaction, we can specify the mapping once and then focus on the business needs. We do need to be careful and check the underlying database interaction to make sure we're optimizing it as we should. In many simple operations, the default behavior is fine. However, there are times when refactoring our code can produce dramatic improvements in the resulting implementation. If we really need control over the data we receive, we do have additional options including stored procedures and user-defined functions, which we will look at in chapter 8. For now, let's move beyond simply fetching data and look at options we have to save our data once we change it.

6.6 *Updating data*

If we were limited to fetching data, the functionality would be no more than a reporting tool. Luckily, updating the data is just as simple as fetching it. As long as we have a persistent `DataContext` object, we can make additions, alterations, and deletions using standard methods on the table objects. The `DataContext` keeps track of the changes and handles updating the database with a single method call.

To begin, let's look at an example that updates the price of our most expensive books so we can offer a discount on them (see listing 6.28). In this case, we fetch only the books that are "expensive"—where the price is greater than $30—and then iterate over them, reducing the price of each by $5. Finally, we persist the changes to our database by calling the SubmitChanges method on our DataContext object.

Listing 6.28 Updating values and committing them to the database

```
DataContext dataContext = new DataContext(liaConnectionString);
var ExpensiveBooks =            ❶
    from b in dataContext.GetTable<Book>()
    where b.Price>30
    select b;

foreach (Book b in ExpensiveBooks)       ❷
{
    b.Price -= 5;
}
dataContext.SubmitChanges();        ❸
```

The code in listing 6.28 is straightforward C# code. We start by fetching the records that we want to modify ❶. We then make the necessary changes by working with the book object just as we would with any other collection ❷. Once we're done, we call SubmitChanges to commit the changes ❸. We don't need to worry about creating a separate mapping to issue an update command. The context takes the same metadata we created for querying and uses it to generate the necessary update statement. Here is the SQL that was generated for our example:

```
UPDATE [Book]
SET [Price] = @p8
WHERE (([ID] = @p0) AND ([Isbn] = @p1) AND ([Notes] IS NULL) AND
  ([PageCount] = @p2) AND ([Price] = @p3) AND ([PubDate] = @p4) AND
  ([Summary] IS NULL) AND ([Title] = @p5) AND ([Subject] = @p6) AND
  ([Publisher] = @p7)
```

Although this code may appear to be excessive, the first two lines accomplish the update. The rest is in place to check for concurrency violations. We will look at concurrency in chapter 8. What is important at this point is to observe that the change manager of the DataContext object recognized that the only column that needs to be changed in our database is the Price field. It does not try to update any other columns or records. This reduces the amount of data we need to transmit across the network. We're also able to queue up multiple updates into a single unit of work and commit them with a single call to SubmitChanges. We've seen how to read and update. Now, let's take a look at the other two parts of the CRUD operation: create and delete.

Typically when working with collections, we'd add and remove objects by using IList's Add and Remove methods. The traditional semantics of Add and Remove imply that the collections immediately reflect the new values. Preview releases of LINQ continued the tradition of using Add and Remove for these functions. However, users were confused when their values were not returned as part of subsequent queries until they were committed to the database. As a result, the names for these methods were changed to InsertOnSubmit and DeleteOnSubmit to reflect the nature of the implementation more accurately.

Creating new items with LINQ to SQL is as simple as calling the InsertOnSubmit method on the table object. To delete, we similarly call the DeleteOnSubmit method. Listing 6.29 demonstrates adding a book to our book collection and subsequently removing it.

Listing 6.29 Adding and removing items from a table

```
DataContext dataContext = new DataContext(liaConnectionString);
Table<Book> books = dataContext.GetTable<Book>();        ◁─┐ Get book
                                                             │ table
                                        ┌─ Create
                                        │  new book
Book newBook = new Book();     ◁──┘
newBook.Price = 40;
newBook.PublicationDate = System.DateTime.Today;
newBook.Title = "Linq In Action";
newBook.PublisherId =
    new Guid("4ab0856e-51f3-4b67-9355-8b11510119ba");
newBook.SubjectId =
    new Guid("a0e2a5d7-88c6-4dfe-a416-10eadb978b0b");

books.InsertOnSubmit(newBook);       ◁─┐ Add and
                                        │ save book
dataContext.SubmitChanges();         ◁─┘

books.DeleteOnSubmit(newBook);       ◁─── Remove from  table

dataContext.SubmitChanges();         ◁─── Remove from database
```

If we check the generated SQL code, we will see that the code to insert a record is a simple INSERT INTO statement. The code to delete the record is a bit more complex than a simple DELETE FROM Table structure. The extra code is required to handle potential concurrency issues. We can perform all of the standard CRUD operations using basic object method calls. The `DataContext` maintains the changes and automatically generates the SQL to accomplish the requested work.

6.7 *Summary*

In this chapter, we demonstrated how to map our relational data to object structures. Once we have the mappings set up, we can perform all of the standard query expressions and extension methods. In previous versions of ADO.NET, we had to manually implement the specific data access implementation for each scenario and separate implementations for each of the CRUD operations. With LINQ to SQL, once the mappings are defined, we can ignore the details of the database interaction. Instead, we work with the objects focusing on the business need rather than the implementation details.

Additionally, LINQ to SQL offers an advantage over LINQ to Objects in that we can capitalize on the power of the database to preprocess our results. The queries are dynamically composed to reduce the amount of network bandwidth and client processing requirements. We recommend taking a moment and trying the examples in this chapter before moving on in order to get a feel for LINQ to SQL in action.

In the next couple of chapters, we will dive deeper into the LINQ to SQL capabilities and tools. We could get started working with the technology now, but to understand how it works or some of the advanced options, keep reading. We will explain how LINQ to SQL performs its magic and explore some more advanced options. If you like what you've seen so far, keep reading. It gets better.

Peeking under the covers of LINQ to SQL

7

This chapter covers:

- Mapping from the database to objects
- Exploring how LINQ to SQL works under the covers
- Translating query expressions into SQL with `IQueryable` and expression trees
- Tracking objects through their life cycle
- Working with disconnected data

In chapter 6, we presented a high-level view of some of the capabilities of LINQ to SQL. By now, you should have enough tools under your belt to start working with LINQ to SQL.

In this chapter, we dive a bit deeper and explore how the technology works under the covers. We'll start by looking at the mapping options at our disposal. We explain not only the mapping options, but also how to employ some of the tools that come with Visual Studio 2008 to make mapping easier. We'll continue by looking at the underlying technologies that make LINQ to SQL behave differently from LINQ to Objects. We won't have enough time to create our own O/R mapper, but we'll discuss how they differ at their core. We'll conclude this chapter by examining the object life cycle and see how LINQ to SQL manages the objects through their changes until they are updated. By combining the mapping, translations, and object life cycle, LINQ to SQL emerges as a powerful extension of the LINQ family of technologies.

7.1   *Mapping objects to relational data*

In the previous chapter, we extended the `Book` and `Subject` objects of our running example using several custom attributes. By decorating the classes and properties, we demonstrated how to eliminate repetitive traditional ADO.NET code and let the framework handle mapping the relational tables to our business entity classes. We're able to specify the mappings once. The framework can determine the SQL necessary to translate our declarative query constructs into a syntax that our database can recognize. By changing the business needs, we do not need to implement an entirely different data tier, potentially with separate code both in our application and on the database itself. We can let the framework manage the language translations based on the mappings we set up.

When we initially presented the mappings, we showed how to manually map the values. The attribute-based mappings provide a direct method of specifying the mappings. In addition to explicitly specifying the mappings with attributes, Visual Studio 2008 offers three other mechanisms to assist with mapping data to your objects. The full list of mapping options consists of

- Attributes declared inline with your classes
- External XML files
- The command-line SqlMetal tool
- The graphical LINQ to SQL Designer tool

In this section, we'll explore all four of these methods and identify how each one has a role. By understanding each method, we'll be able to build and maintain applications quicker and more effectively. In chapter 6, we introduced the concept of mapping with attributes. Since we're already familiar with using the `Table` and `Column` attributes to accomplish mappings, let's begin our exploration by seeing how we can implement more of the capabilities that these attributes offer.

7.1.1 Using inline attributes

In many ways, starting our discussion with the manual method is like learning to ride a unicycle before riding a bicycle with training wheels. However, starting with the basics helps us to better appreciate the other options. We'll also have a better understanding of the code generated by the other tools.

In the previous chapter we identified LINQ to SQL's three main types of attributes—`Table`, `Column`, and `Association`. We can decorate our classes with the `Table` attribute to designate how the object maps to a database table. Properties can be decorated with either the `Column` attribute or the `Association` attribute. The `Column` attribute designates how an individual property maps to a column in the table. The `Association` attribute designates how tables are related to each other via foreign-key relationships. In addition to these three attributes, there are a number of less frequently used attributes. Table 7.1 provides a brief overview of the basic functionality of each of these attributes.

Table 7.1 Custom attributes exposed by `System.Data.Linq.Mapping` for mapping databases to objects

Attribute	Description
Association	Sets up the primary-key and foreign-key relationships between classes.
Column	Identifies the mapping for a column in the database table to the specified property or field.
Database	Specifies the database name used by `CreateDatabase` from your mapping metadata.
Function	Used to map user-defined functions or stored procedures to a method.
InheritanceMapping	Used when mapping to polymorphic objects. We'll discuss this in chapter 8.
Parameter	Designates the parameters for a stored procedure or function.
Provider	Designates the type used to perform the querying. Since LINQ to SQL is limited to SQL Server, this will indicate the version of SQL Server that will be targeted.
ResultType	Indicates the type of object that is returned as the result of a stored procedure or function.
Table	Designates the name of the table you wish to map to a class.

For the moment, let's restrict our focus to the main attributes you'll use with standard tables. We'll explore stored procedures, functions, and inheritance in chapter 8. Let's take a closer look at the `Table`, `Column`, and `Association` attributes.

Table attribute

The `Table` attribute serves as a starting point to bridge the gap between tables and objects. If we don't specify that our class is the representation for a table, any of the other attributes we set on the properties will be useless as there will be no way of knowing what table the class is related to. To indicate that a class named `Author` maps to the `Author` table, decorate the class with the `Table` attribute.

```
[Table()]
public class Author
```

Not only is the `Table` attribute one of the most critical, it is also one of the simplest. By default, just decorating the class with the `Table` attribute indicates that the class name is the same as the name of the table. The `Table` attribute also takes one parameter as an argument called `Name`. Use the `Name` argument to specify the name of the table in the database if they are not the same. For example, if we wanted to modify our `Author` class to use data from a table called `Authors`, change the attribute to include the `Name` parameter as follows:

```
[Table(Name="dbo.Authors")]
```

Column Attribute

Typically, the most frequently used attribute is the `Column` attribute. This attribute maps the columns in the database to the class properties. In mapping a column to a property with the same name, we can get away with decorating the property with the `Column` attribute without specifying any parameter values. In many cases, we'll want to specify some of the parameters in table 7.2 to add functionality to the mappings.

Table 7.2 Listing of parameters used by the `Column` attribute

Parameter name	Description
AutoSync	Enumerated value indicating how LINQ to SQL should handle database columns that change as the result of a `Create` or `Update` method. This is particularly useful for columns with default values. The valid options are `Default`, `Always`, `Never`, `OnInsert`, and `OnUpdate`.
CanBeNull	Indicates if the database column can be null. Remember, a null is not the same as an empty string.

Table 7.2   Listing of parameters used by the `Column` attribute *(continued)*

Parameter name	Description
`DbType`	This attribute is used to specify the database type used when creating a column with the `DataContext.CreateDatabase` method. A valid example would be `NVarChar(50) Not Null Default('')`
`Expression`	This value is only used when generating databases with the `CreateDatabase` method. The value included here is the SQL string specifying how to create a calculated field in the database.
`IsDbGenerated`	Used to indicate if the database generates the value for this property. This parameter should be used for Identity or AutoNumber columns in the database. The value will be populated in your class immediately after the record is updated in the database via the `SubmitChanges` method.
`IsDiscriminator`	Use this to designate that the column in question identifies a specific instance type to be used for the given row. We'll see this in action in section 8.3.3.
`IsPrimaryKey`	Set this value for the column of your table that uniquely identifies the row. Most frequently, this is the primary key column of your table. LINQ to SQL requires at least one column be indicated as the primary key for each class for use by the object identity and change tracking services; for multicolumn keys, set this in each `Column` attribute.
`IsVersion`	Use this attribute on columns that are the timestamp or version number of your record. This value is updated each time the row is changed, and is useful for optimistic concurrency checks.
`Name`	Indicates the name of the column in the table you wish to map to.
`Storage`	To map a column directly to the underlying private field in a class rather than using the public property setter, specify the name of the field as the storage parameter.
`UpdateCheck`	Specifies how LINQ to SQL will use this column when processing the optimistic concurrency (see section 8.1). By default, all mapped columns in the class will be used when evaluating the concurrency. If you're using a timestamp or another technique to manage concurrency, use this parameter to optimize your update and delete methods. This parameter takes an enumerated value with the following options: `Always` (default)—Always check this column `Never`—Never check this column `WhenChanged`—Only check this column if the given property has changed.

Using these attributes, we can map the `Author` class from our running example to the corresponding table. Every `EntitySet` collection requires an identifying property. In the case of `Author`, we'll use a `Guid` called ID. Instead of using the public property set method, we specify that we want to store the value directly in the private

_ID field using the Storage parameter. For clarity, we indicate that the name of the column is ID using the Name parameter. In case we wanted to generate the database dynamically, we specify the DbType for the column as UniqueIdentifier NOT NULL. Perhaps the most critical parameter on this column is the IsPrimaryKey designation that is required for at least one property in each class. The final parameter of the ID column is CanBeNull, which indicates that a value is required for this property. If no value is supplied, a run-time exception will be thrown.

```
private System.Guid _ID;
[Column(Storage = "_ID", Name = "ID",
    DbType = "UniqueIdentifier NOT NULL",
    IsPrimaryKey = true, CanBeNull = false)]
public System.Guid ID { get { return _ID;} set{ _ID = value;} }
```

The next three columns are similar. In each case, we specify the name of the column that corresponds to our property. The data type of each column is VarChar. The FirstName and LastName are optional (NOT NULL and CanBeNull = false). The others allow for null values in the database. If either of these were value types rather than strings, we would need to use the nullable types introduced by the .NET Framework 2.0 for these properties.

```
[Column(Name = "LastName", DbType = "VarChar(50) NOT NULL",
    CanBeNull = false, UpdateCheck=UpdateCheck.Never)]
public string LastName { get; set; }

[Column(Name = "FirstName", DbType = "VarChar(30) NOT NULL",
    CanBeNull = false, UpdateCheck=UpdateCheck.Never)]
public string FirstName { get; set; }

[Column(Name = "WebSite", DbType = "VarChar(200)",
    UpdateCheck=UpdateCheck.Never)]
public string WebSite { get; set; }
```

All three of these columns include the parameter instruction to never perform an update check because of a special feature we're including in this example— the final timestamp column. With SQL Server, a TimeStamp column is changed by the database every time a record is changed. We indicate that the database will assign it by including the IsDbGenerated parameter and setting it to true. We also specify that this column tracks each time the row was changed by setting the IsVersion attribute. We specify that the value is required using the CanBeNull=false designation.

```
[Column(Name="TimeStamp", DbType="rowversion NOT NULL",
    IsDbGenerated=true, IsVersion=true, CanBeNull=false,
    UpdateCheck=UpdateCheck.Always)]
public byte[] TimeStamp { get; set; }
```

We'll discuss concurrency in chapter 8. For now, understand that when making updates, we check to see if values were changed since we last fetched the values. Because the database updates a timestamp each time the row is changed, we don't need to worry about changes to any other column. By combining the previous value of the ID and timestamp, we check to see that someone else didn't make a conflicting change to our record while we were working on it. The rest of the properties are not needed for concurrency checking and thus we can state that we never need to check the values on update (UpdateCheck.Never).

With these mappings in place, we're ready to perform standard queries against our revised Author class. If we wanted to work with object trees to join our authors with the books using the AuthorBooks table, we would need to specify one more set of mapping attributes, Association.

Association attribute

The Association attribute is used to designate how two classes, and by extension their corresponding tables, are related. Unlike the Table and Column attributes, at least one parameter is required in order for our association to work. Table 7.3 lists the parameters used by the Association attribute.

Table 7.3 Listing of parameters used by the Association attribute

Parameter Name	Description
DeleteRule	Indicates the cascading delete policy for the relationship.
DeleteOnNull	Used in 1:1 relationships to indicate the cascading delete policy when the foreign key fields are not nullable.
IsForeignKey	Indicates that the class in question is the child of a parent-child relationship.
IsUnique	Used to indicate a 1:1 relationship where both the foreign key and primary key are unique and contained in both tables. This is not used often, as most relationships are 1:0-1 or 1:n rather than a true 1:1.
Name	Specifies the name of the foreign key that will be used when dynamically creating the database from the metadata.
OtherKey	Used to identify the column(s) in the associated class that contain the related key values. If the parameter is not specified, the ID columns specified in the other class will be assumed.
Storage	Specifies the internal field used to track the related child object EntitySets.
ThisKey	Identifies the property that contains the local ID field. If this is not specified, the column(s) designated by IsPrimary in the Column attribute are used. If the key consists of multiple columns, include each of them in a comma-separated list of the column names.

Given this information, let's take a look at how we can add an association between our new Author class and a BookAuthor class.

```
private EntitySet<BookAuthor> _BookAuthors;
[Association(Name="FK_BookAuthor_Author", Storage="_BookAuthors",
    OtherKey="Author", ThisKey="ID")]
public EntitySet<BookAuthor> BookAuthors
{
    get
    {
        return this._BookAuthors;
    }
    set
    {
        this._BookAuthors.Assign(value);
    }
}
```

The primary key of the Author class is the ID property (ThisKey) and the associated key in the BookAuthor is the Author property (OtherKey). We'll store the collection (Storage) in an EntitySet<BookAuthor> field called _BookAuthors. In case we wish to autogenerate the database from our class attribute metadata, we'll specify the name of the foreign key to be FK_BookAuthor_Author (Name).

So far in this chapter we've focused on the three main attributes—Table, Column, and Attribute. Using these mapping structures, we can declaratively work with our objects using standard query expressions and allow the framework to automatically handle the data access plumbing for us. Directly embedding the mapping in our classes can be seen as a double-edged sword when it comes to code maintenance. When creating a business class, the developer is typically intimately aware of the relationships between the database and the object. Additionally, we can ensure that changes we make are not orphaned as we continue to enhance our system. However, when maintaining an application down the road, quickly locating the attributes can be difficult when interspersed throughout our code. Additionally, polluting our business code with the mapping information makes focusing on the core business requirements more difficult from a readability standpoint.

A bigger issue with using attributes is that they are set at compile time. Breaking changes in our database's schema, including renaming or removing an existing column or table, will require us to rebuild the application in order to synchronize the components. If the attributes specify a mapping that no longer exists in the database, a run-time exception will likely arise. To handle both concerns, LINQ offers a second mapping mechanism—using an external XML file.

7.1.2 *Mapping with external XML files*

Using XML files to specify mappings is similar to using attributes on classes. With XML mapping, the mapping file needs to be specified when instantiating the `DataContext`. Unlike attribute-based mappings, the XML mapping file can be dynamically changed without recompiling. Additionally, attributes can be removed from the business class definitions, which should facilitate focusing on the business requirements. XML mapping files also offer the added benefit of keeping our mappings in a central location, making maintenance of the mapping portions easier.

We don't need to be concerned about learning an entirely different set of properties to use the external file. The XML mapping elements look similar to the attributes we've already discussed. The amount of code that needs to be maintained is reduced. By using the XML mapping, we can eliminate the inline attributes on our class. Instead, we can use the file shown in listing 7.1 to map our `Author` object to the database.

Listing 7.1 XML mapping file for `Author` class

```xml
<?xml version="1.0" encoding="utf-16"?>
<Database Name="lia"
  xmlns="http://schemas.microsoft.com/linqtosql/mapping/2007">
  <Table Name="Author">                    ❶
    <Type Name="LinqInAction.LinqBooks.Common.Author">      ❷
      <Column Name="ID" Member="ID" Storage="_Id"
       DbType="UniqueIdentifier NOT NULL" IsPrimaryKey="True" />    ❸
      <Column Name="LastName" Member="LastName"
       DbType="VarChar(50) NOT NULL" CanBeNull="False" />
      <Column Name="FirstName" Member="FirstName"
       DbType="VarChar(30)" />
      <Column Name="WebSite" Member="WebSite"
       DbType="VarChar(200)" />
      <Column Name="TimeStamp" Member="TimeStamp"
       DbType="rowversion NOT NULL" CanBeNull="False"
       IsDbGenerated="True" IsVersion="True" AutoSync="Always" />
    </Type>
  </Table>
</Database>
```

The resulting `Author` class is similar to the code we set up back in chapter 4. All of the extra mapping work we did has been moved to the XML file. The information in the XML mapping file nearly matches the parameters we previously used in the class's attributes. We do need to specify the `Type` and `Member` information to indicate which class and property we wish to map.

The root node of the XML file is the `Database` element. Here we specify the name of the database we're mapping to. The `Database` can have multiple `Table` elements. Each `Table` ❶ element contains a `Type` element, which indicates the class we use when mapping the given table. The `Type` ❷ can have any number of `Column` and `Association` elements. The attributes for the `Column` ❸ and `Association` element include one additional value not included in the attribute based version we previously used—`Member`.

Since we're not directly decorating individual properties using attributes, we need to specify which property (or `Member`) the column mapping applies to. Given what we learned previously about the `Table`, `Column`, and `Association` attributes, we can transfer the attributes from the class declarations directly into the `Column` and `Association` elements, remembering to add the `Member` attribute.

In order to use our new mapping file, we need to instruct the `DataContext` to use the mapping rather than rely on the default attribute based declaration. In listing 7.2, we show how to attach an external mapping file (lia.xml) to the `DataContext` and then query our undecorated business objects using the XML mappings.

Listing 7.2 Attaching the external XML mapping to the `DataContext`

```
XmlMappingSource map =        ❶
    XmlMappingSource.FromXml(File.ReadAllText(@"lia.xml"));

DataContext dataContext =        ❷
    new DataContext(liaConnectionString, map);

Table<Author> authors = dc.GetTable<Author>();        ❸
```

In the first line of listing 7.2, we create a new `System.Data.Linq.XmlMapping-Source` instance in the lia.xml file in our application directory ❶. We can load this document using any of the following methods: `FromXml`, `FromUrl`, `From-Stream`, or `FromReader`. To attach our `XmlMappingSource` object to the `DataContext`, we add it as the second parameter of the overloaded constructor ❷. Once we've attached the external mapping to the `DataContext`, we're free to use all of the querying techniques we learned in chapter 6 ❸.

As we've mentioned, the XML mapping offers the benefit of centralizing the definitions and allows us to change the mappings dynamically as schema changes are made in the underlying database. The need to load and parse the XML file increases the overhead required to create the `DataContext` compared to using attributes. As with any programming task, test the various options in any situation to determine the most appropriate method. Each method has its positives and negatives.

One of the negatives that both the XML and attribute-based mappings face is the tedium caused by having to manually create and maintain the classes and mappings. Thankfully, Visual Studio includes a couple of options to help generate the mappings—the command-line SqlMetal tool and the LINQ to SQL designer. If you're a masochist who enjoys manually creating your classes and mappings, you can skip the next sections. Otherwise, let's see how we can exploit the tools to do the monotonous work for us, starting with a command-line option—SqlMetal.

7.1.3 *Using the SqlMetal tool*

Microsoft realized developers would be more likely to adopt the technology if tools were provided to automate the mapping process. One such tool is a command-line tool called SqlMetal. We point the tool at our database and it generates the corresponding business classes. The basic syntax for using the tool is `SqlMetal [switches] [input file]`. Let's see what happens if we try to generate classes for the SqlExpress database for this book.

To begin, open the Visual Studio 2008 Command Prompt, located in the Visual Studio Tools folder for Visual Studio 2008. We need to use this command prompt rather than the standard command-line tool in order to set the necessary path settings. To generate our classes, enter the following from the command prompt, making sure to use the correct path to your database:

```
SqlMetal /server:.\sqlexpress
/namespace:LinqInAction.LinqBooks.Common /code:Common.cs
/language:csharp "C:\projects\Lia\lia.mdf"
```

With this command, we specify that we want SqlMetal to generate a set of C# classes (because of the `language` switch) based on the LIA SqlExpress database. The `code` switch indicates that the classes will be generated in a single file called Common.cs and placed in the `LinqInAction.LinqBooks.Common` namespace because of the `namespace` switch. SqlMetal has a number of switches that can specify more advanced capabilities.

The switches we provide to SqlMetal will depend on our specific needs. Perhaps the most useful switch as we begin is the help switch, which is fairly standard with command-line tools. This command displays a listing of all of the switches, along with a description and sample usages.

```
SqlMetal /?
```

As with the first example, generating classes directly from the database may be sufficient. In the following command, we can generate a set of classes in the `Linq-InAction` namespace to a file called Common.cs. The generated code will be in C# and will include stored procedures in addition to the tables.

```
SqlMetal /database:lia.mdf /Namespace:LinqInAction /code:Common.cs
/language:csharp /sprocs
```

Other times, it may be helpful to generate the metadata first. Do this by directing SqlMetal at your database and sending the results to a file called LiaMetadata.xml as follows:

```
SqlMetal /database:lia.mdf /xml:LiaMetadata.xml
```

This generated metadata file is an XML file that can be modified to adjust the names of the classes, properties, and columns. Once the metadata is extracted to the XML file, we can use the following command to generate classes based on the metadata rather than going back to the database again:

```
SqlMetal /namespace:LinqInAction /code:Common.cs
/language:csharp LiaMetadata.xml
```

Regardless of how we arrive at our final code, the generated code uses the same basic patterns. Go ahead and run the first SqlMetal command. Open the Common.cs file in Visual Studio and explore the generated code. The file can be broken down into the following sections:

- DataContext
  - Partial method declarations for custom logic on insert, update, and delete for each table
  - Overloaded constructors
  - Table accessors
  - Stored procedure and function implementations
- Table classes
  - Change notification event args
  - Private fields
  - Partial method declarations for change notification
  - Constructors
  - Public properties with attribute mapping
  - Properties for associated tables
  - Change notification events
- Classes for object types returned by stored procedures and functions

NOTE Partial methods are a new language feature that allows you to insert method stubs that the generated code can optionally call if they are implemented. We'll discuss this more fully in chapter 8.

The Common.cs file contains a number of class definitions. The first class encapsulates the `DataContext` that represents the connection to the database. It also includes methods to access each of the tables and other database objects.

Following the `DataContext` class, the generated file includes class definitions for each table in the database. Unlike the simplistic class definitions we've used thus far, the generated classes have more business functionality. Each class is defined as a partial class. In chapter 8, we'll look at extending this functionality to add custom business logic.

The table definitions also contain built-in functionality to manage robust change tracking. When any property's values are changed, the generated code fires change notification events and calls partial methods that will be called if they are implemented. The table classes also offer accessors and tracking of related child objects.

Following the table definitions, SqlMetal generates classes to represent the result types for the various stored procedures and functions. These classes are used as the return types of the function declarations established in the custom `DataContext` class.

SqlMetal is great if we want to regenerate our entire database model into a single class file. It can even be included as part of a continuous integration practice by scripting it into a custom MSBuild action. The tool does not give the flexibility to pick and choose which elements will be generated. If there are relationships that aren't included in the database implementation, including table relationships beyond primary key-foreign key relationships that can't be predefined in the database, they won't be scripted as part of the SqlMetal implementation. Also, using SqlMetal to directly generate the entities from the database will be restricted to the names defined in your tables and columns. An intermediary database markup language (DBML) file is required to specify mapping changes as necessary. Perhaps the biggest hindrance for SqlMetal is that it's not a flexible, graphical mapping tool. Visual Studio 2008 comes with a visual designer to help bridge this gap.

7.1.4 *The LINQ to SQL Designer*

To help developers visually model their data mappings, Visual Studio provides an integrated designer. This designer allows developers to drag and drop objects from their database or manually add conceptual models and visually manage the mappings. Although some expert programmers may shun designers, the tools can often assist not only in seeing a snapshot of the model, but also in helping to learn a new technology. If we're unsure how to map a specific data relationship, we can try using the design tool. We can always go back and tweak the generated code as long as we don't plan on regenerating it.

Let's try using the designer and see what it produces. To begin, right-click the project in the Solution Explorer and select Add, then New Item. From the list of supplied templates, locate the one named LINQ to SQL Classes. Change the name to Lia.dbml and click the Add button. You'll now be presented with a blank design surface.

With the LINQ to SQL designer visible, open the Server Explorer. If the listing of data connections doesn't already include our lia database, add it by right-clicking on the Data Connections node in the Server Explorer and selecting Add Connection. In the connection wizard, supply the appropriate values for the server name and database name and click OK to add the connection.

Once the database is included in the Data Connections node, expand the tables for the lia database. Select all of the tables by left-clicking the first one and then holding down the Shift key and left-clicking each of the others. With all of the tables selected, drag them onto the middle of the design surface. The designer will interrogate the tables and their relationships, adding them to the design surface.

The designer is fully editable. From the toolbox, we can drag and drop new `Class` and `Association` items. Removing items is done by selecting them and pressing the Delete key. We can also move any of our entities around on the design surface to provide a more coherent representation of our data. Figure 7.1 shows a structured representation of our lia database after we've rearranged the classes and associations.

In figure 7.1, we show several regions that are used with the designers. In the upper-left corner, we show the Server Explorer. We can drag server objects onto the main area in the middle, which includes the method pane. This main area in the center is where we can visually design our class structures and mappings. The design surface is divided into two halves. The left side allows us to graphically

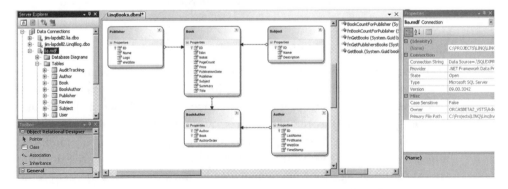

Figure 7.1 Mapping the LINQinAction database using the LINQ to SQL designer tool

design our class relationships, similar to using the Class Designer introduced with Visual Studio 2005. On the right side is the method pane, where we can work with our stored procedures and table-defined functions.

The toolbox is in the lower-left corner. When the designer is visible, we can add classes, associations, and inheritance relationships. At this point, the designer surface includes classes (boxes) and associations (arrows). In chapter 8, we'll add some inheritance as well.

On the right side, we show the context-sensitive property window, which should be familiar. If we need to modify the mapping structures, we do it in the designer or the property window. In this case, we've changed the Book's PubDate column to a property called PublicationDate by setting the Name property for that item. By changing it in the designer, the changes will be retained whenever we regenerate the classes with subsequent changes we make in the designer.

Once we're happy with our modeling view, we can save it and the associated classes will be generated. The designer consists of three files: an XML-based meta-data file (Lia.dbml) specifying how the classes will be generated, another XML file containing visual layout information on the designer surface (Lia.dbml.layout), and the actual generated classes in a single file (Lia.designer.cs). By default, the diagram and designer files are hidden by the Solution Explorer. However, clicking the Show All Files option in the Solution Explorer will expose them. The designer file contains the actual partial class definitions, similar to the code file we generated previously with the SqlMetal tool.

Look at the generated code and use it as a learning tool for creating your own classes by hand. However, resist the temptation to modify the code in the code behind designer file directly. Modifications to the code in the designer file, including adding new tables and associations, will be overwritten if unrelated changes in the actual design surface are made. Instead, try to limit modifying the objects to the graphical designer by using the property window or directly in the DBML file.

So far, this chapter has explored the mapping options. We can do it manually with attributes or XML. If we're not comfortable doing it manually or want to reduce the amount of redundant typing needed to establish the classes, we can use a command-line tool or a visual designer. The command-line tool offers a mechanism to generate the entire database mapping, but it doesn't offer the ability to take parts of the database or customize the mappings for particular business entity needs. The designer gives an easy snapshot of just the pertinent portions of the database and allows for customization. The designer does not offer any easy method to regenerate the classes when the database schema changes. Manually dropping and re-creating the table(s) in question is the current solution.

SqlMetal does offer the option of incorporating it into a regular build process. By using SqlMetal to construct the metadata (DBML) file and modifying that manually as necessary, it can generate your class definitions directly from the DBML file as part of the regular build process and thus achieve the best of both worlds.

7.2 Translating query expressions to SQL

In this chapter, we're attempting to pull back the covers and expose the core of LINQ to SQL. So far, we've peeled back the outer layer by exploring the mapping options. We have to get through some more layers before we can truly understand LINQ. One of the layers we can pull back relatively easily is the query expressions. Since the LINQ querying functionality is built around extending types that implement IEnumerable<T>, all we need is for our EntitySets and Tables to implement IEnumerable<T>.

Naturally, EntitySet<T> and Table<T> do implement IEnumerable<T>. However, if that were as far as they went, all of the querying functionality would be performed on the client, including filtering and sorting. We need a way to advance to a more specialized implementation if we want to translate our expressions to the server. Enter an interface that extends the IEnumerable<T> model called IQueryable<T>.

7.2.1 IQueryable

One of the biggest advantages LINQ to SQL has over LINQ to Objects is the ability to evaluate query expressions and translate them into another format. In order to accomplish this, the objects need to expose additional information regarding the structure of the query. All of the query expressions in LINQ to Objects are built to be able to extend IEnumerable<T>. However, IEnumerable<T> only offers the ability to iterate over *data*. It doesn't include information that would allow us to easily analyze the query's *definition* in order to accomplish the necessary translation. The .NET Framework 3.5 adds a new interface that extends IEnumerable and does include the necessary information—the IQueryable interface. Figure 7.2 shows the relationship between IQueryable and IEnumerable and their generic counterparts.

IQueryable requires the implementing class to inherit IEnumerable. In addition, it requires the class to contain three other pieces of information—the ElementType that it contains, an Expression that represents the actions to be taken, and a Provider that implements the IQueryProvider generic interface.

By containing an interface implementation, IQueryable supports creating additional provider models for other data sources, including specific SQL flavors for databases other than SQL Server. The provider takes the information contained by

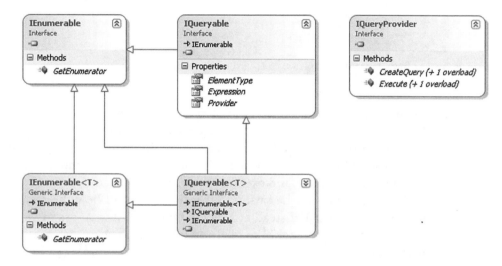

Figure 7.2 Object model for the IQueryable interface

the IQueryable expression and performs the heavy work of translating the structure into an expression that can be consumed. The translation is done by CreateQuery. The Execute method consumes the query that was created.

The Expression property contains the definition of the method. To help understand the difference, let's consider the case of the following query.

```
var query = books.Where(book => book.Price>30);
```

If the books object only implemented IEnumerable<T>, the compiler would translate it into a standard static method call similar to the following:

```
IEnumerable<Book> query =
  System.Linq.Enumerable.Where<Book>(
    delegate(Book book){return book.Price > 30M;});
```

However if the Books object implements IQueryable<T>, the compiler would retain the steps used to create the result as an expression tree (listing 7.3):

Listing 7.3 Query expressed as expressions

```
LinqBooksDataContext context = new LinqBooksDataContext();

var bookParam = Expression.Parameter(typeof(Book), "book");

var query =
  context.Books.Where<Book>(Expression.Lambda<Func<Book, bool>>
    (Expression.GreaterThan(
```

```
Expression.Property(
  bookParam,
  typeof(Book).GetProperty("Price")),
Expression.Constant(30M, typeof(decimal?))),
new ParameterExpression[] { bookParam }));
```

By retaining the steps that were used to create the query, IQueryable's provider implementation can translate the language construct into a format understood by the underlying data source. Also, we can compositionally create and extend the query constructs by adding more functionality (ordering, grouping, aggregating, paging) and then evaluate and execute the results all at once.

At this point, you may be saying, "Okay, I understand how the compiler can know to use LINQ to SQL instead of LINQ to Objects, but what are the expression things you keep mentioning?" I'm glad you asked, as they are the next layer that we must strip away.

7.2.2   *Expression trees*

Expression trees supply the working pieces of LINQ to SQL with the information necessary to work. We introduced expression trees in section 3.5. In section 5.1.3, we demonstrated how to dynamically create expressions and add them to the trees to build a query dynamically.

In contrast to our previous explorations, with LINQ to SQL we take existing expression trees and examine them branch by branch in order to translate our query expressions to a syntax understood by the database. There have been other efforts to make database access more generic so that the same query syntax can be applied to multiple database engines, even though the engines may process the query differently. Often these solutions rely on taking queries as strings and applying a number of string manipulations to convert one string representation into another.

Unlike these other query translation systems, LINQ to SQL distinguishes itself by translating the query expressions into expression trees. By retaining the expressions, we can enhance the queries by adding to them compositionally, keep the queries strongly typed, provide better IDE integration, and retain the necessary metadata. Best of all, we don't have to worry about parsing a string representation of our intent. The expression trees allow us to use similar heuristics that are implemented by the language compilers themselves.

Let's see what happens if we apply this concept to our earlier IQueryable example. In this case, let's focus on the expressions in the example.

```
LinqBooksDataContext context = new LinqBooksDataContext();

var bookParam = Expression.Parameter(typeof(Book), "book");

var query =
  context.Books.Where<Book>(Expression.Lambda<Func<Book, bool>>
    (Expression.GreaterThan(
      Expression.Property(
        bookParam,
        typeof(Book).GetProperty("Price")),
      Expression.Constant(30M, typeof(decimal?))),
    new ParameterExpression[] { bookParam }));
```

By highlighting our expression types, we can see that we have the following kinds of expressions: *Lambda, GreaterThan, Property, Parameter, Constant.* Each of these expression types can be broken down into more granular portions to encapsulate more information. For example, the `GreaterThan` expression is actually a `BinaryExpression` that takes two parts, a left side and a right side. With this, we can compare the value from the left side to see if it is `GreaterThan` the value on the right side. By breaking the expression down, we can then generalize the analysis and allow for variations in the left and right portions. In this example, the left value is the book's price and the right side is the constant value of 30. Figure 7.3 shows a graphical representation of the full expression tree.

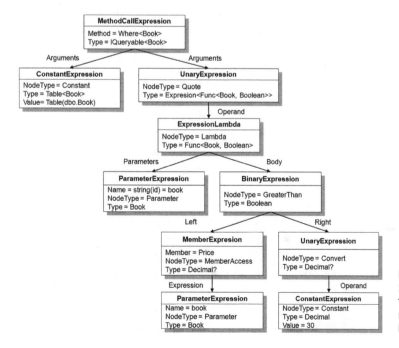

Figure 7.3
`ExpressionTree`
`Visualizer`
representation of the book query

In the figure, we can see that more information is available about the method than was evident in the compiler representation from the `IQueryable` example.[1] Starting at the top, we can see that the `Where MethodCallExpression` takes two arguments, the `ConstantExpression` that contains the source of the data and a `UnaryExpression` that contains the function we'll apply. Because the data context maintains a reference to the metadata information including the mapping (generated from attributes or XML), we can translate the object representation into terms that the database understands.

Looking further down the expression tree, we can see how additional nodes are inserted when applying the `GreaterThan BinaryExpression`. When applying the `GreaterThan` operator on CLR types, we need to compare similar types. Thus, we need to convert the `ConstantExpression` into a nullable `Decimal` type in order to compare it with the data type in the underlying book's `Price` property. However, this additional step is not necessary when we issue a SQL statement to the database.

So, how does LINQ to SQL take all of this information and translate it to the database? When we first try to iterate over the results of our `IQueryable<T>` type, the entire `Expression` value is passed to its assigned `Provider`. The provider then uses a Visitor pattern to walk the expression tree identifying expression types that it knows how to handle, such as `Where` and `GreaterThan`. Additionally, it walks the expression tree from the bottom up to identify nodes that don't need to be evaluated, like lifting the constant to a nullable type. The provider constructs a parallel expression tree that more closely matches the SQL implementation.

Once the expressions are parsed, the provider constructs the resulting SQL statement, substituting the appropriate mappings to translate the objects into table and column names taken from the attributes or XML mapping source. Once all of the pieces are put together, the resulting SQL statement can be sent to the database. The resulting values are then used to populate the necessary object collection, again using the mapping information as appropriate.

Performing the translation from the expression tree to a provider-specific implementation increases in complexity as we add more functions to the tree. It would be impossible to cover all of the possible query permutations in this book. If you're interested in pursuing this further, Matt Warren, one of the original architects of LINQ to SQL, has a detailed explanation demonstrating how to implement an `IQueryable` provider in a blog series starting with http://blogs.msdn.com/mattwar/archive/2007/07/30/linq-building-an-iqueryable-provider-part-i.aspx.

---

[1] The LINQ samples at http://msdn2.microsoft.com/en-us/bb330936.aspx include an expression tree visualizer project that can evaluate an expression tree and display it in a treeview control.

Additionally, we'll dig deeper with the expression trees at the end of this book, when we investigate extending LINQ to use a web service provided by Amazon. For now, the important thing to take away is to understand the difference between LINQ to Objects and LINQ to SQL and how the `IQueryable` interface can be used to perform the key translations that make the technology work.

So far we've shown how LINQ to SQL knows how to map the data to classes. We also have shown how it translates our query expressions into a syntax the database understands. By combining these features, the .NET 3.5 Framework has provided a powerful querying functionality. As we demonstrated in chapter 6, LINQ to SQL is not limited to only viewing data. It also maintains information necessary to persist our changes back to the database. Let's continue our look under the covers by seeing what happens to our objects in their life cycle after we fetch them.

7.3 The entity life cycle

If LINQ to SQL were limited to mapping data between relational data and objects, it would represent yet another in a long line of object-relational mapping solutions. As we've already seen, LINQ offers the capability to construct strongly typed queries directly within the language. Beyond that, the framework includes support to manage object changes and to optimize the database interaction based on those values.

The `DataContext` object continues to play a pivotal role in the entity's life cycle. As we've already seen, the `DataContext` manages the connection to the database. In addition, it evaluates the mappings and translates the expression trees into consumable structures. If we were only concerned with viewing data, the mapping and translation services would be sufficient for our needs. The life cycle would end the moment we fetched the objects.

As applications work with the results of queries, they typically view the data and make changes. We need a mechanism for tracking the changes that are made and maintaining those values until they are no longer needed. Additionally, we need to retain the changes so that we can commit them to the database. To handle the rest of the object's life cycle, the `DataContext` also manages references to the retrieved objects. It watches as changes are made to them by tracking the retrieved object's identities and the changed values. Figure 7.4 illustrates the services offered by the `DataContext`.

The life cycle begins when we first read a value from the database. Prior to passing the resulting object on to the consuming application code, the `DataContext` retains a reference to the object. An identity management service tracks the

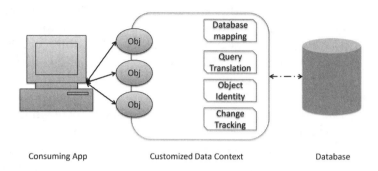

Figure 7.4 `DataContext` **services to maintain the object life cycle between the application and database**

object in a list indexed by the identity designated in the mapping. By retaining this value, we can refer back to the object based on its object identity.

Each time we query values from the database, the `DataContext` checks with the identity management service to see if an object with the same identity has already been returned in a previous query. If so, the `DataContext` will return the value stored in the internal cache rather than remapping the row to the table. By retaining the original value, we can allow clients to make changes to their copy of the data without regard for changes that other users have made. We won't worry about concurrency issues until the changes are submitted.

You may expect that if the context is caching the returned values, separate database queries will not be issued each time you request information. Assuming you don't prefetch your results using the `ToList` or similar extension methods, the database *will* be queried each time. The distinction here is that if the context is already aware of the object, only the identifying column(s) will be used. The additional columns will be ignored.

There are a couple of instances where the object identity implementation may catch you off guard. Using the `Single` extension method is an exception to this caching behavior. With `Single`, the internal cache is checked first. If the requested object is not in the cache, the database will be queried.

Additionally, you may expect that an item inserted into or removed from a table will be available for querying. Since the database is hit and only items that the database knows about are returned, objects added or removed using `InsertOnSubmit` or `DeleteOnSubmit` are not included in the results until they are actually submitted. This is the key reason why the xxxOnSubmit methods were used instead of the typical `IList` method names. The at times counterintuitive behavior of the object identity is important to understand as we use LINQ to change data.

7.3.1 *Tracking changes*

As we make changes to our objects, the `DataContext` maintains both the original value of that property and the newly changed value by a change tracking service. By retaining both the original and new values, we can optimize the submission back to the database and only update the changed records. In listing 7.4, we establish two different `DataContext` objects. Each of them manages its own set of object identities and change tracking.

Listing 7.4   Identity management and change tracking

```
LinqBooksDataContext context1 = new LinqBooksDataContext();      ❶
LinqBooksDataContext context2 = new LinqBooksDataContext();

context1.Log = Console.Out;      ❷
context2.Log = Console.Out;

Guid Id = new Guid("92f10ca6-7970-473d-9a25-1ff6cab8f682");

Subject editingSubject =         ❸
    context1.Subjects.Where(s => s.ID == Id).SingleOrDefault();

ObjectDumper.Write(editingSubject);
ObjectDumper.Write(context2.Subjects.Where(s => s.ID == Id));

editingSubject.Description = @"Testing update";      ❹

ObjectDumper.Write(context1.Subjects.Where(s => s.ID == Id));
ObjectDumper.Write(context2.Subjects.Where(s => s.ID == Id));
```

As we did in listing 7.3, we begin by setting up our two data context objects ❶. We use two contexts for the purpose of this example to simulate two separate users. Each context manages the identity and change tracking services separately. In this example, we retrieve the subject that corresponds to a given `Guid`. In order to demonstrate the identity management, we fetch the same record from our database in two separate contexts. We also include logging ❷ for each context to output the results to the console (or output) window to prove that we're actually requesting information from the database.

We fetch the `editingSubject` from the first context and display the values in both the `editingSubject` and the database in the second context ❸. As shown in table 7.4, the output for both values should be identical. We then change the description on the editing subject, but we don't commit the change to the database ❹. At this point, the change is only retained in memory via the change tracking service of the `context1` instance. `Context2` has no knowledge of the change.

Table 7.4 State of values returned by queries before and after changes

Action	Context1	Context2	Database
Value returned from original query	Original	Original	Original
Make change and requery	Changed	Original	Original

When we output the results by reissuing the original query, we now see that the description returned by the query on `context1` returns our new description value, but the one using `context2` still returns the original value. Remember, since each context mimics a different user, this would mean that two users would see different representations of the data. If we were to check the value in the database, we would see that it still retains the original values as well.

It is important to realize the difference between the value stored in memory for each context object and the value stored in the database. The results of the query on the second context object are not surprising. However, what is not expected is that requerying the first context returns the object from the identity tracking service instead of a new object from the database. Actually, the second context is returning the object it has retained as well, but since we haven't made any change to the object tracked by the second context, it appears to be identical to the values stored in the database for that row.

In addition to tracking changes in column-mapped properties, the change-tracking service also monitors changes in object associations. Thus if we were to move a comment from one book to another, the change tracking would maintain that change in memory until we actually submit the change back to the database.

7.3.2 Submitting changes

So far, all of the changes we've made have been retained in memory and not persisted to the database. It only appears that the changes have been applied on subsequent queries due to the identity tracking on the `DataContext`. As we demonstrated in chapter 6, submitting changes to the database is done with a single call of `SubmitChanges` on the context. When `SubmitChanges` is called, the context compares the original values of the objects that it is tracking with the current values. If these differ, the context packages up the changes and creates the necessary query string to be executed by the database.

Assuming no conflicts occurred in the update and the appropriate records are updated, the context flushes its list of changes. If there are problems, the changes are rolled back in the database based on the concurrency management selected. Listing 7.5 extends the previous example by actually saving the data to the database.

Listing 7.5 Submitting changes with identity and change tracking management

```
LinqBooksDataContext context1 = new LinqBooksDataContext();
LinqBooksDataContext context2 = new LinqBooksDataContext();

Guid Id = new Guid("92f10ca6-7970-473d-9a25-1ff6cab8f682");

Subject editingSubject =
    context1.Subjects.Where(s => s.ID == Id).SingleOrDefault();

Console.WriteLine("Before Change:");
ObjectDumper.Write(editingSubject);
ObjectDumper.Write(context2.Subjects.Where(s => s.ID == Id));

editingSubject.Description = @"Testing update";

Console.WriteLine("After Change:");
ObjectDumper.Write(context1.Subjects.Where(s => s.ID == Id));
ObjectDumper.Write(context2.Subjects.Where(s => s.ID == Id));

context1.SubmitChanges();               ❶

Console.WriteLine("After Submit Changes:");
ObjectDumper.Write(context1.Subjects.Where(s => s.ID == Id));    ❷
ObjectDumper.Write(context2.Subjects.Where(s => s.ID == Id));

LinqBooksDataContext context3 = new LinqBooksDataContext();     ❸
ObjectDumper.Write(context3.Subjects.Where(s => s.ID == Id));
```

This results in the following output:

```
Before Change:
ID=92f10ca6-7970-473d-9a25-1ff6cab8f682
Name=Novel
Description=Initial Value
ObjectId=448c7362-ca4e-4199-9e4f-0a0d029b9c8d

ID=92f10ca6-7970-473d-9a25-1ff6cab8f682
Name=Novel
Description=Initial Value
ObjectId=5040810a-eca9-4850-bcf6-09e42837fe92

After Change:
ID=92f10ca6-7970-473d-9a25-1ff6cab8f682
```

```
Name=Novel
Description=Testing Update
ObjectId=448c7362-ca4e-4199-9e4f-0a0d029b9c8d

ID=92f10ca6-7970-473d-9a25-1ff6cab8f682
Name=Novel
Description=Initial Value
ObjectId=5040810a-eca9-4850-bcf6-09e42837fe92

After Submit Changes:
Id=92f10ca6-7970-473d-9a25-1ff6cab8f682
Name=Novel
Description=Testing update
ObjectId=bc2d5231-ed4e-4447-9027-a7f42face624

Id=92f10ca6-7970-473d-9a25-1ff6cab8f682
Name=Novel
Description=Original Value
ObjectId=18792750-c170-4d62-9a97-3a7444514b0b

Id=92f10ca6-7970-473d-9a25-1ff6cab8f682
Name=Novel
Description=Testing update
ObjectId=207eb678-0c29-479b-b844-3aa28d9572ac
```

Listing 7.5 begins just as the previous example did. Up until we call Submit-Changes on the first context ❶, any changes we made were retained only in memory. Calling SubmitChanges on context1 commits the changes to the database and flushes the change tracking on context1. Following SubmitChanges, we issue the same LINQ query on context1 and context2 ❷. Additionally, for the purposes of this example, we create a new third context that is oblivious to the identity and change tracking of the other two contexts ❸. The final three queries are identical except for the context that is issuing the request. In Table 7.5 we summarize the results before and after submitting the changes.

Table 7.5   Values returned before and after submitting changes from each DataContext

Action	Description1	Description2	Description3	Id1	Id2	Id3
Initial fetch	Original	Original	n/a	Guid1	Guid2	n/a
After change	Changed	Original	n/a	Guid1	Guid2	n/a
After commit	Changed	Original	Changed	Guid1	Guid2	Guid3

In order to explicitly identify the objects, we've added a new Guid property called ObjectId. The value of this column is assigned as part of the Subject's constructor. This way, the value should change each time we have a different object instance. In the resulting output, compare the values in each object before changes, after changes, and after submitting. Notice that the `ObjectId` in the subject returned by first context is retained for the life of the context. Even after we submit changes, `context1` continues to track the same object through the identity-tracking service. To prove that the value actually exists in the database following the submit changes, we compare the results from `context1` and the local context instance (Description3 and Id3). Notice that the fetched values are identical, but the `ObjectId` differs between these objects. Also notice that the subject returned from `context2` is still maintaining the values from its identity service.

It is important to realize how your objects work in relation to the data context. The `DataContext` is intended to be a short-lived object. We need to be aware of the context(s) we're using and how the identity- and change-tracking services work in order to avoid unexpected results. When only fetching data, we can create the context as we fetch the values and then throw it away. In that case, we can optimize the context by setting the `ObjectTrackingEnabled` property to false. This increases performance by disabling the change- and identity-tracking services, but disables the ability to update the changes.

If we need to be able to update the data, be aware of the context's scope and manage it appropriately. In Windows applications, it may be acceptable to retain a context as changes are made, but realize the performance and memory overhead that come with retaining all objects and the changed values. The intended usage pattern for LINQ to SQL is as a *unit of work*, which uses the following pattern: Query – Report – Edit – Submit – Dispose. As soon as we no longer need to maintain changes on an object, we should clean up the context and create a new one.

7.3.3 *Working with disconnected data*

Occasionally, working in a connected environment with the context is either inadvisable or impossible. This situation typically occurs when updating values from an ASP.NET page, web service, or other similar disconnected model, including Workflow (WF) and Windows Communication Foundation (WCF). When fetching records in the disconnected model, we need to encapsulate the results. We cannot cache the context or transmit it to the disconnected user.

Since the object must be divorced from the context, we can no longer rely on the context's change-tracking or identity-management services. Transmission to the client is limited to simple objects (or an XML representation of the objects). Managing changes becomes a bigger challenge in the disconnected model.

To support the disconnected model, LINQ to SQL offers two alternatives to apply changes. If you're just adding a row to a table, you can call the InsertOn-Submit[2] method on the appropriate DataContext's table object. Change tracking is not necessary for new records, only for changing existing ones, thus calling InsertOnSubmit works fine since we don't need to worry about conflicts with existing records.

However, if we need to change an existing record, we need to associate the changes with the existing record. Several options exist to attach the changed object to the context. The easiest and preferred method is to use the Attach method to introduce the record to a DataContext as if it were loaded via a normal query. The example in listing 7.6 uses the Attach method to connect an object to a new DataContext.

Listing 7.6 Updating records in a disconnected environment

```
public void UpdateSubject(Subject cachedSubject)
{
  LinqBooksDataContext context = new LinqBooksDataContext();
  context.Subjects.Attach(cachedSubject);          ❶
  cachedSubject.Name = @"Testing update";          ❷
  context.SubmitChanges();
}
```

In this example, we begin with the existing, unchanged object. This object could have been cached in an ASP.NET Session object or supplied as a parameter of our method. We connect the object to the DataContext using the Attach method ❶. Once it is attached, the context's change- and identity-tracking service can monitor the changes we're going to apply. Any subsequent changes ❷ will be tracked by the change-tracking service and updated accordingly. Remember that the object must be attached *prior* to making the changes or else the change tracking will not be aware of the changes.

If you try to attach a value already updated, as is typical in a web service scenario, you can't just attach this already-changed version unless the object has some special characteristics. If you implement a TimeStamp column in your object, as we did with the Author object, you can attach the author object using the overloaded Attach method as follows:

```
context.Authors.Attach(cachedAuthor, True)
```

---

[2] LINQ releases through the beta cycle used the Add and Remove methods on the table objects. When Visual Studio 2008 was finished, the names for these methods were changed to InsertOnSubmit and RemoveOnSubmit. Earlier documentation may still refer to the earlier API.

The second parameter indicates that the object should be considered dirty and forces the context to add the object to the list of changed objects. If you don't have the liberty of enhancing your database schema to include timestamp columns and you need to use `Attach` like this, you can set the `UpdateCheck` property on the mapping so that the values are not checked. In both of these cases, all properties will be updated, regardless of whether or not they have been changed.

If you retain a copy of the original object (either via a cache or by keeping a copy inside the entity itself), attach the new object by using the `Attach` method and including both the changed version along with the original version:

```
context.Subjects.Attach(changedSubject, originalSubject);
```

In this case, only the changed columns will be included in the `Update` clause, rather than an update being forced on all columns. The original values will be used in the `Where` clause for concurrency checking.

If you can't take advantage of any of these `Attach` scenarios, you can replace the `originalSubject` with one newly fetched from the database as part of the update transaction as shown in listing 7.7.

Listing 7.7 Updating a disconnected object that has already been changed

```
public static void UpdateSubject(Subject changingSubject)
{
    LinqBooksDataContext context = new LinqBooksDataContext();
    Subject existingSubject = context.Subjects        ❶
                         .Where(s => s.ID == changingSubject.ID)
                         .FirstOrDefault<Subject>();
    existingSubject.Name = changingSubject.Name;      ❷
    existingSubject.Description = changingSubject.Description;
    context.SubmitChanges();                          ❸
}
```

In the case of objects that have already been updated, simply attaching them to the `DataContext` will fail. No values would be flagged as needing to be updated, as the change-tracking service will have been unaware of the changes. Here, we need to fetch the record from the database based on the ID of the object that we're trying to update ❶. Then, we need to update each property as necessary ❷. If the values in the properties are the same, the change-tracking service will continue to exclude those properties from needing to be updated. When we call `Submit-Changes`, only the properties and objects that have changed will be submitted. ❸

Be aware that the object we're updating may have been based on values that have been subsequently changed in the database. In order to manage concurrency tracking, our best option is to supply a timestamp that indicates the database version when originally fetching the record. If adding the timestamp column is not an option, we can retain a copy of the original values or a hash of the original values. We can then compare the appropriate values and manage the concurrency ourselves.

The `DataContext`'s object identity and change-tracking services play a crucial role in the object's life cycle. If we simply need to read the values, we can set the `DataContext` to a read-only mode by setting the `ObjectTrackingEnabled` to false, thus bypassing these services. However, if we need to be able to change and persist the values, tracking the objects and changes is critical.

7.4   Summary

On the surface, LINQ to SQL allows for easy access to querying and updating abilities without the need to manually define the database access. Under the covers, it offers a powerful set of mapping structures, expression parsing, and entity management. You can use the technology without fully understanding how everything works under the covers. The more you understand how it works, the less likely you are to find yourself experiencing unexpected results. If nothing else, it is important to understand how the `DataContext` manages the object identity and change management so that you make sure you update the correct information.

At this point, we've covered the core concepts behind LINQ to SQL and pulled back the covers to get an understanding of how it works. In the next chapter, we'll continue to examine LINQ to SQL by exploring some more advanced functionality. By the time we're done, you should have a full tool belt for using LINQ with the SQL Server family of databases.

Advanced LINQ to SQL features

8

This chapter covers:

- Handling concurrency
- Working directly with the database using pass-through queries, stored procedures, and user defined functions
- Improving the business tier with compiled queries, partial classes, partial methods, and object inheritance
- Comparison of LINQ to SQL with LINQ to Entities

In the last couple of chapters, we discussed the core components of working with relational data using LINQ to SQL. We saw how the mapping metadata combined with the `IQueryable` interface and expression trees to enable us to apply the same LINQ to Objects query expressions to relational data stores. By leveraging common APIs, we can eliminate vast amounts of data plumbing code and focus more directly on the business needs.

In this chapter, we're going to extend the basic concepts and see some of LINQ to SQL's more advanced features. We'll begin by expanding on our discussion of the object life cycle, focusing on concurrency and transaction issues. We'll continue by exploring how we can work more directly with the database and take advantage of some of the more specific functionality offered by SQL Server. Moving beyond the data tier, we'll look at options LINQ to SQL gives us to customize the business tier, including precompiling query expressions, using partial classes, and polymorphism via inheritance. We'll conclude by briefly exploring the upcoming Entity Framework as an alternative to LINQ to SQL for accessing relational data.

8.1   Handling simultaneous changes

When designing systems for a single user, the developer doesn't need to worry about how changes that one person makes affect other users. In actuality, it is rare for a production system to be used by only one user, as they typically grow and take on lives of their own. As the system grows to support multiple users, we need to take into account the conflicts that arise when two users try to change the same record at the same time. In general, there are two strategies to handle this: *pessimistic concurrency*, which locks a second user out of changing a record until the first user has released a lock, and *optimistic concurrency*, which allows two users to make changes. In the case of optimistic concurrency, the application designer needs to decide whether to retain the first user's values, retain the last update, or somehow merge the values from both users. Each strategy offers different advantages and disadvantages.

8.1.1   Pessimistic concurrency

Prior to .NET, many applications maintained open connections to the database. With these systems, developers frequently wrote applications that would retrieve a record in the database and retain a lock on that record to prevent other users from making changes to it at the same time. This kind of locking is called pessimistic concurrency. Small Windows-based applications built with this pessimistic concurrency worked with few issues. However, as those systems needed to scale to larger user bases, the locking mechanisms caused systems to bog down.

At the same time the scalability issues started emerging, many systems began moving from client-server architectures toward more stateless, web-based architectures in order to alleviate deployment challenges. The demands of stateless web applications required that they no longer rely on long-held pessimistic locks.

As an attempt to keep developers from falling into the scalability and locking traps posed by pessimistic concurrency models, the .NET Framework was designed to target the disconnected nature of web-based applications. The data API for .NET, ADO.NET, was created without the capability to hold cursors to the tables and thus eliminated automated pessimistic concurrency options. Applications could still be designed to add a "checked out" flag on a record that would be evaluated when subsequent attempts were made to access the same record. However, these checked out flags were frequently not reset, as it became difficult to determine when the user was no longer using it. Due to these issues, the pessimistic concurrency model began to unravel in the disconnected environment.

8.1.2 *Optimistic concurrency*

As a result of the problems encountered in a disconnected environment, an alternative strategy was typically used. The alternative, optimistic concurrency model allowed any user to make changes to their copy of the data. When the values were saved, the program would check the previous values to see if they were changed. If the values were unchanged, the record would be considered unlocked, thus the record would be saved. If there was a conflict, the program would need to know whether to automatically overwrite the previous changes, throw away the new changes, or somehow merge the changes.

The first half of determining optimistic concurrency is relatively simple. Without a concurrency check, the SQL statement to the database would consist of the following syntax: UPDATE TABLE SET [field = value] WHERE [Id = value]. To add optimistic concurrency, the WHERE clause would be extended to not only include the value of the ID column, but also compare the original values of each column in the table. Listing 8.1 demonstrates a sample SQL statement to check for optimistic concurrency on our running example's Book table.

> **Listing 8.1 SQL Update statement to perform optimistic concurrency on Book**

```
UPDATE dbo.Book
SET Title = @NewTitle,        ◁──┐  New
  Subject = @NewSubject,             values
  Publisher = @NewPublisher,
  PubDate = @NewPubDate,
  Price = @NewPrice,
```

```
   PageCount = @NewPageCount,
   Isbn = @NewIsbn,
   Summary = @NewSummary,
   Notes = @NewNotes                                          Compare
WHERE ID = @ID AND Title = @OldTitle AND    ◁──┘            original values
   Subject = @OldSubject AND
   Publisher = @OldPublisher AND
   PubDate = @PubDate AND
   Price = @Price AND
   PageCount = @PageCount AND
   Isbn = @OldIsbn AND
   Summary = @OldSummary AND
   Notes = @OldNotes
RETURN @@RowCount    ◁──── Update successful?
```

Using the code in listing 8.1, we attempt to update a record and check the Row-Count to see if the update succeeded. If it returns 1, we know that the original values did not change and the update worked. If it returns 0, we know that someone changed at least one of the values since they were last fetched, because we can't find a record that still has the same values we originally loaded. In this case, the record is not updated. At that point, we can inform the user that there was a conflict and handle the concurrency violation appropriately. As with the rest of LINQ to SQL, handling concurrency issues is built in.

Configuring classes to support optimistic concurrency is extremely easy. In fact, by establishing the table and column mappings, we're already set to use optimistic concurrency. When calling SubmitChanges, the DataContext will automatically implement optimistic concurrency. To demonstrate the SQL generated for a simple update, let's consider an example where we get the most expensive book in our table ❶ and attempt to discount it by 10% ❷. (See listing 8.2.)

Listing 8.2   Default concurrency implementation with LINQ to SQL

```
Ch8DataContext context = new Ch8DataContext()
Book mostExpensiveBook = (from book in context.Books        ❶
                          orderby book.Price descending
                          select book).First();

decimal discount = .1M;
mostExpensiveBook.Price -= mostExpensiveBook.Price * discount;      ❷

context.SubmitChanges();       ❸
```

This produces the SQL to select the book, as well as the following SQL to update:

```
UPDATE [dbo].[Book]
SET [Price] = @p8
FROM [dbo].[Book]
WHERE ([Title] = @p0) AND ([Subject] = @p1) AND ([Publisher] = @p2)
      AND ([PubDate] = @p3) AND ([Price] = @p4) AND ([PageCount] = @p5)
      AND ([Isbn] = @p6) AND ([Summary] IS NULL) AND ([Notes] IS NULL)
      AND ([ID] = @p7)
```

When SubmitChanges is called on the DataContext ❸, the Update statement is generated and issued to the server. If no matching record is found based on the previous values passed in the WHERE clause, the context will recognize that no records are affected as part of this statement. When no records are affected, a ChangeConflictException is thrown.

Depending on the situation, the number of parameters needed to implement optimistic concurrency can cause performance issues. In those cases, we can refine our mappings to identify only the fields necessary to ensure that the values didn't change. We can do this by setting the UpdateCheck attribute. By default, UpdateCheck is set to Always, which means that LINQ to SQL will always check this column for optimistic concurrency. As an alternative, we can set it to only check if the value changes (WhenChanged) or to never check (Never).

If we really want to draw on the power of the UpdateCheck attribute and have the ability to modify the table schema, we can add a RowVersion or TimeStamp column to each table. The database will automatically update the value of the Row-Version each time the row is changed. Concurrency checks only need to run on the combination of the version and ID columns. All other columns are set to UpdateCheck=Never and the database will assist with the concurrency checking. We used this scheme for the Author class mapping back in chapter 7. Listing 8.3 illustrates the revised Author class, applying the same change as we did in the previous example. Using the TimeStamp column, we can see a streamlined WHERE clause in the Update statement.

Listing 8.3 Optimistic concurrency with Authors using a timestamp column

```
Ch8DataContext context = new Ch8DataContext();
Author authorToChange = (context.Authors).First();

authorToChange.FirstName = "Jim";
authorToChange.LastName = "Wooley";

context.SubmitChanges();
```

This results in the following SQL: **Perform update**

```
UPDATE      [dbo].[Author]        ←──────┘
SET         [LastName] = @p2, [FirstName] = @p3
FROM        [dbo].[Author]
WHERE       ([ID] = @p0) AND ([TimeStamp] = @p1)


SELECT      [t1].[TimeStamp]      ←──── Get updated timestamp
FROM        [dbo].[Author] AS [t1]
WHERE       ((@@ROWCOUNT) > 0) AND ([t1].[ID] = @p4)
```

In addition to changing the standard optimistic concurrency by setting all fields to check always or using a timestamp, there are a couple of other concurrency models available. The first option is to simply ignore any concurrent changes and always update the records, allowing the last update to be accepted. In that case, set UpdateCheck to Never for all properties. Unless you can guarantee that concurrency is not an issue, this is not a recommended solution. In most cases, it is best to inform the user that there was a conflict and provide options to remedy the situation.

In some cases, it is fine to allow two users to make changes to different columns in the same table. For example, in wide tables, we may want to manage different sets of columns with different objects or contexts. In this case, set the UpdateCheck attribute to WhenChanged rather than Always.

This is not recommended in all cases, particularly when multiple fields contribute to a calculated total. For example, in a typical OrderDetail table, columns may appear for quantity, price, and total price. If a change was made in either the quantity or price, the total price will need to be changed. If one user changes the quantity while another changes the price, the total price would not be modified properly. This form of automatic merge concurrency management does have its place. Business demands should dictate if it is appropriate in any given situation.

With LINQ to SQL, concurrency checking can be set on a field-level basis. The framework was designed to provide the flexibility to allow for various customized implementations. The default behavior is to fully support optimistic concurrency. So far, we've identified how to recognize when there is a conflict. The second part of the equation is what we do with the knowledge that there was a concurrency exception.

8.1.3 Handling concurrency exceptions

In using the Always or WhenChanged options for UpdateCheck, it is inevitable that two users will modify the same values and cause conflicts. In those cases, the DataContext will raise a ChangeConflictException when the second user issues an `SubmitChanges` request. Because of the likelihood of running into an exception, we need to make sure we wrap the updates inside a structured exception-handling block.

Once an exception is thrown, several options to resolve the exception exist. The `DataContext` helps discover not only the object(s) that are in conflict, but also which properties are different between the original value, the changed value, and the current value in the database. In order to provide this level of information, we can specify the `RefreshMode` to determine whether the conflicting record is first refreshed from the database to determine the current values. Once we have the refreshed values, we can determine whether we want to retain the original values, the current database values, or our new values. If we want to take the last option and make sure our values are the ones that are retained, we resolve the change conflicts of the context object specifying that we want to keep the changes. Listing 8.4 illustrates a typical try-catch block to make sure our changes are retained.

> **Listing 8.4   Resolving change conflicts with `KeepChanges`**

```
try
{
    context.SubmitChanges(ConflictMode.ContinueOnConflict);
}
catch (ChangeConflictException)
{
    context.ChangeConflicts.ResolveAll(RefreshMode.KeepChanges);

    context.SubmitChanges();
}
```

If we use the `KeepChanges` option, we don't need to inspect the changed values. We assert that our values are correct and go ahead and force them into the appropriate row. This last-in-wins method can be potentially dangerous. Columns that we didn't update will be refreshed from the current value in the database.

If the business needs demand it, we could merge the changes with the new values from the database; simply change `RefreshMode` to `KeepCurrentValues`. This way, we'll incorporate the other user's changes into our record and add our changes. However, if both users changed the same column, the new value will overwrite the value that the first user updated.

To be safe, we can overwrite the values that the second user tried to change with the current values from the database. In that case, use `RefreshMode.OverwriteCurrentValues`. At this point, it would not be beneficial to submit the changes back to the database again, as there would be no difference between the current object and the values in the database. We would present the refreshed record to the user and have them make the appropriate changes again.

Depending on the number of changes that the user made, they may not appreciate having to reenter their data. Since `SubmitChanges` can update multiple records in a batch, the number of changes could be significant. To assist with this, the `SubmitChanges` method takes an overloaded value to indicate how we wish to proceed when a record is in conflict. We can either stop evaluating further records or collect a listing of objects that were conflicted. The `ConflictMode` enumeration specifies the two options: `FailOnFirstConflict` and `ContinueOnConflict`.

With the `ContinueOnConflict` option, we'll need to iterate over the conflicting options and resolve them using the appropriate `RefreshMode`. Listing 8.5 illustrates how to submit all of the nonconflicting records and then overwrite the unsuccessful records with the current values in the database.

Listing 8.5   Replacing the user's values with ones from the database

```
try
{
  context.SubmitChanges(ConflictMode.ContinueOnConflict);
}
catch (ChangeConflictException)
{
  context.ChangeConflicts.ResolveAll(RefreshMode.OverwriteCurrentValues);
}
```

With this method, we can at least submit some of the values and then prompt the user to reenter his information in the conflicting items. This could still cause some user resentment, as he would need to review all of the changes to see what records need to be changed.

A better solution would be to present the user with the records and fields that were changed. LINQ to SQL not only allows access to this information, but also supports the ability to view the current value, original value, and database value for the conflicting object. Listing 8.6 demonstrates using the `ChangeConflicts` collection of the `DataContext` to collect the details of each conflict.

Listing 8.6   Displaying conflict details

```
try
{
    context.SubmitChanges(ConflictMode.ContinueOnConflict);
}
```

```
catch (ChangeConflictException)
{
    var exceptionDetail =
        from conflict in context.ChangeConflicts      ❶
        from member in conflict.MemberConflicts       ❷
        select new
        {
                TableName = context.GetTableName(conflict.Object),
                MemberName = member.Member.Name,
                CurrentValue = member.CurrentValue.ToString(),
                DatabaseValue = member.DatabaseValue.ToString(),    ❸
                OriginalValue = member.OriginalValue.ToString()
        };
    ObjectDumper.Write(exceptionDetail);
}
```

Each item in the ChangeConflicts collection ❶ contains the object that conflicted as well as a MemberConflicts collection ❷. This collection contains information about the Member, CurrentValue, DatabaseValue, and OriginalValue ❸. Once we have this information, we can display it to the user in whatever method we choose.

Using this code, we can display details of the concurrency errors that the user creates. Consider the possibility where two users try to change the price of a book at the same time. If the first user were to raise the price by 2 dollars while a second tries to discount it by a dollar, what would happen? The first user to save the changes would have no problems. As the second user tries to commit her changes, a ChangeConflictException will be thrown. We could easily display the exceptionDetail list as shown in figure 8.1.

Once presented with the details of the conflicts, the second user can elect how she wants to resolve each record individually. The key point to realize is that the

	TableName	MemberName	CurrentValue	DatabaseValue	OriginalValue
▶	dbo.Book	Price	38.5000	41.5000	39.5000
	dbo.Book	Price	38.5000	41.5000	39.5000
	dbo.Book	Price	28.5500	31.5500	29.5500
	dbo.Book	Price	15.0000	18.0000	16.0000
	dbo.Book	Price	32.0000	35.0000	33.0000

Figure 8.1   Displaying the original, current, and database value to resolve concurrency exceptions

`DataContext` is more than a connection object. It maintains full change tracking and concurrency management by default. We have to do extra work to turn the optimistic concurrency options off.

In designing systems that allow for multiple concurrent users, we need to consider how to handle concurrency concerns. In most cases, it is not a matter of *if* a `ChangeConflictException` will be thrown. It is only a matter of *when*. By catching the exception, we can either handle it using one of the resolution modes or roll the entire transaction back. In the next section, we'll look at options for managing transactions within LINQ to SQL.

8.1.4   *Resolving conflicts using transactions*

As we were discussing concurrency options, we noted that updating the database with `SubmitChanges` could update a single record or any number of records (even across multiple tables). If we run into conflicts, we can decide how to handle the conflict. However, we didn't point out previously that if some effort is not made to roll back changes, any records that were successfully saved prior to the exception will be committed to the database. This could leave the database in an invalid state if some records are saved and others are not.

Why is it a bad thing to save some of the records and not others? Consider going to a computer store to purchase the components for a new computer. We pick up the motherboard, case, power supply, hard drives, and video card, and then head to the counter to check out. The astute salesperson notices the missing memory and processor. After looking around for a bit, he finds the store doesn't have a compatible processor. At this point, we're left with a decision: go ahead and purchase the pieces we picked out and hope to find the remaining pieces somewhere else, change the motherboard to one with a matching processor, or stop the purchase.

Now, consider that this computer is your database. The components are the records in the business objects that need to be updated and the salesperson is the `DataContext`. The salesperson noticing the problem can be compared to the `DataContext` throwing a `ChangeConflictException`. If we choose the first option (buy what we can now), we could use `ConflictMode.ContinueOnConflict` and then ignore the conflicts. Naturally, the `DataContext` needs to be told how to handle the conflicts before they arise. If we choose the third option (give up and go home), any changes would need to be rolled back (get your money back). If we choose the middle option, we would need to roll back the changes from the database, then decide what changes we need to make. Once the appropriate changes are made, we could try to submit the changes again.

LINQ to SQL offers three main mechanisms to manage transactions. In the first option, used by default, the `DataContext` will create and enlist in a transaction when `SubmitChanges` is called. This will roll back changes automatically depending on the selected `ConflictMode` option.

If we wish to manually maintain the transaction, the `DataContext` also offers the ability to use the transaction on the connection already maintained by the `DataContext`. In this case, we call `BeginTransaction` on `DataContext.Connection` before we try to submit the changes. After we submit the changes, we can either commit them or roll them back. Listing 8.7 demonstrates this alternative.

Listing 8.7 Managing the transaction through the `DataContext`

```
try
{
    context.Connection.Open();
    context.Transaction = context.Connection.BeginTransaction();
    context.SubmitChanges(ConflictMode.ContinueOnConflict);
    context.Transaction.Commit();
}
catch (ChangeConflictException)
{
    context.Transaction.Rollback();
}
```

The downside of managing the transactions directly through the `DataContext` is that it cannot span multiple connections or multiple `DataContext` objects. As a third option, the `System.Transactions.TransactionScope` object that was introduced with the .NET 2.0 Framework was specifically designed to seamlessly span connections. To use it, add a reference to the `System.Transactions` library.

This object will automatically scale the transaction based on the objects that it covers. If the scope only covers a single database call, it will use a simple database transaction. If it spans multiple classes with multiple connections, it will automatically scale up to an enterprise transaction. Additionally, the `TransactionScope` doesn't require us to explicitly begin the transaction or roll it back. The only thing you need to do is complete it. Listing 8.8 illustrates using the `Transaction-Scope` with LINQ to SQL.

Listing 8.8 Managing transactions with the `TransactionScope` object

```
using (System.Transactions.TransactionScope scope =
        new System.Transactions.TransactionScope())
{
```

```
    context.SubmitChanges(ConflictMode.ContinueOnConflict);
    scope.Complete();
}
```

Unlike the other transaction mechanisms, we don't need to wrap the code in a try-catch block solely to roll the transaction back. With the `TransactionScope`, the transaction will automatically get rolled back *unless* we call the `Complete` method. If an exception is thrown in `SubmitChanges`, the exception will bypass the `Complete` method. We don't need to explicitly roll the transaction back. It still needs to be wrapped in an exception-handling block, but the exception handling can be done closer to the user interface.

The true joy of the `TransactionScope` object is that it automatically scales based on the given context. It works equally well with local transactions and with heterogeneous sources. Because of the flexibility and scalability, using the `TransactionScope` object is the preferred method of handling transactions with LINQ to SQL.

Managing transactions and concurrency are important tasks that most applications need to consider. Even though LINQ to SQL provides baseline implementations of these important concepts, it allows the programmer to customize the implementation to refine it to the customized business needs. The customizations do not end with transactions and concurrency. They extend to a number of database-specific capabilities that we can work with. Let's continue by looking at some of these more advanced capabilities.

8.2 Advanced database capabilities

In many cases, the default mapping between tables and objects is fine for simple CRUD operations. But sometimes a direct relationship is not sufficient. In this section, we'll explore some of the additional options LINQ to SQL provides to customize your data access. In each case, the programming model dramatically reduces the amount of custom plumbing code. We'll start by looking at issuing statements directly to the database. We'll continue by looking at how we can call upon the programmatic options of SQL Server, including stored procedures and user-defined functions.

8.2.1 SQL pass-through: Returning objects from SQL queries

Although the querying functionality in LINQ presents us with a revolutionary way of working with data, there is a major downside to the concept. The object-based query structures need to be compiled. In cases of ad hoc reporting or other user-defined data access, we often need more flexible models. To achieve this end, LINQ to SQL offers the ability to send dynamic SQL statements directly to the database without the need to compile them. To use this, we only need a `DataContext` object. From it, we can call the `ExecuteQuery` method passing the SQL string we want to execute. In listing 8.9, we ask the user to supply the fields they want to include and concatenate that value to the end of the SQL statement. We then display the results.

Listing 8.9 Dynamic SQL pass-through

```
string searchName;
string sql = @"Select ID, LastName, FirstName, WebSite, TimeStamp " +
    "From dbo.Author " +
    "Where LastName = '" + searchName + "'";

IEnumerable<Author> authors = context.ExecuteQuery<Author>(sql);
```

The amount of data access code is greatly reduced as compared to standard ADO.NET. When using the `ExecuteQuery` method, the source of the data is not important. All that is important is that the column names returned by the `select` statement match the names of the properties in the class. As long as these values match, the pass-through query can return the strongly typed objects that we specify.

Since the entire query is weakly typed when working with pass-through queries, special care needs to be taken to validate the user-supplied values. In addition, we also need to check the syntax. In listing 8.9, if the user enters a value for the `SearchName` that is not a valid field name, the framework will throw an exception. Even worse, a malicious user could easily initiate a SQL injection attack. For example, consider the results that would be returned if the user enters the following string in the textbox: `Good' OR ''='`. In this case, we would effectively be returning all records where the author last name is "Good" *and* any records where an empty string equals an empty string. Since the second clause would always return true, all authors would be returned rather than just the requested author.

As an alternative, the pass-through query can be constructed using the same curly notation that is used by the `String.Format` method. Follow the SQL string with a list of parameters that will be used by the query. In this case, the values are added into the statement as parameters rather than relying on string concatenation. Listing 8.10 extends the previous example with a parameter array replacing the inline concatenation. Rather than performing a direct `String.Format` method, which would result in a concatenation, the `DataContext` translates the expression into a parameterized query. In this case, we can thwart users trying to inject commands into the query string.

Listing 8.10 Dynamic SQL pass-through with parameters

```
string searchName = "Good' OR ''='";

Ch8DataContext context = new Ch8DataContext();
string sql =
    @"Select ID, LastName, FirstName, WebSite, TimeStamp " +
    "From dbo.Author " +
    "Where LastName = {0}";

ObjectDumper.Write(context.ExecuteQuery<Author>(sql, SearchName));
```

Looking at the generated SQL, we can see that the query is now parameterized, which will prevent the dreaded SQL injection attack.

```
Select ID, LastName, FirstName, WebSite, TimeStamp
From dbo.Author
Where LastName = @p0
```

Dynamic SQL can be a powerful tool. It can also be dangerous if placed in the hands of the wrong users. Even for users who aren't malicious, the dynamic SQL option can allow them to create queries that cause poor performance due to a lack of proper indexing for the query in question. Many database administrators will object to the overuse of dynamic SQL. While it definitely has its place, try to come up with other options before traversing down this route.

8.2.2 Working with stored procedures

At the opposite end of the spectrum from dynamic SQL lies the precompiled stored procedures that are included with SQL Server. Although standard LINQ to SQL methods can often be fine for simple CRUD operations, often business forces demand the use of stored procedures. The most typical reasons for reliance on stored procedures revolve around security, performance, auditing, or additional functionality.

In some cases, LINQ to SQL's use of parameterized queries reduces the concerns from a performance and security perspective. From the performance perspective, the parameterized queries' execution plans are evaluated once and cached, just as they are for stored procedures. From the security perspective, parameterized queries eliminate the possibility of SQL injection attacks. LINQ to

SQL still requires server permissions at the table level, which some database administrators (DBAs) are reluctant to allow.

Also, stored procedures allow the DBA to control the data access and customize the indexing schemes. However, when using stored procedures, we can't rely on the `DataContext` dynamically creating the CRUD SQL statements and limiting the number of properties that need to be updated. The entire object needs to be updated each time. Nonetheless, if the application requires stored procedures, they are relatively easy to use.

Reading data with stored procedures

When your environment requires stored procedures for accessing data, a bit more work is necessary as opposed to using just the basic LINQ query syntax. The first step is to create the stored procedure to return results. Once the procedure is set up in your database, we can access it the same as any other method call. Let's consider a procedure to fetch a single book from the database based on a value passed in by the user. To demonstrate the kind of additional functionality we can do inside the stored procedure, we'll add a bit of logging into an `AuditTracking` table. The sample project that comes with this book includes this table and the `GetBook` stored procedure that we'll be using.

To add the stored procedure, we open the LINQ to SQL design surface that contains our `Books` class. Next, expand the Stored Procedures node of the Server Explorer and find the `GetBook` procedure. Drag the `GetBook` procedure onto the design surface and drop it on top of the `Book` class. The result is shown in figure 8.2.

When we were working with tables, we mapped the tables directly to classes. When we query the data, we use extension methods or query syntax to define our

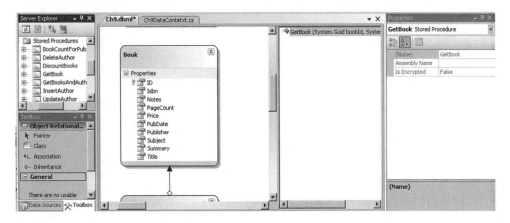

Figure 8.2 Adding the `GetBook` stored procedure to the LINQ to SQL Designer

queries. Stored procedures, on the other hand, are implemented as method calls that return objects. Since the designer defines the stored procedure as a method in the custom data context, we call it as shown in listing 8.11.

Listing 8.11   Using a stored procedure to return results

```
Guid bookId = new Guid("0737c167-e3d9-4a46-9247-2d0101ab18d1");
Ch8DataContext context = new Ch8DataContext();
IEnumerable<Book> query =
    context.GetBook(bookId,
    System.Threading.Thread.CurrentPrincipal.Identity.Name);
```

Returning results from a stored procedure is as easy as calling the generated method passing in the appropriate values. The values we pass in are strongly typed. As long as the column names returned in the stored procedure's result set correspond to the destination object type, the values will be automatically matched up. Note that the results of the stored procedure are returned as an IEnumerable<T> rather than IQueryable<T> type. Because we cannot consume the results of stored procedures in other server-side queries, there is no need to worry about the expression tree parsing required by IQueryable. We can, however, consume the results on the client in a LINQ to Objects query if we want.

Before moving on, let's take a quick peek under the covers and see how the DataContext actually calls into the stored procedure. If we look at the generated Ch8.designer.cs file, we can see the underlying generated method call, as shown in listing 8.12.

Listing 8.12   Generated `GetBook` code to call the stored procedure

```
[Function(Name="dbo.GetBook")]
public ISingleResult<Book> GetBook(          ❶
  [Parameter(Name="BookId", DbType="UniqueIdentifier")]
  System.Nullable<System.Guid> bookId,                    ❷
  [Parameter(Name="UserName", DbType="NVarChar(50)")]
  string userName)
{
  IExecuteResult result = this.ExecuteMethodCall(        ❸
    this,
    ((MethodInfo)(MethodInfo.GetCurrentMethod())),
    bookId,
    userName);

  return ((ISingleResult<Book>)(result.ReturnValue));    ❹
}
```

Implementation of the stored procedure proxies requires us to not only import the System.Data.Linq namespace, but also System.Data.Linq.Mapping and System.Reflection. For this method, we want to get a book that uses the given ID. We name our method GetBook ❶ and pass two parameters, a Guid called BookId and a string called UserName ❷. The method will return an object typed ISingleResult<Book>. ISingleResult does not return a single object, but rather a single list of objects. If our stored procedure returned multiple result sets, we would use IMultipleResult.

In order to map our method to the stored procedure, we need to specify a number of attributes.[1] The first attribute maps the Function called dbo.GetBook to this method by specifying the Name parameter.

Next, we need to identify how we're going to map the method's parameters to the stored procedure's parameters. We do this by decorating each method with a System.Data.Linq.Mapping.Parameter attribute. Once we have the mappings in place, all we need to do is call the method.

In order to call a stored procedure, the DataContext class includes a method called ExecuteMethodCall ❸. We can use this method to return result sets, scalar values, or issue a statement to the server. Since we've already created our method inside a class that inherits from DataContext, we can call the ExecuteMethodCall directly by calling into the DataContext base class itself.

ExecuteMethodCall takes three parameters. The first parameter is the Data-Context object instance that is calling it. The second parameter is a reference to the information about the method that is calling it. Using reflection, the Method-Info needs to be passed in order for the framework to recognize our attributes and map them appropriately. Typically we can just set the first parameter to this and the second to MethodInfo.GetCurrentMethod.

The final parameter is a parameter array that takes a list of values. These remaining parameters are the actual values that we'll be sending to our stored procedure. The order of the parameters must match the order in which they appear in the Parameter attributes in the method's declaration. If they don't match, a runtime exception will be thrown. Figure 8.3 shows the interfaces that ExecuteMethodCall returns.

---

[1] We could use an external mapping file here as well. Attributes are used to facilitate explanation for the purpose of the text. Chapter 7 includes a full discussion of mapping options available with LINQ to SQL.

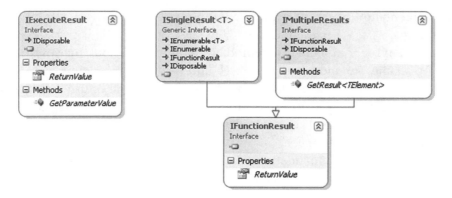

Figure 8.3   Interfaces return as a result of `ExecuteMethodCall`

`IExecuteResult` exposes a `ReturnValue` of type `Object` and the ability to access parameter values to the parameters. If the procedure returns a list of objects that we can strongly type, we'll typically cast the `ReturnValue` as an `ISingle-Result<T>` ❹. If it can return different types based on internal processing, we would use the `IMultipleResults` implementation, which allows us to access a specific type via the generic `GetResult<TElement>` method.

Retrieving data via stored procedures is not limited to returning tables and result sets. They can just as easily return scalar values. Listing 8.13 demonstrates consuming the `BookCountForPublisher` stored procedure to return the count of the books for a given publisher. We don't return a result set, but rather rely on the return parameter, which contains the resulting count. As in the previous example, we call the procedure using the `ExecuteMethodCall` method of the `DataContext`.

Listing 8.13   Returning a scalar value

```
[Function(Name="dbo.BookCountForPublisher")]
public int BookCountForPublisher(
  [Parameter(Name="PublisherId", DbType="UniqueIdentifier")]
  System.Nullable<System.Guid> publisherId)
{
  IExecuteResult result = this.ExecuteMethodCall(
    this,
    ((MethodInfo)(MethodInfo.GetCurrentMethod())),
    publisherId);
  return ((int)(result.ReturnValue));
}
```

In this case, we retrieve our scalar value through the return parameter of our stored procedure. LINQ to SQL realizes that there are no result sets being sent back. Instead, it presents the value that the stored procedure returns as the `ReturnValue` of the result. All we need to do is cast the value to the appropriate type. The `ReturnValue` will change depending on what kinds of data the procedure returns. In listing 8.14, we consume this method as we would any other method.

Listing 8.14 Consuming a scalar stored procedure

```
Guid publisherId = new Guid("851e3294-145d-4fff-a190-3cab7aa95f76");
Ch8DataContext context = new Ch8DataContext();
Console.WriteLine(String.Format("Books found: {0}",
    context.BookCountForPublisher(publisherId).ToString()));
```

The fetching examples shown here are admittedly rudimentary. In actuality, we could perform the same queries using standard LINQ to SQL and avoid the need to define our own custom stored procedures. Depending on the application's business needs, directly accessing the table may be fine. Other business situations require the use of stored procedures for accessing data to meet security, performance, or auditing needs or to otherwise perform more advanced server-side processing before returning the results. Few changes are necessary to call stored procedures for these operations.

Updating data with stored procedures

Updating data is perhaps a more frequent use of stored procedures. Because a user making changes to data often requires more complex logic, security, or auditing, applications frequently rely on stored procedures to handle the remainder of the CRUD operations. As we've observed already, LINQ to SQL covers some of the same concerns that lead many applications to use stored procedures. In many cases, the dynamic SQL created by calling `SubmitChanges` on the `DataContext` is sufficient. In other cases, using stored procedures is still necessary.

If the use of stored procedures for updating data is required, using it is almost as easy as fetching records. However, we'll no longer be able to take advantage of the dynamic optimization that LINQ provides by only updating changed columns. Additionally, we'll be responsible for handling concurrency conflicts explicitly. Let's take look at what we need to do to replace the standard LINQ update method for our `Author` class.

In listing 8.15 we see the definition of the stored procedure we can create to handle the update for the `Author` class. To illustrate how we can add additional

functionality using stored procedures, this procedure will not only update the
`Author` table, but also insert a record into the `AuditTracking` table.

Listing 8.15   Stored procedure to update an `Author`

```
CREATE PROCEDURE [dbo].[UpdateAuthor]
  @ID UniqueIdentifier output,        ❶
  @LastName varchar(50),
  @FirstName varchar(50),
  @WebSite varchar(200),
  @UserName varchar(50),
  @TimeStamp timestamp                ❷
AS

DECLARE @RecordsUpdated int           ❸

-- Save values
UPDATE dbo.Author                     ❹
SET LastName=@LastName,
    FirstName=@FirstName,
    WebSite=@WebSite
WHERE ID=@ID AND
    [TimeStamp]=@TimeStamp

SELECT @RecordsUpdated=@@RowCount        ❺

IF @RecordsUpdated = 1 BEGIN          ❻

  -- Add auditing record
  INSERT INTO dbo.AuditTracking
    (TableName, UserName, AccessDate)
  VALUES ('Author', @UserName, GetDate())

END

RETURN @RecordsUpdated                ❼
```

This script is fairly standard. In it, we define a parameter for each value we're going
to update ❶. Since we're using a timestamp column ❷, we don't need to send the
original values for each column as well. This will help to optimize our network
bandwidth to the server. We also declare an internal parameter called `@RecordsUp-`
`dated` that will help us track whether records were updated ❸. If no records are
updated, we'll assume that there is a concurrency problem. Once we set up our values, we can try to call the update method ❹. Immediately after calling the update,
we need to get the number of rows that were changed ❺. If we wait, `@@RowCount`
will not return a reliable result.

If records are updated, we add a record to our tracking table ❻. We don't care about tracking changes that aren't successful. At the end, we make sure to return the number of rows updated so that our client code can raise a concurrency exception if necessary ❼.

With this code in place, we can create a method in our `DataContext` class that will consume the procedure (see listing 8.16). We can create this method manually or using the designer by dragging our stored procedure into the method pane. Here we see the code generated by the designer.

Listing 8.16 Consuming the update stored procedure using LINQ

```
[Function(Name="dbo.UpdateAuthor")]            ❶
public int AuthorUpdate(
  [Parameter(Name="ID")] Guid iD,              ❷
  [Parameter(Name="LastName")] string lastName,
  [Parameter(Name="FirstName")] string firstName,
  [Parameter(Name="WebSite")] string webSite,
  [Parameter(Name="UserName")] string userName,
  [Parameter(Name="TimeStamp")] byte[] timeStamp)
{
  if (userName == null)             ❸
    {userName=Thread.CurrentPrincipal.Identity.Name;}
  IExecuteResult result = this.ExecuteMethodCall(      ❹
    this, ((MethodInfo)(MethodInfo.GetCurrentMethod())),
    iD, lastName, firstName, webSite, userName, timeStamp);
  iD = (Guid)(result.GetParameterValue(0));
  int RowsAffected = ((int)(result.ReturnValue));      ❺
  if (RowsAffected==0){throw new ChangeConflictException();}
  return RowsAffected;
}
```

The basic pattern we use in this update method is almost identical to the one we used when accessing data. We start by defining our method, decorating it with the `Function` attribute ❶ and its parameters with the `Parameter` attribute ❷ so that we can map them to our stored procedure and the stored procedure's parameters. Since our procedure needs the name of the current user in order to perform the logging, we include it as well. We check to see if it is populated, and if not, set it to the currently logged-in user ❸.

The meat of the method follows. Here we call `ExecuteMethodCall` to access the database ❹. As we did before, we pass the instance of the `DataContext` and the calling method's `MethodInfo` so that `ExecuteMethodCall` will be able to determine the appropriate mappings. We follow that with a parameter array of the values that we're sending to the database. Make sure to keep the order of the parameters in the method signature identical to the order in the parameter array.

ExecuteMethodCall will return the return value from our stored procedure as part of its result. We check this ReturnValue, making sure to cast it to an integer **⑤**. In order to check for concurrency issues, we determine whether any records were updated. If not, we throw a ChangeConflictException so that our client code can handle the concurrency exception. This first implementation of UpdateAuthor does the dirty work of calling the stored procedure.

If we want to automatically use this procedure in place of the run-time generated method whenever we update this table, we create a second method with a special signature as shown in listing 8.17.

Listing 8.17 UpdateT(T instance) **method to replace the run-time implementation**

```
private void UpdateAuthor(Author instance)
{
  this.UpdateAuthor(instance.ID,
      instance.LastName, instance.FirstName,
      instance.WebSite, null, instance.TimeStamp);
  }
}
```

In the UpdateAuthor(Author instance) method, we use a predefined signature designating that this method be used to update records on this object type rather than creating the update method dynamically. If we define methods in our Data-Context with the following signatures, they will be used instead of the dynamic SQL: InsertT(T instance), UpdateT(T instance), and DeleteT(T instance). In this case, since we're updating an Author instance, we define our method as UpdateAuthor(Author instance). If we have a method with this signature in the context attached to the objects we're updating, it will be called when Submit-Changes is called on that DataContext instance rather than dynamically creating the update SQL statement.

So far, we've demonstrated coding the procedures manually. In many cases, it may be easier to at least start with the designer and then use the generated code to learn now to do it manually. In figure 8.4, we show the Visual Studio designer again. This time, pay attention to each of the four panes: the Server Explorer, both sides of the Method pane, and the Properties window. To generate a method from a stored procedure, we simply drag and drop the procedure in question from the Server Explorer into the Method pane. The generated method's signature will appear.

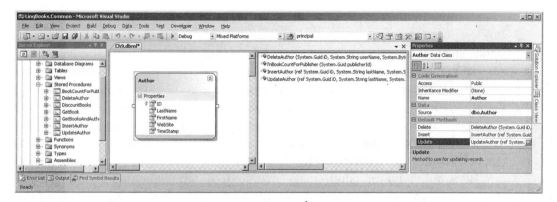

Figure 8.4 LINQ to SQL Designer to map stored procedures to the data context as methods

Once we've added the stored procedures, we can configure the custom `Insert`, `Update`, and `Delete` methods. Click on the `Author` class in the Method pane and observe the Properties window. Entries for each of these custom procedure functions will appear. If we select the `Update` property, we can click on a button that opens the designer shown in figure 8.5. Alternatively, right-click the class in the designer and select Configure Behavior.

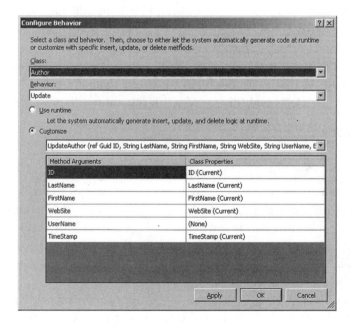

**Figure 8.5
Update procedure designer window to assign the custom stored procedures with CRUD operations**

By default, the behavior for the methods is set to Use Runtime. As long as it is set to Use Runtime, the `DataContext` will dynamically generate the `Insert`, `Update`, and `Delete` methods and issue them directly against the tables. To change the functionality, select the Customize option for the behavior you wish to replace. From the drop-down option under Customize, select the desired method. If the stored procedures are already defined, they can be selected at this point. Once set, the mapping of the method arguments can be customized. In the case of this method, we'll leave the class property for the `UserName` set to None and then set it in our actual implementing method.

Be aware that if we want to make changes to the implementation, they need to be done in the partial class and not in the designers. Any changes made to the .designer.cs file will be overwritten as the designers regenerate the code due to other changes. In this example, we did the implementation in a partial class definition of the data context in order to specify the user name based on the current thread's identity.

Traditionally, stored procedures make up the bulk of the custom database code when working with SQL Server. In fact, there are a number of books and best practice guides that argue in favor of limiting all database access to go through stored procedures rather than allowing direct access to the underlying tables. Familiarity with the technology and business requirements will help determine whether stored procedures are still necessary for individual applications or whether the native LINQ to SQL behavior is sufficient.

The functionality offered by SQL server does not stop with stored procedures. It also offers the ability to define user-defined functions that can return both scalar values and tables. The next section explores the capabilities that these offer.

8.2.3 *User-defined functions*

Many data-centric applications currently limit themselves to tables and stored procedures for data access. An additional area that may offer benefits and is easier to use than stored procedures is user-defined functions. The two main flavors of user-defined functions are scalar and table-valued functions. Scalar functions return a single value, which is handy for quick lookup translations. Table-valued functions return results that can be consumed as if they were returned by the table directly. Similar to stored procedures, additional functionality can be added to the function within certain limitations. Unlike stored procedures, you can reuse the return results natively on the server as part of other server-side queries. When building new components and applications, consider how user-defined functions may offer additional functionality and flexibility over stored procedures for fetching results.

To see how we can use user-defined functions, let's revisit our stored procedure from listing 8.13, which returned the count of books by publisher. To begin, we need to establish the function that we're going to use. To avoid naming conflicts, we'll name our database function fnBookCountForPublisher. (See listing 8.18.)

Listing 8.18 User-defined scalar function

```
CREATE FUNCTION dbo.fnBookCountForPublisher
  ( @PublisherId UniqueIdentifier )
  RETURNS int
AS
BEGIN
        DECLARE @BookCount int

        SELECT @BookCount = count(*)
        FROM dbo.Book
        WHERE dbo.Book.Publisher=@PublisherId

        Return @BookCount
END
```

The definition of the function is nearly identical to the one we used in listing 8.13. Most of the differences are syntactic. Instead of focusing on the differences in the server implementation, we'll concentrate on the differences in the LINQ code. Luckily, the differences are relatively minor. Using the LINQ to SQL Designer, we can drag our new function onto the design surface and the function will appear in the right column. Once we save the changes in the designer, we can take a peek at the generated code, as shown in listing 8.19.

Listing 8.19 LINQ code generated for the scalar function

```
[Function(Name = "dbo.fnBookCountForPublisher",
    IsComposable = true)]
public int? fnBookCountForPublisher1(
    [Parameter(Name = "PublisherId")] Guid? publisherId)
{
    return (int?)(this.ExecuteMethodCall(
        this,
        ((MethodInfo)(MethodInfo.GetCurrentMethod())),
        publisherId).ReturnValue);
}
```

Comparing the client code in listings 8.13 and 8.19, we see that they are very similar. We execute the function the same way we did with the stored procedure, using the `ExecuteMethodCall` of the `DataContext` instance and returning the `ReturnValue`.

The key change between functions and stored procedures is the use of the `IsComposable` attribute on the method signature. With functions, we set this to `True`. By doing this, we can use the function within a LINQ query and the call will be executed on the server. With the function translated to the server, consider the results of the sample in listing 8.20.

Listing 8.20   Using a scalar user-defined function in a query

```
var query =
    from publisher in context.GetTable<Publisher>()
    select new
    {
        publisher.Name,
        BookCount = context.fnBookCountForPublisher(publisher.ID)
    };
```

Checking the generated SQL statement, we can see that the function is translated to run directly on the server rather than the client as we iterate over each result.

```
SELECT      Name, CONVERT(Int, dbo.fnBookCountForPublisher(ID)) AS value
FROM        Publisher AS t0
```

If it weren't for the composability that LINQ and deferred execution offer, the query would need to return the list of publishers to the client and then issue separate function calls to the database to evaluate each row. Due to LINQ's composability, the entire query is executed directly on the server. As a result, we minimize round-trips to the database and maximize performance due to optimized execution plans on the server.

Returning a table is similar. Consider a business situation where we want to horizontally partition our book table by publishers. Suppose we don't want users to have direct access to fetch all records from the table, only the records for their publisher code. But we still want to work with the results as a table for query purposes. In that case, we could create different views for each publisher and configure security based on those views. Alternatively, our sample database includes a table-defined function to return the books based on their publisher ID. We consume this using the code shown in listing 8.21.

Listing 8.21 Defining and consuming a table-valued function

```
[Function(Name = "dbo.fnGetPublishersBooks",
    IsComposable = true)]
public IQueryable<Book> fnGetPublishersBooks(
    [Parameter(Name = "Publisher", DbType = "UniqueIdentifier")]
    System.Nullable<System.Guid> publisher)
{
    return this.CreateMethodCallQuery<Book>(
        this,
        ((MethodInfo)(MethodInfo.GetCurrentMethod())),
        publisher);
}
```

In this example, the SQL function returns a table rather than a single value. We send a single parameter—publisher—and return all books that are assigned to the given publisher. In order for LINQ to consume this function, we need to set up our familiar mappings for the function and the parameters. Instead of calling ExecuteMethodCall, we use a new method on the context—CreateMethod-CallQuery<T>. The main distinction between these two methods is the fact that CreateMethodCallQuery returns an IQueryable rather than just IEnumerable, which allows us to compose larger expression trees. As a result, we can use this result just as we would any other LINQ to SQL table. Listing 8.22 illustrates how we can use both of our user-defined functions within a single LINQ query to return an anonymous type of the name of a book along with how many other books are published by that publisher.

Listing 8.22 Consuming user-defined functions

```
Guid publisherId = new Guid("855cb02e-dc29-473d-9f40-6c3405043fa3");
var query1 =
  from book in context.fnGetPublishersBooks(publisherId)
  select new
        {
            book.Title,
            OtherBookCount =
                context.fnBookCountForPublisher(book.Publisher) - 1
        };
```

In this code, we consume both the fnPublishersBooks and the fnBookCountFor-Publisher methods that we set up previously. Executing this query results in the following SQL expression:

```
SELECT     Title,
     CONVERT(Int, dbo.fnBookCountForPublisher(Publisher)) - @p1 AS value
     FROM        dbo.fnGetPublishersBooks(@p0) AS t0
```

We can consume functions in much the same way as we consume data from tables. Functions offer the added benefit of allowing custom logic to be run on the server in conjunction with fetching the data. Functions also offer the added benefit that they can be used inside queries, both on the server and when using LINQ on the client. The power and flexibility of functions make them a viable alternative to stored procedures and views when designing LINQ-enabled applications.

At this point, we've explored how LINQ to SQL handles working with the major portions of the database engine. These capabilities allow us to perform operations on tables, views, stored procedures, and user-defined functions.

We've been focusing not on the database capabilities, but rather on alternative methods of programmatically accessing the data in a client or business tier. At this point, we'll move from looking at LINQ to SQL in the database-centric mode and instead focus on the advanced options available from an object-oriented perspective on the business and/or client tier.

8.3   Improving the business tier

When working on the business tier, we begin to focus on areas of performance, maintainability, and code reuse. This section looks at some of the advanced functionality LINQ to SQL offers in these areas. We begin by focusing on improving performance by caching the frequently used query structures. We continue by looking at three options for improving maintainability and reuse through the use of partial classes, partial methods, and object inheritance. Obviously we'll only be able to scratch the surface of the later topics, as they are often subjects of complete books in themselves.

8.3.1   Compiled queries

Any time complex layers are added, performance can potentially decrease. The architectural dilemma when designing systems is determining the trade-off between performance and maintainability. Working with LINQ is no exception. There is overhead in determining the translation between the LINQ query syntax and the syntax the database understands. This translation requires reflecting on the mapping metadata, parsing the query into an expression tree, and constructing a SQL string based on the results.

With queries that will be performed repeatedly, the structure can be analyzed once and then consumed many times. To define a query that will be reused, use the `CompiledQuery.Compile` method. We recommend using a static field and a nonstatic method to the data context. Instead of returning a value type or simple class, this method will return a generic function definition. Listing 8.23 demonstrates creating a precompiled query to return expensive books. In this case, we can pass in a threshold amount, which we'll call `minimumPrice`. We can use this `minimumPrice` parameter to determine what constitutes an expensive book. The entire query structure will be precompiled with the exception of the value of the parameter. All the runtime will need to do is specify the `DataContext` instance and the value of the `minimumPrice`, and the compiled query will return the list of books that meet the criteria.

Listing 8.23   Precompiling a query

```
public static Func<CustomContext, decimal, IQueryable<Book>>        ❶
   ExpensiveBooks = CompiledQuery.Compile(
     (Ch8DataContext context, decimal minimumPrice) =>
     from book in context.Books
     where book.Price >= minimumPrice
     select book);

public IQueryable<Book>        ❷
    GetExpensiveBooks(decimal minimumPrice)
{
    return ExpensiveBooks(this, minimumPrice);
}
```

Listing 8.23 includes the two new members. The first, `ExpensiveBooks`, is a static field that contains the compiled query definition ❶. The second method acts as a helper method to encapsulate the call to `ExpensiveBooks`, passing in the containing `DataContext` instance ❷. The real work is done in the first method. The function stored in `ExpensiveBooks` defines a signature that takes a `Ch8DataContext` and a decimal as input parameters and returns an object that implements the generic `IQueryable<Book>` interface.

We define the function as the result of `System.Data.Linq.CompiledQuery.Compile`. `Compile` takes a lambda expression defining our query. It evaluates the structure and prepares the function for use. Since the function is defined as static, it will be evaluated only once in the lifetime of our `AppDomain`. After that, we're free to use it as much as we want without worrying about most of the evaluation overhead.

Any time we want to fetch the listing of expensive books, we can call the `GetExpensiveBooks` method. The framework no longer needs to reevaluate the mappings between the database and the objects, nor will it need to parse the query into an expression tree. This work has already been done.

If you're unsure of the impact of using compiled queries, read the series of posts by Rico Mariani beginning with http://blogs.msdn.com/ricom/ archive/2007/06/22/dlinq-linq-to-sql-performance-part-1.aspx. He shows how using a compiled query offers nearly twice the performance of noncompiled queries and brings the performance to within 93 percent of using a raw `Data-Reader` to populate objects. As LINQ continues to evolve, there will continue to be more performance enhancements.

The other business tier components that we'll discuss are less focused on performance and more focused on code maintainability and reuse. The fine art of programming is all about making trade-offs between these two areas. Often a small performance penalty is outweighed by greatly increased maintainability.

8.3.2   *Partial classes for custom business logic*

Using object-oriented programming practices adds functionality to the business domain by taking base object structures and extending them to add the custom business logic. Prior to .NET 2.0, the main way to extend those structures was by inheriting from a base class. With .NET 2.0, Microsoft introduced the concept of *partial classes*. With partial classes, we can isolate specific functionality sets in separate files and then allow the compiler to merge them into a single class. The usefulness of partial classes is particularly evident when dealing with generated code.

By default, both of the automated generation tools we've explored (the designer and SqlMetal) generate the class definitions as partial classes. As a result, we can use either tool to dynamically generate our entities and enforce customized business logic in separate classes. Let's explore a simple use case that will entail adding a property to concatenate and format the author's name based on the existing properties in the `Author` object.

In chapter 7, we defined the mapped version of our `Author` class. When we defined it manually, we set it up as `public class Author`. When we later let the tools generate our `Author` class, they defined it as a partial class. Because it was created as a partial class, we can create a second class file to define the other part. Listing 8.24 shows the code to add functionality to our `Author` class by using a partial class definition.

Listing 8.24 Adding functionality with partial classes

```
public partial class Author
{
  public string FormattedName
  {
    get { return this.FirstName + ' ' + this.LastName; }
  }
}
```

The code in listing 8.24 is not earth-shattering, but shows how easy it is to add customized logic to an existing class in our project. This is particularly important if the mapping portion of the class is going to be regenerated by Visual Studio. Some other areas that already use the partial code methodology within Visual Studio include the WinForms and ASP.NET designers. In both cases, Microsoft split the functionality between two files to keep the development focused on the custom business logic and hide the details and fragility of the designer-generated code.

With the combined class, we can now create a LINQ query leveraging both the mapped class and our new FormattedName property as shown in listing 8.25. Be aware that you cannot project into an anonymous type containing an unmapped property. Thus we have to select the entire Author object in the Select clause when working with LINQ to SQL.

Listing 8.25 Querying with a property from the partial class

```
var partialAuthors = from author in context.Authors
                        select author;
```

Note that our client code is oblivious to the fact that the portions are defined in separate files. We just consume it as if it were defined as a standard class.

Partial classes are not limited to adding simple calculated fields. We can include much more functionality than that. As an example, consider the ability to extend a class by implementing an interface in the partial class. Listing 8.26 shows some sample code that we could use to implement the IDataErrorInfo interface.

Listing 8.26 Implementing IDataErrorInfo in the custom partial class

```
partial class Publisher : System.ComponentModel.IDataErrorInfo
  {
      private string CheckRules(string columnName)        ❶
      {
```

```
            //See the download samples for the implementation
            //All rules are ok, return an empty string
             return string.Empty;
        }

        #region IDataErrorInfo Members
        public string Error
        {
            get { return CheckRules("Name") +
                CheckRules("WebSite"); }
        }

        public string this[string columnName]
        {
            get { return CheckRules(columnName); }
        }

        #endregion
    }
```

IDataErrorInfo is used by the ErrorProvider in WinForm applications to provide immediate feedback to the user that an object doesn't meet a set of business
logic. The implementation in this example is not intended to be a full-featured
rules management application, only to demonstrate the possibilities that arise by
leveraging the partial class implementation.

In this case, we can centralize the business logic of our class to a single Check-
Rules method ❶. Then whenever the UI detects a change in the business object,
it checks the validity of the object and the changing property. If the resulting
string returned from the Error or the column name indexer contains values, an
error icon is displayed as shown in figure 8.6.

In this grid, the rules we place in the CheckRules method are checked as users
change values. If the user-supplied value does not agree with the business rules,
the user is shown a nonintrusive notification that he needs to change his value.
The key thing to take away here is that we can use the LINQ to SQL Designer to
generate our business class and put our logic in the partial class implementation.

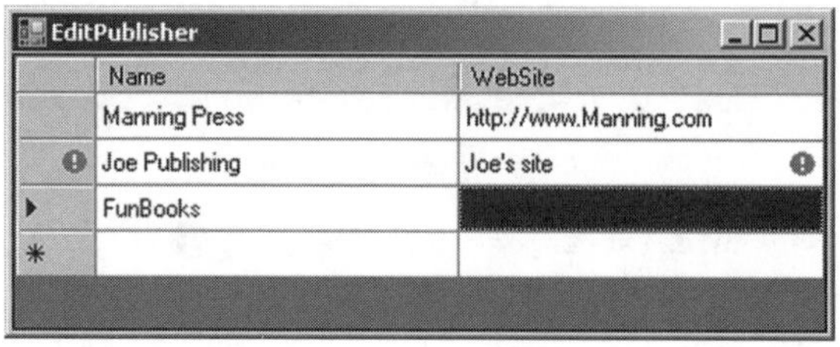

Figure 8.6
**DataGridView for editing Publishers
implementing IDataErrorInfo in
the partial class**

When we need to regenerate our entities, the business functionality will be retained. When we compile our application, the compiler combines the generated code with our custom code into a single class definition.

Partial classes were introduced as a way to add physically separate methods into isolated files. If we want to optionally inject functionality within a given generated method, it does not give us the hooks that we could use. C# 3.0 and VB 9.0 include a new language feature called *partial methods* to allow injecting functionality within a method.

8.3.3 *Taking advantage of partial methods*

Typically when working with business entities, we need to provide additional processing as part of a constructor or during a property change. Prior to C# 3.0 and VB 9.0, we would need to create base abstract classes and allow our properties to be overridden by implementing classes. Such a class would then implement the desired custom functionality. As we'll discuss briefly, using this form of inheritance can be problematic with LINQ to SQL due to the inheritance implementation model. Thankfully, C# 3.0 and VB 9.0 bring us the option of partial methods.

With partial methods, we can insert method stubs into our generated code. If we implement the method in our business code, the compiler will add the functionality. If we don't implement it, the complier will remove the empty method. Listing 8.27 shows some of the partial methods that the LINQ to SQL Designer and SqlMetal insert into our class definitions and how we can take advantage of them.

Listing 8.27 Partial signature of the generated class including partial methods

```
[Table(Name="dbo.Publisher")]
public partial class Publisher :
    INotifyPropertyChanging, INotifyPropertyChanged
{
#region Extensibility Method Definitions
  partial void OnCreated();                        ❶ Partial method
  partial void OnNameChanging(string value);         stubs
  partial void OnNameChanged();
 #endregion

public Publisher()
{
  this._Books = new EntitySet<Book>(
    new Action<Book>(this.attach_Books),
    new Action<Book>(this.detach_Books));
  OnCreated();
}
```

```
[Column(Storage="_Name", DbType="VarChar(50) NOT NULL",
  CanBeNull=false)]
public string Name
{
  get
  {
    return this._Name;
  }
  set
  {
    if ((this._Name != value))
    {
      this.OnNameChanging(value);              ◄─────┐
      this.SendPropertyChanging();                   │  Call
      this._Name = value;                            │  partial
      this.SendPropertyChanged("Name");              │  method
      this.OnNameChanged();                    ◄─────┘
    }
  }
}
```

For the `Publisher` object and most of the entities generated by the LINQ to SQL tools, you'll find a number of method stubs that allow you to inject functionality ❶. In this example, if we wanted to perform some initialization on our properties, we could add that by implementing an `OnCreated` method as follows:

```
partial void OnCreated()
{
  this.ID = Guid.NewGuid();
  this.Name = string.Empty();
  this.WebSite = string.Empty();
}
```

With the `OnCreated` method implemented, we can now make sure that we initialize our values as the object is being instantiated. If we wanted, we could also take the opportunity to hook the `PropertyChanging` and `PropertyChanged` events to a more robust rules engine or change-tracking engine (like the one the `DataContext` includes).

Speaking of property changing, the generated code offers two partial method stubs in each property set that allow us to perform actions both before and after a given property is changed. This would allow us to implement a change-tracking system or other business logic based on the user input.

Remember, if we don't implement the partial methods, they will not clutter up the compiled business object with needless processing cycles. They are helpful otherwise to allow beneficial extensibility points for injecting custom business logic.

Partial classes and methods offer powerful abilities to extend otherwise generic entities. However, more defined customized logic for related object instances often requires a more polymorphic inheritance model. For example, in cases where we have different kinds of users, we would want to have a base user type and then inherit from that to provide the additional functionality of each specific user type. Naturally, LINQ to SQL offers this kind of polymorphic inheritance behavior.

8.3.4 *Using object inheritance*

As with .NET, LINQ has objects and OOP at its heart. One of the pillars of OOP is the ability to inherit from base classes and extend the functionality based on customized business needs. Frequently, inheriting objects extend base classes by exposing new properties. As long as the needed properties are contained in the same table as the base class, LINQ to SQL supports mapping the specialized objects. For this section, we'll continue extending our running example. In this case, we'll consider the users of the system.

When we started, we only had a single user object that contained the user name and an ID. We may find as we work that we want to have some specialized users with additional functionality. In particular, we may want to give Authors and Publishers special rights to be able to edit information that applies to them. Other users would have more restrictive rights. In order to link users with their roles, we could add columns to the User table to specify the Publisher's and Author's IDs. We'll set both of these as Nullable, as users that are not one of the specialized types won't have values in these fields. Figure 8.7 shows a representative set of the revised User table to support these specialized user types.

In our new table, we've added three columns. The last two columns contain the foreign key values of the ID columns in the Publisher and Author tables respectively. The additional column UserType identifies what kind of user the row

ID	Name	UserType	Publisher	Author
4b3-0f2a86b11754	Joe	S	NULL	NULL
a064f1c0-99e8-...	Steve	A	NULL	fec5d55d-8762-...
9ca4918f-cf91-4...	Jim	A	NULL	41fd8c54-6191-...
b1ad7c85-1500-...	Mike	P	851e3294-145d-...	NULL
493c9f8a-1e68-...	Fabrice	A	NULL	9b7822c6-4f22-...

Figure 8.7 User table sample data to support inheritance based on the distinguishing UserType **column**

represents. In our case, if the type is A, the user is an Author. If it is P the user is a Publisher. Standard users are designated with S as their UserType. In the sample data, the first user is a standard user and doesn't have a publisher or author foreign key value. Mike is a publisher and has a Publisher foreign key. The other users are all authors and include the appropriate Author foreign key.

With this structure in mind, we can think about how we want to model our objects to reflect the new table structure. Since we have three types of users, we'll have three classes to represent the different behavior of each user. We'll call the standard user UserBase, as it will serve as the base user type for the other two types. The other users we'll call AuthorUser and PublisherUser. Each of these custom user types will inherit from UserBase. Figure 8.8 shows the full object structure.

We begin building our structure by opening the LINQ to SQL Designer. In the designer, add the Publisher, Book, BookAuthor, and Author tables by dragging them from the Server Explorer to the design surface. To add the users, drag the

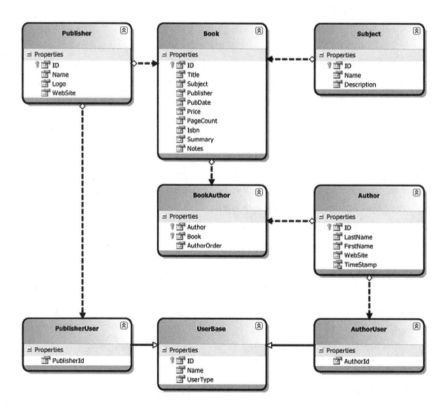

Figure 8.8 LINQ to SQL Designer with inherited users

modified User table to the design surface. Since our UserBase object will not include the fields for the customized objects, remove the Author and Publisher properties from the User object. From the Properties window, change the Name of the User object to UserBase.

Once our UserBase class is configured, we need to add our two customized user objects. To do this, drag two new objects onto the design surface from the toolbar. Name the first one PublisherUser and the second one AuthorUser. In the PublisherUser object, right-click the Properties heading and select Add, then Property. Set the Name of the property to PropertyId. Set the Source property to the Publisher column of the table. Do the same for the AuthorUser object, but this time, name the property AuthorId and set the source to the Author column.

With your classes defined, click on the Inheritance tool in the toolbox. Drag an inheritance line from the PublisherUser to the UserBase class. The inheritance arrow will appear in the designer. Do the same again to set up the inheritance between AuthorUser and UserBase.

We're almost done setting up our inheritance model. At this point, we need to identify which object type we want to load for each row in our table. For example, if we load a User with a UserType of A, we should get an instance of the AuthorUser instead of just the simple UserBase instance. To do so, we need to enhance our mappings. We could do this by adding more attributes to our class definition indicating the InheritanceMapping value. Since we're making these modifications using the designer, let's see how we can do it from there.

To specify the mapping, select the inheritance arrow line between the PublisherUser and UserBase and open the Properties window. The Properties window has four values: Base Class Discriminator, Derived Class Discriminator, Discriminator Property, and Inheritance Default. Let's start by setting the Discriminator Property. This will identify which property in our base class indicates which type of object to instantiate. Our UserBase class maintains this in the UserType property, so set the Discriminator Property to UserType. The Base Class Discriminator is used to indicate what value in the UserType will be used for objects of UserBase. In our case, that will be the Standard user, so we'll add the value S. The next property is for the Derived Class Discriminator. Since we want to load the PublisherUser when the UserType is P, enter the value P for this property. From this window, we can also specify that the default class implementation is the UserBase class when no match can be found on the discriminator.

We have one final step. We need to identify under which circumstances we want to instantiate the AuthorUser object. Similar to PublisherUser, we click the arrow between the AuthorUser and UserBase classes and open the Properties window.

Notice this time, since we already assigned the Base Class Discriminator, Discriminator Property, and Inheritance Default, these values are retained. All we need to do is set the Derived Class Code. Since we want `AuthorUsers` loaded when the type is `A`, enter the value `A`. With the inheritance mappings set, save the changes to the designer. Viewing the generated code in the .designer.cs file shows the attributes that were added to your class definition.

```
[InheritanceMapping(Code="S", Type=typeof(UserBase), IsDefault=true)]
[InheritanceMapping(Code="A", Type=typeof(AuthorUser))]
[InheritanceMapping(Code="P", Type=typeof(PublisherUser))]
[Table(Name="dbo.[User]")]
Public partial class UserBase
{
  //Implementation code omitted
}
```

The runtime relies on the attributes (or the XML mapping file) to indicate which objects to load. In addition to the `InheritanceMapping` attributes defined on the class, there is one other parameter we set when we made the changes in the designer. The attribute in question is not on the table, but on the `UserType`'s `Column` attribute. Note that the `IsDiscriminator` parameter is now set to true.

```
[Column(Storage="_UserType", IsDiscriminator=true)]
public char UserType
```

As we fetch records, LINQ to SQL will check the property decorated by the `IsDiscriminator` attribute. It will then compare the underlying value against the list of `InheritanceMapping` codes in the base class to determine which type to instantiate. With this value set, we've completed the necessary steps to create our inheritance trees.

Before we consume our new inherited objects, let's use the designer to establish one more set of relationships. At this point, we can use the designer to assign associations between the `Publisher` and `Author` objects and our newly customized `AuthorUser` and `PublisherUser` objects. This will allow us to drill into the object hierarchies even though we don't have foreign key indexes associated between the tables in our database. The designer makes adding this functionality a breeze. Select the Association tool from the toolbox. Click on the `ID` property of the `Author` class, followed by the `AuthorId` property of the `AuthorUser`. Do the same for the `Publisher` and `PublisherUser`. The designer should now look something like the illustration we started with in figure 8.4.

We're done with the changes to our designer. Let's move on to actually using our hard work. Listing 8.28 demonstrates several ways we can access our user lists.

Listing 8.28   Consuming inherited LINQ to SQL objects

```
var query =           ❶
    from user in context.UserBases
    select user.Name;

var authors =         ❷
    from user in context.UserBases
    where user is AuthorUser
    select user.Name;

var publishers =      ❸
    from user in context.UserBases.OfType<PublisherUser>()
    select user.Name;
```

In the first example ❶, we can select all users from our user table regardless of the implementing type. We can iterate over the list even though each row is represented by a different object type because each of the objects inherits from the same UserBase class. Here is the SQL that is generated for this first query:

```
SELECT [t0].[Name]
FROM [dbo].[User] AS [t0]
```

In the second query, we limit the records we want to retrieve based on the object type. To fetch just the AuthorUser objects (where the UserType=A) we can use strong typing and specify we only want users where the implementing type is AuthorUser in the where clause ❷. The final example illustrates another method of filtering. In this case, we use the OfType extension method to retrieve only objects that match the PublisherUser type ❸. Since we're selecting just the user name, both of these queries result in the same generated SQL:

```
SELECT [t0].[Name]
FROM [dbo].[User] AS [t0]
WHERE [t0].[UserType] = @p0
```

One thing to keep in mind, if you have columns that apply to some derived classes but not others, they need to be marked as Nullable in the database. Otherwise, updating values in the table on objects that don't implement those properties will throw an exception because the values were not supplied.

We've only scratched the surface of the capabilities that inheritance can offer. As long as the data is limited to a single table, implementing inheritance with LINQ to SQL is relatively painless. The InheritanceMapping attributes on the base class and Discriminator column on the table are all that we need.

The inheritance model supported by LINQ to SQL does suffer from a couple of weaknesses. First, the runtime requires that the base class of the object hierarchy include the definition for the base table mappings. Thus, using a base framework for business objects may limit the ability to define mappings in the base class implementation, as each object will likely come from a different table.

The second weakness in the LINQ to SQL inheritance model lies in the fact that the columns for the object's properties cannot cross multiple tables. It is not uncommon to have a set of database entities where a portion of the data, like a postal address, is included in a referential table. This may be fine from a relational database perspective, but including the address information within the entity class may fit better with the business model. Alternatively, the address information could be included within the same table as the entity's data, but having a shared `Address` class could offer better maintainability due to code reuse. In both cases (1 class encompassing 2 tables, and 2 classes pointing to the same table) LINQ to SQL fails to support a direct mapping structure at this time.

In those cases, we need to look beyond LINQ to SQL and investigate another portion of the new data access stack—the ADO.NET Entity Framework, which is scheduled to ship after the rest of the LINQ technologies. At this point, let's take a brief diversion into what this technology will offer us for more advanced mapping relationships.

8.4   A brief diversion into LINQ to Entities

In many cases, LINQ to SQL may serve the need for CRUD operations in our applications. As we've already pointed out, direct table access can be insufficient. To accommodate this, LINQ to SQL allows access to extra processing power via stored procedures and user-defined functions in the database. Other times, the business model requires more complex entity structures than are available with one-to-one table to object data mappings.

Frequently with larger database structures, the database will perform better with a more normalized structure. That normalized structure may or may not represent an optimal structure for our business entities. In those cases, we can flatten our table structures by using database views. Figure 8.9 illustrates such a case. In this example, we add one more table to our running database structure. This new table stores addresses. With it, we can store addresses for any number of associated tables. In figure 8.9, we show how the `Address` table can store information for both the `Author` and `Publisher`.

> **NOTE**   We're not arguing here whether the schema shown in figure 8.9 is the best. We're using it as an example. You need to determine how your data is best stored in terms of normalization.

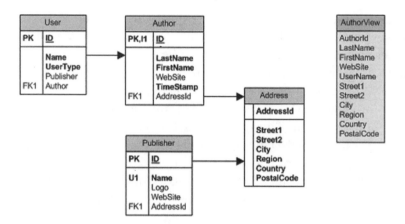

Figure 8.9   Adding a shared address table for both the `Author` and `Publisher` tables

In this example, we may want to store our data with the address information normalized into a separate table. However, our business entity may want to combine the author, user, and address information into a single class to reflect the full information about the `Author` in a single class. If we only want to view this flattened information, we could easily create a server view. The view would isolate the business from needing to remember how to join the tables.

The challenge with a view is that once flattened, the metadata needed in order to update records in the original tables is lost. In 1976, Dr. Peter Chen wrote a seminal paper outlining the theory of an entity-relationship model.[2] In it, he outlines a separation between the physical model (from the database) and the logical model (in the objects) by inserting a conceptual model.

In some ways, this conceptual model is similar to a view in that it can consolidate information from multiple sources. It goes beyond a view in several ways. First, unlike a view, the conceptual Entity Data Model (EDM) includes information about the source of the data so that the tools have enough information about the creation. This metadata indicates where the values came from and consequently where they will go when updated. Additionally, the EDM includes the ability to store both objects and relationships necessary to create fully dynamic object hierarchies in a conceptual model.

At the same time that the language teams were designing LINQ, the Microsoft data teams were working on implementing this conceptual model to handle these

---

[2] http://portal.acm.org/citation.cfm?id=320440

more complex entity structures. They are calling this technology the ADO.NET Entity Framework (EF). The EF separates the physical from the logical models by using a series of XML-based mapping files (see figure 8.10).

In the EF, the physical database is mapped to a logical model using a one-to-one relationship between the tables and logical layer entities. The logical entities are defined through an XML-based Store Schema Definition Language (SSDL) file. These mappings are similar to those we defined in LINQ to SQL.

The EF moves beyond LINQ to SQL by using another XML-based file (Mapping Schema Language or MSL) to map the logical model to a conceptual model. The conceptual model is yet another XML file using a Conceptual Schema Definition Language (CSDL). These conceptual entities can be further converted into strongly typed objects if desired.

With the EDM established, we can query it with a string-based query language called Entity SQL. In addition, our LINQ knowledge can be applied against the EDM by using LINQ to Entities. Since the EDM represents a true abstraction layer between the application and database, we can modify our database and EDM mapping file and restructure the data store without having to recompile the application.

The separation of layers we get from the EDM allows for an increased separation between the physical and logical. This allows us to change our data model and mapping structures and leave our application intact. Additionally, since the

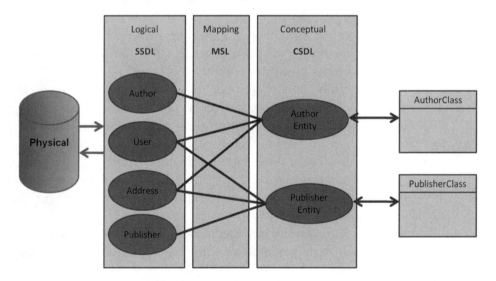

Figure 8.10 Layers of the Entity Framework

EF is built on top of the existing ADO provider model, the EF can work against data stores other than SQL Server. If you can't wait for native LINQ support for other databases, you may want to look into the LINQ to Entities and the EF for your data access tier.

As of the writing of this book, the EF is scheduled to be released after the official release of the LINQ technologies. Due to the release schedule and the scope of the project itself, we're unable to cover it with the sufficient attention it deserves. More information about the entity framework is available at http://msdn2.microsoft.com/en-us/data/aa937723.aspx.

8.5   *Summary*

LINQ to SQL offers the capability to manage the interaction between relational data stores and application logic based in objects through the object's full life cycle. We no longer need to manually write hundreds of lines of ADO.NET plumbing code. In fact, with the supplied tools, most of the code can be automatically generated. Once the objects and mapping structures are established, we can work with the data using the same query syntax used in LINQ to Objects.

Because we set up the metadata about the source and destination of the data, we can let the framework manage the entire life cycle. Let's summarize what we've covered in the past three chapters by stepping through the typical object life cycle. See figure 8.11.

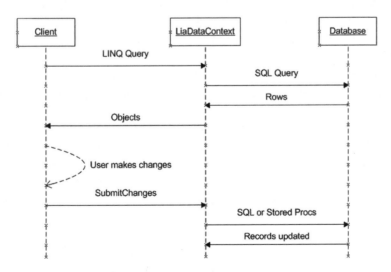

Figure 8.11   LINQ to SQL sequence diagram

In the typical scenario, our objects are created when we first query them. The client defines a query using query syntax or method calls and passes the resulting expression tree to the DataContext. The DataContext parses the expression tree and translates it into a query syntax that the database understands. As we ask for results, the DataContext opens the connection to the database and fetches the rows. The rows returned from the database are translated into a collection of objects. As it evaluates the returned values, it checks them against the versions already in memory by checking the objects' identities. If it has a copy of the object, it returns the copy the user has been working with. The resulting objects are then returned to our client to consume.

> **NOTE** In this case, we're referring to the client in a generic sense. The client does not have to be a person or presentation layer. The client is anything that consumes the LINQ to SQL entities. This can include a SOA service or data access tier.

The process can end here by just displaying the resulting objects to the consumer. If necessary, the user can make changes to the objects and submit those changes back via the DataContext. The DataContext evaluates the submitted data and compares it against the change-tracking store to determine which values need to be sent back to the database. The DataContext packages these changes up and issues the appropriate statements back to the server either using parameterized queries or stored procedures. If it uses parameterized queries, it automatically manages concurrency control. If problems occur during the update, they are handled by the transaction mechanisms that are implicitly or explicitly defined. Once the data is committed, the cycle is ready to start all over again.

At this point, we should be equipped with the tools needed to use LINQ to work with relational data. As with any tool, the ability to use the tool will depend on how much it is used. We could spend several chapters going over numerous usage permutations, but it would be impossible to cover every situation. Before moving on to LINQ to XML in the next chapter, take some time to work with LINQ to SQL, try the examples included in this book, and then extend them to meet business needs. Increased familiarity will help you identify the capabilities of the tool and decide where it fits in your data access toolkit.

Part 4

Manipulating XML

XML has become an important piece of technology within the applications we build. Whether we're integrating with a third-party web site via its public XML API, building RSS capabilities into our application, or reading an XML configuration file, XML has become an integral component within our applications. In this section, we explore how we can use LINQ against our XML data. We'll explore how to query XML using the standard LINQ query syntax covered in the first three parts of this book, as well as how we can use the new XML API provided with LINQ to manipulate XML documents.

Chapter 9 introduces you to LINQ to XML and the new lightweight XML programming API it provides. In chapter 10, we look at how we can use LINQ to query XML, as well as how LINQ to XML can be used to transform XML into alternate formats. Chapter 11 covers many of the common scenarios that you'll encounter as you begin to work with LINQ to XML.

Introducing
LINQ to XML

9

This chapter covers

- LINQ to XML design principles
- LINQ to XML class hierarchy
- Loading, parsing, and manipulating XML

In the first three parts of this book, we introduced you to the new language features in C# and VB that help enable LINQ, the default implementation of the standard query operators that work over objects—LINQ to Objects—as well as the implementation of LINQ for working with relational data—LINQ to SQL. In this chapter, we introduce you to another import piece of LINQ—LINQ to XML.

LINQ to XML allows you to use the powerful query capabilities offered by LINQ with XML data. Rather than learn a new API for querying XML, we can stick with the familiar query syntax that we've already learned for querying objects and relational data.

In addition to allowing us to query XML using LINQ, LINQ to XML also provides developers with a new XML programming API. The programming API is a lightweight, in-memory API that has been designed to take advantage of the latest .NET Framework. It provides functionality similar to the DOM, but does so with a redesigned API that is more intuitive.

In this chapter, we're going to focus on the new XML programming API offered with LINQ. Understanding the LINQ to XML API will give us a foundation that we'll build upon as we dive deeper later in this chapter, as well as in chapters 10 and 11. Once we have a firm understanding of the LINQ to XML API, we'll see how we can begin to query and transform XML data with LINQ to XML in chapter 10.

To become experts in the LINQ to XML API, we first need to back up and become familiar with its key design principles. In this chapter, we'll introduce those design principles, along with several of the key concepts that are at the heart of the API. Once we understand why Microsoft chose to create LINQ to XML, we'll plunge into the LINQ to XML class hierarchy. As we look at the class hierarchy, we'll identify several of the key constructors and methods that we'll use when working with the LINQ to XML API toward the end of this chapter. Once we have an overview of the classes provided by LINQ to XML, we'll look at how we can begin to use the LINQ to XML classes to perform the key operations necessary for building applications that use XML data, such as how to load, parse, create, update, delete, and save XML.

Before we get too deep into the details of the LINQ to XML API, we first need to understand what an XML API is, and what it's good for.

9.1   *What is an XML API?*

An XML API provides developers with a programming interface for working with XML data. By utilizing an XML API, we can build applications that make use of XML. To illustrate our need for such an API, think about how we might build an application that makes use of an XML file that contains a list of web site links, as shown in listing 9.1.

Listing 9.1   Sample XML file containing web site links

```
<links>
  <link>
    <url>http://linqinaction.net</url>
    <name>LINQ in Action</name>
  </link>
  <link>
    <url>http://hookedonlinq.com</url>
    <name>Hooked on LINQ</name>
  </link>
  <link>
    <url>http://msdn.microsoft.com/data/linq/</url>
    <name>The LINQ Project</name>
  </link>
</links>
```

To build an application that uses this XML file, we need a way to open the XML file and read its contents. We also might need a way to create a file with the same structure as the file shown, as well as a way to modify specific links contained within the XML file. If you've done any work with XML, you already know that these scenarios are exactly what an XML API is designed for. Rather than resorting to brute force string manipulation, we use an API that is designed to make loading, manipulating, and saving XML easy for programmers.

Over the years we've seen many different implementations of APIs for working with XML. While they all share some common attributes, they each have a different style and approach that make them unique. Today, when working with XML in .NET, we can choose from a variety of APIs. Our choice largely depends upon what we're trying to accomplish. If we're interested in the low-level parsing of XML, we can use the XmlTextReader class. If we're dealing with large documents, we might choose a streaming API such as XmlReader. And if we're interested in an API that will make it easy to traverse the XML, we might choose to use the DOM available via the XmlNode class, or the XPathNavigator class, which allows traversal of XML nodes via XPath expressions. Each API provides unique advantages and has specific strengths and weaknesses. But what they all have in common is their goal of allowing developers to build applications that use XML.

With so many .NET XML API choices available today, you might be wondering why we need LINQ to XML at all. After all, it appears we have a lot of specialized XML APIs that are designed for working with XML data. Let's now take a look at why we need yet another XML programming API.

9.2 *Why do we need another XML programming API?*

With existing APIs, developers have too much to think about. We have to know when to choose between XSLT, XPath, XQuery, and XML DOM. We have to worry about the subtle points of a lot of different APIs and need to learn technologies that have completely different conceptual models. For those working with XML day in and day out, this might not be a problem, but for the majority of developers, the depth and breadth of technological choices for working with XML is overwhelming.

LINQ to XML aims to solve these problems by providing mainstream developers with a simple, yet powerful, XML programming API. It provides the query and transformation power of XQuery and XPath integrated into .NET programming languages, as well as an in-memory programming API that makes working with XML data consistent and predictable.

In addition to providing developers with a more usable XML API, LINQ to XML also aims to take advantage of the advancements in programming languages that have occurred since the DOM/SAX was created nearly a decade ago. Language features such as nullable types and functional construction are in wide use today, and developers working with XML should be able to leverage these language advancements in their daily work. Additionally, LINQ itself brings many language advancements such as extension methods, anonymous types, and lambda expressions. In order for LINQ to fulfill its goal of providing a single query API for all data, Microsoft needed to ensure the LINQ story surrounding XML was compelling.

It could be argued that instead of creating a brand-new API, Microsoft should have reworked its existing APIs. Although Microsoft considered adding LINQ support to the existing APIs, retrofitting them would be difficult without breaking existing applications. An attempt to do so would cause a great deal of confusion among developers and would raise the complexity of those APIs to a point that they'd be unusable for most tasks. Since one of the primary goals was to make a more usable XML API, the complexity that changing existing APIs would bring made it a less viable option.

If what we've just said has yet to convince you, don't worry, because as you begin to work with LINQ to XML you'll quickly see why Microsoft chose to create a new XML API. LINQ to XML has been designed for LINQ, and it shows!

Let's now look at the core LINQ to XML design principles to get a better understanding of how LINQ to XML differs from existing .NET XML APIs.

9.3   *LINQ to XML design principles*

To make working with XML more productive and enjoyable for the average XML programmer, Microsoft has taken a completely new approach with the design of LINQ to XML. It has been designed to be a lightweight XML-programming API, both from a conceptual as well as from a memory and performance perspective. As we'll see in section 9.4, the LINQ to XML data model has been closely aligned with the W3C Information Set.[1]

To fully appreciate how the design principles that we're about to discuss make a difference when working with XML, let's create a simple XML document using today's most prominent XML-programming API, the DOM, then compare it against how we create the same XML document using LINQ to XML. Our simple example will show how LINQ to XML can make our lives as XML developers easier and more productive.

Our aim is to create an XML document that contains the details of the books contained within our `LINQBooks` sample application. Let's start with a simple document that contains the most important book in anyone's library (see listing 9.2).

Listing 9.2   The most important book in anyone's library

```
<books>
  <book>
    <title>LINQ in Action</title>
    <author>Fabrice Marguerie </author>
    <author>Steve Eichert</author>
    <author>Jim Wooley</author>
    <publisher>Manning</publisher>
  </book>
</books>
```

---

[1] The W3C Information Set is a specification that provides a consistent set of definitions for the information in an XML document. For more information, visit the W3C Information Set web site: http://www.w3.org/TR/xml-infoset/.

Listing 9.3   Create an XML document using the DOM

```
XmlDocument doc = new XmlDocument();
XmlElement books = doc.CreateElement("books");
XmlElement author1 = doc.CreateElement("author");
author1.InnerText = "Fabrice Marguerie";
XmlElement author2 = doc.CreateElement("author");
author2.InnerText = "Steve Eichert";
XmlElement author3 = doc.CreateElement("author");
author3.InnerText = "Jim Wooley";
XmlElement title = doc.CreateElement("title");
title.InnerText = "LINQ in Action";
XmlElement book = doc.CreateElement("book");
book.AppendChild(author1);
book.AppendChild(author2);
book.AppendChild(author3);
book.AppendChild(title);
books.AppendChild(book);
doc.AppendChild(books);
```

As we can see, creating XML documents using the DOM requires us to use an imperative construction model. First, we create our element within the context of our document, and then we append it to its parent. The imperative construction model results in code that looks nothing like the resulting XML. Rather than being hierarchical like the XML we're trying to produce, the code is flat with everything at a single level. Additionally, we need to create a lot of temporary variables to hold onto each element we create. The result is a block of code that is hard to read, debug, and maintain. The structure of the code has no relationship to the structure of the XML we're creating. In contrast, let's look at the code required to create the same XML using LINQ to XML.

Listing 9.4   Create an XML document using LINQ to XML

```
new XElement("books",
  new XElement("book",
    new XElement("author", "Fabrice Marguerie"),
    new XElement("author", "Steve Eichert"),
    new XElement("author", "Jim Wooley"),
    new XElement("title", "LINQ in Action"),
    new XElement("publisher", "Manning")
  )
);
```

By providing convenient constructors for creating elements within the context of a document-free environment, we can quickly write the code necessary for creating our document using the LINQ to XML programming API. We no longer have to worry about creating our elements within the context of a parent document, and we can construct our XML using a structure very similar to that of the resulting XML.

Our simple example demonstrated several of the key design differences between LINQ to XML and the DOM. To highlight the difference even more, we're now going to explore LINQ to XML's key concepts and examine the underlying design principles of LINQ to XML in detail.

9.3.1 *Key concept: functional construction*

LINQ to XML provides a powerful approach to creating XML elements, referred to as *functional construction*. Functional construction allows a complete XML tree to be created in a single statement. Rather than imperatively building up our XML document by creating a series of temporary variables for each node, we build XML in a functional manner, which allows the XML to be built in a way that closely resembles the resulting XML.

When working with the DOM, notice how much code we need to write just to keep our elements around so we can assign them values and append them to the appropriate parent element. Not only do we need to write a lot more code, but also the code doesn't look at all like the resulting XML. In order to build XML using the imperative model that the DOM requires, we need to stop thinking about our XML and instead think about how the XML DOM works.

The goal of functional construction is to allow programmers to build XML in a way that fits with how they think about XML. By allowing developers to stay focused on the XML and not have to switch gears, the LINQ to XML API makes developers' lives more pleasant and enjoyable. Isn't happiness in life defined by how nicely your XML API lets you create XML documents?

As we can see in figure 9.1, the LINQ to XML code on the left closely resembles the resulting XML that's shown on the right.

```
new XElement("book",                              <book>
  new XElement("title", "LINQ in Action"),          <title>LINQ in Action</title>
  new XElement("author", "Fabrice Marguerie"),      <author>Fabrice Marguerie</author>
  new XElement("author", "Steve Eichert"),          <author>Steve Eichert</author>
  new XElement("author", "Jim Wooley"),             <author>Jim Wooley</author>
  new XElement("publisher", "Manning")              <publisher>Manning</publisher>
);                                                </book>
```

Figure 9.1   LINQ to XML's functional construction allows the code for creating XML to closely resemble the resulting XML.

When we start discussing how to create XML in section 9.5.3, we'll revisit and reexamine how functional construction is made possible in LINQ to XML. For now, let's move on to the second key concept of LINQ to XML, context-free XML creation.

9.3.2 *Key concept: context-free XML creation*

When creating XML using the DOM, everything must be done within the context of a parent document. This document-centric approach to creating XML results in code that is hard to read, write, and debug. Within LINQ to XML, elements and attributes have been granted first-class status. They're standalone values that can be created outside the context of a document or parent element. This allows programmers to work with XML in a much more natural way. Rather than going through factory methods to create elements and attributes, they can be created using the compositional constructors offered by the XElement and XAttribute class.

The result is code that is much more readable and understandable. In addition, it is easier to create methods that accept and return elements and attributes, since they no longer have to be constructed within the context of their parent document.

Although documents have lost their elite status within LINQ to XML, they still have their place. When creating full XML documents that have XML declarations, document type definitions, and XML processing instructions, LINQ to XML offers the XDocument class.

As we work through the rest of this chapter, you'll begin to see the benefits of working within a context-free API. We know you're excited to see more key concepts, so now let's move on to simplified names.

9.3.3 *Key concept: simplified names*

One of the most confusing aspects of XML is all the XML names, XML namespaces, and namespace prefixes. When creating elements with the DOM, developers have several overloaded factory methods that allow them to include details of the fully expanded name of an element. How the DOM figures out the name, namespace, and prefix is confusing and complicates the API unnecessarily. Within LINQ to XML, XML names have been greatly simplified. Rather than having to worry about local names, qualified names, namespaces, and namespace prefixes, we can focus on a single fully expanded name. The XName class represents a fully expanded name, which includes the namespace and local name for the elements. When a namespace is included as part of an XName, it takes the following form: {http://schemas.xyxcorp.com/}localname.

In addition to simplifying the process of creating elements that use namespaces, LINQ to XML also makes it much easier to query an XML tree for elements that have a namespace specified. Let's look at the code for querying the following RSS feed (which has namespaces), shown in listing 9.5.

Listing 9.5   An RSS feed that uses XML namespaces

```
<?xml-stylesheet href=http://iqueryable.com/friendly-rss.xsl
 type="text/xsl" media="screen"?>
<rss version="2.0" xmlns:dc="http://purl.org/dc/elements/1.1/"
 xmlns:slash="http://purl.org/rss/1.0/modules/slash/"
 xmlns:wfw="http://wellformedweb.org/CommentAPI/">
  <channel>
    <title>Steve Eichert</title>
    <link>http://iqueryable.com/</link>
    <generator>ActiveType CMS v0.1</generator>
    <dc:language>en-US</dc:language>
    <description />
    <item>
      <dc:creator>Steve Eichert</dc:creator>
      <title>Parsing WordML using LINQ to XML</title>
      <link>http://iqueryable.com/LINQ/ParsingWordMLusingLINQ to XML</link>
      <pubDate>Wed, 02 Aug 2006 15:52:44 GMT</pubDate>
      <guid>http://iqueryable.com/LINQ/ParsingWordMLusingLINQ to XML</guid>
      <comments>
      http://iqueryable.com/LINQ/ParsingWordMLusingLINQ to XML#comments
      </comments>
      <wfw:commentRss>
      http://iqueryable.com/LINQ/ParsingWordMLusingLINQ to
XML/commentRss.aspx
      </wfw:commentRss>
      <slash:comments>1</slash:comments>
      <description>Foo…</description>
    </item>
  </channel>
</rss>
```

Note that the RSS feed uses several XML namespaces: `http://purl.org/dc/ele-ments/1.1/`, `http://purl.org/rss/1.09/modules/slash/`, and `http://well-formedweb.org/commentapi/`. Listing 9.6 shows the code for using the DOM to select values out of elements that use a namespace prefix for the aforementioned namespaces.

Listing 9.6   Working with XML containing namespaces via the DOM

```
XmlDocument doc = new XmlDocument();
doc.Load("http://iqueryable.com/rss.aspx");

XmlNamespaceManager ns = new XmlNamespaceManager(doc.NameTable);
```

```
ns.AddNamespace("dc", "http://purl.org/dc/elements/1.1/");
ns.AddNamespace("slash", "http://purl.org/rss/1.0/modules/slash/");
ns.AddNamespace("wfw", "http://wellformedweb.org/CommentAPI/");

XmlNodeList commentNodes = doc.SelectNodes("//slash:comments", ns);
foreach(XmlNode node in commentNodes) {
    Console.WriteLine(node.InnerText);
}
```

When querying the RSS feed using the DOM, we need to create an XMLNamespace-Manager and remember to use it every time we do a search on the document. Unless of course we don't plan on querying for elements that have a prefix, in which case we can get rid of the namespace manager altogether:

```
XmlNodeList titleNodes = doc.SelectNodes("/rss/channel/item/title");
foreach(XmlNode node in titleNodes) {
  Console.WriteLine(node.InnerText);
}
```

Depending on what we're querying, we have slightly different APIs. We have to remember when to use a namespace manager and when to forgo it. LINQ to XML provides a more natural way of handling namespaces. Instead of working with an XMLNamespaceManager and having to remember when to use it, we remember one simple rule:

Always use fully expanded names when working with elements and attributes.

If the element that you're interested in has a namespace associated with it, use it when constructing your XName; if it doesn't, then don't. Listing 9.7 shows the LINQ to XML code for querying our sample XML.

Listing 9.7 Querying XML containing namespaces with LINQ to XML

```
XElement rss = XElement.Load("http://iqueryable.com/rss.aspx");
XNamespace dc = "http://purl.org/dc/elements/1.1/";
XNamespace slash = "http://purl.org/rss/1.0/modules/slash/";
XNamespace wfw = "http://wellformedweb.org/CommentAPI/";

IEnumerable<XElement> comments = rss.Descendants(slash + "comments");  ⟵
foreach(XElement comment in comments) {
  Console.WriteLine((int)comment);                    Fully expanded query using
}                                                      an XNamespace and XName

IEnumerable<XElement> titles = rss.Descendants("title");  ⟵  Query using
foreach(XElement title in titles) {                         only a local
  Console.WriteLine((string)title);                         name
}
```

As you can see, the way we deal with namespaces in LINQ to XML is straightforward. In our first query, we build our fully expanded name (XName) by appending the element's local name to our XNamespace (slash). In the second query for the titles of the items in the RSS feed, we use just the local name (title) since it doesn't have any namespace associated with it. By combining the namespace and the local name into a single concept, LINQ to XML makes working with XML documents that use namespaces and namespace prefixes much simpler. Everything is wrapped up into a single concept and encapsulated in a single class, XName.

That completes our quick tour of the key concepts within LINQ to XML. Throughout the next chapters, you'll see many examples of these key concepts, as well as how they can make your life easier when working with XML. Now let's jump into the class hierarchy itself so that we can see how everything we've talked about thus far manifests itself in the classes and objects we'll use to build XML applications.

9.4   LINQ to XML class hierarchy

Before moving on to look at how we can use the LINQ to XML programming API to load, create, and update XML, we need to understand the major classes we'll be using. Fortunately, LINQ to XML has a relatively small hierarchy, and only a handful of classes that you'll work with day to day. The class hierarchy is figure 9.2 shows the major classes defined in the LINQ to XML API.

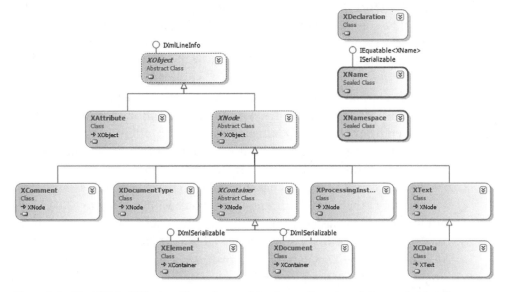

Figure 9.2   The LINQ to XML class hierarchy consists of a small number of classes, but together they provide developers with a powerful programming API for working with XML.

LINQ to XML is a small, focused API that has been designed to allow programmers to work with XML in a more productive and intuitive manner.

At the top of figure 9.2 we have the abstract `XObject` class. The `XObject` class serves as a base class for the majority of the classes within the LINQ to XML class hierarchy. It provides an `AddAnnotation` method for adding user-defined information, such as line numbers, to LINQ to XML objects, as well as a `RemoveAnnotation` for getting rid of an annotation when it's no longer desired. To retrieve annotations, `XObject` offers the `Annotation`, `Annotation<T>`, `Annotations`, and `Annotations<T>` axis methods.

Just below `XObject` in the class diagram is the abstract `XNode` class. `XNode` is the base class for all LINQ to XML classes that represent element nodes. It provides common operations for updates using the imperative style such as `AddAfterSelf`, `AddBeforeSelf`, and `Remove`, as well as axis methods such as `Ancestors`, `ElementsAfterSelf`, `ElementsBeforeSelf`, `NodesAfterSelf`, and `NodesBeforeSelf`.

Just below `XNode` in the class hierarchy is the `XContainer` class. `XContainer` is an abstract base class for all `XNode` objects that can contain other `XNode` objects. `XContainer` adds additional imperative update methods such as `Add`, `AddFirst`, `RemoveNodes`, and `ReplaceNodes`. It also adds axis methods such as `Nodes`, `Descendants`, `Element`, and `Elements`. `XContainer` serves as the base class of two of the most important classes within the LINQ to XML hierarchy, `XElement` and `XDocument`.

Although it appears low in the class hierarchy, the most fundamental class within LINQ to XML is `XElement`. The `XElement` class represents XML element nodes that contain other elements as child nodes. It adds further axis methods such as `Attributes`, `AncestorsAndSelf`, and `DescendantAndSelf`, as well as additional imperative update methods such as `RemoveAll`, `RemoveAttributes`, `SetElementValue`, and `SetAttributeValue`. As the fundamental class within LINQ to XML, `XElement` also provides a static `Load` method, which allows XML to be loaded from external sources, as well as a static `Parse` method that allows an `XElement` to be created from a string of XML. Finally, `XElement` offers a `Save` method for saving the XML tree that it represents to disk, as well as a `WriteTo` method that allows the XML to be written to an `XmlWriter`. In addition to being able to contain other `XNode` objects, `XElement` also has the ability to have attributes assigned.

The `XAttribute` class represents attributes within LINQ to XML. Unlike many of the other core classes within LINQ to XML, `XAttribute` does not inherit from `XNode`. `XAttribute` objects are name/value pairs that are associated with `XElement` objects. The `XAttribute` class provides a `Parent` axis property, as well as a single imperative `Remove` method.

As we mentioned earlier in this chapter, the importance of XML documents has been greatly deemphasized in LINQ to XML, but they're still needed from time to time. It's for this purpose that LINQ to XML provides the XDocument class. The XDocument class represents a complete XML document. Like the XElement class, it offers both a static Load method for loading XML documents from external sources and a static Parse method that allows XML documents to be created from a string. It also offers the same Save and WriteTo methods that allow the actual XML document that they represent to be saved. The primary difference between the XElement and XDocument classes is that an XDocument contains a single root XElement, as well as the ability to contain

- One XML declaration
- One XML document type
- XML processing instructions

As mentioned earlier, one of the key concepts of LINQ to XML is the simplification of XML names. The two classes that help with this simplification are the XName and XNamespace classes. XName represents a fully expanded name for an XElement or XAttribute. The fully expanded name is represented in the string format {namespace}localname. The XNamespace class represents the namespace portion of an XName, and as such can be retrieved using the Namespace property of an XName. The XName and XNamespace classes have an implicit operator overload defined that allows a string formatted in expanded XML Name format to automatically be converted into an XName and XNamespace. The implicit overloads allow us to use strings in place of XName and XNamespace objects when constructing XElement and XAttribute objects.

While there are several other classes within the LINQ to XML hierarchy, they're complementary classes that you likely won't see in your everyday programming efforts. See table 9.1.

Table 9.1 Complementary LINQ to XML classes

Class	Description
XDeclaration	Represents an XML declaration. An XML declaration is used to declare the XML version, the encoding, and whether or not the XML document is standalone.
XComment	Represents an XML comment.
XDocumentType	Represents an XML DTD.

Table 9.1   Complementary LINQ to XML classes *(continued)*

Class	Description
XProcessingInstruction	Represents an XML processing instruction. A processing instruction is intended to convey information to an application that processes the XML.
XStreamingElement	Allows elements to be streamed on input and output.
XText and XCData	The LINQ to XML text node classes. Text nodes are used when creating CData sections or working with mixed content

The simplicity of LINQ to XML can be seen in the low number of classes within the API, and in how few classes you need to be intimately familiar with to complete common XML programming tasks. Now that we have a base understanding of the core classes within the LINQ to XML object hierarchy, let's start to get our hands dirty with LINQ to XML.

9.5   *Working with XML using LINQ*

Now that we've seen the LINQ to XML class hierarchy, it's time to look at how we use the API provided by the LINQ to XML classes to perform the common XML operations we encounter when developing applications. The LINQ to XML API provides developers with an in-memory programming interface for reading, parsing, creating, and manipulating XML. Using the LINQ to XML API, we can quickly build applications that leverage XML data throughout.

In this section, we're going to cover all the fundamental operations that are required for building applications that use XML. As we work our way through the API, we're not going to cover every class within the LINQ to XML hierarchy, and we're not going to cover every method available. Instead we'll focus on the key classes and methods that will be the most valuable when building applications with LINQ to XML.

We're going to start by looking at how to load data from a file on disk, as well as from an external web site. Once we have a firm understanding of how to read XML, we'll be able to leverage the various XML data feeds available on the web within our applications. While it's nice to have a well-formatted XML document, we'll sometimes need to parse a string of text formatted as XML into a LINQ to XML object. Because of this, we'll explore the Parse methods available on XElement and XDocument.

Next, we'll learn how to create our own XML, and we'll finish by looking at how we can alter and modify existing XML trees using the LINQ to XML API. By the time we finish, we'll have covered all the common operations that you'll need to start building applications that use XML. Without further ado, let's take a look at how to load existing XML documents with LINQ to XML.

9.5.1 *Loading XML*

LINQ to XML allows XML to be loaded from a variety of input sources. These sources include a file, a URL, and an XmlReader. To load XML, the static Load method on XElement can be used. To load an XML file from a file on your hard drive into an XElement, you can use the following C# code:

```
XElement x = XElement.Load(@"c:\books.xml");
```

Loading XML from a web site (or any URL) is also supported by the Load method. To load the RSS feed from the MSDN web site, we can alter the Load method to take in a URL instead of a file path.

```
XElement x = XElement.Load("http://msdn.microsoft.com/rss.xml");
```

By default, when XML is loaded into a XDocument or XElement, the whitespace within the document is removed. If you want to preserve the whitespace within the source document, you can overload the Load method so it takes a Load-Options flag. The LoadOptions flag can be used to indicate the options to use when loading the XML. The available options are None, PreserveWhitespace, SetBaseUri, and SetLineInfo. Let's load the RSS from MSDN again, but this time preserve whitespace by passing the LoadOptions.PreserveWhitespace flag.

```
string xmlUrl = "http://msdn.microsoft.com/rss.xml";
XElement x = XElement.Load(xmlUrl, LoadOptions.PreserverWhitespace);
```

When loading XML from a file or URL, LINQ to XML uses the XmlReader class. The XmlReader first retrieves the XML requested in the Load method, either by reading the file from the local filesystem or by requesting the file with the provided URL. Once the file is retrieved, the XmlReader reads the XML within the file and parses it into an in-memory tree of LINQ to XML objects. Given XElement's use of XmlReader for loading XML, it's not surprising that LINQ to XML also supports loading XML directly from an existing XmlReader. To load XML from an XmlReader, you must first position the XmlReader on an element node.

In listing 9.8, we load our books.xml file into an XmlReader using its static Create method. We then read each node within the XmlReader until we find a node with a NodeType of XmlNodeType.Element. Once our XmlReader is positioned on an element node, we then use the static ReadFrom method that accepts an XmlReader as a parameter to create an XElement from the existing XmlReader instance.

Listing 9.8   Creating an `XElement` from an existing `XmlReader`

```
using(XmlReader reader = XmlReader.Create("books.xml")) {
  while(reader.Read()) {
    if(reader.NodeType == XmlNodeType.Element)
      break;
  }
  XElement booksXml = (XElement) XNode.ReadFrom(reader);
}
```

If you want to create an `XElement` object from a fragment of XML contained within an `XmlReader`, you need to navigate to the proper node using the `Xml-Reader` API and once again pass the reader to the `ReadFrom` method. For example, to load the first book element within our books.xml file, we can use listing 9.9.

Listing 9.9   Creating an `XElement` object from a fragment of XML contained within an `XmlReader`

```
using(XmlReader reader = XmlTextReader.Create("books.xml")) {
  while (reader.Read()) {
    if (reader.NodeType == XmlNodeType.Element && reader.Name == "book")
      break;
  }
  XElement booksXml = (XElement) XNode.ReadFrom(reader);
}
```

Thus far we've only explored how to load XML into `XElement` objects. If you're interested in accessing the XML declarations (`XDeclaration`), top-level XML processing instructions (`XProcessingInstruction`), XML document type definitions (`XDocumentType`), or XML comments (`XComment`) within an XML document, you'll need to load your XML into an `XDocument` object instead of an `XElement`. To load XML into an `XDocument` object, you can use the same mechanisms that we just discussed. The static `Load` method on `XDocument` has the same overloads as `XElement` and provides the same basic behavior. The only difference is that `XDocument` can contain additional nodes types as children. If we again want to load the MSDN RSS feed, but this time we're interested in being able to access every child node (including the XML declarations, DTDs, processing instructions, and comments) we can load the RSS feed into an `XDocument` object using the following code:

```
XDocument msdnDoc = XDocument.Load("http://msdn.microsoft.com/rss.xml");
```

Now that we've discussed how to load XML from external sources such as files, URLs, and `XmlReader` objects, let's look at how we can deal with XML that is contained within a simple string rather than a file.

9.5.2 *Parsing XML*

In some cases the XML that we want to use won't be in a file, or located at a URL. It will be a simple string that is being built by some other part of our application. For these cases, the XElement class provides a static Parse method that creates a new XElement from a string of XML. The Parse method has a similar interface to the Load method, so there isn't much new to learn. Listing 9.10 shows how we can use the Parse method to create an XElement from a string of XML.

Listing 9.10   Parsing a string of XML to an XElement

```
XElement x = XElement.Parse(
@"<books>
    <book>
      <author>Don Box</author>
      <title>Essential .NET</title>
    </book>
    <book>
      <author>Martin Fowler</author>
      <title>Patterns of Enterprise Application Architecture</title>
    </book>
  </books>");
```

Just like the Load method, the Parse method allows you to control whether whitespace is preserved by passing LoadOptions.PreserveWhitespace as the second parameter:

```
XElement x = XElement.Parse("<books/>", LoadOptions.PreserveWhitespace);
```

As noted earlier, LINQ to XML uses an XmlReader to parse XML. If malformed XML is passed to Parse then the underlying XmlReader will throw an exception. The Load and Parse methods do not catch the exceptions thrown by XmlReader; instead the exception bubbles up so that application code can catch the exception and handle it appropriately. The following code shows the general structure that should be followed when loading or parsing XML:

```
try {
  XElement xml = XElement.Parse("<bad xml>");
}
catch (System.Xml.XmlException e) {
  // log the exception
}
```

As we've seen throughout this section, the way we load and parse XML hasn't changed much with LINQ to XML. Under the covers, LINQ to XML leverages the power of the existing XmlReader infrastructure to perform all the XML parsing.

This allows the LINQ to XML classes to focus on providing an intuitive API for working with XML, rather than on the nitty-gritty details required to parse the XML.

Now that we've covered the basics of loading and parsing existing XML, let's move on to creating XML from scratch.

9.5.3 Creating XML

As we discussed earlier in this chapter, LINQ to XML provides a powerful approach to creating XML elements, referred to as functional construction. Functional construction allows a complete XML tree to be created in a single statement. As an example, let's look at how we can create the following XML using functional construction.

```
<books>
    <book>
        <author>Don Box</author>
        <title>Essential .NET</title>
    </book>
</book>
```

To create this XML, we can use one of the XElement constructors that allow us to pass in an entire XML fragment as a set of nested XElement objects. See listing 9.11.

Listing 9.11 Creating an XElement with functional construction

```
XElement books = new XElement("books",
  new XElement("book",
    new XElement("author", "Don Box"),
    new XElement("title", "Essential .NET")
  )
);
```

By indenting the C# code used to create the XML, we can see it take the shape of the resulting XML. Compare this to listing 9.12, which creates the same XML using the imperative construction model provided by LINQ to XML.

Listing 9.12 Creating an XElement using the imperative construction model provided by LINQ to XML

```
XElement book = new XElement("book");
book.Add(new XElement("author", "Don Box"));
book.Add(new XElement("title", "Essential .NET"));

XElement books = new XElement("books");
books.Add(book);
```

While the overall number of lines to create the XML in the two code samples is comparable, the first sample that used functional construction is more readable and more closely resembles the resulting XML. When creating XML using the imperative model, we need to create temporary variables for the various elements that make up the resulting XML. The result is code that is less readable and more prone to errors.

When thinking about XML, we often visualize the hierarchy of nodes that make up the XML. When building XML using imperative `Add` method calls, the code can't easily take on a shape similar to the resulting XML. With functional construction, we can write code that has a shape and feel similar to the resulting XML. This allows us to stay focused on the XML and not have to switch gears. The end result is a more pleasant and enjoyable programming experience.

To enable functional construction, the following three constructors are available on `XElement`.

```
public XElement(XName name)
public XElement(XName name, object content)
public XElement(XName name, params object[] content)
```

The `content` parameter can be any type of object that is a legitimate child of an `XElement`. Legitimate child content includes

- A `string`, which is added as text content. This is the recommended pattern to add a `string` as the value of an element; the LINQ to XML implementation will create the internal `XText` node.

- An `XText`, which can have either a `string` or `CData` value, added as child content. This is mainly useful for CData values; using a `string` is simpler for ordinary string values.

- An `XElement`, which is added as a child element.

- An `XAttribute`, which is added as an attribute.

- An `XProcessingInstruction` or `XComment`, which is added as child content.

- An `IEnumerable`, which is enumerated, and these rules are applied recursively.

- Anything else, in which case `To String()` is called and the result is added as text content.

- `null`, which is ignored.

The simplest way to create an `XElement` is by using a constructor that takes an `XName`.

```
XElement book = new XElement("book");
```

To make working with the LINQ to XML API more usable, the XName class has an implicit conversion from string. This means that LINQ to XML can convert a string, such as "book", into an XName object without you explicitly specifying a cast or creating a new XName object. Because of this, we can pass the name of the element ("book") directly to the XElement constructor. Under the covers, LINQ to XML implicitly converts the string into an XName and initializes the XElement with the XName.

Creating leaf elements that have text content is as easy as passing the content as the second parameter to the XElement constructor.

```
XElement name = new XElement("name", "Steve Eichert");
```

Which will produce

```
<name>Steve Eichert</name>
```

As you would expect, the string could have been stored in a variable or returned from a method call.

```
XElement name = new XElement("name", usersName);
XElement name = new XElement("name", GetUsersName());
```

To create an XML element with child nodes, we can take advantage of the third XElement constructor that is declared with the params keyword. The params keyword allows a variable number of arguments to be passed as content. To create this XML:

```
<books>
  <book>LINQ in Action</book>
  <book>Ajax in Action</book>
</books>
```

We can use the following code:

```
XElement books = new XElement("books",
  new XElement("book", "LINQ in Action"),
  new XElement("book", "Ajax in Action")
);
```

Since each child node in the previous sample is itself an XElement, we can extend the code to create an entire XML tree, as in listing 9.13.

Listing 9.13 Creating an XML tree using LINQ to XML

```
XElement books = new XElement("books",
  new XElement("book",
    new XElement("title", "LINQ in Action"),
    new XElement("authors",
```

```
      new XElement("author", "Fabrice Marguerie"),
      new XElement("author", "Steve Eichert"),
      new XElement("author", "Jim Wooley")
    ),
    new XElement("publicationDate", "January 2008")
  ),
  new XElement("book",
    new XElement("title", "Ajax in Action"),
    new XElement("authors",
      new XElement("author", "Dave Crane"),
      new XElement("author", "Eric Pascarello"),
      new XElement("author", "Darren James")
    ),
    new XElement("publicationDate", "October 2005")
  )
);
```

Of course, as you encounter real-life scenarios for creating XML, it's pretty unlikely that you'll be dealing with XML that doesn't contain namespaces and namespace prefixes. To create an element with a namespace, you can either pass the fully expanded XML name as the first parameter to the XElement constructor or you can create an XNamespace and append the local name when creating the element. Listing 9.14 shows how to create an XElement with a full XML name, as well as with an XNamespace.

Listing 9.14 Creating an XElement with a full XML name and an XNamespace

```
XElement book = new XElement("{http://linqinaction.net}book");   ◁─┐  Create
                                                                      XElement
XNamespace ns = "http://linqinaction.net";        ◁─┐ Create with     with fully
XElement book = new XElement(ns + "book");           │ XNamespace      expanded
                                                       │ and local name  XName
```

If you're creating a single element that uses a namespace, you'll most likely pass the fully expanded name and not explicitly create an XNamespace. If you're creating several elements that all use the same namespace, your code will look a lot cleaner if you declare the XNamespace once and use it throughout all the relevant elements, as shown in listing 9.15.

Listing 9.15 Creating several elements that all use an XNamespace

```
XNamespace ns = "http://linqinaction.net";
XElement book = new XElement(ns + "book",
  new XElement(ns + "title", "LINQ in Action"),
```

```
    new XElement(ns + "author", "Fabrice Marguerie"),
    new XElement(ns + "author", "Steve Eichert"),
    new XElement(ns + "author", "Jim Wooley"),
    new XElement(ns + "publisher", "Manning")
);
```

This will produce the following XML:

```
<book xmlns="http://linqinaction.net">
  <title>LINQ in Action</title>
  <author>Fabrice Marguerie</author>
  <author>Steve Eichert</author>
  <author>Jim Wooley</author>
  <publisher>Manning</publisher>
</book>
```

If you need to include namespace prefixes in your XML, you'll have to alter your code to explicitly associate a prefix with an XML namespace. To associate a prefix with a namespace, you can add an XAttribute object to the element requiring the prefix and append the prefix to the XNamespace.Xmlns namespace, as seen in listing 9.16.

Listing 9.16 Associating a prefix with a namespace

```
XNamespace ns = "http://linqinaction.net";
XElement book = new XElement(ns + "book",
  new XAttribute(XNamespace.Xmlns + "l", ns)
);
```

The resulting XML will look like this:

```
<l:book xmlns:l="http://linqinaction.net" />
```

Thus far we've primarily focused on producing XML that contains elements. When creating XML in real-world scenarios, the XML that we produce may include attributes, processing instructions, XML DTDs, comments, and more.

To include any of these in our XML is simply a matter of passing them in at the appropriate place within the functional construction statement. For example, to add an attribute to our book element, we can create a new XAttribute and pass it as one of the content parameters of our XElement, as in listing 9.17.

Listing 9.17   Creating XML with an attribute

```
XElement book = new XElement("book",
  new XAttribute("publicationDate", "October 2005"),
  new XElement("title", "Ajax in Action")
);
```

In this section we've focused exclusively on using functional construction and the LINQ to XML API for creating XML. We've also focused on doing so with C# as our programming language. Those VB programmers in the crowd will be excited to know that you're privy to a nice feature called *XML literals*, which allows you to embed XML directly within your Visual Basic 9.0 code.

9.5.4   *Creating XML with Visual Basic XML literals*

When creating XML in Visual Basic 9.0 using LINQ to XML, we can use the functional construction pattern as well as the imperative methods available within the LINQ to XML API. In addition, XML can be embedded directly within VB code using the XML literal syntax. To illustrate the power of the XML literals feature, let's look at how we can construct XML using functional construction and compare it against the code for creating the same XML using XML literals. Let's start by taking a look at the XML we're going to produce.

```
<book>
  <title>Naked Conversations</title>
  <author>Robert Scoble</author>
  <author>Shel Israel</author>
  <publisher>Wiley</publisher>
</book>
```

Before checking out how to create this XML using XML literals let's first do so using functional construction. The VB code to construct the XML using functional construction is shown in listing 9.18.

Listing 9.18   Creating XML using Visual Basic and functional construction

```
Dim xml As New XElement("book", _
  New XElement("title", "Naked Conversations"), _
  New XElement("author", "Robert Scoble"), _
  New XElement("author", "Shel Israel"), _
  New XElement("publisher", "Wiley") _
)
```

As you can see, the code for creating the XML using functional construction is exactly the same as the code we've already seen when creating XML using C# (besides the minor syntactical differences). Let's now take a look at listing 9.19, which shows the code for creating the XML using the XML literal syntax offered by VB9.

Listing 9.19 Creating XML using XML literals

```
Dim xml As XElement = <book>
  <title>Naked Conversations</title>
  <author>Robert Scoble</author>
  <author>Shel Israel</author>
  <publisher>Wiley</publisher>
</book>
```

With XML literals, we can embed XML directly into our Visual Basic code. Rather than creating LINQ to XML object hierarchies that represent the XML, we instead can define the XML using XML syntax. The result is code that exactly mirrors the resulting XML and is more clear and concise.

In listing 9.19, we create a static XML fragment using XML literals. When building real applications, we need to build XML in a more dynamic fashion. XML literals allow us to embed expressions into the XML literal code using syntax that is similar to the syntax used in ASP.NET. Let's modify the code to create an XML fragment using values stored in a set of local variables to illustrate how we can embed expressions in our XML. See listing 9.20.

Listing 9.20 Embedding expressions in XML literal expression holes

```
Dim title as String = "NHibernate in Action"
Dim author as String = "Pierre Kuate"
Dim publisher as String = "Manning"

Dim xml As XElement = <book>
  <title><%= title %></title>
  <author><%= author %></author>
  <publisher><%= publisher %></publisher>
</book>
```

In the listing code, we use an expression hole, which is expressed with the <%= statement %> syntax to embed dynamic values into our XML literals. While our expressions use local variables, we could just as easily use values returned from a function or pulled from a database. By allowing us to embed our own expressions within the XML literal code, VB9 provides us with an intuitive method for dynamically creating XML fragments using familiar XML syntax.

In addition to supporting expression holes as the content of XML tags, we can also use expression holes to create XML elements dynamically. For instance, if we wanted to store the element name for the root element within our XML in a variable, we can modify our code to look like listing 9.21.

Listing 9.21 Using expression holes to populate the element name of an XML element

```
Dim elementName as String = "book_tag"
Dim title as String = "NHibernate in Action"
Dim author as String = "Pierre Kuate"
Dim publisher as String = "Manning"

Dim xml As XElement = <<%= elementName %>>
  <title><%= title %></title>
  <author><%= author %></author>
  <publisher><%= publisher %></publisher>
</>
```

Which results in the following output:

```
<book_tag>
  <title>NHibernate in Action</title>
  <author>Pierre Kuate</author>
  <publisher>Manning</publisher>
</book_tag>
```

As we can see, using expression holes as element names is a matter of placing the expression that builds the tag inside the expression hole. Since tags created with expression holes aren't known until run-time, VB9 allows an empty tag `</>` to denote the close of an element.

In addition to supporting expression holes as element names and as content of elements, expressions can also be used in place of attribute values:

```
Dim linkXml = _
      <link updatedDate=<%=Now()%>>http://www.linqinaction.net/</link>
```

The addition of XML literals provides an intuitive syntax for creating XML in Visual Basic. Rather than having to learn the details of an XML API, XML literals allow programmers to embed XML directly within their code. Under the covers, the Visual Basic compiler coverts the XML literals into the corresponding LINQ to XML API calls that we discussed earlier in this chapter. This allows XML code created within

XML literals to interoperate with code written in languages that don't support XML literals, such as C#.

Now that we've covered how to create XML using functional construction, as well as Visual Basic's XML literals, let's move on to look at how we can create full XML documents using LINQ to XML's XDocument class.

9.5.5 *Creating XML documents*

When working with XDocument objects, you'll find yourself in familiar territory. All of the methods that we've talked about thus far, within the context of elements, apply equally to XDocument. The main difference between the two is what is considered allowable content. When working with XElement objects, we allow XElement objects, XAttribute objects, XText, IEnumerable, and strings to be added as content. XDocument allows the following to be added as child content:

- One XDocumentType for the DTD.

- One XDeclaration object, which allows you to specify the pertinent parts of an XML declaration: the XML version, the encoding of the document, and whether the XML document is standalone.

- Any number of XProcessingInstruction objects. A processing instruction conveys information to an application that processes the XML.

- One XElement object. This is the root node of the XML document.

- Any number of XComment objects. The comments will be siblings to the root element. The XComment object can't be the first argument in the list, as it is invalid for an XML document to start with a comment.

In most usage scenarios, XML documents will be created using the functional construction pattern, as shown in listing 9.22.

Listing 9.22 Create an XML document using the XDocument class and functional construction

```
XDocument doc = new XDocument(
  new XDeclaration("1.0", "utf-8", "yes"),
  new XProcessingInstruction("XML-stylesheet", "friendly-rss.xsl"),
  new XElement("rss",
    new XElement("channel", "my channel")
  )
);
```

Now that we've constructed our initial XDocument, let's talk about some of the classes that we may use during its construction.

XDeclaration

The `XDeclaration` class represents an XML declaration. An XML declaration is used to declare the version and encoding of the document, as well as to indicate whether the XML document is standalone.[2] As such, the `XDeclaration` class has the following constructor:

```
public XDeclaration(string version, string encoding, string standalone)
```

The `XDeclaration` class can be constructed using an existing `XDeclaration` or `XmlReader`. When an existing `XmlReader` is passed into the constructor, the XML declaration from the `XmlReader` is read into the `XDeclaration`. In order for the XML declaration to be read from the `XmlReader`, it must be positioned on the XML declaration. If the `XmlReader` is not positioned on an XML declaration, an `Invalid-OperationException` will be thrown.

XProcessingInstruction

The second class that becomes relevant when we start working with XML documents is `XProcessingInstruction`. The `XProcessingInstruction` class represents an XML processing instruction. Processing instructions convey information to an application that processes the XML. Like the `XDeclaration` class, the `XProcessingInstruction` class can be constructed with an existing `XmlReader` instance. Another way an `XProcessingInstruction` can be constructed is via the following constructor:

```
public XProcessingInstruction(string target, string data)
```

One of the most common uses of XML processing instructions is to indicate what XSLT stylesheet should be used to display an XML document. For example, to display a human-readable page when visitors click the RSS feed for your blog, you may want to add an XML-stylesheet processing instruction to tell browsers to apply a custom XSL stylesheet when displaying the raw XML feed, as in listing 9.23.

Listing 9.23 Create an XML document with an XML stylesheet processing instruction

```
XDocument d = new XDocument(
  new XProcessingInstruction("XML-stylesheet",
    "href='http://iqueryable.com/friendly-rss.xsl' type='text/xsl'
    media='screen'"),
  new XElement("rss", new XAttribute("version", "2.0"),
```

[2] A standalone XML document does not rely on information from external sources, such as external DTDs, for its content.

```
      new XElement("channel",
        new XElement("item", "my item")
      )
    )
  );
```

As we can see, the process of adding XML processing instructions to XML documents is easy as pie when we have the powerful functional construction capabilities offered by LINQ to XML at our disposal. Let's now move on to the next class that may be necessary for the XML document you're creating, XDocumentType.

XDocumentType

The XDocumentType class represents an XML document type definition. When constructing XML, we can use a DTD to define the rules for the document, such as what elements are present, as well as the relationships that exist between elements. Like every other class we've talked about in this section, XDocumentType has one constructor that allows it to be constructed from an XmlReader and another that gives it the freedom to be created without an XmlReader object. Here is the constructor definition:

```
public XDocumentType(string name, string publicId, string systemId, string
internalSubset)
```

To see an example of the XDocumentType class, let's create a valid HTML page using LINQ to XML. For an HTML document to be considered valid, it must declare the version of HTML that is used in the document; we'll do so using an XDocumentType object. When we're finished we'll end up with the following HTML document:

```
<!DOCTYPE HTML PUBLIC "-//W3C//DTD HTML 4.01//EN"
  "http://www.w3.org/TR/html4/strict.dtd">
<html>
  <body>This is the body!</body>
</html>
```

To create this HTML, we can create a new XDocument object using functional construction and pass along an XDocumentType, as well as an XElement as in listing 9.24.

> **Listing 9.24 Create an HTML document with a document type via the XDocumentType class**

```
XDocument html = new XDocument(
  new XDocumentType("HTML", "-//W3C//DTD HTML 4.01//EN",
                    "http://www.w3.org/TR/html4/strict.dtd", null),
```

```
    new XElement("html",
      new XElement("body", "This is the body!")
    )
  );
```

Now that we've seen how to add XML document type declarations to our XML documents, let's finish off our discussion of the classes that we'll use when creating XML documents by looking at how we can include XML comments.

XComment
Like the comments that we place within our C# and VB.NET code, XML comments can be added to XML documents to provide an explanation of what is contained within the document. An XML comment can be constructed with a string or by reading the XML comment that an XmlReader is currently positioned on. The XComment class is not limited to use within XDocument classes, but we don't see it as important so we've buried it down here where nobody except you will ever see it. After all, XML is supposed to be human readable, why should we need comments?

Now that we've covered how to use LINQ to XML to create XML from scratch using XElement and XDocument, it's time to look at how we can update and modify the XML we've created.

9.5.6 *Adding content to XML*

LINQ to XML provides a full set of methods for manipulating XML. Let's start by looking at how we can insert new elements and attributes into an existing XElement.

After loading or constructing an XElement, you may want to add additional child items to the element. The Add method allows content to be added to an existing XElement. The definition of the Add method is similar in nature to the constructors offered by XElement. It provides two overloads. The first overload takes in a single object, while the second allows a variable number of items to be added as content. The following are the two overloads for Add:

```
public void Add(object content)
public void Add(params object[] content)
```

These two overloads on Add allow content to be added using the functional construction pattern we discussed in section 9.5.3. To add a single child element to an existing XElement, we can use the following code:

```
XElement book = new XElement("book");
book.Add(new XElement("author", "Dr. Seuss"));
```

Of course the content parameter can be anything that is allowable as a child of XElement. We can add an attribute to our XElement by passing an XAttribute to our Add method instead of an XElement.

```
XElement book = new XElement("book");
book.Add(new XAttribute("publicationDate", "October 2005"));
```

As shown in listing 9.25, we can also use the second overload that accepts a variable number of objects to assign as content.

Listing 9.25 Add content to an `XElement` using the `Add` method

```
XElement books = new XElement("books");
books.Add(new XElement("book",
    new XAttribute("publicationDate", "May 2006"),
    new XElement("author", "Chris Sells"),
    new XElement("title", "Windows Forms Programming")
  )
);
```

It's also important to note that Add will properly handle content that implements IEnumerable. When a content item that implements IEnumerable is passed to the Add method, each item within the IEnumerable is recursively added to the XElement. This allows LINQ queries to be used to construct XML, since the standard query operators, as well as all of the XML query axis methods provided by LINQ to XML, return IEnumerable<XElement>. In chapter 10, we'll discuss the querying capabilities of LINQ to XML in depth and show how the functional construction pattern of creating XML can be combined with query expressions to create and transform XML. For the time being, let's look at the following example, which shows how we can leverage the support for IEnumerable within the Add method to add all the child elements in an existing XML document to an XElement.

```
XElement existingBooks = XElement.Load("existingBooks.xml");
XElement books = new XElement("books");
books.Add(existingBooks.Elements("book"));
```

By default, when an item is added to an XElement, it is added as the last child of the element. If the content being added is an XElement, the element is added as the last child element. If the content is an XAttribute, the attribute is the last attribute defined within the element. If this isn't the behavior you're after, don't worry. XElement offers several alternate methods. To add the child as the first child, you can call AddFirst. Alternatively, if you know precisely where you want the element placed, you can navigate to an element and call AddAfterSelf or

`AddBeforeSelf`. For example, to add a book element as the second child of our books `XElement`, we can do the following:

```
XElement newBook = new XElement("book", "LINQ in Action");
XElement firstBook = books.Element("book");
firstBook.AddAfterSelf(newBook);
```

The `AddFirst`, `AddAfterSelf`, and `AddBeforeSelf` methods all provide the same two overloads as `Add`, and they all process the content parameter in the same way. As you explore the LINQ to XML API, you'll see that it has been designed to work the same way throughout. Rather than finding unexpected behavior when exploring new methods, you'll find that they work just as you would expect.

Now that we've figured out how to add content to our XML, let's look at how we can remove it.

9.5.7 Removing content from XML

`XElement` provides several methods for removing child content. The most straightforward approach is to navigate to the item to be deleted and call `Remove`. `Remove` works over a single element as well as with an `IEnumerable`. Calling it on an `IEnumerable` will remove all elements within the `IEnumerable` with a single call. In listing 9.26, we show how to delete a single book element, as well as how to remove all book elements.

> **Listing 9.26 Removing one or many elements from an `XElement` with `Remove`**
>
> ```
> books.Element("book").Remove();   // remove the first book
> books.Elements("book").Remove();  // remove all books
> ```

Although not as straightforward, the `SetElementValue` method on `XElement` can also be used to remove elements. To remove an element using `SetElementValue`, pass null as the parameter.

```
books.SetElementValue("book", null);
```

If you're interested in keeping your element around but removing all of its content, you can use the `Value` property. To delete the content of the author element ("Steve Eichert") in the following XML:

```
<books>
  <book>
    <author>Steve Eichert</author>
  </book>
</books>
```

You can navigate to the element and then set the `Value` property to an empty string.

```
books.Element("book").Element("author").Value = String.Empty;
```

Which results in the following XML:

```
<books>
  <book>
    <author></author>
  </book>
</books>
```

Several of the methods mentioned in this section can also be used to update XML. We explore their use within that context next. Before moving on, let's take a deep breath. We've been covering a lot of ground and realize that you may be getting tired. Luckily we only have two more sections before we're finished with our introduction to the LINQ to XML API.

Let's move on to take a look at how we can update XML content using LINQ to XML.

9.5.8 *Updating XML content*

LINQ to XML offers several alternatives when it comes to updating XML. The most direct approach is to use the `SetElementValue` method defined on `XElement`. `SetElementValue` allows simple content of child elements to be replaced. Let's replace Steve Eichert as the author of this book with someone a little more prominent. Let's first take a look at the XML we'll be updating.

```
<books>
  <book>
    <title>LINQ in Action</title>
    <author>Steve Eichert</author>
  </book>
</books>
```

To update the `<author/>` element, we navigate to the first book element using the `Element` axis method. Once we're positioned on the `<book/>` element, we call `SetElementValue` and pass the name of the element that we want to update (author), as well as the new value.

```
XElement books = new XElement("books.xml");
books.Element("book").SetElementValue("author", "Bill Gates");
```

After calling `SetElementValue`, the value of the author element has been updated to `Bill Gates`:

```
<books>
  <book>
    <title>LINQ in Action</title>
    <author>Bill Gates</author>
  </book>
</books>
```

It's important to remember that SetElementValue only supports simple content. If we try to pass more advanced content, SetElementValue will attempt to convert the content to a string using the GetStringValue method on XContainer. For example, if we update our code to pass an XElement as the value for our author element instead of the string, like so:

```
books.Element("book").SetElementValue("author", new XElement("foo"));
```

we'll end up with an exception being thrown by XContainer, since it does not accept anything that inherits from XObject to be used as content.

To handle more complex content, the ReplaceNodes method that is defined on XContainer should be used. ReplaceNodes supports passing in all different types of content and provides overloads for passing in a variable number of content items. If we update our code to use ReplaceNodes instead of SetElementValue, we end up with the results we're after. The following code:

```
books.Element("book").Element("author").ReplaceNodes(new XElement("foo"));
```

results in

```
<books>
  <book>
    <title>LINQ in Action</title>
    <author>
      <foo/>
    </author>
  </book>
</books>
```

Calling ReplaceNodes on an XElement results in all existing content being removed and the content parameter passed to ReplaceNodes being added. The content parameter can be any valid child element of XElement, as well as an IEnumerable. If an IEnumerable is encountered, each item in the enumeration is added as a child content item. ReplaceNodes also has an overload that accepts a variable number of content parameters. This allows multiple child content items to be used as the replacement for the existing content. If we want to replace the entire contents of a <book/> element with a new set of child elements, we can use listing 9.27.

Listing 9.27 Replacing the contents of a element with new content

```
books.Element("book").ReplaceNodes(
  new XElement("title", "Ajax in Action"),
  new XElement("author", "Dave Crane")
);
```

Both `SetElementValue` and `ReplaceNodes` operate over the content of an element. If you need to replace an entire node rather than update its contents, you can use the `ReplaceWith` method defined on XNode. `ReplaceWith` operates over the element itself, rather than its content. This allows entire elements to be replaced. For example, if we want to replace all the <title/> elements within our XML file with <book_title/> elements, we could use listing 9.28.

Listing 9.28 Replace an entire node with `ReplaceWith`

```
var titles = books.Descendants("title").ToList();
foreach(XElement title in titles) {
  title.ReplaceWith(new XElement("book_title", (string) title));
}
```

In the listing, we first select all the <title/> elements using the `Descendants` axis method (which we'll discuss in the next chapter). Once we have all of the elements, we loop over each element and call the `ReplaceWith` method, passing a new XElement with book_title as its XName and the value of the current element as the value. This results in all the <title/> elements being replaced with <book_title/> elements.

As we've seen, when updating XML, we have several options at our disposal. `ReplaceWith` allows entire nodes to be replaced and is ideal for scenarios where we need to replace all instances of a given element with a new element. `SetElementValue` and `ReplaceNodes` offer us the ability to replace the contents of elements. `SetElementValue` is only meant for simple content, while `ReplaceNodes` supports more advanced content.

Throughout the last several sections, we've focused on how to add, delete, and update XML with a strong focus on elements. Since elements are the fundamental building block that we use to build XML, it's understandable that they've received most of our attention. Now that we have a firm grasp of how to work with elements, we need to look into how we can annotate our elements with attributes. After all, attributes are used in the majority of XML documents today. If we're going to be able to create and read real-world XML documents, we'll need to understand how LINQ to XML makes that possible. In the next section, we provide a complete run down of how to deal with attributes when working with LINQ to XML.

9.5.9   *Working with attributes*

The `XAttribute` class is used to represent an attribute within LINQ to XML. Unlike earlier XML APIs, attributes are not within the same class hierarchy as elements and nodes. In LINQ to XML, attributes are simply name-value pairs. As such, it's not surprising to find a constructor that allows `XAttribute` objects to be constructed with a name and value.

```
public XAttribute(XName name, object value)
```

During the creation of XML, we can include attributes within our XML by passing them as one of the parameters to the functional construction statements and/or the `Add` method. To create a book element with a publication date attribute, we can either add the attribute during construction time:

```
new XElement("book", new XAttribute("pubDate", "July 31, 2006"));
```

or we can add the attribute after the fact by calling `Add` and passing the attribute as the content parameter.

```
book.Add(new XAttribute("pubDate", "July 31, 2006"));
```

In either case, we end up with the following XML:

```
<book pubDate="July 31, 2006"/>
```

In addition to the `Add` method, we also have the ability to add attributes to elements with `SetAttributeValue`. `SetAttributeValue` is similar to the `SetElementValue` method we discussed earlier. `SetAttributeValue` can be used to add or update an attribute on an existing `XElement`. If the attribute already exists on the element, it will be updated, and if it doesn't exist, it will be added. If we need to update the `pubDate` attribute, we can use the `SetAttributeValue` method.

```
book.SetAttributeValue("pubDate", "October 1, 2006");
```

Again, like its closely related friend `SetElementValue`, `SetAttributeValue` can also be used to remove attributes by passing null as the value parameter. In addition to allowing attributes to be removed with `SetAttributeValue`, the `XAttribute` class has a `Remove` method.

```
book.Attribute("pubDate").Remove();
```

Remove can be called on a single XAttribute as well as on an IEnumerable<XAttribute>. Calling Remove on the latter results in all the attributes within the IEnumerable being removed from their associated elements.

As you can see, the way we work with attributes within LINQ to XML closely parallels how we work with elements. The key difference is that XAttribute objects are not nodes in the element tree, but are name-value pairs associated with an XML element.

We've gotten to a point where we can create XML from scratch using functional construction as well as manipulate that XML in all ways possible. As we continue, we'll likely want to figure out how our modified XML can be saved. Lucky for us, that's the focus of our next section.

9.5.10 *Saving XML*

The process of saving XML is extremely straightforward. The XElement and XDocument classes provide a Save method that will save your XML to a file, an XmlText-Writer, or an XmlWriter. To save an XElement to disk, we can call Save and pass a file path as a parameter, as in listing 9.29.

Listing 9.29 Saving an XElement to disk with the Save method

```
XElement books = new XElement("books",
  new XElement("book",
    new XElement("title", "LINQ in Action"),
    new XElement("author", "Steve Eichert"),
    new XElement("author", "Jim Wooley"),
    new XElement("author", "Fabrice Marguerie")
  )
);
books.Save(@"c:\books.XML");
```

That's it! Well, not entirely; you do have the ability to disable formatting of the XML during save by passing SaveOptions.DisableFormatting as a second parameter to the Save method, but it doesn't get much simpler than that, does it?

Now that we can save our XML, we've come full circle with the LINQ to XML programming API. We've covered how to load and parse XML from files, URLs, and text, as well as how to create XML using functional construction. Additionally, we've covered how we can use the imperative update methods available on XElement and XAttribute (such as Add, SetElementValue, and Remove) to add, update, and delete XML. We finished by looking at how we can use the Save method on XElement and XDocument to save our XML to a file. While we haven't covered every detail of every class, we've covered the major classes and methods that will allow you to start building applications with LINQ to XML. As with any new technology, the best way to learn the intricacies of the LINQ to XML programming API is to start writing applications that use it today.

9.6   *Summary*

LINQ to XML builds on the infrastructure provided by LINQ to allow XML to be queried using the standard query operators. LINQ to XML provides several XML axis methods that make retrieving elements or attributes easily. While the query capabilities offered by LINQ to XML are significant, just as significant if not more so is the LINQ to XML programming API. It provides a much better programming experience for developers working with XML and has an intuitive API that makes building applications that use XML simpler and more enjoyable.

The LINQ to XML programming API is a new lightweight XML API that was designed for LINQ. It builds on the language innovations brought by LINQ and introduces several new key concepts such as functional construction, context-free XML creation, and simplification of XML names. While Microsoft could have retrofitted existing XML APIs to work with LINQ, creating a new API designed and tuned specifically for LINQ has resulted in an API that makes working with XML productive and enjoyable.

At the heart of the LINQ to XML class hierarchy is `XElement`. It is the fundamental class that you work with in LINQ to XML. In addition to `XElement`, the `XAttribute`, `XDocument`, and `XName` classes are prominent. These core classes, as well as the rest of the programming API, have been designed with the programmer in mind, and as such provide an intuitive API for loading, parsing, creating, updating, and saving XML.

Now that we've introduced you to LINQ to XML and provided a detailed overview of the XML class hierarchy and programming API, it's time to move on to a detailed discussion of querying and transforming XML using LINQ to XML. We do that in the next chapter.

Query and transform
XML with LINQ to XML

10

This chapter covers:

- LINQ to XML query axis methods
- Querying XML documents using LINQ to XML
- Transforming XML

Over the last several years, many websites have begun to offer public XML web services that allow developers to access the data inside their site. Amazon.com provides a set of e-commerce web services that allow you to search their product catalog, Flickr lets you grab photographs that people have identified as interesting, and del.icio.us exposes XML feeds that allow you to keep abreast of websites that users have added to their bookmarks. By providing this data to clients as XML, Amazon, Flickr, and del.icio.us have enabled third-party developers to tie into their platforms to create compelling applications.

In order to do interesting things with the data contained in the XML, developers need a toolset that allows them to query the XML for the individual pieces of data that are of interest. With Amazon, they need to be able to read product details out of the XML feed, with Flickr it's the photograph details, and with del.icio.us it's the URL of the site that's been bookmarked.

In this chapter, we explore the querying and transformation capabilities offered by LINQ to XML. After a full chapter focusing on the LINQ to XML API, you might be wondering how LINQ to XML fits in with the rest of the LINQ toolset. After all, the previous chapter was primarily focused on learning about the XML API, and as such didn't include any discussion about how we can query XML data using LINQ. Now that we understand the core class library and have a feel for the XML API, it's time to look at how we can leverage the tremendous querying capabilities offered by LINQ when working with XML data.

We'll start by looking at parts of the XML API that we intentionally brushed over in the previous chapter, the LINQ to XML axis methods. The axis methods are made available by the LINQ to XML programming API and allow us to retrieve particular elements, attributes, and nodes within an XML tree. In order to do anything productive with XML data, we need this basic capability.

Once we've covered the LINQ to XML axis methods, we'll take a look at how the axis methods can be combined with the standard query operators and LINQ query expressions to provide the powerful querying capabilities that we've come to expect from LINQ. In addition to looking into the LINQ to XML axis methods and standard query operators, we'll also show how to query LINQ to XML objects using XPath.

Finally, we'll switch gears and examine how we can use LINQ to XML to transform XML into alternate formats. In a perfect world, the XML data we receive would already be in the exact format that we require, but sadly that's rarely the case. In order for us to use XML, we often need to transform it into alternate XML formats or into a format that can be displayed to a user, such as HTML. By combining the powerful query capabilities offered with LINQ to XML with functional construction and/or XML literals, we can transform XML documents into alternate formats quickly and easily.

In the LINQ to Objects and LINQ to SQL sections of this book, you've seen how the standard query operators allow a common set of query expressions to be used against objects as well as relational data. In this chapter, we'll show how the same standard query operators enable the querying of XML. Before we get to the standard query operators, we need to dive into the LINQ to XML axis methods, since they're the key to enabling the standard query operators to work against XML data. Let's get started.

10.1 *LINQ to XML axis methods*

The standard query operators provided by the LINQ framework allow queries to be a first-class language construct in C# and VB.NET. As we learned earlier in this book, the standard query operators operate over a sequence, where the sequence is an object whose type implements the IEnumerable<T> or IQueryable<T> interface. In the case of LINQ to XML, the "some type T" is typically an XElement, XAttribute, or XNode.

In order to use the standard query operators with our XML data, we need to be able to search our XML for a sequence of objects that can then be queried using the standard query operators. The LINQ to XML axis methods provide a means by which we can find the elements, attributes, and nodes that we want to work with within our XML.

Throughout this section we're going to introduce you to the various axis methods and explain when to use each. Once we have a firm handle on the axis methods, we'll look at how we can use them along with the standard query operators. To get started, let's look at the sample XML file that we'll use throughout this section for learning about the axis methods. The XML in listing 10.1 represents a subset of the books within our LINQ Books catalog.

Listing 10.1 A sample XML file, illustrating the tree-like structure of XML

```
<category name="Technical">
  <category name=".NET">
    <books>
      <book>CLR via C#</book>
      <book>Essential .NET</book>
    </books>
  </category>
  <category name="Design">
    <books>
      <book>Refactoring</book>
      <book>Domain Driven Design</book>
      <book>Patterns of Enterprise Application Architecture</book>
    </books>
```

```
    </category>
    <books>
      <book>Extreme Programming Explained</book>
      <book>Pragmatic Unit Testing with C#</book>
      <book>Head First Design Patterns</book>
    </books>
  </category>
```

As we look at this XML, we can see that it contains information about categories and books. In order for this data to be useful, we need to figure out how we can get it out of the XML and into a set of objects that we can query using LINQ.

Like most XML, this XML is hierarchical in nature. It contains a parent <category> element that contains a series of children (either other <category> elements or <books>), which themselves contain their own children (<book>s). With the LINQ to XML axis methods, we can select the elements and attributes that we're interested in. In this XML, we might be interested in the name of the root category element, or perhaps we're interested in the names of all the books within the .NET category. Or maybe we don't care at all about the categories and just want a list of every book, no matter where it lives in the XML tree.

Before we get any further, we should quickly mention that context is important when discussing the axis methods. Let's take a step away from the LINQ to XML axis methods for a second and imagine that we've decided to take a trip to the grocery store to pick up something to eat in anticipation for a long night of LINQ coding. When we get to the store, we realize we have no idea where anything is. Luckily, we find a lovely lady at the front of the store who seems willing to help. We walk up and tell her our problem. We need to get a pack of Mountain Dew, a bag of chips, and some donuts to fuel our coding frenzy. As the lady tells us where everything is, she does so by using our current location as a point of reference. She tells us the Mountain Dew is three aisles to the left, chips are two aisles to the right, and the donuts are all the way at the other end of the aisle right in front of us. Without knowing our current location, or context, those instructions wouldn't mean a thing.

The same applies to the LINQ to XML axis methods. In order to understand the results they're going to produce, we need to know our current location within the XML tree. We'll remind you of this as we move through our discussion of each method, but since it's important to understand, we wanted to call your attention to it now before getting started.

With that out of the way, let's get started with the LINQ to XML axis methods. To explore what the LINQ to XML axis methods provide, let's try to produce the following output with the help of the axis methods:

```
.NET
- CLR via C#
- Essential .NET
```

To produce this output, we'll need to learn a bit about the `Element`, `Attribute`, and `Elements` axis methods. Once we have a good grasp on these three core axis methods, we'll move on to look at a few other axis methods such as `Descendants` and `Ancestors`.

Let's get started by showing how the `Element` axis method can be put into action and get us on our way to accomplishing our goal.

10.1.1 *Element*

The first thing that we need to do to produce our desired output is select the .NET category element within our XML. The `Element` axis method allows us to select a single XML element by name. In our case, we're looking to select the first XML element with the `category` name. We can use listing 10.2 to do just that.

> **Listing 10.2 Selecting an element by name using the `Element` query axis method**

```
XElement root = XElement.Load("categorizedBooks.xml");
XElement dotNetCategory = root.Element("category");
Console.WriteLine(dotNetCategory);
```

As you can see, we start by loading our XML into an `XElement` using the static `Load` method we introduced in chapter 9. Once we have our XML loaded, we call the `Element` axis method on the root `XElement` and pass `category` as a parameter. The `Element` axis method accepts an `XName` as a parameter and returns the first matching `XElement` with the provided name that is a child of the current element. As we learned in the previous chapter, the implicit operator overloads defined on `XName` allow us to pass `category` instead of new `XName("category")`. The implicit operator overload automatically turns the string `"category"` into a full `XName` object with the local name set to `category`. The code in listing 10.2 results in the following output being printed to the console:

```
<category name=".NET">
  <books>
    <book>CLR via C#</book>
    <book>Essential .NET</book>
  </books>
</category>
```

If no elements are found with the name provided to the `Element` axis method, null will be returned.

Now that we have the .NET category XElement, we need to print out the name of the category rather than the entire XML fragment. As we can see, the name of the category is stored in the name attribute. As such, now seems like the perfect opportunity to introduce the Attribute axis method.

10.1.2 *Attribute*

Now that we have the .NET category element in the form of an XElement, we want to query the XElement for the value of the name attribute. To retrieve the name attribute, we use the Attribute axis method. Like the Element axis method, Attribute returns the first matching attribute with the provided XName. In our case, we only have a single attribute defined on the XElement, but you can be sure that won't always be the case. Since we're interested in the name of the category, we'll call the Attribute axis method and pass name as a parameter, as shown in listing 10.3.

Listing 10.3 Retrieve an attribute from an XML element with the Attribute method

```
XElement root = XElement.Load("categorizedBooks.xml");
XElement dotNetCategory = root.Element("category");
XAttribute name = dotNetCategory.Attribute("name");
```

Just like the Element axis method, Attribute returns the first attribute with the provided XName. If no attributes with the provided name are found, null is returned. Now that we have the name XAttribute in hand, we can output the title of the category to the console by casting the XAttribute to a string, as shown:

```
Console.WriteLine((string) name);
```

This results in the following output:

```
.NET
```

Once we have the category name printed to the console, we can stop and celebrate. We've accomplished part of our goal, and at the same time learned about both the Element and Attribute axis methods! Okay, you're right; perhaps we shouldn't celebrate just yet. We still have a ways to go.

With the Element and Attribute methods in our arsenal, we're on our way to being able to use LINQ query expressions and standard query operators with our XML data. We can select individual elements that we're interested in, as well as read individual attributes of an XElement. We're not quite ready to show how what we've learned can be used in a LINQ query, but you need not worry: It's coming shortly.

Before moving on to our next LINQ to XML axis method, let's revisit the XML fragment that we're working with and talk about what's next. We started our journey by selecting the first `category` under the root element in listing 10.1. The following XML fragment is the result:

```
<category name=".NET">
  <books>
    <book>CLR via C#</book>
    <book>Essential .NET</book>
  </books>
</category>
```

Once we have the `XElement` in hand, we output the name of the category to the console with the help of the `Attribute` query axis method. Next we need to query the category `XElement` for all the book elements contained within it. Unfortunately, we need to select multiple elements, so we can't use the `Element` method that we've already learned about. It looks like it's time to learn about the `Elements` axis method.

10.1.3 *Elements*

The `Elements` axis method is similar to the `Element` query axis method; the primary difference is that rather than returning the first matching `XElement`, `Elements` returns all matches. Given this, it shouldn't be surprising that `Elements` returns an `IEnumerable` of `XElement` objects, rather than a single `XElement`. Like `Element`, `Elements` accepts an `XName` as a parameter.

In our case, we're looking for all `<book>` elements so we'll provide `book` as our parameter to `Elements`. Since the `<book>` elements aren't directly under the category `XElement` that we selected in sections 10.1.1 and 10.1.2, we'll need to select the `<books>` element with the `Element` query axis method, and then call `Elements` as shown in listing 10.4.

Listing 10.4   Select all the child book elements using the `Elements` query axis method

```
XElement root = XElement.Load("categorizedBooks.xml");
XElement dotNetCategory = root.Element("category");
XAttribute name = dotNetCategory.Attribute("name");

XElement books = dotNetCategory.Element("books");
IEnumerable<XElement> bookElements = books.Elements("book");

Console.WriteLine((string) dotNetcategory);
foreach(XElement bookElement in bookElements) {
  Console.WriteLine(" - " + (string)bookElement);
}
```

When we run the code, we get the following results:

```
.NET
- CLR via C#
- Essential .NET
```

In addition to allowing us to find all elements with a given name, the `Elements` method also has a parameterless overload that can be used to retrieve all the children of an `XElement`. In the listing, we could have called the parameterless version of `Elements` since the `<books>` element only contains `<book>` elements as children.

By leveraging the `Element`, `Attribute`, and `Elements` axis methods, we've successfully read a set of details out of our sample XML and accomplished our goal. We didn't set our sights that high, but nevertheless we've learned about three essential LINQ to XML axis methods that we'll use when constructing more complex LINQ to XML queries.

It's important to remember that `Elements` only searches the elements that are direct children of the `XElement` that it's called on. Sometimes rather than needing just the children of the current element, we want to look at all the elements that exist at any level beneath the current element. It's for these scenarios that the LINQ to XML API provides the `Descendants` axis method.

10.1.4 *Descendants*

The `Descendants` axis method works in the same way as the `Elements` method, but instead of limiting the elements returned to those that are direct children of the current element, `Descendants` will traverse all the elements underneath the current element.

The `Descendants` axis method is helpful when you want to retrieve all the elements with a particular `XName`, but you're not sure where in the tree they live. The `Descendants` axis method has two overloads. The first overload accepts an `XName` and returns all elements anywhere underneath the current element with the provided `XName`. To retrieve every descendant, regardless of `XName`, you can call `Descendants` without any parameters.

We're once again going to use the XML we introduced in listing 10.1. This time, instead of looking for all the books within a single category, we'd like to return every book, no matter what category it's in. Since the book elements exist at different levels within the XML, we can't use the `Elements` axis method. Instead, we'll use the `Descendants` axis method. To retrieve every book within our XML, we can write the code shown in listing 10.5.

Listing 10.5   Retrieve every book within the XML with the `Descendants` method

```
XElement books = XElement.Load("categorizedBooks.xml");
foreach(XElement bookElement in books.Descendants("book")) {
  Console.WriteLine((string)bookElement);
}
```

This will output

```
CLR via C#
Essential .NET
Refactoring
Domain Driven Design
Patterns of Enterprise Application Architecture
Extreme Programming Explained
Pragmatic Unit Testing with C#
Head First Design Patterns
```

As you can see, the `Descendants` axis method makes it easy to retrieve all the book elements within the XML. Rather than having to navigate the tree ourselves using a combination of the `Element` and `Elements` methods, we can use the `Descendants` method to return all the elements that fall underneath the current element with a given `XName` ("book").

Closely related to the `Descendants` axis method is the `DescedantNodes` axis method. The only difference between the two is that `DescendantNodes` includes nonelement nodes (such as `XComment` and `XProcessingInstruction`) and as such returns an `IEnumerable` of `XNode` objects rather than an `IEnumerable` of `XElement` objects.

It's important to note that the `Descendants` axis method does not include itself in the tree of elements that are searched. If you need to include the current element, use the `DescendantsAndSelf` axis method. Just like the `Descendants` axis method, the `DescendantsAndSelf` method returns an `IEnumberable` of `XElement` objects. The only difference is that `DescendantsAndSelf` includes itself within the set of `XElement` objects that will be returned. Let's once again return to the XML introduced in listing 10.1, which is shown here:

```
<category name="Technical">
  <category name=".NET">
    <books>
      <book>CLR via C#</book>
      <book>Essential .NET</book>
    </books>
  </category>
  <category name="Design">
```

```
    <books>
      <book>Refactoring</book>
      <book>Domain Driven Design</book>
      <book>Patterns of Enterprise Application Architecture</book>
    </books>
  </category>
  <books>
    <book>Extreme Programming Explained</book>
    <book>Pragmatic Unit Testing with C#</book>
    <book>Head First Design Patterns</book>
  </books>
</category>
```

Now let's compare the `Descendants` and `DescendantsAndSelf` methods with the code shown in listing 10.6.

Listing 10.6   Comparing the `Descendants` and `DescendantsAndSelf` query axis methods

```
XElement root = XElement.Load("categorizedBooks.xml");
IEnumerable<XElement> categories = root.Descendants("category");

Console.WriteLine("Descendants");
foreach(XElement categoryElement in categories) {
  Console.WriteLine(" - " + (string)categoryElement.Attribute("name"));
}

categories = root.DescendantsAndSelf("category");
Console.WriteLine("DescendantsAndSelf");
foreach (XElement categoryElement in categories) {
  Console.WriteLine(" - " + (string)categoryElement.Attribute("name"));
}
```

As we can see, the way we call `Descendants` and `DescendantsAndSelf` is identical. If we examine the following output, we can see that `DescendantsAndSelf` included the root category (`Technical`) in its output.

```
Descendants
 - .NET
 - Design
DescendantsAndSelf
 - Technical
 - .NET
 - Design
```

Using `Descendants` and `DescendantsAndSelf`, we can quickly retrieve all the elements that we're interested in within a given XML tree as long as the elements are under the current node. When querying XML, you'll find that `Element`, `Elements`, `Attribute`, and `Descendants` are the primary axis methods that you use for finding the elements and attributes that are of interest in an XML tree. Since `Elements` and `Descendants` return `IEnumerable<XElement>` objects, they work nicely with the standard query operators and query expressions. We'll be digging into how the standard query operators work with LINQ to XML in section 10.2, but to give you a small taste, let's rewrite our earlier query using the LINQ query expression syntax. See listing 10.7.

Listing 10.7 Using LINQ query expression syntax for querying XML

```
XElement root = XElement.Load("categorizedBooks.xml");
var books = from book in root.Descendants("book")
            select (string)book;

foreach(string book in books) {
  Console.WriteLine(book);
}
```

As you can see, with a little help from the `Descendants` axis method, LINQ to XML allows us to write a query against our XML data using the same syntax that we use for querying our objects and relational data. Before further investigating how we can use the standard query operators and query expressions, let's finish off our discussion of the remaining LINQ to XML axis methods as well as show the more compact syntax Visual Basic provides for several of the axis methods already discussed.

While not as commonly used as the axis methods we've already covered, the remaining axis methods provide important functionality to developers. Let's start by exploring an axis method that shares many similarities with the `Descendants` axis method, `Ancestors`.

10.1.5 *Ancestors*

The `Ancestors` axis method works exactly like the `Descendants` method, except instead of searching down the XML tree, it searches up the tree. It offers the same signature and has the same related methods, `AncestorsAndSelf` and `Ancestor-Nodes`. Unlike all the other axis methods we've discussed so far, `Ancestors` searches for matching elements that are above the current node within the XML tree.

So far, we've learned how to get a list of books within a category element using a combination of `Element` and `Elements`, as well as how to get every book within our XML using `Descendants`. In this section, we're going to learn how we can use `Ancestors` to get the list of categories that a given book is in. Since the category elements are nested, we'll look to get the full category path for a book in the following form:

Domain Driven Design is in the: Technical/Design category.

The first thing we'll need to do is select the book that we're interested in. To do this, we can use the `Descendants` axis method to select all the books in our XML. Once we have all the books, we can filter the list of books down to the single one we're interested in using the `Where` and `First` standard query operators, like so:

```
XElement root = XElement.Load("categorizedBooks.xml");
XElement dddBook =
        root.Descendants("book")
            .Where(book => (string)book == "Domain Driven Design")
            .First();
```

In the code, we select the Domain Driven Design book element. Once we have the book element in hand, we can call the `Ancestors` axis method to select all the parent categories for the book element. Once we have the list of parent elements, we'll do some special processing with `Reverse` and `String.Join` to get the categories formatted as we desire. When all is said and done, we end up with listing 10.8.

Listing 10.8 Using `Ancestors` to query an XML document for elements above a particular element

```
XElement root = XElement.Load("categorizedBooks.xml");
XElement dddBook = root.Descendants("book")
                        .Where(book =>
                            (string)book == "Domain Driven Design"
                        ).First();

IEnumerable<XElement> ancestors = dddBook.Ancestors("category").Reverse();  ⟵──

string categoryPath =   ⟵── Build the category path
    String.Join("/", ancestors.Select(e =>
  (string)e.Attribute("name")).ToArray());

Console.WriteLine((string)dddBook + " is in the: " + categoryPath +
" category.");
```

Reverse the order, since we want the topmost category first

The result printed to the console includes everything we expect:

Domain Driven Design is in the: Design/Technical category.

The final set of axis methods available within the LINQ to XML API allow you to retrieve all the elements or content that occur before or after the current element. Let's look at them next.

10.1.6 ElementsAfterSelf, NodesAfterSelf, ElementsBeforeSelf, and NodesBeforeSelf

The `ElementsAfterSelf`, `ElementsBeforeSelf`, `NodesAfterSelf`, and `Nodes-BeforeSelf` methods provide an easy way for us to retrieve all the elements or content that exist before or after the current element. As is evident from their names, the `ElementsBeforeSelf` and `ElementsAfterSelf` axis methods return all the `XElement` objects that occur before or after the current element in the XML tree, respectively. If you need to retrieve all nodes, and not just the elements, then the `NodesBeforeSelf` and `NodesAfterSelf` methods are what you're after. Let's return to our previous example to see how the `ElementsBeforeSelf` and `ElementsAfterSelf` axis methods work. Once again we'll be working with the XML shown in Listing 10.1.

When we examined the `Ancestors` axis method, we looked at how we could retrieve the category path for a book within the XML tree. With the `Elements-BeforeSelf` and `ElementsAfterSelf` methods, we can look at the book elements that sit before or after the Domain Driven Design book element. It's important to note that unlike the `Ancestors` and `Descendants` axis methods, the `Elements-BeforeSelf`, `ElementsAfterSelf`, `NodesBeforeSelf`, and `NodesAfterSelf` methods only look at the elements and nodes at the same level as the current element. In listing 10.9, we'll use the `ElementsBeforeSelf` axis method to retrieve all the elements that are before the Domain Driven Design book element.

> **Listing 10.9 Finding all element nodes at the same level as an element using ElementsBeforeSelf**

```
XElement root = XElement.Load("categorizedBooks.xml");
XElement dddBook =
          root.Descendants("book")
          .Where(book => (string)book == "Domain Driven Design")
          .First();

IEnumerable<XElement> beforeSelf = dddBook.ElementsBeforeSelf();
foreach (XElement element in beforeSelf) {
  Console.WriteLine((string)element);
}
```

Not surprisingly, we end up with the following output:

```
Refactoring
```

The Refactoring book element is the only element that exists before the Domain Driven Design book element in our sample XML. As we can see from our output,

`ElementsBeforeSelf` is limited to elements on the same level as the current node. It will not traverse up or down the tree like the `Ancestors` and `Descendants` axis methods.

As you can see, the way that we navigate the XML tree using the LINQ to XML axis methods is simple, consistent, and powerful. The LINQ to XML axis methods provide us with an easy-to-use API that allows us to navigate to whatever it is we might be looking for within our XML. Before moving on to look at how we can use the LINQ to XML axis methods along with the standard query operators, let's look at a couple of unique features available within Visual Basic for accessing the axes within an XML tree.

10.1.7 *Visual Basic XML axis properties*

As we saw in chapter 9, Visual Basic has a few unique features for working with XML, most notably XML literals. XML literals allow XML to be created inside Visual Basic code using XML syntax. To complement this feature, the VB team has added several XML axis properties to Visual Basic that allow LINQ to XML axis methods to be called using a more compact syntax.

Let's get started by looking at the Visual Basic child axis property.

Child axis property

The child axis property is equivalent to the `Elements` axis method that we discussed earlier in this chapter. It allows you to return all the child elements with a particular element name. To use the child axis property, the `XName` of the element is enclosed like this: `<element>`. To illustrate, let's compare how we query the RSS feed in listing 10.10 using the child axis property with how we would query it with the `Elements` axis method.

> **Listing 10.10 The RSS feed that we'll query using the Visual Basic XML axis properties**

```xml
<?xml version="1.0" encoding="utf-8" ?>
<rss>
  <channel>
    <title>LINQ</title>
    <description>This is the LINQ channel!</description>
    <item>
      <title>Learning LINQ</title>
      <description>Learning LINQ is best done by reading the fantastic LINQ
in Action book that's currently in your hands.  It's simply amazing, and
has such wonderful code samples, don't you agree?</description>
    </item>
    <item>
      <title>LINQ to XML Axis methods make XML LINQable</title>
```

```
        <description>Without the LINQ to XML Axis methods LINQ to XML would
simply be one of the many XML APIs available in .NET land.  With axis
methods, we get an extremely powerful XML API, as well as a killer query
story that puts XPath, XSLT, and friends to shame.</description>
    </item>
  </channel>
</rss>
```

Let's start by looking at how we can query this RSS using the `Elements` axis method that we used in the previous section, but this time in Visual Basic. See listing 10.11.

Listing 10.11   Querying an RSS feed for all items using the `Elements` query axis method

```
Dim rss = XElement.Load("rss.xml")
Dim items = rss.Element("channel").Elements("item")

For Each item As XElement In items
  Console.WriteLine(CType(item.Element("title"), String))
Next
```

If we convert this code to use the child axis property rather than the `Elements` axis method, we end up with listing 10.12.

Listing 10.12   Querying an RSS feed for all items using the child axis property

```
Dim rss = XElement.Load("rss.xml")
Dim items = rss.<channel>(0).<item>

For Each item As XElement In items
  Console.WriteLine(CType(item.<title>.Value, String))
Next
```

Under the covers, the child axis property is converted into a call to the `Elements` axis method. Given this, it shouldn't be surprising that it returns an `IEnumerable(Of XElement)` with the provided name.

As we discussed when we examined the `Elements` and `Descendants` axis methods, often we don't want to limit the elements that are returned to the immediate children of our current element. If you need to include all the descendant elements in your search, you can use the descendants axis property.

Descendants axis property

As you might have guessed, the descendants axis property is equivalent to the `Descendants` axis method. It returns all the elements with a particular name that occur anywhere below the current element within the XML tree. The syntax for the descendants axis property is the same as the child axis property, except for one slight difference. Rather than calling the axis property with a single dot, the descendants axis property is accessed with triple-dot notation (...). For instance, to return all <item> elements within an RSS XML feed, you can use code in listing 10.13.

Listing 10.13 Retrieving all descendant nodes with the descendants axis property

```
Dim rss = XElement.Load("rss.xml")
Dim items as IEnumerable<XElement> = rss...<item>
```

Like the child axis property, the descendants axis property returns an `IEnumerable(Of XElement)`. If you need to access a particular item within the list of returned `XElement` objects, you can use the extension indexer or the value extension properties, which we'll look at next.

Extension indexer and Value extension

Visual Basic provides the extension indexer and `Value` extension to complement the child and descendants axis properties. The extension indexer allows you to retrieve a particular item in the resulting list of `XElement` objects. If we want to use the second <item> element in our RSS feed, we can use the element indexer along with the descendants axis property:

```
Dim secondItem = rss...<item>(1)
```

The element indexer is converted into a call to the `ElementAt` extension method. Since we often want to work with the value of the first item within the list of matches, VB provides another extension property to support just that. The `Value` extension property returns the value of the first `XElement` returned by the child or descendants axis property. See listing 10.14.

Listing 10.14 Using the `Value` extension property to return the value of the first `XElement`

```
Dim books = <books>
               <book>LINQ in Action</book>
               <book>Art of Unit Testing</book>
            </books>

Console.WriteLine(books.<book>.Value)
```

The code results in "LINQ in Action" being printed to the console.

Now that we've covered the various axis properties available within Visual Basic for retrieving elements, let's look at the final axis property, the attribute axis property.

Attribute axis property

The attributes axis property is equivalent to the `Attribute` axis method we talked about earlier, and can be used by placing a @ before the name of the attribute that you wish to retrieve. Let's look at listing 10.15 to see an example of the attribute axis property in action.

Listing 10.15 Selecting the value of an attribute using the attribute axis property

```
Dim book = <book publisher='Manning'>LINQ in Action</book>

Console.WriteLine(book.@publisher)
```

The attribute axis property returns the string value of the attribute, so listing 10.15 will result in "Manning" being printed to the console. If you need to access the actual `XAttribute` object, you'll need to resort to the standard `Attribute` axis method.

By providing a shorthand syntax for accessing the primary XML axes that developers use when querying XML, Visual Basic allows developers to stay focused on the XML they're trying to consume. While the same result can be achieved using the LINQ to XML axis methods, the Visual Basic axis properties provide a more concise syntax for querying XML.

We've completed our discussion of the various axis methods available in LINQ to XML. With these methods, you have the knowledge necessary to begin querying XML documents using LINQ. Now that we have a solid understanding of the LINQ to XML axis methods, we can further explore how we can use the axis methods along with the standard query operators and LINQ query expressions to query our XML data.

10.2 Standard query operators

In addition to providing the ability to select specific elements, attributes, and nodes within an XML tree, the axis methods are also a key enabler of the standard query operators. As we saw in chapter 4, the standard query operators operate over any sequence of objects that implement the `IEnumerable<T>` or `IQueryable<T>` interface. The axis methods enable the use of the standard query operators by returning an IEnumerable of XElement, XAttribute, or XNode objects. By enabling the use of the standard query operators, the LINQ to XML axis methods allow us to leverage everything we've already learned about querying objects and relational data to our XML data. Rather than having to learn a completely new language or syntax as we switch from objects to relational data to XML, we can instead use LINQ to query all three using the exact same set of standard query operators and query expressions!

Since you're reading this book, we're going to go out on a limb and bet that you're a .NET programmer. What can we say; we like to live on the edge! In this next section, we're going to find some great .NET books by using the standard query operators and LINQ to XML. We'll use the standard query operators to explore XML containing the top 20 most-tagged .NET books on Amazon.com. We're going to use the standard query operators to examine the list of books, filter the list down to those that we think are most interesting, and organize them into logical groupings (such as by publisher). Before we can get started, we need to learn about how we're going to access the XML containing the top-tagged .NET books on Amazon.com.

Amazon provides a number of web services that allows for data contained within Amazon.com to be accessed via a web service API. To access Amazon's web services, you have to register with their web services program.[1] After registering, an access key will be assigned to your account that grants you access to the Amazon web services. Once you have the registration complete, you can start using the web services to retrieve information from Amazon. Amazon provides both SOAP and REST versions of their web services. For this section we'll be accessing the TagLookup web service operation via the REST interface. The REST version of the TagLookup service can be accessed with the following URL:

```
http://ecs.amazonaws.com/onca/xml?Service=AWSECommerceService
        &AWSAccessKeyId={Your Access Key Here}
        &Operation=TagLookup
        &ResponseGroup=Tags,Small
        &Version=2007-07-16
        &TagName={Tag}
        &Count=20
```

If you replace "{Your Access Key Here}" with the key provided to you by Amazon and "{Tag}" with the tag that you're interested in, you can point your web browser

---

[1] http://www.amazon.com/gp/aws/registration/registration-form.html

to the URL to see the XML returned by Amazon. The screenshot in figure 10.1 shows a fragment of the XML returned for the "dotnet" tag.

As we can see, the XML returned contains a `<Tag>` element for the "dotnet" category, along with a series of `<TaggedItems>` elements representing each of the books that have been tagged with "dotnet" on Amazon.com. Let's get started by seeing how we can use the `Select` standard query operator to read the title of each of the books within the XML.

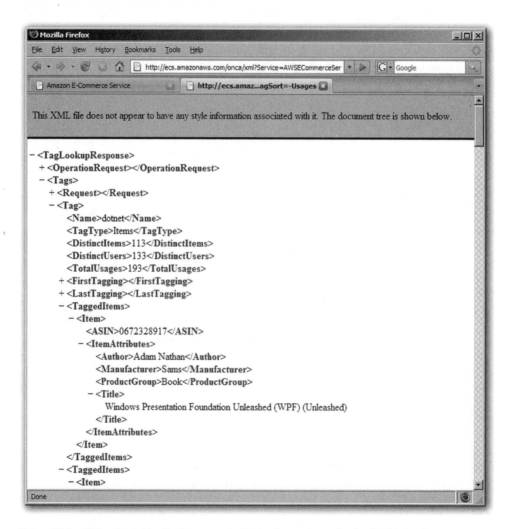

Figure 10.1   XML returned by the Amazon.com TagLookup web service for the "dotnet" tag

10.2.1 *Projecting with Select*

The most commonly used standard query operator may be Select. The Select operator performs a projection over a sequence. In our case, the sequence will be an IEnumerable<XElement>. Let's look at how we can use the Select operator along with the Descendants query axis method that we discussed in the previous section to retrieve the titles of all the books in our XML. In listing 10.16, we build the URL to the Amazon REST Tag Lookup service, define the namespace used in the resulting XML, and finally select the books from the XML using Descendants and the Select operator.

Listing 10.16   Using the Select standard query operator to apply a projection to an XML document

```
string url =
    "http://ecs.amazonaws.com/onca/xml?Service=AWSECommerceService" +
    "&AWSAccessKeyId={Your Access Key Here}" +
    "&Version=2007-07-16" +
    "&Operation=TagLookup" +
    "&ResponseGroup=Tags,Small" +
    "&TagName=dotnet" +
    "&Count=20";

XNamespace ns =
    "http://webservices.amazon.com/AWSECommerceService/2007-07-16";

XElement tags = XElement.Load(url);
var titles = tags.Descendants(ns + "Title")
                .Select(titleElement => (string)titleElement);

foreach (string title in titles) {
  Console.WriteLine(title);
}
```

To select all the <Title> elements within the XML, we use the Descendants axis method. Since the XML returned by Amazon has a default namespace, we declare a local XNamespace variable to be used when we call Descendants. Once we have all the elements, we then call the Select operator and pass it a selector that reads the title out of the <Title> element. The result is a sequence of strings containing the titles for all the books in the source XML. As we learned in chapter 3, the Select operator can also be called using LINQ query expression syntax as shown in listing 10.17.

Listing 10.17   Calling the `Select` standard query operator using LINQ query expression syntax

```
XElement tags = XElement.Load(url);
var titles = from title in tags.Descendants(ns + "Title")
             select (string)title;
```

At the end of the day, the same code gets run whether we call the standard query operators using the direct method call syntax or using the query expression syntax. Due to the expressiveness and compactness of query expressions, they're generally preferred. As we discussed in chapter 3, not all standard query operators have an equivalent query expression clause. Throughout the remainder of this chapter, we'll use the query expressions syntax to express our queries whenever possible.

While it's nice to be able to view all the books within the source XML, it would be even nicer if we could filter the list of books to those that we're most interested in. With listing 10.17, we don't have many attributes to filter on, so we'll keep things simple and filter the list by searching for keywords within the title of the book. As you can tell by our extensive use of `Console.WriteLine` within our code samples, we're in desperate need of a couple of books on Windows Presentation Foundation. Hopefully, after we learn how to filter our list of books down to those specifically about Windows Presentation Foundation, you'll be able to pick out one or two to order so next time around you can create a snazzy 3D GUI for our sample! Let's see how we can filter our list of books using the `Where` standard query operator.

10.2.2   Filtering with Where

We're going to try to find a book on Windows Presentation Foundation so we can expand my UI expertise beyond the simple `Console.WriteLine` paradigm, which we've clearly mastered. To filter our list of books, we'll use the `Where` standard query operator. The `Where` operator is a restriction operator, and as such can be used to filter our list of books down to those that are of interest. Before looking at our query, let's examine the XML for a single book within our XML.

```
<TaggedItems>
  <Item>
    <ASIN>0201734117</ASIN>
    <ItemAttributes>
      <Author>Don Box</Author>
      <Manufacturer>Addison-Wesley Professional</Manufacturer>
      <ProductGroup>Book</ProductGroup>
      <Title>Essential .NET, Volume I: The Common Language Runtime</Title>
    </ItemAttributes>
  </Item>
</TaggedItems>
```

As we can see, we don't have many attributes by which we can filter our books, so we'll stick to filtering the books by looking for "Windows Presentation Foundation" in the title. Listing 10.18 loads the XML from Amazon.com and filters the list of books using the `where` query expression clause.

Listing 10.18   Load XML from Amazon.com and filter the book list using the `where` clause

```
string url =
    "http://ecs.amazonaws.com/onca/xml?Service=AWSECommerceService" +
    "&AWSAccessKeyId={Your Access Key Here}" +
    "&Version=2007-07-16" +
    "&Operation=TagLookup" +
    "&ResponseGroup=Tags,Small" +
    "&TagName=dotnet" +
    "&Count=20";

XNamespace ns =
    "http://webservices.amazon.com/AWSECommerceService/2007-07-16";

XElement tags = XElement.Load(url);

var wpfBooks =
  from book in tags.Descendants(ns + "Item")
  let bookAttributes = book.Element(ns + "ItemAttributes")
  let title = ((string)bookAttributes.Element(ns + "Title"))
  where title.Contains("Windows Presentation Foundation")
  select title;

foreach (string title in wpfBooks) {
  Console.WriteLine(title);
}
```

At the time of this writing, listing 10.18 results in the following books being printed to the console:

```
Windows Presentation Foundation Unleashed (WPF) (Unleashed)
Programming Windows Presentation Foundation (Programming)
```

As we can see by examining our output, our query successfully filtered the list of books down to only those that have "Windows Presentation Foundation" in the title. To filter the list of books, we first selected all the `<Item>` elements in the XML with the `Descendants` axis method. Once all the `<Item>` elements were selected, we used the `let` clause to assign the `<ItemAttributes>` element to a query variable (`bookAttributes`). Finally, we constructed a `where` clause to filter the list of books to only those with "Windows Presentation Foundation" in the title.

In order to express our `where` clause predicate, we needed to cast the `<Title>` element to a `string`. You'll often find that in order to express the `where` clause predicate for LINQ to XML queries, you'll need to cast `XElement` or `XAttribute` objects to other .NET types. Luckily, LINQ to XML makes this easy by providing explicit operator overloads for `XElement` and `XAttribute` objects. Once the `<Title>` element is cast to a `string`, we can complete our predicate definition by calling the `Contains` method on the string with "Windows Presentation Foundation" as the parameter.

Now that we've filtered our list down to a couple of Windows Presentation Foundation books, it's time to jump over to www.amazon.com to place an order. Hopefully once those books arrive, we'll be able to start creating more compelling user interfaces within our code samples.

In the meantime, let's continue to explore a couple more standard query operators to see how they work with LINQ to XML. In addition to applying projections and filtering our XML data, we often want to group the results of our query, as well as order the results. Let's look at how we can use the `OrderBy` and `GroupBy` standard query operators with LINQ to XML.

10.2.3 *Ordering and grouping*

In the previous section, we used the `Where` operator to filter our list of books down to those with "Windows Presentation Foundation" in the title. In this section, we're going to go back to working with all the books in the XML. We're going to learn about how we can sort the books, as well as how we can group the books by their publisher.

LINQ provides two standard query operators for sorting sequences. The `OrderBy` standard query operator sorts the elements within a sequence in ascending order. If you want to sort in descending rather than ascending order, the `OrderByDescending` standard query operator is available. Both the `OrderBy` and `OrderByDescending` standard query operators have equivalent query expression clauses. Table 10.1 shows the query expression equivalent for both C# and Visual Basic.

Table 10.1 Standard query operators and their query expression equivalents

Standard query operator	C# equivalent	VB equivalent
OrderBy	orderby ...	Order By ...
OrderByDescending	orderby ... descending	Order By ... Descending

Let's go back to our query from the previous section, but instead of filtering the books, let's order them instead. Listing 10.19 selects the title of the books from the XML and sorts them in ascending order.

Listing 10.19 Ordering the results of a query using the `orderby` expression

```
XNamespace ns =
      "http://webservices.amazon.com/AWSECommerceService/2007-07-16";

string url =
      "http://ecs.amazonaws.com/onca/xml?Service=AWSECommerceService" +
      "&AWSAccessKeyId={Your Access Key Here}" +
      "&Version=2007-07-16" +
      "&Operation=TagLookup" +
      "&ResponseGroup=Tags,Small" +
      "&TagName=dotnet" +
      "&Count=20";

XElement tags = XElement.Load(url);
var groups =
  from book in tags.Descendants(ns + "Item")
  let bookAttributes = book.Element(ns + "ItemAttributes")
  let title = (string)bookAttributes.Element(ns + "Title")
  orderby title
  select title;
```

Sorting the books in descending rather than ascending order is a matter of changing the `orderby title` class to `orderby title descending`. As with the other operators that we've discussed, the `orderby` operator is used with XML data the same as it's used by objects and relational data. The only difference is that the key that is used for the sorting will come from a LINQ to XML object such as `XElement`, `XAttribute`, or `XNode`. The `orderby` clause allows multiple keys to be specified, which allows one or more secondary sorts to be performed.

Now that we've seen how to sort our data, we're going to investigate one final standard query operator before moving on to look at how we can query LINQ to XML trees using XPath. The last standard query operator that we're going to cover is the `GroupBy` operator.

The `GroupBy` standard query operator allows a sequence of data to be grouped. To illustrate how we can use the `GroupBy` standard query operator with LINQ to XML, let's group the books in our XML by their publisher. To group our books by publisher, we'll modify our query as shown in listing 10.20.

Listing 10.20   Grouping the results of a query using the `group` expression

```
XElement tags = XElement.Load(url);
var groups =
  from book in tags.Descendants(ns + "Item")
  let bookAttributes = book.Element(ns + "ItemAttributes")
  let title = (string)bookAttributes.Element(ns + "Title")
  let publisher = (string)bookAttributes.Element(ns + "Manufacturer")
  orderby publisher, title
  group title by publisher;
```

In the query, we start by selecting all the books with the `Descendants` axis method. We then retrieve the title and publisher of the book using the `Element` axis method. With the title and publisher in hand, we order our results by publisher and then title, and finally group the books by the publisher. The `group by` query expression results in our query returning an object that implements the `IGrouping<K, T>` and `IEnumerable<T>` interfaces. The type `K` is the type of the value we group by, and the type `T` is the type of object that we're putting into our group. In our query, we can determine type `K` and `T` by looking at our `group by` expression.

```
group title by publisher;
      T          K
```

In our `group by` expression, types `T` and `K` are both strings. Now that our results are grouped by publisher, let's loop over the results returned by our query and output them to the console.

```
foreach (var group in groups) {
  Console.WriteLine(group.Count() + " book(s) published by " + group.Key);
  foreach (var title in group) {
    Console.WriteLine(" - " + title);
  }
}
```

When we put everything together and run our code, we end up with the following results.

```
4 book(s) published by Addison-Wesley Professional
 - Essential .NET, Volume I: The Common Language Runtime
 - Framework Design Guidelines: Conventions, Idioms, and Patterns for
Reusable .NET Libraries (Microsoft .NET Development Series)
 - The .NET Developer's Guide to Directory Services Programming (Microsoft
.NET Development Series)
 - The .NET Developer's Guide to Windows Security (Microsoft .NET
Development Series)
5 book(s) published by Apress
```

```
 - Foundations of F#
 - Pro .NET 2.0 Windows Forms and Custom Controls in C#
 - Pro C# 2005 and the .NET 2.0 Platform, Third Edition
 - Pro C# with .NET 3.0, Special Edition (Pro)
 - Pro WF: Windows Workflow in .NET 3.0 (Expert's Voice in .Net)
1 book(s) published by Cambridge University Press
 - Data Structures and Algorithms Using C#
3 book(s) published by Microsoft Press
 - Applications = Code + Markup: A Guide to the Microsoft  Windows
Presentation Foundation (Pro - Developer)
 - CLR via C#, Second Edition (Pro Developer)
 - Inside Windows  Communication Foundation (Pro Developer)
4 book(s) published by O'Reilly Media, Inc.
 - C# Cookbook, 2nd Edition (Cookbooks (O'Reilly))
 - Programming .NET Components, 2nd Edition
 - Programming WCF Services (Programming)
 - Programming Windows Presentation Foundation (Programming)
1 book(s) published by Sams
 - Windows Presentation Foundation Unleashed (WPF) (Unleashed)
2 book(s) published by Wrox
 - Professional .NET Framework 2.0 (Programmer to Programmer)
 - Professional C# 2005 (Wrox Professional Guides)
```

As we've seen by exploring the Select, Where, GroupBy, and OrderBy standard query operators, LINQ to XML fully leverages the LINQ framework and allows you to fully express XML queries using the familiar LINQ query expression syntax. While we haven't explored every standard query operator, rest assured that LINQ to XML fully supports them all. As we discussed earlier in this chapter, not all standard query operators have an equivalent query expression clause. As with LINQ to Objects and LINQ to SQL, LINQ to XML requires you to call those operators using the traditional standard query operator methods.

Now that we've introduced the LINQ to XML axis methods, shown how to use a few of the standard query operators with LINQ to XML, and shown how LINQ to XML queries can be expressed using LINQ query expressions syntax, you should have all you need to start building applications that query XML data with LINQ. The consistent query experience for objects, databases, and XML provided by LINQ offers significant advancements for developers. They no longer have to switch gears as they work with different types of data. Instead, they can learn one common set of standard query operators, along with the LINQ to XML axis methods, and begin to build applications that combine all different types of data.

Until now, we've completely ignored the primary method for querying XML that existed before LINQ to XML, the standard query operators, and the axis methods came to be: XPath.

10.3 *Querying LINQ to XML objects with XPath*

XPath is a language for finding information in an XML document, much like the axis methods and standard query operators. However, instead of offering an API for navigating the XML tree and finding the desired elements and attributes, XPath provides a text-based query language that can be used to define the information that should be selected with the query.

As we've already seen, the primary means for querying XML data when using LINQ to XML are the standard query operators and LINQ to XML axis methods. Still, there may be times when an existing XPath query will need to be used. To enable this, a number of bridge classes have been added to the `System.Xml.XPath` namespace that enable the use of XPath with LINQ to XML objects. To use XPath against LINQ to XML objects, a reference will need to be added to the `System.Xml.XPath` namespace.

```
using Sytem.Xml.XPath;
```

Adding a reference to `System.Xml.XPath` adds a number of extension methods to classes that derive from `XNode`. The first method added is the `CreateNavigator` method, which allows an `XPathNavigator` to be created from an existing `XNode`. In addition to being able to create an `XPathNavigator`, the extension methods also allow XPath expressions to be evaluated against an `XNode` via the `XPathEvaluate` method. Finally, the `XPathSelectElement` and `XPathSelectElements` extension methods allow LINQ to XML objects to be searched via XPath expressions. `XPathSelectElement` returns the first element matching the XPath expression and `XPathSelectElements` returns all elements matching the expression.

Let's see how we can use these extension methods to query the XML with XPath.

```
<category name="Technical">
  <category name=".NET">
    <books>
      <book>CLR via C#</book>
      <book>Essential .NET</book>
    </books>
  </category>
  <category name="Design">
    <books>
      <book>Refactoring</book>
      <book>Domain Driven Design</book>
      <book>Patterns of Enterprise Application Architecture</book>
    </books>
  </category>
```

```
<books>
  <book>Extreme Programming Explained</book>
  <book>Pragmatic Unit Testing with C#</book>
  <book>Head First Design Patterns</book>
</books>
</category>
```

As we did in an earlier example, let's start by querying the XML for every book within the XML. The `Descendants` query axis method is ideal for this type of query, since it traverses the entire XML tree. The equivalent XPath expression for retrieving every book element anywhere within the XML tree is `//book`. Since the `XPathSelectElements` extension method returns an `IEnumerable<XElement>`, we can use the familiar query expression syntax for creating our query, as shown in listing 10.21.

Listing 10.21 Querying `XElement` objects with XPath

```
XElement root = XElement.Load("categorizedBooks.xml");
var books = from book in root.XPathSelectElements("//book")
            select book;

foreach(XElement book in books) {
    Console.WriteLine((string)book);
}
```

When this code is run, we get the following results printed to the console:

```
CLR via C#
Essential .NET
Refactoring
Domain Driven Design
Patterns of Enterprise Application Architecture
Extreme Programming Explained
Pragmatic Unit Testing with C#
Head First Design Patterns
```

By providing a set of extension methods for the `XNode` object, the LINQ to XML team has allowed developers to use the same basic API for querying XML data whether it's via the axis methods and standard query operators or via XPath expressions. Additionally, the extension methods for running XPath queries against LINQ to XML objects allow for a much smoother migration path for applications that we want to move from code based on `System.Xml`.

Now that we've covered how to query XML data using axis methods, the standard query operators, query expressions, and XPath, its time to explore how we can use LINQ to XML to transform XML into alternate formats.

10.4 *Transforming XML*

When working with XML data, we often find that it needs to be transformed or manipulated in order to support our internal systems. This might be because of the way we need to present the data to our users or due to requirements of other systems within our infrastructure for the XML. No matter the reason, XML often needs to be transformed into alternate formats. Luckily, LINQ to XML provides an intuitive and powerful method for transforming XML that leverages its support for LINQ's standard query operators, its implementation of the LINQ to XML axis methods, and its support for functional construction.

10.4.1 *LINQ to XML transformations*

To see the powerful transformational capabilities offered by LINQ to XML, let's transform the XML from listing 10.22 into an XHTML document that can be shown in a browser.

Listing 10.22 The XML to be transformed

```
<?xml version="1.0" encoding="utf-8" ?>
<books>
  <book>
    <title>Linq in Action</title>
    <author>Fabrice Marguerie</author>
    <author>Steve Eichert</author>
    <author>Jim Wooley</author>
    <publisher>Manning</publisher>
  </book>
  <book>
    <title>Ajax in Action</title>
    <author>Dave Crane</author>
    <publisher>Manning</publisher>
  </book>
  <book>
    <title>Enterprise Application Architecture</title>
    <author>Martin Fowler</author>
    <publisher>APress</publisher>
  </book>
</books>
```

When we're finished with our transformation, we'll end up with the following XHTML:

```
<html>
  <body>
    <h1>LINQ Books Library</h1>
```

```
<div>
  <b>LINQ in Action</b>
  By: Fabrice Marguerie, Steve Eichert, Jim Wooley
  Published By: Manning
</div>
<div>
  <b>AJAX in Action</b>
  By: Dave Crane
  Published By: Manning
</div>
<div>
  <b>Patterns of Enterprise Application Architecture</b>
  By: Martin Fowler
  Published By: APress
</div>
  </body>
</html>
```

In order to transform the XML shown in listing 10.22 into this XHTML, we'll need to take advantage of the axis methods provided by LINQ to XML as well its functional construction capabilities. Let's start by examining how we can create the resulting XHTML using functional construction and for the moment ignore the XML that we're going to transform. To get a jump start, we can copy the resulting XHTML to the clipboard and use the Paste XML as LINQ Visual Studio .NET add-in to create our functional construction code for building the desired XML. When we do so, we end up with listing 10.23.

NOTE The Paste XML as LINQ Visual Studio add-in is shipped as a sample. To use it in Visual Studio 2008, you have to compile and install the add-in from the source code provided. The add-in can be found in the LinqSamples directory of the \Program Files\Visual Studio 9.0\Samples\CSharpSamples.zip file.

> **Listing 10.23   The LINQ to XML code created via the Paste XML as LINQ Visual Studio .NET add in**

```
XElement xml =
  new XElement("html",
    new XElement("body",
        new XElement("h1", "LINQ Books Library"),
        new XElement("div",
            new XElement("b", "LINQ in Action"),
            "        By: Fabrice Marguerie, Steve Eichert, Jim Wooley\n" +
            "        Published By: Manning\n"
        ),
        new XElement("div",
            new XElement("b", "AJAX in Action"),
```

```
            "        By: Dave Crane\n" +
            "        Published By: Manning\n"
        ),
        new XElement("div",
            new XElement("b", "Patterns of Enterprise Application
Architecture"),
            "        By: Martin Fowler\n" +
            "        Published By: APress\n"
        )
    )
);
```

As we can see, the Paste XML as LINQ add-in converted the XHTML into a single functional construction statement that creates each item contained within the XML. While the XML isn't perfect, it provides a good starting point.

When transforming XML, you may often find it beneficial to start with the end in mind and work your way backward. Now that we have a template for the XHTML we want to produce, we can incorporate LINQ to XML queries and take advantage of the rich support for embedding query expressions within functional construction statements. Before incorporating our query expressions with the functional construction statements, lets write a query to retrieve the data out of our XML. See listing 10.24.

Listing 10.24 Retrieve the title, publisher, and authors for each book within the XML

```
var books = from book in booksXml.Descendants("book")
            select new {
                Title = (string)book.Element("title"),
                Publisher = (string)book.Element("publisher"),
                Authors = String.Join(", ",
                        book.Descendants("author")
                        .Select(a => (string)a).ToArray())
            };
```

With this query, we've selected the title, publisher, and authors out of the XML file. We've done extra work to format the list of author names as a comma-separated list to match our desired output format. Now that we have our functional construction statements and our query, it's time to combine the two into a single LINQ to XML transformation. See listing 10.25.

Listing 10.25 Transform XML into XHTML with LINQ to XML transformations

```
XElement html =
  new XElement("html",
  new XElement("body",
    new XElement("h1", "LINQ Books Library"),
    from book in booksXml.Descendants("book")
    select new XElement("div",
      new XElement("b", (string)book.Element("title")),
      "By: " + String.Join(", ", book.Descendants("author")
                                    .Select(b => (string)b).ToArray()) +
      "Published By: " + (string)book.Element("publisher")
    )
  )
);
```

The resulting XHTML can be seen in figure 10.2.

As we've illustrated, LINQ to XML provides powerful transformation capabilities. Rather than having to learn a new language, such as XSLT, developers can leverage the knowledge they've already gained for creating XML using functional construction and their knowledge for querying XML using LINQ queries. By providing a single construction method for creating XML from scratch as well as creating XML from other XML via transformations, LINQ to XML provides a consistent programming model.

While LINQ to XML offers powerful transformations, the LINQ to XML team also recognized that a lot of existing applications have large investments in XSLT as a transformation technology. As such, they've provided support for transforming LINQ to XML objects using XSLT. Let's explore how we can use XSLT to produce the same output that we've produced in figure 10.2 with LINQ to XML transformations.

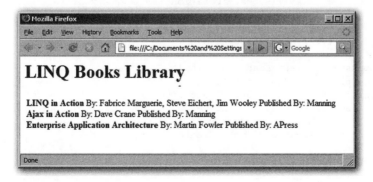

Figure 10.2 The XHTML result from our LINQ to XML query

10.4.2 *Transforming LINQ to XML objects with XSLT*

In order to use XSLT with LINQ to XML objects, a reference to the System.Xml.Xsl namespace must be added to the class handling the transformation. Once a reference has been made to System.Xml.Xsl, an XDocument needs to be created to hold the output of the transformation. From there, you create an XmlWriter using the CreateWriter method on XDocument, load your XSL, then apply the XSL to the XElement. Since the XslCompiledTransform object expects an XmlReader, not an XElement, we need to use the CreateReader() method on XElement and pass the resulting XmlReader on to the transform object. When we put this all together, we end up with listing 10.26.

Listing 10.26   Transforming an XElement using XSLT

```
string xsl = @"<?xml version='1.0' encoding='UTF-8' ?>
                <xsl:stylesheet version='1.0'
                    xmlns:xsl='http://www.w3.org/1999/XSL/Transform'>
                <xsl:template match='books'>
                  <html>
                    <title>Book Catalog</title>
                    <ul>
                      <xsl:apply-templates select='book'/>
                    </ul>
                  </html>
                </xsl:template>
                <xsl:template match='book'>
                  <li>
                    <xsl:value-of select='title'/> by
                    <xsl:apply-templates select='author'/>
                  </li>
                </xsl:template>
                <xsl:template match='author'>
                  <xsl:if test='position() > 1'>, </xsl:if>
                  <xsl:value-of select='.'/>
                </xsl:template>
                </xsl:stylesheet>";

XElement books = XElement.Load("books.xml");
XDocument output = new XDocument();
using (XmlWriter writer = output.CreateWriter()) {
    XslCompiledTransform xslTransformer = new XslCompiledTransform();
    xslTransformer.Load(XmlReader.Create(new StringReader(xsl)));
    xslTransformer.Transform(books.CreateReader(), writer);
}
Console.WriteLine(output);
```

The output is exactly the same as that shown in section 10.5.1. In order to make the transform code we used in the code reusable, we can pull the transformation logic into an extension method like in listing 10.27.

Listing 10.27   An extension method for transforming an XNode using XSL

```
public static class XmlExtensions {
    public static XDocument XslTransform(this XNode node, string xsl) {
        XDocument output = new XDocument();
        using (XmlWriter writer = output.CreateWriter()) {
            XslCompiledTransform xslTransformer = new XslCompiledTransform();
            xslTransformer.Load(XmlReader.Create(new StringReader(xsl)));
            xslTransformer.Transform(node.CreateReader(), writer);
        }
        return output;
    }
}
```

With this extension method in place, we can apply our transformation using the following code:

```
XElement.Load("books.xml").XslTransform(xsl));
```

In this section we've shown how to transform XML from one format to another by using the transformational capabilities of functional construction, as well as with XSLT. But often we need to transform XML data into in-memory objects. In the next chapter, we tackle this common scenario as well as many others.

10.5   *Summary*

In this chapter, we've shown you how to query and transform XML using LINQ to XML. We started by looking at the LINQ to XML axis methods and examined how the different axis methods allow elements and attributes within the XML to be selected. Next, we examined how we can use the axis methods along with the standard query operators and LINQ query expressions to express our XML queries using the same syntax as we use for querying objects and relational data. By enabling developers to use a single query syntax for objects, relational data, and XML, LINQ has completely changed how developers work with data. Rather than learn multiple technologies, developers can instead focus on mastering a single technology that covers all their data needs.

In addition to having strong XML-querying features, LINQ to XML has strong transformation features. By combining the powerful XML-creating capabilities offered by LINQ to XML with the advanced querying capabilities of LINQ, LINQ to XML provides developers an easy and intuitive method for transforming XML. Rather than learn a new transformation language, such as XSLT, developers can stay focused on a single set of techniques that can be used for creating, querying, and transforming XML.

With that, we've completed our overview of LINQ to XML. While we've provided you with the information necessary for building applications with LINQ to XML, we haven't covered many of the common scenarios that you might encounter. We rectify that in our next and final chapter on LINQ to XML.

Common LINQ
to XML scenarios

11

This chapter covers:

- Building objects from XML
- Creating XML from objects
- Creating XML from data in a database
- Creating XML from a CSV file

Now that we've learned about the LINQ to XML API and seen how to query and transform XML using LINQ to XML, it's time to explore some common scenarios that you may come across when working with LINQ to XML. These include building objects from XML, creating XML from a set of objects, creating XML with data from a database, filtering and mixing data from a database with XML data, updating a database with data read from an XML file, and transforming text files into XML using LINQ to XML. As we explore these common scenarios, you'll witness the powerful capabilities offered by LINQ to XML.

In addition to using LINQ to XML, we'll also make extensive use of the capabilities offered by LINQ to Objects and LINQ to SQL in this chapter. At times, you might forget that we're even talking about LINQ to XML because of the strong focus on LINQ to Objects and LINQ to SQL. Our ability to intertwine discussions of LINQ to XML along with LINQ to Objects and LINQ to SQL shows how well the LINQ technologies work together and how important it is to understand each one. In the end, our goal is to help you understand LINQ to XML and how it can be used to solve the common scenarios we've outlined, so we'll try to stay on course.

Within each section of this chapter, we'll start by defining the goal that we're looking to achieve. Once our goal is defined, we'll look at the techniques that we'll use to accomplish our goal. Finally, we'll look at the implementation and examine the code necessary for meeting our goal.

As you'll see throughout this chapter, LINQ to XML provides an intuitive XML programming API that, combined with the LINQ framework, provides a lot of powerful capabilities for building applications.

Let's get started by looking at how we can build objects from an XML file.

11.1   *Building objects from XML*

As we already mentioned, the first scenario that we're going to cover is building objects from XML. Before we look at the specifics of how we go about building objects from XML with LINQ to XML, let's talk briefly about why we would want to do it in the first place. When we build applications today, we do so using objects. Objects allow us to encapsulate the logic and data that exist in our software. Since XML is a data format and not a programming language, we need to read the data out of the XML files if we want to use it in our applications. To ensure our application doesn't get too tightly coupled to the format of an XML file, we'll convert the data within the XML file into a set of objects using the powerful capabilities offered by LINQ to XML.

As we'll see, LINQ to XML allows us to convert XML into objects using the same transformation techniques we learned about in the previous chapter. No matter what format we need to transform our XML into, LINQ to XML is up to the challenge. With that said, let's get started by examining our goal for this scenario.

11.1.1 Goal

Our goal in the section is to create a collection of objects that contain the data within the XML document shown in listing 11.1 using the capabilities offered by LINQ to XML.

Listing 11.1 Book data in XML format

```xml
<?xml version="1.0" encoding="utf-8" ?>
<books>
  <book>
    <title>LINQ in Action</title>
    <authors>
      <author>
        <firstName>Fabrice</firstName>
        <lastName>Marguerie</lastName>
        <website>http://linqinaction.net/</website>
      </author>
      <author>
        <firstName>Steve</firstName>
        <lastName>Eichert</lastName>
        <webSite>http://iqueryable.com</webSite>
      </author>
      <author>
        <firstName>Jim</firstName>
        <lastName>Wooley</lastName>
        <webSite> http://devauthority.com/blogs/jwooley/</webSite>
      </author>
    </authors>
    <subject>
      <name>LINQ</name>
      <description>LINQ shall rule the world</description>
    </subject>
    <publisher>Manning</publisher>
    <publicationDate>January 15, 2008</publicationDate>
    <price>44.99</price>
    <isbn>1933988169</isbn>
    <notes>Great book!</notes>
    <summary>LINQ in Action is great!</summary>
    <reviews>
      <review>
        <user>Steve Eichert</user>
        <rating>5</rating>
        <comments>What can I say, I'm biased!</comments>
```

```
        </review>
      </reviews>
  </book>
  <book>
    <title>Patterns of Enterprise Application Architecture</title>
    ...
  </book>
</books>
```

As we can see, the XML contains a set of information about books. If we move our attention to the classes shown in figure 11.1, we can see that we have a series of objects that correlate to the data contained in the XML file in listing 11.1.

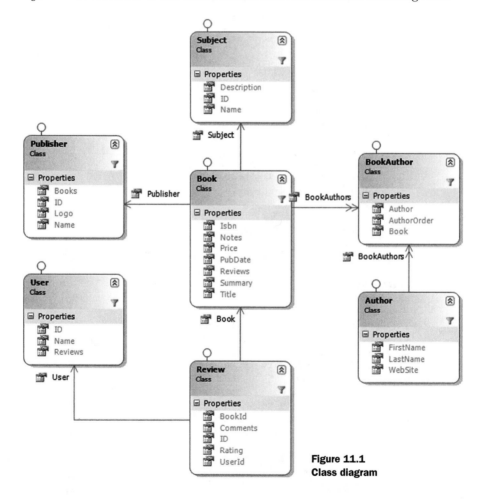

Figure 11.1
Class diagram

Our goal is to take the data contained in the XML file and create a list of Book objects. In addition to populating the Book object, we'll also populate the Subject, Publisher, Authors, and Reviews properties of the Book with the corresponding information in the XML file.

With our goal of creating book objects from the XML out of the way, let's a look at the technique we'll use to accomplish our goal.

11.1.2 *Implementation*

As we saw in the previous chapter, LINQ to XML provides powerful transformation capabilities. In addition to being able to transform XML to alternate XML formats, LINQ to XML also allows us to transform XML into other data structures, such as in-memory objects.

To build our objects from XML, we'll write several queries that leverage the axis methods provided by LINQ to XML. The queries will retrieve the baseline book information out of the XML document, as well as the publishers, authors, and reviews. We'll build our objects using the new object initializer syntax available in C# 3.0. We'll also explore how we can nest query expressions to read data that is in repeating elements, such as the authors and reviews. Before diving into the details of how we can construct objects from XML, let's figure out how to load our XML document into an XElement.

To load the XML document, we can use the static Load method on the XElement class.

```
XElement booksXml = XElement.Load("books.xml");
```

Once the XML is loaded, we need to figure out how we can get the data within the XML into our Book objects. Since the book details are contained within the <book> element, our first step is to retrieve all the <book> elements within the XML document. As we learned in the previous chapter, the Elements query axis method can be used to select all elements with a particular name, so we'll select every book element with the following code:

```
IEnumerable<XElement> bookElements = booksXml.Elements("book");
```

Our call to the Elements query axis method will return an IEnumerable<XElement> that represents the books within our XML document. In order to build our Book object from the XElement objects, we'll need to read data out of the relevant child elements. The easiest way to construct our book object with the data in our XML is to alter our code to use the object initializer syntax available in C# 3.0. Rather than simply selecting the XElement objects as we did earlier, we'll update our query to create new book instances by adding a select clause to our query.

We'll assign the values contained in the child elements of the <book> element to the corresponding property on the Book object, as shown in listing 11.2.

Listing 11.2   Create Book objects from the XML using object initializers

```
var books =
    from bookElement in booksXml.Elements("book")
    select new Book {
        Title = (string)bookElement.Element("title"),
        PublicationDate = (DateTime)bookElement.Element("publicationDate"),
        Price = (decimal)bookElement.Element("price"),
        Isbn = (string)bookElement.Element("isbn"),
        Notes = (string)bookElement.Element("notes"),
        Summary = (string)bookElement.Element("summary")
    };
```

To read the details of the book contained in the child elements, we select the relevant element with the Elementaxis method and use the explicit cast operators defined on XElement to convert the value to the proper data types.

While this query gives us the basic details for our books, it doesn't include the data that is nested within child nodes, such as the list of authors and reviews. To include the authors, we can update our query to include a nested query that returns a list of Author objects that matches the author's details contained in the XML. Since the <author> elements are not directly below the <book> element, we can use the Descendants query axis method and once again use the object initializer syntax to build our author object with the data contained within the XML.

```
...
Authors =                                                          ◁──────┐  Select all
    from authorElement in bookElement.Descendants("author")               │  authors and
    select new Author {                                                    │  create Author
        FirstName = (string)authorElement.Element("firstName"),            │  objects
        LastName = (string)authorElement.Element("lastName")
    }
...
```

Since our query expression returns an IEnumerable<Author>, we can assign the results of the query expression directly to the Authors property on the book instance. To include the reviews, we can take the same approach. We write a query expression that reads the reviews out of the XML and into a list of Review objects:

```
...
Reviews =                                                          ◁──────┐  Select all reviews
    from reviewElement in bookElement.Descendants("review")                │  and create
    select new Review {                                                    │  Review objects
```

```
          User = new User { Name = (string)reviewElement.Element("user") },
          Rating = (int)reviewElement.Element("rating"),
          Comments = (string)reviewElement.Element("comments")
      }
  ...
```

If we wrap everything together, we end up with the program in listing 11.3, which creates a list of books from our XML document and prints them to the console using `ObjectDumper`

Listing 11.3   Creating objects from XML

```
using System;
using System.Linq;
using System.Xml.Linq;
using LinqInAction.LinqBooks.Common;

namespace Chapter11.CreateObjectsFromXml {
  class Program {
    static void Main(string[] args) {                          Load the XML
                                                               document
      XElement booksXml = XElement.Load("books.xml");   ◁┘

      var books =                                      ◁────   Build our objects
        from bookElement in booksXml.Elements("book")          using query
        select new Book {                                      expressions and
        Title = (string)bookElement.Element("title"),          object initializers
        Publisher = new Publisher {
          Name = (string)bookElement.Element("publisher")
        },
        PublicationDate = (DateTime)bookElement.Element("publicationDate"),
        Price = (decimal)bookElement.Element("price"),
        Isbn = (string)bookElement.Element("isbn"),
        Notes = (string)bookElement.Element("notes"),
        Summary = (string)bookElement.Element("summary"),
        Authors =
          from authorElement in bookElement.Descendants("author")
          select new Author {
            FirstName = (string)authorElement.Element("firstName"),
            LastName = (string)authorElement.Element("lastName")
          },
        Reviews =
          from reviewElement in bookElement.Descendants("review")
          select new Review {
            User = new User {
              Name = (string)reviewElement.Element("user")
            },
            Rating = (int)reviewElement.Element("rating"),
            Comments = (string)reviewElement.Element("comments")
          }
```

```
        };

        ObjectDumper.Write(books);     ⊲⏋ Print the
    }                                      results
  }
}
```

With LINQ to XML we can transform our XML data into alternate data formats quickly and easily. By combining query expressions with the new object initializer syntax offered by C# 3.0, we can build objects from XML using familiar LINQ language constructs. As you'll see throughout the remainder of this chapter, LINQ to XML provides a simple and consistent API for transforming data to and from XML.

Now that we've covered how to create objects from XML, let's look at how we can handle our next common scenario, creating XML from objects using VB9's XML literals.

11.2 Creating XML from object graphs

As we discussed in chapter 9, XML literals is a Visual Basic feature that allows XML to be created using familiar XML syntax. Our XML will be created from a set of in-memory objects that contain details about books within our LinqBooks catalog, as well as reviews for those books. Let's dig into more specifics regarding our goal for this scenario.

11.2.1 Goal

No application is complete without a little RSS sprinkled in. In this section, our goal is to create an RSS feed that contains all the book reviews within our Linq-Books catalog. To keep things simple, we're going to assume that we already have a set of objects loaded with the book and review data, and that the RSS feed that we create will be constructed directly from those objects.

Since we often deal with in-memory objects when developing applications, this section will provide a good overview of how in-memory objects can be transformed into XML using XML literals.

Before getting started with the code, let's look at a sample of the XML document that we'll produce.

```
<?xml version="1.0" encoding="UTF-8"?>
<rss version="2.0">
  <channel>
    <title>Book Reviews</title>
    <description>LINQBooks Book Reviews</description>
```

```
  <item>
    <title>Review of LINQ in Action by Steve Eichert</title>
    <description>This is an amazing book!...and I'm not biased!
    </description>
  </item>
  </channel>
</rss>
```

The XML that we produce will be a standard RSS 2.0 feed that contains the reviews for our books. The final XML will contain one `<item>` element for each review within the data used to produce the feed.

Now that we've determined our goal for this scenario, let's look at how we're going to use XML literals to achieve it.

11.2.2 Implementation

By allowing XML to be directly embedded in code, XML literals reduce the ambiguity that often exists when creating XML. Rather than focusing on the programming API required to create XML, XML literals allow developers to focus on the XML that they want to produce.

In this scenario, we're going to use XML literals to create an RSS feed that contains the reviews within a set of in-memory objects. We'll construct a query to return the book and review data and use the support for embedding expressions inside XML literals to produce our final XML.

To create our RSS feed, we'll query our in-memory objects for all the books that have at least one review, and create an RSS feed containing the reviews for the books using XML literals. We're going to use the objects that we reviewed in section 11.1 (see figure 11.1) as well as the `SampleData` class introduced in chapter 4.

As a reminder, listing 11.4 shows how the `SampleData` class is defined.

> **Listing 11.4   The `SampleData` class introduced in chapter 4**

```
using System;
using System.Collections.Generic;
using System.Text;

namespace LinqInAction.LinqBooks.Common {
    static public class SampleData {

        static public User[] Users ={
            new User { Name="Steve Eichert"},
            new User { Name="Fabrice Marguerie"},
            new User { Name="Jim Wooley"}
        };
```

```
static public Publisher[] Publishers = {
    new Publisher {Name="FunBooks"},
    new Publisher {Name="Joe Publishing"},
    new Publisher {Name="I Publisher"}
};

static public Author[] Authors = {
    new Author {FirstName="Johnny", LastName="Good"},
    new Author {FirstName="Graziella", LastName="Simplegame"},
    new Author {FirstName="Octavio", LastName="Prince"},
    new Author {FirstName="Jeremy", LastName="Legrand"}
};

static public Book[] Books = {
    new Book {
        Title="Funny Stories",
        Publisher=Publishers[0],
        Authors=new[]{Authors[0], Authors[1]},
        Price=25.55M,
        Isbn="0-000-77777-2",
        Reviews=new Review[] {
            new Review {
                User=Users[0],
                Rating=5,
                Comments="It was very funny indeed!"
            },
            new Review {
                User=Users[1],
                Rating=4,
                Comments="It was Fabulous."}
        }
    },
    new Book {
        Title="LINQ rules",
        Publisher=Publishers[1],
        Authors=new[]{Authors[2]},
        Price=12M,
        Isbn="0-111-77777-2"
    },
    new Book {
        Title="C# on Rails",
        Publisher=Publishers[1],
        Authors=new[]{Authors[2]},
        Price=35.5M,
        Isbn="0-222-77777-2",
        Reviews=new Review[] {
            new Review {
                User=Users[0],
                Rating=5,
```

```
                                Comments="Say goodnight to the Rails Party,
                                    Microsoft is here!"},
                        new Review {
                            User=Users[1],
                            Rating=5,
                            Comments="Don Box said he likes Ruby, little
                                did we know he'd turn C# into Ruby.NET!"}
                    }
                },
                new Book {
                    Title="All your base are belong to us",
                    Publisher=Publishers[1],
                    Authors=new[]{Authors[3]},
                    Price=35.5M,
                    Isbn="0-333-77777-2"
                },
                new Book {
                    Title="Bonjour mon Amour",
                    Publisher=Publishers[0],
                    Authors=new[]{Authors[1], Authors[0]},
                    Price=29M,
                    Isbn="2-444-77777-2"
                }
            };
        }
    }
```

To build our RSS feed; we want to select the books from the `SampleData.Books` array shown in listing 11.4. Since the RSS will have details of the reviews, we want to limit the list of books to those that have at least one review. To limit the set of books returned to only those with reviews, we'll check that the `Reviews` property on the book is not null and that at least one review exists using listing 11.5.

Listing 11.5 Limit the set of books returned to only those with reviews

```
Dim reviews =
    From book In SampleData.Books _
    Where Not IsNothing(book.Reviews) AndAlso book.Reviews.Count > 0 _
    From review In book.Reviews _
    Select book, review
```

Since we can have multiple reviews per book, we've created a second-level query that selects each review from the `book.Reviews` property. To create our XML feed, we'll need to embed this query into our XML literals code.

Now that we've defined a query for retrieving the necessary data, we need to create the XML literal code that will produce the desired XML. With XML literals, VB allows us to create XML using familiar XML syntax. Now we can focus on the desired XML output rather than on the details of the XML programming API. As mentioned in chapter 9, under the covers, XML literals get turned into functional construction statements, which allow them to be interoperable with other languages that don't support XML literals.

Creating the XML literals is a matter of copying and pasting the desired XML into our class that will be responsible for the XML creation. We can, of course, hand-code the XML as well, but since we've already done that once to create the sample document, we might as well leverage all that typing here. We'll use listing 11.6 as a template for building our desired XML.

Listing 11.6   XML literals template for building RSS

```
Dim rss = _
<?xml version="1.0" encoding="utf-8"?>
<rss version="2.0">
  <channel>
    <title>Book Reviews</title>
    <description>LINQBooks Book Reviews</description>
    <item>
      <title>Review of LINQ in Action by Steve Eichert</title>
      <description>
        This is an amazing book!...and I'm not biased!
      </description>
    </item>
  </channel>
</rss>
```

With the XML literals code in place, we're ready to integrate the query that selects the book and review data from the `SampleData.Books` array, as well as place "holes" within the XML literals that we can use to plug in the proper values from our query. As mentioned in chapter 9, we can place expression holes in our XML literals using the `<%= Expression %>` and `<% Statement %>` syntax.

To create our full RSS feed, we're going to replace the single `<item>` element in listing 11.6 with our query for retrieving the book and review data. Once we have our queries and XML literal code in place, we replace the hard-coded book name, reviewer name, and review with embedded expressions that place the proper values from the book and review objects into the resulting XML. The complete code for creating our RSS feed is shown in listing 11.7.

Listing 11.7 Creating XML from an object graph using XML literals

```
Imports LinqInAction.LinqBooks.Common

Module XmlFromObjectsUsingXmlLiterals
  Sub Main()
    Dim rss = _
    <?xml version="1.0" encoding="utf-8"?>
    <rss version="2.0">
      <channel>
        <title>Book Reviews</title>
        <description>LINQBooks Book Reviews</description>
        <%= From book In SampleData.Books _
            Where Not IsNothing(book.Reviews) _
            AndAlso book.Reviews.Count > 0 _
            Select _
            From review In book.Reviews _
            Select _
              <item>
                <title>
                  Review of <%= book.Title %> by <%= review.User.Name %>
                </title>
                <description><%= review.Comments %></description>
              </item> %>
      </channel>
    </rss>

    Console.WriteLine(rss)
  End Sub
End Module
```

When we run this code, we end up with the following XML printed to the console:

```
<rss version="2.0">
  <channel>
    <title>Book Reviews</title>
    <description>LINQBooks Book Reviews</description>
    <item>
      <title>Review of Funny Stories by Steve Eichert</title>
      <description>It was very funny indeed!</description>
    </item>
    <item>
      <title>Review of Funny Stories by Fabrice Marguerie</title>
      <description>It was Fabulous.</description>
    </item>
    <item>
      <title>Review of C# on Rails by Steve Eichert</title>
      <description>Say goodnight to the Rails Party, Microsoft is here!
        </description>
```

```
    </item>
    <item>
      <title>Review of C# on Rails by Fabrice Marguerie</title>
      <description>Don Box said he likes Ruby, little did we know he'd turn
C# into Ruby.NET!</description>
    </item>
  </channel>
</rss>
```

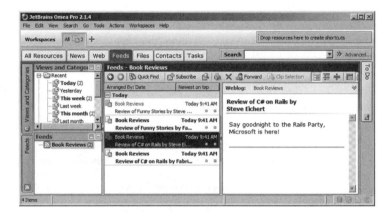

**Figure 11.2
The resulting
Reviews RSS feed**

Now that we have our RSS feed created, we can deploy it to our web host and start sharing our reviews with the world. See figure 11.2.

In this section, we created an RSS feed from our in-memory book objects. By utilizing XML literals, we were able to stay focused on the end goal and plug in data from our objects as necessary. The result is a more productive programming environment for developers. While it was a fun exercise to convert our in-memory objects to XML, it's more likely that we'll need to pull information from our database. In the next section, we explore what LINQ to XML offers for such a case.

11.3 Creating XML with data from a database

The relational database is at the heart of many of the applications we build. It provides a reliable means for storing, aggregating, and processing our data. Often the data within our applications need to be shared with others, and more often than not the format chosen for the interchange is XML. In this scenario, we'll explore how we can take data within our relational database and create an XML representation of it that can be shared with others. As we learned in chapters 6, 7, and 8, LINQ to SQL provides powerful capabilities for working with our relational data via LINQ. In this scenario, we'll get a chance to see how nicely LINQ to XML can be used in conjunction with LINQ to SQL to combine relational and XML data within a single query. Let's get started by looking at our goal for this scenario.

11.3.1 Goal

Our goal is to export XML of the books within our book catalog database (see figure 11.2). This will allow us to share our catalog with other LinqBooks users. We're going to start by creating the desired XML with the Paste XML as LINQ Visual Studio Add-In that is shipped as a sample with Visual Studio 2008, and then define our queries to retrieve the data from the database. Once we have the stub code for our XML and the queries for retrieving the data, we'll combine the two to create our desired XML.

Listing 11.8 shows the XML that we'll create.

Listing 11.8 The XML that will be created from our database

```
<books>
  <book>
    <title>LINQ in Action</title>
    <authors>
      <author>
        <firstName>Steve</firstName>
        <lastName>Eichert</lastName>
        <webSite>http://iqueryable.com</webSite>
      </author>
      <author>
        <firstName>Fabrice</firstName>
        <lastName>Marguerie</lastName>
        <webSite>http://linqinaction.net/</website>
      </author>
      <author>
        <firstName>Jim</firstName>
        <lastName>Wooley</lastName>
        <webSite>http://devauthority.com/blogs/jwooley</website>
      </author>
    </authors>
    <subject>
      <name>LINQ</name>
      <description>LINQ shall rule the world</description>
    </subject>
    <publisher>Manning</publisher>
    <publicationDate>January, 2008</publicationDate>
    <price>43.99</price>
    <isbn>1933988169</isbn>
    <notes>Great book!</notes>
    <summary>LINQ in Action is great!</summary>
    <reviews>
      <review>
```

```
            <user>Steve Eichert</user>
            <rating>5</rating>
            <comments>What can I say, I'm biased!</comments>
          <review>
        <reviews>
      </book>
   </books>
```

To create this XML we'll need to query data from the database tables shown in figure 11.3.

Now that we've seen the structure of the XML we're trying to produce as well as the schema for the database tables we'll be pulling our data from, let's look at the technique we'll use to accomplish our goal.

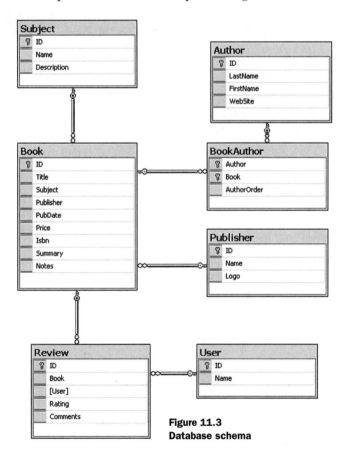

Figure 11.3
Database schema

11.3.2 *Implementation*

Functional construction provides a powerful means by which we can create XML. By embedding query expressions within functional construction statements, XML trees can be built from a database or any other data source. Since LINQ to SQL provides an implementation of the standard query operators for querying relational databases, we can use familiar LINQ query expressions to retrieve the data for creating the desired XML.

The XML tree that we're going to produce requires information from every table within the database schema shown in figure 11.3. To retrieve the data, we'll generate a set of objects from our database using LINQ to SQL. As we discussed in chapter 6, LINQ to SQL creates a class for every table in the database. In addition to generating properties that map to each column in the database, LINQ to SQL also generates properties to represent the relationships within the database. This allows all the relevant information required for creating our XML to be retrieved via the Book class.

Before diving into the code necessary for creating the XML from the database, we need to generate our LINQ to SQL objects. There are several options available for generating our objects. To keep things simple, we'll use the SqlMetal.exe command-line executable that ships with LINQ to SQL.

```
CMD>Sqlmetal /server:localhost /database:LinqInAction /pluralize
/namespace:LinqInAction.LinqToSql /code:LinqInAction.cs
```

While the details of SqlMetal are outside the scope of this chapter, you can find more information about how to leverage it to create LINQ to SQL objects by checking out chapter 7 or by browsing to \Program Files\Microsoft SDKs\Windows\v6.0A\Bin and executing SqlMetal.exe without any command-line switches.

```
usage: sqlmetal [options] [<input file>]
options:
  /server:<name>      database server name
  /database:<name>    database catalog on server
  /user:<name>        login user id
  /password:<name>    login password
  /views              extract database views
  /functions          extract database functions
  /sprocs             extract stored procedures
  /xml[:file]         output as xml
  /code[:file]        output as source code
  /map[:file]         generate xml mapping file instead of attributes
  /language:xxx       language for source code (vb,csharp)
  /namespace:<name>   namespace used for source code
  /pluralize          auto-pluralize table names
  /dataAttributes     auto-generate DataObjectField and Precision attributes
  /timeout:<seconds>  timeout value in seconds to use for database commands
```

Once we have our LINQ to SQL objects generated, we can write the code for creating our XML tree. To get started, we can copy the XML in our sample XML document to the clipboard and use the Paste XML as LINQ Visual Studio add-in to give us the C# code shown in listing 11.9.

Listing 11.9 Stub code via copy and paste `XElement`

```
XElement xml = new XElement("books",
  new XElement("book",
    new XElement("title", "LINQ in Action"),
    new XElement("authors",                    ❶ Replace the authors element
      new XElement("author",                       with a query expression that
        new XElement("firstName", "Steve"),        returns all the authors
        new XElement("lastName", "Eichert"),
        new XElement("webSite", "http://iqueryable.com")
      ),
      new XElement("author",
        new XElement("firstName", "Fabrice"),
        new XElement("lastName", "Marguerie"),
        new XElement("website", "http://linqinaction.net/")
      ),
      new XElement("author",
        new XElement("firstName", "Jim"),
        new XElement("lastName", "Wooley"),
        new XElement("website", "http://devauthority.com/blogs/jwooley/")
      )
    ),                            ❷ Replace the hard-coded subject with the subject
    new XElement("subject",          name and description from the Subject table
      new XElement("name", "LINQ"),
      new XElement("description", "LINQ shall rule the world")
    ),
    new XElement("publisher", "Manning"),      Replace the publisher
    new XElement("publicationDate", "January, 2008),   name with the proper
    new XElement("price", "43.99"),            publisher name from
    new XElement("isbn", "1933988169"),      ❸ the publishers table
    new XElement("notes", "Great book!"),
    new XElement("summary", "LINQ in Action is great!"),
    new XElement("reviews",
      new XElement("review",
        new XElement("user", "Steve Eichert"),
        new XElement("rating", "5"),
        new XElement("comments", "What can I say, I'm biased!")
      )
    )             Replace the hard-coded list of
  )               reviews with a query expression
)                 that returns all the reviews ❹
);
```

In the listing, we've identified four sections of XML that will need to be replaced with LINQ expressions. The author element ❶ will need to be replaced with a query expression that returns an `IEnumerable<XElement>` containing the author elements. We'll need to replace the hard-coded name and description on the Subject ❷ with the name and description from the `Subject` table that the `Book` table links to. Next we'll need to replace the publisher name ❸ with the proper publisher name from the `Publisher` table. Finally, the hard-coded lists of reviews ❹ will need to be replaced with a query expression that returns an `IEnumerable <XElement>` built from the `Reviews` table.

Now that we have the stub code in listing 11.9, we need to plug in query expressions for retrieving information about the book, as well as its publisher, subject, authors, and reviews. To express our queries, we can use query expressions or explicit dot notation. Since query expressions are more readable and compact and work better when embedding queries within functional construction statements, we'll use them to create our XML.

The first query expression that we need returns all the books within our database. Although the sort order of the books doesn't matter, we'll sort them by title to make our query more interesting.

```
LinqInActionContext ctx = new LinqInActionContext();
var books = from book in ctx.Books
    orderby book.Title
    select book;
```

To retrieve the other details necessary for building the XML, we can traverse the relationships that SqlMetal creates on the Book class. Figure 11.4 shows a class diagram of the classes created by SqlMetal to see what relationships are available.

As we can see in figure 11.4, the Book class has relationships that allow us to retrieve all the related data using properties such as `book.BookAuthors`, `book.Subject`, `book.Reviews`, and `book.Publisher`. Utilizing these properties, we can create queries for returning the data necessary for building our complete XML document, as in listing 11.10.

Listing 11.10 Retrieve the data necessary for building our XML document using LINQ to XML queries

```
var authors =                          ◁──────────┐  Retrieve the authors
    from bookAuthor in book.BookAuthors            │  through the BookAuthors
    orderby bookAuthor.AuthorOrder
    select bookAuthor.Author;
                                   ┌─ Review the data from
                                   │  the l-to-l relationships
var subject = book.Subject;    ◁───┘
```

```
var publisher = book.Publisher;

var reviews =
    from review in book.Reviews
    orderby review.Rating
    select review;
```

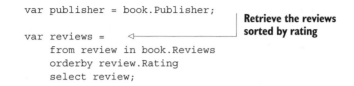

**Retrieve the reviews
sorted by rating**

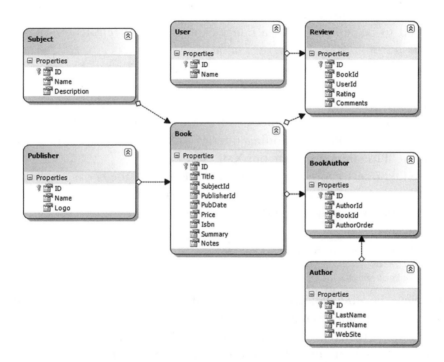

**Figure 11.4   A class diagram showing the classes and relationships created by SqlMetal
for the LinqBooks database**

Once we have these queries, we can plug them into our original statement that
creates our XML. In listing 11.11, we update the hard-coded element values with
the appropriate value from the book instance and replace the repeating elements—such as the authors and reviews—with query expressions that return an
IEnumerable<XElement> that represents the items.

Listing 11.11   Code to create our full XML tree

```
using System;
using System.Linq;
using System.Xml.Linq;
```

```csharp
using System.Data.Linq;
using LinqInAction.LinqToSql;

namespace Chapter11.CreateXmlFromDatabase {
  class Program {
    static void Main(string[] args) {

      LinqInActionDataContext ctx = new LinqInActionDataContext();

      XElement xml = new XElement("books",
        from book in ctx.Books
        orderby book.Title
        select new XElement("book",
          new XElement("title", book.Title),
          new XElement("authors",
            from bookAuthor in book.BookAuthors
            orderby bookAuthor.AuthorOrder
            select new XElement("author",
              new XElement("firstName", bookAuthor.Author.FirstName),
              new XElement("lastName", bookAuthor.Author.LastName),
              new XElement("webSite", bookAuthor.Author.WebSite)
            )
          ),
          new XElement("subject",
          new XElement("name", book.Subject.Name),
            new XElement("description", book.Subject.Description)
          ),
          new XElement("publisher", book.Publisher.Name),
          new XElement("publicationDate", book.PubDate),
          new XElement("price", book.Price),
          new XElement("isbn", book.Isbn),
          new XElement("notes", book.Notes),
          new XElement("summary", book.Summary),
          new XElement("reviews",
            from review in book.Reviews
            orderby review.Rating
            select new XElement("review",
              new XElement("user", review.User.Name),
              new XElement("rating", review.Rating),
              new XElement("comments", review.Comments)
            )
          )
        )
      );

      Console.WriteLine(xml.ToString());
    }
  }
}
```

Create DataContext to retrieve data from database

Create XML

Print XML to console

With the powerful creation capabilities offered by functional construction, as well as its tight integration with other LINQ-enabled technologies such as LINQ to SQL, LINQ to XML is primed to become the runaway winner when it comes to selecting an XML stack to build applications on top of. Not only does it offer all the query advantages that we've seen time and time again from the LINQ framework, it also provides the most powerful and user friendly XML API available!

Now that we've seen how to create XML from a database, it's time to move on to our next scenario.

11.4 Filtering and mixing data from a database with XML data

Now that we've seen how we can create XML from a database, it's time to further explore how we can integrate XML and relational data within a single LINQ query. In this scenario, we're going to look at how we can mix the data within our database with XML data retrieved from Amazon's e-commerce web services. As we'll see in this example, LINQ to XML makes it easy to join XML data with data from a relational database. Before we jump into how we accomplish this, let's review our goal.

11.4.1 Goal

The Amazon e-commerce web services provide developers with a set of APIs for retrieving data from the Amazon catalog. In this scenario, we'll query the Item-Lookup service for the reviews that have been submitted for a set of books within our LinqBooks catalog. With our XML data in hand, we'll then query our relational database for additional book details. Finally, we'll integrate the two data sources with a single query and display the results on screen.

The following is a sample of the output:

```
Book: CLR via C#, Second Edition
-------------------------
Rating: 5
-------------------------
Jeffrey Richter is my hero, he really is. This guy is simply amazing. I just
cant imagine how he pulls it off - the toughest topics explained in the
clearest manner.Moreover, he has achieved this feat over and over again. Any
book he has written is testimony for this.
<br />In his books, you would find information where you wouldnt find in any
other place. You would also find information you can find elsewhere, but
not as clear as his. He has the advantage of working closely with Microsoft
and consulting with the .NET team, but I would say he would be a great author
and teacher even without that advantage.
<br />As about this book, it should not be your first C# book. I suggest you
```

```
get beginner's C# book first (if you dont know any C#), I suggest Jesse
Liberty's book, and then come to this book. You would get a tremendous
advantage over people who havent read this book and your understanding of the
building blocks of .NET platform would be in depth. His chapters on Threading
alone is worth the price of the book. This book is an absolute pleasure to
read, just like any other book from Richter. Grab your copy today!
If there really is a 5 star book,this one is it.
<br />Nobody writes like Richter, nobody.
------------------------
Rating: 5
------------------------
I echo the positive reviews below. If you already know the .Net platform
fairly well and want to understand the internals of the CLR, this is the best
place to start. This edition is as good or better than his 1.0/1.1 version,
Applied .Net Framework Programming.
```

By allowing us to easily load XML data from a web service and mix that data with data from a LINQ to SQL query, LINQ to XML provides a powerful method for creating XML content. Let's look at the technique we'll use for creating our desired result.

11.4.2 *Implementation*

LINQ provides several mechanisms for mixing XML and relational data. To allow users to see the reviews on Amazon for a given book, we'll be joining the data available within our relational database with XML data returned by a call to the Amazon `ItemLookup` service. Although the data is in completely different formats and from completely different sources, LINQ allows us to easily mix the data by joining the two sources on the common data points, in this case the ISBN, then selecting the data we're interested in from each source within our `select` clause. In order to get the data that we want to display to users, we'll need to perform two queries. The first query will retrieve XML data from Amazon and the second query will retrieve information from the database.

Let's start by loading the XML data from Amazon. Amazon provides several different ways to access its web services. Developers can request data from Amazon using either the REST or SOAP APIs offered by Amazon. Since LINQ to XML is ideally suited to work as a client for REST web services, we'll leverage that strength here and use the REST web service API.

As we briefly mentioned in chapter 10, to access the Amazon web services, you're required to register with the Amazon Web Services program.[1] After registering with Amazon, you'll be assigned a key, which grants you access to the Amazon

---

[1] http://www.amazon.com/gp/aws/registration/registration-form.html

web services. Once you have the registration complete, you can start using the web services to retrieve information from Amazon.

Now that we have that disclaimer out of the way, let's figure out how to retrieve data from the Amazon `ItemLookup` service. To retrieve data from the `ItemLookup` service, we create a request URL that includes all the request parameters that detail the information that we're interested in retrieving from Amazon. To retrieve the reviews, we use the following request URL:

```
http://webservices.amazon.com/onca/xml?Service=AWSECommerceService&
    AWSAccessKeyId={AccessKey}&
    Operation=ItemLookup&
    ItemId={ItemID}&
    ResponseGroup=Reviews
```

Table 11.1 shows the common request parameters that are included in Amazon web services calls. For more detailed information on the parameters available, refer to the Amazon Web Service documentation at http://aws.amazon.com/.

Table 11.1 Common Amazon e-commerce web service operation request parameters

Parameter	Value	Description
Service	AWSECommerceService	Specifies the ECS service.
AWSAccessKeyId	Your Amazon-assigned Access Key ID	You can register for an access key ID from the Amazon web site if you do not have one. Every ECS 4.0 request must contain either an access key ID or a subscription ID, but not both.
SubscriptionId	Your Amazon-assigned subscription ID	Every ECS 4.0 request must contain either an access key ID or a subscription ID, but not both. Starting with version 2006-06-28, ECS stopped distributing subscription IDs. If you already have one, it will continue to work.
Operation	Operation you wish to perform	One of the ECS operation types.[a]
ResponseGroup	Reviews	Specifies what data is to be returned by the current operation; allows you to control the volume and content of returned data.
ItemId	The list of ASINs for the products to return data for	Product(s) you would like information about. You may specify up to 10 IDs using a comma-separated list (REST) or multiple elements (SOAP). By default the item IDs are assumed to be ASINs, unless you specify the `IdType` parameter.

a. http://docs.amazonwebservices.com/AWSEcommerceService/2006-06-28/PgOverviewArticle.html#Summary

Now that our request URL is created, we can load the XML response using the
Load method of XElement, as shown in listing 11.12.

Listing 11.12 Load XML from Amazon's e-commerce web service

```
string requestUrl =
    "http://webservices.amazon.com/onca/xml?Service=AWSECommerceService&" +
    "AWSAccessKeyId={AccessKey}&" +
    "Operation=ItemLookup&" +
    "ItemId=0735621632&" +
    "ResponseGroup=Reviews";

XElement amazonReviews = XElement.Load(requestUrl);
```

Before moving on, let's look at the XML that is returned for our request, shown in
figure 11.5.

As you can see in the figure, the reviews are returned within the <CustomerRe-
views> element. We're particularly interested in the <Rating> and <Content> elements, as they contain the information that we're going to display on screen.

Now that we've covered some of the basics regarding how we'll retrieve the Amazon reviews, let's look at how to retrieve the books from our relational database. As
we saw in section 11.3, LINQ to SQL makes it easy to retrieve data from our database.

```
 1  <?xml version="1.0" encoding="utf-8"?>
 2  <ItemLookupResponse xmlns="http://webservices.amazon.com/AWSECommerceService/2005-10-05">
 3     <OperationRequest>...
17     <Items>
18       <Request>...
25       <Item>
26         <ASIN>0735621632</ASIN>
27         <CustomerReviews>
28           <AverageRating>5.0</AverageRating>
29           <TotalReviews>13</TotalReviews>
30           <TotalReviewPages>3</TotalReviewPages>
31           <Review>
32             <ASIN>0735621632</ASIN>
33             <Rating>4</Rating>
34             <HelpfulVotes>1</HelpfulVotes>
35             <CustomerId>AOPOVBBO6EVP6</CustomerId>
36             <TotalVotes>2</TotalVotes>
37             <Date>2006-08-16</Date>
38             <Summary>For advanced developers</Summary>
39             <Content>This book gives a deep view of the CLR and framework. You can find tips for
40           </Review>
41           <Review>...
51           <Review>...
64           <Review>...
74           <Review>...
86         </CustomerReviews>
87       </Item>
88     </Items>
89  </ItemLookupResponse>
```

Figure 11.5 Amazon.com reviews XML

As we did in section 11.3, we'll retrieve the details of our book with the `LinqIn-ActionDataContext.Books` property.

```
LinqInActionDataContext ctx = new LinqInActionDataContext();
var books = ctx.Books;
```

With the details of our queries out of the way, it's time we move on to joining them together and displaying the details onscreen. To join the XML data returned by Amazon and the book details within our database, we use the `Join` operator provided by LINQ. As discussed in chapter 3, the `Join` and `GroupJoin` operators allow us to join two sequences on matching keys extracted from each sequence. In our case, the two sequences are the sequence of book elements returned by `amazon-Reviews.Elements(ns + "Items").Elements(ns + "Item")` and the sequence of books within the database that we access through the `Books` property on the `Linq-InActionDataContext` class. We'll extract the `ASIN` element out of our XML and the ISBN out of our `Book`, and use them to join our two sequences together.

When we put everything together we end up with the program in listing 11.13.

Listing 11.13   Mixing XML and relational data within a single query

```
using System;
using System.Linq;
using System.Xml.Linq;
using System.Data.Linq;
using LinqInAction.LinqToSql;

namespace Chapter11.MixXmlAndRelationalData {
  class Program {
    public const string AmazonAccessID = "15QN7X0P65HR0X975T02";

    static void Main(string[] args) {
      string requestUrl =
➥"http://webservices.amazon.com/onca/xml?Service=AWSECommerceService" +
          "&AWSAccessKeyId=" + AmazonAccessID +
          "&Operation=ItemLookup&" +
          "ItemId=0735621632&" +
          "ResponseGroup=Reviews";

      XNamespace ns =
        "http://webservices.amazon.com/AWSECommerceService/2005-10-05";
      LinqInActionDataContext ctx = new LinqInActionDataContext();

      XElement amazonReviews = XElement.Load(requestUrl);

      var results =
        from bookElement in amazonReviews.Element(ns + "Items")
                                    .Elements(ns + "Item")
```

```
        join book in ctx.Books on
            (string)bookElement.Element(ns + "ASIN") equals book.Isbn.Trim()
        select new {
            Title = book.Title,
            Reviews =
            from reviewElement in bookElement.Descendants(ns + "Review")
            orderby (int)reviewElement.Element(ns + "Rating") descending
            select new Review {
              Rating = (int)reviewElement.Element(ns + "Rating"),
              Comments = (string)reviewElement.Element(ns + "Content")
              }
                };

    string seperator = "--------------------------";
    foreach (var item in results) {
      Console.WriteLine("Book: " + item.Title);
      foreach (var review in item.Reviews) {
        Console.WriteLine(seperator + "\r\nRating: " +
                          review.Rating + "\r\n" +
            seperator + "\r\n" + review.Comments);
      }
    }
  }
 }
}
```

By leveraging the built-in join support offered by LINQ, we can build queries that select from multiple data sources and create new objects from subsets of the data within each data source. It should be noted that in order to do the join between our XML and database, LINQ enumerates each element returned by `ctx.Books`. This results in a query being run that returns every book within our database. In our particular scenario, we're not concerned with the performance impact of that operation, but it's something you should keep in mind when designing queries that join XML and relational data.

At this point, we've covered several common scenarios involving XML and our database. In the next section, we cover the most obvious remaining scenario, updating our database with information contained within XML.

11.5 *Reading XML and updating a database*

In the previous two sections, we've looked at how we can use LINQ to XML to create XML from a database as well as how we can join XML and relational data within a single LINQ query. In this section, we go a step further and investigate how we can use LINQ to XML and LINQ to SQL to update our database with information contained within XML. Before getting started with our goal, we should mention that this scenario is a little more involved than those that we've covered thus far. As such, this scenario is a bit longer, but also a bit more interesting. The real power of LINQ is shown when all the different LINQ-enabled technologies are used together. In this scenario, we use LINQ to XML, LINQ to Objects, and LINQ to SQL. Additionally, we query a web service, a database, and a UI for data, and learn about how we can update our relational data with information returned from a web service!

Now that we've whetted your appetite with what's to come, let's get started by identifying our goal for this scenario.

11.5.1 *Goal*

In this section, we're going to add an exciting new feature to our sample application. We're going to allow users to add new books to their LinqBooks catalog directly from Amazon. To enable this, we'll build a simple GUI screen that can be used to search Amazon for books. See figure 11.6.

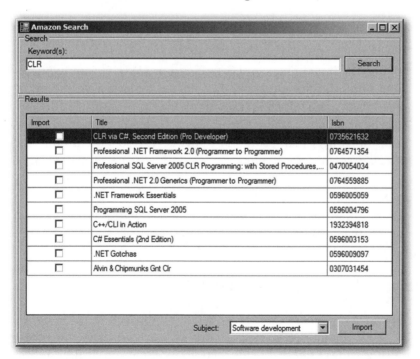

Figure 11.6   Amazon search UI

As shown in the figure, a search box at the top of the UI will allow users to enter the keywords to search on. After entering keywords, users will be able to click the Search button. When the Search button is clicked, a web service call will be made to Amazon for all books that match the entered keywords. The results provided by Amazon will be displayed in the grid, where users will be able to select the book(s) to be imported by checking the Import check box. Before importing the selected books, they need to be classified. The Subject combo box, at the bottom of the form, lists all the subjects currently in the database. Once the appropriate subject is selected and the Import button is clicked, the books will be inserted into the LinqBooks database.

11.5.2 *Implementation*

In order to accomplish our goal, we'll need to leverage a lot of what we've learned throughout the last several chapters. We're going to query the Amazon web service using LINQ to XML, query our relational database using LINQ to SQL, build objects from XML, and finally create new records in our database with information within the XML.

As we saw in the previous section, LINQ provides a Join operator that allows XML and relational data to be included in a single LINQ query. In this section, we're going to go a step further and join XML, relational data, and in-memory objects. When we're through, we'll have a simple Windows Forms application that allows users to search Amazon.com for books and import them into their Linq-Books database.

After creating our basic UI, which we'll skip here since we have a lot of ground to cover, we need to start creating our LINQ queries for retrieving information from Amazon, as well as our database. We'll once again use the REST service to retrieve books that match the keywords entered into the UI.

We need to formulate a URL with all the details of our query before making our request. The URL that we use to retrieve the books matching our keywords is shown in listing 11.14.

> **Listing 11.14 Amazon.com REST URL for retrieving books by a keyword**

```
http://webservices.amazon.com/onca/xml?Service=AWSECommerceService&
    AWSAccessKeyId={AccessKey}&
    Operation=ItemSearch&
    SearchIndex=Books&
    Keywords={keywords}&
    ResponseGroup=Large
```

Once our request URL is formulated, we make our service call to Amazon by calling the static `Load` method on `XElement`. When we call `Load`, the `XElement` class asks `System.Xml.XmlReader` to load the URL. This results in a web request being made to Amazon's server, which in turn constructs an XML document that contains the results of our search. The following is the code to retrieve the books matching the keywords supplied in the `keywords` text box:

```
string requestUrl =
    "http://webservices.amazon.com/onca/xml?Service=AWSECommerceService" +
    "&AWSAccessKeyId=" + AmazonAccessKey +
    "&Operation=ItemSearch" +
    "&SearchIndex=Books" +
    "&Keywords=" + keywords.Text +
    "&ResponseGroup=Large";

XElement amazonXml = XElement.Load(requestUrl);
```

Now that we have a loaded XML tree, we need to read the books out of the XML and display them to the user. Before investigating how we can display the books, let's look at the XML that is returned, shown in listing 11.15

Listing 11.15 Amazon XML for a book

```xml
<?xml version="1.0" encoding="utf-8"?>
<ItemSearchResponse
xmlns="http://webservices.amazon.com/AWSECommerceService/2005-10-05">
  <Items>
    <TotalResults>1389</TotalResults>
    <TotalPages>139</TotalPages>
    <Item>
      <ASIN>0977326403</ASIN>
      <DetailPageURL>http://www.amazon.com/gp/redirect.html%3FASIN=0977326403%
26tag=ws%261code=xm2%26cID=2025%26ccmID=165953%261ocation=/o/ASIN/
0977326403%253FSubscriptionId=15QN7X0P65HR0X975T02</DetailPageURL>
      <SalesRank>49</SalesRank>
      <ItemAttributes>
        <Author>Jim Collins</Author>
        <Binding>Paperback</Binding>
        <DeweyDecimalNumber>658.048</DeweyDecimalNumber>
        <EAN>9780977326402</EAN>
        <ISBN>0977326403</ISBN>
        <Label>Collins</Label>
        <ListPrice>
          <Amount>1195</Amount>
          <CurrencyCode>USD</CurrencyCode>
          <FormattedPrice>$11.95</FormattedPrice>
        </ListPrice>
```

```
      <Manufacturer>Collins</Manufacturer>
      <NumberOfItems>1</NumberOfItems>
      <NumberOfPages>42</NumberOfPages>
      <PackageDimensions>
        <Height Units="hundredths-inches">13</Height>
        <Length Units="hundredths-inches">916</Length>
        <Weight Units="hundredths-pounds">21</Weight>
        <Width Units="hundredths-inches">642</Width>
      </PackageDimensions>
      <ProductGroup>Book</ProductGroup>
      <PublicationDate>2005-11-30</PublicationDate>
      <Publisher>Collins</Publisher>
      <Studio>Collins</Studio>
      <Title>Good to Great and the Social Sectors:
             A Monograph to Accompany Good to Great</Title>
    </ItemAttributes>
   </Item>
  </Items>
 </ItemSearchResponse>
```

After reviewing the XML returned by Amazon and taking a quick peek at the grid we're using to display the results of our search, we find that the two primary pieces of information we need to read from the XML are within the `<Title>` and `<ISBN>` elements. Both elements live inside the `<ItemAttributes>` element. With this knowledge in hand, let's start to put the pieces in place for our GUI. We'll start by adding an event handler for the `Click` event of our search button.

```
private void searchButton_Click(object sender, EventArgs e) {
    ⟵── Do cool Amazon search here!
}
```

Once our event handler is in place, we add the code for constructing our request URL and then make the web service call to Amazon by calling `XElement.Load(requestUrl)`. Since we're going to be using the Amazon results outside the scope of the `searchButton_Click` handler, we assign the results of our web service call to a class-level variable named `amazonXml`. Finally, we construct a query expression that creates a sequence of `Books` by reading the title and ISBN out of the XML returned by Amazon. See listing 11.16.

> **Listing 11.16 When Search button is clicked, query Amazon for books matching our keywords**

```
private void searchButton_Click(object sender, EventArgs e) {
                                      │  Create a request URL for calling
                                      └─ the ItemSearch Amazon service
    string requestUrl =    ⟵
        String.Format(Amazon.AmazonSearchRestUrl, keywords.Text);
```

```
amazonXml = XElement.Load(requestUrl);          ◁─┐  Load the XML
                                                    │  from Amazon
                          │ Query the XML returned by │
                          │ Amazon for the title and ISBN
var books =        ◁──┘
      from amazonItem in amazonXml.Descendants(ns + "Item")
      let attributes = amazonItem.Element(ns + "ItemAttributes")
      select new Book {
        Isbn = (string)attributes.Element(ns + "ISBN"),
        Title = (string)attributes.Element(ns + "Title"),
      };

  bookBindingSource.DataSource = books;
}
```

Before moving on, let's dig into our query expression and examine how we're building our list of books. The first thing to point out is that we create an `XNamespace` instance with the default namespace used in the XML returned by Amazon. As we mentioned in previous chapters, all queries in LINQ to XML use the full expanded name (namespace + local name) of elements. We declare our namespace once, before constructing our query expression, to keep our query clean and concise. Once our namespace is declared, we can move on to constructing our query expression. The XML returned by Amazon contains one `<Item>` element for each book that matches our search. We use the `Descendants` query axis method available on `XElement` to retrieve each `<Item>` element and build a new `Book` instance using an inline object initializer. We set the `Title` and `ISBN` properties on the book instance to the values within the `<Title>` and `<ISBN>` elements of the XML. Also of note is our use of the `let` clause. Rather than typing the full expression for reading the title and ISBN out of the `/Item/ItemAttributes/Title` and `/Item/ItemAttributes/ISBN` elements, we instead use a `let` clause to assign the `ItemAttributes` element to a query variable called `attributes`. This allows us to use `attributes` in our `select` clause, which results in less typing and a more readable query. Finally, we bind our query defined in the `books` variable to the binding source for our grid, which populates the grid with the books returned by Amazon. Now that we have the books matching our keywords in our grid, let's move on to figuring out how we can get them imported into our database.

Once the books returned from Amazon are shown in the grid, users can select the books to import by checking the check box in the first column. Once the user has checked the books she would like to import, she clicks the Import button to put them into the LinqBooks database.

The first thing that we need to do when the user clicks the Import button is fig-ure out what items in the grid have been checked. To get the books that have been selected, we want to find all the rows within our grid that have the check box in the first cell checked. To determine whether the check box in the first cell of our grid is checked, we examine the `EditedFormattedValue` of the `DataGrid-ViewCell`. If we were still stuck in the olden days of programming, we would loop over every row in the grid and check whether the `EditedFormattedValue` of the first cell was true. If so, we'd then add the `Book` that was bound to the row to a list of some sort. Lucky for us, we're not stuck in the olden days. Rather than looping over the rows in the grid, we can construct a query expression to select the rows that match a predicate, which we've defined. The code to do just that follows:

```
var selectedBooks =
    from row in bookDataGridView.Rows.OfType<DataGridViewRow>()
    where ((bool) row.Cells[0].EditedFormattedValue) == true
    select (Book) row.DataBoundItem;
```

Notice our use of the `OfType<>` extension method. `OfType<>` allows us to turn an old-school `DataGridViewRowCollection` into an `IEnumerable` of `DataGridView-Row` objects. Once we have the `DataGridViewRow` objects in an `IEnumerable`, we can query them using LINQ.

Once we have the books that have been checked for import, we can begin to write the code that will import the books into our database. It's important to remember that the books bound to the `DataGridView` only contain the title and ISBN of the book. In order to get all the details for the book, we're going to need to return to the XML that we retrieved from Amazon.

As we saw when we built the list displayed in the grid, most of the details of the book are contained within the `<ItemAttributes>` element of the XML. We need to match the item attributes contained in the XML with the columns that we have in our database (see figure 11.2 to review the database schema). The mapping of the XML to the database can be seen in table 11.2.

Table 11.2 Mapping of XML to database for `Book` attributes

Book attribute	Location in XML	Location in database
Title	/Items/Item/ItemAttributes/Title	Book.Title
ISBN	/Items/Item/ItemAttributes/ISBN	Book.ISBN
Publication Date	/Items/Item/ItemAttributes/PublicationDate	Book.PubDate
Price	/Items/Item/ItemAttributes/ListPrice/FormattedPrice	Book.Price

Table 11.2   Mapping of XML to database for `Book` **attributes** *(continued)*

Book attribute	Location in XML	Location in database
Publisher	/Items/Item/ItemAttributes/Publisher	Publisher.Name
Author(s)	/Items/Item/ItemAttributes/Author *(repeated for each author)*	Author.FirstName & Author.LastName

In table 11.2 we define the mapping between the XML and our database. Since the title, ISBN, publication date, and price have a straightforward mapping; let's start by constructing a query that will read those values out of the XML and into our `Book` objects.

Listing 11.17   Read the values out of the XML returned by Amazon into our `Book` **objects**

```
var booksToImport =
    from amazonItem in amazonXml.Descendants(ns + "Item")
    let attributes = amazonItem.Element(ns + "ItemAttributes")
    select new Book {
        Isbn = (string)attributes.Element(ns + "ISBN"),
        Title = (string)attributes.Element(ns + "Title"),
        PubDate = (DateTime)attributes.Element(ns + "PublicationDate"),
        Price = ParsePrice(attributes.Element(ns + "ListPrice"))
    };
```

With this query in place, we need to start thinking about how we're going to filter the list of books to only those that we checked in the grid. Additionally, we need to figure out how we're going to set the `Publisher` for our book, as well as the list of authors. Let's start by figuring out how we can filter our list of books to only those that the user selected.

To filter the list of books, we need to join the results of the query for finding books from Amazon with the query for retrieving the list of selected books from the grid. See listing 11.18.

Listing 11.18   Joining the results returned by Amazon with the books selected in the grid

```
var selectedBooks =
    from row in bookDataGridView.Rows
    where ((bool)row.Cells[0].EditedFormattedValue) == true
    select (Book)row.DataBoundItem;

var booksToImport =
    from amazonItem in amazonXml.Descendants(ns + "Item")
    join selectedBook in selectedBooks on
```

```
        (string)amazonItem.Element(ns + "ItemAttributes")
                          .Element(ns + "ISBN")
      equals selectedBook.Isbn
    let attributes = amazonItem.Element(ns + "ItemAttributes")
    select new Book {
        Isbn = (string)attributes.Element(ns + "ISBN"),
        Title = (string)attributes.Element(ns + "Title"),
        PubDate = (DateTime)attributes.Element(ns + "PublicationDate"),
        Price = ParsePrice(attributes.Element(ns + "ListPrice"))
    };
```

As you can see, we again use the Join operator provided by LINQ for joining our two data sources together. This provides the results we're looking for, a list of books built from the data returned by Amazon filtered down to only those that were checked for import in the grid. Now that we have the books we're interested in, let's explore how we can include the additional details such as the Publishers and Authors.

At first glance, including the Publishers and Authors seems like a simple task. Since the data from Amazon includes the publisher and authors, it's simply a matter of updating our query expression to select the values out of the XML and assign them to the appropriate properties on our book instance. Unfortunately, nothing in life is as easy as it first seems.

As we import books into our catalog, we'll slowly build up a list of authors and publishers. If we're not careful, we could end up with duplicate authors and publishers within our database. If we go to import a book that has the same publisher or author as a book already in the database, we'll end up with duplicates if we don't specifically handle that case. We could ignore this fact and insert a new publisher and author for every book, but that would result in data integrity issues, which we'd rather not introduce. If the publisher or author already exists in the database, we want to assign that existing publisher or author to the book. If the publisher or author does not exist, we want to create a new instance and insert them into the database. When building objects in an imperative manner, this wouldn't be too hard to solve, but how do we handle this when our objects are getting built within a query expression?

Let's start by looking at how we can include the publisher in our query. The XML returned by Amazon has the publisher stored in the /Item/ItemAttributes/Publisher element. We need to perform a search on the Publisher table to see if a publisher with a Name equal to the value in our <Publisher> element exists. If so, the existing publisher needs to be pulled out of the database and assigned to the `Publisher` property on our book instance. If a publisher doesn't exist, we need to create a new `Publisher` instance with the publisher's name that is in the XML and assign it to our book. To accomplish this, we'll use the grouping join support in LINQ as well as the `DefaultIfEmpty` operator.

```
from amazonItem in amazonXml.Descendants(ns + "Item")
join p in ctx.Publishers on
     (string)amazonItem.Element(ns + "ItemAttributes")
                  .Element(ns + "Publisher")
     equals p.Name into publishers
     from existingPublisher in publishers.DefaultIfEmpty()
...
```

> Perform a left outer join between our XML and the Publisher table

By combining a grouping join with the `DefaultIfEmpty` operator, we are able to create a left outer join between our XML and `Publisher` table. Once we have our left outer join in place, we can use the null coalescing operator (`??`) and object initializers to get our desired behavior. If our join results in a null publisher, we'll create a new `Publisher`; otherwise, we'll assign our existing publisher to the `Publisher` property on our book.

```
...
Publisher=(existingPublisher ??
     new Publisher {
          ID = Guid.Empty,
          Name = (string)attributes.Element(ns + "Publisher")
     }
)
...
```

> Assign the publisher if it's not null; otherwise create a new Publisher

When we put everything together, we end up with a query expression that joins our Amazon item with the `Publisher` table in our database and either assigns the existing publisher to our book or creates a new one. See listing 11.19.

Listing 11.19 Populate the book publisher by joining to the `Publisher` table

```
var booksToImport =
  from amazonItem in amazonXml.Descendants(ns + "Item")
  join selectedBook in selectedBooks on
    (string)amazonItem.Element(ns + "ItemAttributes").Element(ns + "ISBN")
    equals selectedBook.Isbn
  join p in ctx.Publishers on
    (string)amazonItem.Element(ns + "ItemAttributes").Element(ns +
"Publisher")
    equals p.Name into publishers
  let existingPublisher = publishers.SingleOrDefault()
  let attributes = amazonItem.Element(ns + "ItemAttributes")
  select new Book {
    Isbn = (string)attributes.Element(ns + "ISBN"),
```

```
    Title = (string)attributes.Element(ns + "Title"),
    Publisher = (existingPublisher ??
      new Publisher {
        ID = Guid.Empty,
        Name = (string)attributes.Element(ns + "Publisher")
      }
    ),
    PubDate = (DateTime)attributes.Element(ns + "PublicationDate"),
    Price = ParsePrice(attributes.Element(ns + "ListPrice"))
};
```

Now that we have the publisher out of the way, it's time to move on to the authors. To include the authors, we're going to use some of the same methods we just covered for including the publisher. The primary difference is that a book can have multiple authors. Since our existing query expression is getting a little more complex than we'd like, we'll separate out the logic for assigning the authors into a separate method.

Before diving into the code for creating our authors, let's quickly review what we need to accomplish. The XML returned for a book can have one-to-many <Author> elements. We need to ensure that when we import our book, we don't re-create an author that is already in our database. As we can see in figure 11.7, we also need to map each author element into an Author object, which will be placed inside a BookAuthor object. The BookAuthor object is an association object that represents the link between a book and the authors who wrote the book. For more details about how one-to-many relationships are represented in LINQ to SQL, refer to chapter 7. Figure 11.7 shows the relationship between the Book class and the Author class.

Figure 11.7 Author and Book **class diagram**

After reviewing the class diagram in figure 11.7, we see that our `Author` class has `FirstName` and `LastName` properties. That means that we'll need to map the full author name within our XML to two properties on our object. To make our lives easy, we'll take a naïve approach and assume that the author element in the XML contains the first and last names of the author separated by a space. Once we have all these details out of the way, we can construct our query expression for retrieving our authors, as in listing 11.20.

Listing 11.20   Query our XML for the authors of the book

```
var bookAuthors =
  from authorElement in amazonItem.Elements(ns + "Author")
  join a in ctx.Authors on
  (string)authorElement equals a.FirstName + " " + a.LastName into authors
  let existingAuthor = authors.SingleOrDefault()
  let nameParts = ((string)authorElement).Split(' ')
  select new BookAuthor {
    Author = existingAuthor ??
      new Author {
        ID = Guid.Empty,
        FirstName = nameParts[0],
        LastName = nameParts[1]
      }
  };
```

We again use a grouping join and the `DefaultIfEmpty` operator to create a left outer join between our `<Author>` element and the `Author` table. We don't have a unique key to join on in this case, so we do the best we can by joining the full author name contained in the `<Author>` element to the first and last name in the `Author` table. After creating the query expression to retrieve the authors, we need to encapsulate it inside a method that we can call from our main query expression. Additionally, we need to use the results of the `authors` query expression to create an `EntitySet<BookAuthor>`, which we'll assign to the `BookAuthors` property on our book instance. After a bit of work, we end up with the `GetAuthors` method shown in listing 11.21.

Listing 11.21   Retrieving the authors from the XML and converting them into an `EntitySet`

```
private EntitySet<BookAuthor> GetAuthors(IEnumerable<XElement>
  authorElements) {
  LinqInActionDataContext ctx = new LinqInActionDataContext();
  var bookAuthors =
```

```
      from authorElement in authorElements
      join a in ctx.Authors on
        (string)author equals a.FirstName + " " + a.LastName into authors
      from existingAuthor in authors.DefaultIfEmpty()
      let nameParts = ((string)authorElement).Split(' ')
      select new BookAuthor {
        Author = existingAuthor ?? new Author {
          ID = Guid.Empty,
          FirstName = nameParts[0],
          LastName = nameParts[1]
        }
      };

    EntitySet<BookAuthor>set = new EntitySet<BookAuthor>();
    set.AddRange(bookAuthors);
    return set;
}
```

With the `GetAuthors()` method in place, we can update our query expression to incorporate the authors into our query:

```
var booksToImport =
  from amazonItem in amazonXml.Descendants(ns + "Item")
  join selectedBook in selectedBooks on
    (string)amazonItem.Element(ns + "ItemAttributes").Element(ns + "ISBN")
      equals selectedBook.Isbn
  join p in ctx.Publishers on
    (string)amazonItem.Element(ns + "ItemAttributes")
                      .Element(ns + "Publisher")
      equals p.Name into publishers
  from existingPublisher in publishers.DefaultIfEmpty()
  let attributes = amazonItem.Element(ns + "ItemAttributes")
  select new Book {
    Isbn = (string)attributes.Element(ns + "ISBN"),
    Title = (string)attributes.Element(ns + "Title"),
    Publisher = (existingPublisher ??
      new Publisher {
        ID = Guid.Empty,
        Name = (string)attributes.Element(ns + "Publisher")
      }),
    Subject = (Subject)categoryComboBox.SelectedItem,
    PubDate = (DateTime)attributes.Element(ns + "PublicationDate"),
    Price = ParsePrice(attributes.Element(ns + "ListPrice")),
    BookAuthors = GetAuthors(attributes.Elements(ns + "Author"))
  };
```

We've now completed the process of writing a query expression to create a list of books that should be imported from the XML returned by Amazon.

Thankfully, LINQ to SQL handles the majority of the work once we have our objects created. We do have a small preparatory step that we need to take before we can let LINQ to SQL run with our list of books and save them to the database. In order for our books to get saved, we need to tell the `DataContext` to add the books to the database. Telling the `DataContext` to add our books is simply a matter of calling `ctx.Books.InsertAllOnSubmit(booksToImport)`.[2] Once we have all our books added, we call `SubmitChanges()`.

```
ctx.Books.InsertAllOnSubmit(booksToImport);

try {
    ctx.SubmitChanges();
    MessageBox.Show(booksToImport.Count() + " books imported.");
} catch(Exception ex) {
    MessageBox.Show("An error occurred while attempting to import the
selected books. " + Environment.NewLine + Environment.NewLine +
    ex.Message);
}
```

With everything now in place, we can run our application and begin to import books into our LinqBooks database from Amazon.com. The complete code listing is shown in listing 11.22.

Listing 11.22   Full code for importing books from Amazon.com

```
using System;
using System.Collections.Generic;
using System.Data.Linq;
using System.Drawing;
using System.Linq;
using System.Windows.Forms;
using System.Xml.Linq;
using Chapter11.Common;
using LinqInAction.LinqToSql;

namespace Chapter11.WinForms {
  public partial class ImportForm : Form
  {

    LinqInActionDataContext ctx;
    XNamespace ns =
        "http://webservices.amazon.com/AWSECommerceService/2005-10-05";
    XElement amazonXml;
```

---

[2] The `InsertOnSubmit` method was named `Add` in Beta1 and Beta2 of LINQ to SQL.

```csharp
public ImportForm()
{
    InitializeComponent();
    this.Load += new EventHandler(ImportForm_Load);
    ctx = new LinqInActionDataContext();
}

void ImportForm_Load(object sender, EventArgs e)
{
    subjectComboBox.DataSource = ctx.Subjects.ToList();
}

void searchButton_Click(object sender, EventArgs e)
{
    string requestUrl =
      String.Format(Amazon.AmazonSearchRestUrl, keywords.Text);
    amazonXml = XElement.Load(requestUrl);

    var books =
        from result in amazonXml.Descendants(ns + "Item")
        let attributes = result.Element(ns + "ItemAttributes")
        select new Book
        {
            Isbn = (string)attributes.Element(ns + "ISBN"),
            Title = (string)attributes.Element(ns + "Title"),
        };

    bookBindingSource.DataSource = books;
    var rows =
    from row in bookDataGridView.Rows.OfType<DataGridViewRow>()
    let dataBoundBook = ((Book)row.DataBoundItem)
    join book in ctx.Books
      on dataBoundBook.Isbn equals book.Isbn.Trim()
    select row;

    foreach (DataGridViewRow row in rows)
    {
      row.DefaultCellStyle.BackColor = Color.LightGray;
      row.Cells[0].ReadOnly = true;
      row.Cells[1].Value =
        "** Already Exists ** - " + row.Cells[1].Value;
    }
}

void importButton_Click(object sender, EventArgs e)
{
  var selectedBooks =
    from row in bookDataGridView.Rows.OfType<DataGridViewRow>()
    where ((bool)row.Cells[0].EditedFormattedValue) == true
    select (Book)row.DataBoundItem;
```

```
using (var newContext = new LinqInActionDataContext())
{
    var booksToImport =
        from amazonItem in amazonXml.Descendants(ns + "Item")
        join selectedBook in selectedBooks
            on (string)amazonItem
               .Element(ns + "ItemAttributes")
               .Element(ns + "ISBN")
                equals selectedBook.Isbn
        join p in newContext.Publishers
            on ((string)amazonItem
               .Element(ns + "ItemAttributes")
               .Element(ns + "Publisher")).ToUpperInvariant()
                equals p.Name.Trim().ToUpperInvariant()
            into publishers
        from existingPublisher in publishers.DefaultIfEmpty()
        let attributes =
            amazonItem.Element(ns + "ItemAttributes")
        select new Book
        {
          ID = Guid.NewGuid(),
          Isbn = (string)attributes.Element(ns + "ISBN"),
          Title = (string)attributes.Element(ns + "Title"),
          Publisher = (existingPublisher ??
                      new Publisher
                      {
                        ID = Guid.NewGuid(),
                        Name = (string)attributes
                              .Element(ns + "Publisher")
                      }
          ),
          Subject = (Subject)subjectComboBox.SelectedItem,
          PubDate =
            (DateTime)attributes.Element(ns + "PublicationDate"),
          Price = ParsePrice(attributes.Element(ns + "ListPrice")),
          BookAuthors =
            GetAuthors(attributes.Elements(ns + "Author"))
        };

    newContext.Subjects.Attach((Subject)
    ➥subjectComboBox.SelectedItem);

    newContext.Books.InsertAllOnSubmit(booksToImport);

    try
    {
        newContext.SubmitChanges();
        MessageBox.Show(booksToImport.Count() + " books imported.");
    }
```

```
                    catch (Exception ex)
                    {
                        MessageBox.Show(
                            "An error occurred while attempting to import the
                        selected books."
                          + Environment.NewLine + Environment.NewLine + ex.Message);
                    }
                }
            }

        private EntitySet<BookAuthor> GetAuthors(IEnumerable<XElement>
    authorElements)
        {
            var bookAuthors =
                from authorElement in authorElements
                join author in ctx.Authors
                  on (string)authorElement
                  equals author.FirstName + " " + author.LastName
                into authors
                from existingAuthor in authors.DefaultIfEmpty()
                let nameParts = ((string)authorElement).Split(' ')
                select new BookAuthor
                {
                  ID = Guid.NewGuid(),
                  Author = existingAuthor ??
                    new Author
                    {
                      ID = Guid.NewGuid(),
                      FirstName = nameParts[0],
                      LastName = nameParts[1]
                    }
                };

            EntitySet<BookAuthor> set = new EntitySet<BookAuthor>();
            set.AddRange(bookAuthors);
            return set;
        }

        private decimal ParsePrice(XElement priceElement)
        {
            return Convert.ToDecimal(
                    ((string)priceElement.Element(ns + "FormattedPrice"))
                    .Replace("$", String.Empty)
            );
        }
    }
}
```

In this section, we pulled together many of the features available within LINQ and LINQ to XML to create an application that allows users to import books from Amazon.com. The application demonstrates the powerful capabilities available within LINQ for joining together data from in-memory objects, XML, and the database, as well as shows how LINQ to XML and LINQ to SQL can be used together to integrate data from disparate systems.

The past three scenarios have all involved integrating LINQ to XML with a relational database via LINQ to SQL. In our next scenario, we'll take a step away from the database and look at how we can use LINQ to XML to transform text files into XML. Although text files may not be as glamorous as databases, the LINQ framework and LINQ to XML manage to make programming against text files just as fun!

11.6 *Transforming text files into XML*

In today's modern world that's ruled by XML, you'd think everybody would've upgraded their internal systems to the latest and greatest, and done away with their arcane flat files. Unfortunately, many internal systems still rely heavily on text files. Rather than stay in the dark ages, we'd like to upgrade all of our internal systems to speak XML. To that end, let's see what LINQ to XML offers when it comes to converting text files into XML. As you should be accustomed to by now, we'll get started by exploring our goal for this scenario.

11.6.1 *Goal*

In this section, we aim to transform a text file into a hierarchical XML document. As shown in listing 11.23, the text file will contain the following book information: the ISBN, title, author(s), publisher, publication date, and price.

Listing 11.23   CSV of Books

```
01 0735621632,CLR via C#,Jeffrey Richter,Microsoft Press,02-22-2006,59.99
02 0321127420,Patterns Of Enterprise Application Architecture,Martin
➥Fowler,Addison-Wesley,11-05-2002,54.99
03 0321200683,Enterprise Integration Patterns,Gregor Hohpe,Addison-Wesley,
➥10-10-2003,54.99
04 0321125215,Domain-Driven Design,Eric Evans,Addison-Wesley,08-22-2003,
➥54.99
05 1932394613,Ajax In Action,Dave Crane;Eric Pascarello;Darren James,
➥Manning Publications,10-01-2005,44.95
```

This text file is the same file that we used in the LINQ to Text Files section of chapter 5. You'll notice some similarities between the code here and that presented in chapter 5, since not only are we using the same file, but both sections are using functional construction to convert the text file into alternate formats. In this scenario, our goal is to parse the data in the text file and produce a hierarchy of XML, as shown in listing 11.24.

Listing 11.24   The XML output that will be created from the transformation

```xml
<?xml version="1.0" encoding="utf-8" ?>
<books>
  <book>
    <title>CLR via C#</title>
    <authors>
      <author>
        <firstName>Jeffrey</firstName>
        <lastName>Richter</lastName>
      </author>
    </authors>
    <publisher>Microsoft Press</publisher>
    <publicationDate>02-22-2006</publicationDate>
    <price>59.99</price>
    <isbn>0735621632</isbn>
  </book>
  <book>
    <title>Patterns Of Enterprise Application Architecture</title>
    <authors>
      <author>
        <firstName>Martin</firstName>
        <lastName>Fowler</lastName>
      </author>
    </authors>
    <publisher>Addison-Wesley Professional</publisher>
    <publicationDate>11-05-2002</publicationDate>
    <price>54.99</price>
    <isbn>0321127420</isbn>
  </book>
  ...
</books>
```

Now that we have an idea of the XML we'll be producing, let's look at the technique we'll use to create the XML.

11.6.2 *Implementation*

The technique used in this scenario is similar to the previous examples we've covered. The XML is constructed in a bottom-up manner using LINQ to XML's functional construction capabilities, along with a set of query expressions that selects the relevant data out of the individual lines of the CSV file. Once again, we see that LINQ to XML allows us to intertwine results from varying data sources, in this case a flat file, with LINQ to XML functional construction statements to create XML.

In order to create our desired XML, we need to open the text file, split each line in the file into an array, and place each item in the array into the appropriate XML element. Let's start with opening the file and splitting it into parts.

```
from line in File.ReadAllLines("books.txt")
let items = line.Split(',')
```
    Add functional construction statements for creating the XML

We leverage the static `ReadAllLines` method available on the `File` class to read each line within the text file. Since `ReadAllLines` returns a string array, we can safely use it in our `from` clause. To split each line, we use the `Split` method available on `string`, as well as the `let` clause that is available in C#. The `let` clause allows us to perform the split operation once and refer to the result in subsequent expressions. Once we have our line split apart, we can wrap each item into the appropriate XML element, as in listing 11.25.

> **Listing 11.25   Read the lines from the text file into `XElement` objects**

```
var booksXml = new XElement("books",
  from line in File.ReadAllLines("books.txt")
  let items = line.Split(',')
  select new XElement("book",
    new XElement("title", items[1]),
    new XElement("publisher", items[3]),
    new XElement("publicationDate", items[4]),
    new XElement("price", items[5]),
    new XElement("isbn", items[0])
  );
```

We conveniently left the authors out of the query, since they require extra work. Unlike the other fields in our text file, there can be more than one author specified for a single book. If we go back and review the sample text file, we see that the authors are delimited by a semicolon (;).

```
Dave Crane;Eric Pascarello;Darren James
```

As we did with the entire line, we can `Split` the string of authors into an array, with each author being an individual element in the array. To be sure we get our fill of `Split`, we use it one final time to break the full author name into first and last name parts. Finally, we place the statements for parsing out the authors into a query and wrap the results of our many splits into the appropriate XML.

```
...
new XElement("authors",
  from authorFullName in items[2].Split(';')
  let authorNameParts = authorFullName.Split(' ')
  select new XElement("author",
    new XElement("firstName", authorNameParts[0]),
    new XElement("lastName", authorNameParts[1])
  )
)
...
```

When we add it all together we get the final solution, which can be seen in listing 11.26.

Listing 11.26 Flat file to XML implementation

```
using System;
using System.Linq;
using System.Xml.Linq;
using System.IO;

namespace Chapter11.FlatFileToXml {
  class Program {
    static void Main(string[] args) {
      XElement xml =
        new XElement("books",
        from line in File.ReadAllLines("books.txt")
        where !line.StartsWith("#")
        let items = line.Split(',')
        select new XElement("book",
          new XElement("title", items[1]),
          new XElement("authors",
            from authorFullName in items[2].Split(';')
            let authorNameParts = authorFullName.Split(' ')
            select new XElement("author",
              new XElement("firstName", authorNameParts[0]),
              new XElement("lastName", authorNameParts[1])
            )
          ),
          new XElement("publisher", items[3]),
          new XElement("publicationDate", items[4]),
          new XElement("price", items[5]),
          new XElement("isbn", items[0])
        )
      );
      Console.WriteLine(xml);
    }
  }
}
```

We'd be remiss if we didn't point out that the code presented here isn't recommended if the file that is being processed is large. In this scenario, we used the `File.ReadAllLines` method in our LINQ to XML query. When working with large files, and/or when performance is critical, the file should be read using a streaming approach like that presented in section 5.3.1.

As we've seen over and over again, LINQ to XML allows us to mix and match data from varying data sources into functional construction statements. The result is a consistent programming API for developers, which makes the way XML is created from other data sources—whether they be relational, object, or a text file—consistent and predictable.

11.7 Summary

In this chapter, we took a whirlwind ride through many of the common scenarios you'll run into when building applications that use XML. Along the way, we explored many of the powerful capabilities that LINQ to XML offers.

We started by exploring LINQ to XML's transformation capabilities, by building a set of objects from XML. Since we often work with objects, this scenario provided a good overview of how we can read data from XML into a set of objects. It also showed how similar the code is for transforming XML to alternate data formats when using LINQ to XML.

Next we moved on to look at how to create XML from objects using the XML literals support in Visual Basic. By allowing developers to embed XML directly into VB code, XML literals help reduce the confusion that often arises when creating XML.

In addition to having solid support for transforming XML into objects, LINQ to XML also has strong integration with LINQ to SQL. We explored this integration by creating XML from data within a database as well as by filtering and mixing data from a database with XML data in a single query. We rounded out our exploration of LINQ to XML's integration with LINQ to SQL by looking at how to read information out of an XML file to update a database.

Finally, we completed our common scenarios by exploring how a flat CSV file could be transformed into XML, once again using LINQ to XML's powerful transformation capabilities.

In this chapter, we were able to create XML from in-memory objects, a relational database, and flat files. We also transformed our XML into other data sources—such as LINQ to SQL objects—and saw how functional construction solves many of our data transformation scenarios.

In the first four parts of this book, we've provided you with detailed coverage of all the major pieces of the LINQ puzzle. In the next chapter, we explore how you can extend LINQ to support additional scenarios that it doesn't support out of the box.

Part 5

LINQing it all together

The first purpose of this part of the book is to show how LINQ can be extended to adapt to your own application domains. The second purpose is to show how different flavors of LINQ can be used in every layer of applications.

Chapter 12 is devoted to LINQ's extensibility. It demonstrates how you can create custom query operators and even complete LINQ providers. Chapter 13 discusses using all the flavors of LINQ and their extensibility options in the context of a complete application, our LinqBooks example.

Extending LINQ

12

This chapter covers:

- LINQ's extension mechanisms
- Custom query operators
- The query expression pattern
- `IQueryable` and `IQueryProvider`
- LINQ to Amazon

When we introduced LINQ, we pointed out that one of its major features is its ability to query several kinds of data and data sources. In the chapters that followed, we focused on LINQ to Objects, LINQ to SQL, and LINQ to XML. In this chapter, we'll analyze how these flavors of LINQ extend LINQ with support for data sources such as in-memory collections, XML, or relational databases. This will allow you to determine the techniques you can use to extend LINQ and use it with your own data sources. LINQ's extensibility features will allow you to adapt it to particular needs. They will also enable novel use cases that expand the LINQ spectrum.

LINQ's extensibility allows you to create your own flavor of LINQ by creating a LINQ provider. Of course, this can be a lot of work. Most of the time you won't need to create a complete LINQ flavor. You may simply need small adaptations of LINQ's behavior. Fortunately, LINQ is flexible enough that you can add new query operators or redefine some of the default ones according to your needs. Whether you're a framework provider who wants to give your users the power of LINQ or simply a developer who wants to adapt LINQ to your own business context, you'll find that LINQ is flexible enough to adapt to your needs.

The goal of this chapter is to show the available extensibility options that LINQ offers to help you pick the technique best for your situation. We'll also show you how to use these extensibility options through demonstrations. In order to demonstrate LINQ's extensibility, we'll cover several examples. We'll start by creating custom query operators and using them as utility methods that can simplify your LINQ queries. We'll also create domain-specific query operators. These will allow you to work closely with your own business objects. We'll then see how we can rewrite the basic operators used by query expressions, such as `Where` or `OrderBy`. Finally, we'll create a new LINQ provider: LINQ to Amazon. This example will demonstrate how to encapsulate calls to a web API into a LINQ provider that you'll use in LINQ queries. We'll then review advanced extensibility features that involve expression trees and the `System.Linq.IQueryable<T>` interface.

To get started, let's review how LINQ was designed to be extensible.

12.1 Discovering LINQ's extension mechanisms

As we explained when we introduced LINQ, it is not a closed package that allows working only with in-memory collections, XML, or relational databases. In fact, LINQ is based on extensibility from the ground up. In other words, LINQ isn't exclusive. It can be adapted to work with the data sources you have to deal with.

The core of LINQ consists of query operators and query expressions. This is where the magic happens. The great news is that the query syntax offered by

LINQ's query expressions is by no means hard-wired to the standard query operators we introduced in chapters 3 and 4. Query expressions are purely a syntactic feature that applies to anything that fulfills what is known as the *LINQ query expression pattern*. This pattern defines the set of operators required to fully support query expressions and how they must be implemented. Implementing this pattern consists of providing methods with appropriate names and signatures. The standard query operators you are used to working with provide an implementation of the LINQ query expression pattern. They're implemented as extension methods (see chapter 2) that augment the IEnumerable<T> interface. This is just one possible implementation of the LINQ query expression pattern.

The standard query operators implement the LINQ query expression pattern to enable querying any .NET array or collection. Developers may apply the query syntax to any class they want, as long as they make sure their implementation adheres to the LINQ pattern. Third parties are free to replace the standard query operators with their own implementations that are appropriate for a target domain or technology. Custom implementation may provide additional services such as remote evaluation, query translation, or optimization. By adhering to the conventions of the LINQ pattern, such implementations can enjoy the same language integration and tool support as the standard query operators.

Before looking at how we can extend LINQ, it's important to understand how Microsoft's official flavors of LINQ are built on the LINQ foundation. This will allow us to highlight the different extensibility options that are available.

12.1.1 *How the LINQ flavors are LINQ implementations*

The extensibility of the query architecture is used in LINQ to provide implementations that work over various data sources such as XML or SQL data. The query operators over XML (LINQ to XML) use an efficient, easy-to-use in-memory XML facility to provide XPath/XQuery functionality in the host programming language. The query operators over relational data (LINQ to SQL) build on the integration of SQL-based schema definitions into the CLR type system. This integration provides strong typing over relational data while retaining the expressive power of the relational model and the performance of query evaluation directly in the underlying data store.

The flavors of LINQ provided by Microsoft are all made possible thanks to LINQ's extensibility. These flavors include LINQ to Objects, LINQ to XML, LINQ to DataSet, LINQ to SQL, and LINQ to Entities. In terms of implementation, each flavor comes in the form of a LINQ *provider*. Each provider relies on specific extensibility techniques supported by LINQ. Depending on what you wish to achieve, you'll reuse one of the techniques that the default providers use. Reviewing how each provider is implemented will help you determine which technique to use to create your own *LINQ to Whatever.*

LINQ to Objects

LINQ to Objects allows us to query arrays or other collections that implement the IEnumerable<T> interface. LINQ to Objects relies on the standard query operators, which are extension methods for the IEnumerable<T> type. When we use LINQ to Objects, we're using the set of query operators implemented by the System.Linq.Enumerable class. That's all there is to LINQ to Objects. It's pretty straightforward.

LINQ to DataSet

LINQ to DataSet allows us to query DataSets using LINQ. It is not much more complicated than LINQ to Objects. LINQ to DataSet is also based on the same standard query operators, but it adds a small set of extension methods for the types involved in DataSets, mostly the System.Data.DataRow class.

See our online chapter to learn more about LINQ to DataSet.

LINQ to XML

LINQ to XML is also based on the standard query operators, but adds a set of classes to deal with XML objects. LINQ to XML is used the same way LINQ to Objects is used, but this time you query and create objects such as XNode, XElement, XAttribute, and XText.

LINQ to SQL

LINQ to SQL works differently than the previous providers. While the standard query operators used with LINQ to Objects and LINQ to XML use delegates, all the query operators used by LINQ to SQL are implemented using expression trees. The implementation of the operators is provided by the System.Linq.Queryable class this time. Also, these operators don't deal with IEnumerable<T> but with IQueryable<T>. The use of expression trees and IQueryable<T> enables LINQ to SQL queries obtained by numerous calls to query operators to be converted into a single SQL query that gets sent to the database.

LINQ to Entities

LINQ to Entities is implemented using the same technique as LINQ to SQL. LINQ to Entities translates LINQ expressions into the canonical query trees used throughout the ADO.NET Entity Framework. These trees are handed out to the Entity Framework query pipeline for mapping and SQL generation.

The way the official Microsoft LINQ providers are implemented should give you a good idea of what can be achieved through LINQ's extensibility features. Here are the options we can use to improve LINQ or to create a new LINQ provider:

- Create query operators that implement the LINQ query expression pattern using delegates.

- Provide classes that can be used with the standard query operators but that allow working with a specific data source or with specific data types.

- Create query operators that implement the LINQ query expression pattern using expression trees.

- Implement the IQueryable<T> interface.

We'll soon demonstrate how to put these techniques into practice. Before this, let's suggest additional usages for LINQ's extensibility features.

12.1.2 *What can be done with custom LINQ extensions*

The range of possibilities offered by LINQ's extensibility features goes from querying your custom business objects to querying...anything! LINQ has extension mechanisms suitable for the level of customization you desire.

As we'll demonstrate through examples, you can start by simply creating additional query operators. And if you have a need for it, you can even create a custom implementation of the standard query operators. By writing extension methods that mimic what the implementation from System.Linq.Enumerable provides, you can adapt the behavior of the standard operators to your needs.

In advanced cases, you can resort to the technique used for LINQ to SQL: resorting to expression trees and implementing the IQueryable<T> interface. This is more difficult than creating simple query operators, but this is what you'll need to do if you want to use LINQ queries with complex or remote data sources. For example, web sites and web services don't support the kind of intensive interaction LINQ to Objects implies with the standard query operators. This means that other techniques are required. Similar to the way LINQ to SQL works, you can take advantage of expression trees and deferred query execution to be able to query remote sources.

It may be difficult to imagine what your needs will be, but we can give you an idea of what can be achieved through extensibility. Let's review potential uses of LINQ to help you see how far you can go with it.

Suggested use cases for LINQ's extensibility

Here are some scenarios that could require putting LINQ's extensibility into action:

- Querying a custom data source (such as a filesystem, Active Directory, WMI, or Windows's Event Log)

- Querying web services (Amazon, other public web services, or in-house web services)

- Allowing the developers who use your product to take advantage of LINQ—if you are a tool provider or sell a development framework (examples include object-relational frameworks)

Some of these scenarios are more difficult than others. Querying the Windows Event Log may not require more than implementing some query operators, which is not very difficult. In comparison, integrating LINQ with an object-relational framework is more involved and implies dealing with the `IQueryable<T>` interface and expression trees. This is what LINQ to SQL uses to generate SQL queries from LINQ queries. This is also what a framework like NHibernate could use to generate HQL queries from LINQ queries.

> **NOTE** The custom query operators we'll demonstrate here apply to in-memory queries only. This means that they can work with LINQ to Objects, LINQ to DataSet, and LINQ to XML, but not with LINQ to SQL or LINQ to Entities. This is because for a query operator to be supported by LINQ to SQL or LINQ to Entities, it must be translatable into SQL or Entity SQL. LINQ to SQL and LINQ to Entities have no knowledge about your additional operators, so they wouldn't know what to do with them.
>
> Techniques exist to create custom query operators that can be used in LINQ to SQL, but we won't discuss them here.

Enough with the preliminaries! It's time to get our hands dirty. We'll cover the various extensibility options, from the simplest ones to the richer and more difficult ones. We'll use a gradual approach, starting with "light" extensions and finishing with our advanced LINQ to Amazon example. To get started, let's see how to implement additional query operators.

12.2 Creating custom query operators

In this section, we'll focus on LINQ to Objects. Even though LINQ comes with 51 standard query operators, in some situations this may not be enough, as you'll see.

The first way to extend LINQ is to create additional query operators. You can use this technique to overcome the limitations that you may run into when working with the standard query operators. We'll lead you through examples that will show you how to create additional operators that supplement the standard operators. We'll also demonstrate how custom query operators may be used to enrich your LINQ queries with domain-specific processing.

12.2.1 *Improving the standard query operators*

Since we're looking at how you can overcome limitations of the standard query operators, the best example to look at is a custom implementation of the Sum operator. When using the standard query operators in his code, a C# developer named Troy Magennis noticed some limitations (see http://aspiring-technology.com/ blogs/troym/archive/2006/10/06/24.aspx). One of the limitations comes from the Sum query operator. There is a high chance for overflow when working with big numbers and the variant of Sum that operates on a sequence of integers.

The following simple piece of code demonstrates this problem:

```
Enumerable.Sum(new int[] {int.MaxValue, 1});
```

Understandably, this code yields an OverflowException with the message "Arithmetic operation resulted in an overflow."[1] The problem is that the sum of two integers can be too big to fit in an int (System.Int32) object. This is why Troy wrote LongSum, which returns a long (System.Int64) object instead of an int object, as with Sum.

Let's re-create the LongSum operator together. As you saw when we introduced the standard query operators in chapter 3, they consist of extension methods for the IEnumerable<T> type.

Listing 12.1 shows how the Sum operator for int comes out of the box in the System.Linq.Enumerable class.

> **Listing 12.1 Standard implementation of the Sum operator for int**

```
namespace System.Linq
{
  public static class Enumerable
  {
```

---

[1] C# statements can execute in either checked or unchecked context, depending on the use of the checked or unchecked keywords. In a checked context, arithmetic overflow raises an exception. In an unchecked context, arithmetic overflow is ignored and the result is truncated. The Sum operator is implemented using the checked keyword, hence the OverflowException.

```
. . .

public static int Sum(this IEnumerable<int> source)
{
  if (source == null)
    throw new ArgumentNullException("source");
  int sum = 0;
  checked
  {
    foreach (int v in source)
      sum += v;
  }
  return sum;
}

public static int? Sum(this IEnumerable<int?> source)
{
  if (source == null)
    throw new ArgumentNullException("source");
  int? sum = 0;
  checked
  {
    foreach (int? v in source)
      if (v != null)
        sum += v;
  }
  return sum;
}

public static int Sum<T>(this IEnumerable<T> source,
  Func<T, int> selector)
{
  return Enumerable.Sum(Enumerable.Select(source, selector));
}

public static int? Sum<T>(this IEnumerable<T> source,
  Func<T, int?> selector)
{
  return Enumerable.Sum(Enumerable.Select(source, selector));
}

  . . .
}
}
```

As you can see in the code, the Sum operator is implemented as four method overloads. These methods can be easily adapted to create the LongSum operator. Listing 12.2 shows the source code that implements the same four methods but with longs as the results.

Listing 12.2 `LongSum,` **improved implementation of the** `Sum` **operator for** `int` **(SumExtensions.cs)**

```csharp
using System;
using System.Collections.Generic;
using System.Linq;

namespace LinqInAction.Extensibility
{
  public static class SumExtensions
  {
    public static long LongSum(this IEnumerable<int> source)
    {
      if (source == null)
        throw new ArgumentNullException("source");
      long sum = 0;
      checked
      {
        foreach (int v in source)
          sum += v;
      }
      return sum;
    }

    public static long? LongSum(this IEnumerable<int?> source)
    {
      if (source == null)
        throw new ArgumentNullException("source");
      long? sum = 0;
      checked
      {
        foreach (int? v in source)
          if (v != null)
            sum += v;
      }
      return sum;
    }

    public static long LongSum<T>(this IEnumerable<T> source,
      Func<T, int> selector)
    {
      return SumExtensions.LongSum(Enumerable.Select(source, selector));
    }

    public static long? LongSum<T>(this IEnumerable<T> source,
      Func<T, int?> selector)
    {
      return SumExtensions.LongSum(Enumerable.Select(source, selector));
    }
  }
}
```

The new `LongSum` operator we've just created in listing 12.2 returns the numerical sum of a sequence of `int`s or nullable `int`s as a `long` or nullable `long`. This gives more range for the results compared to the default `Sum` operator.

This demonstrates how you can improve your LINQ experience with query operators that work the way they should, or at least the way you want them to work. This kind of extensibility ensures that you are not stuck with a static predefined set of operators.

The example we've just seen shows how to fix a problem with a standard query operator. But this isn't the only way we can extend LINQ to solve a problem or to improve our code. Creating custom query operators can be useful in other situations, as you'll see next.

12.2.2 *Utility or domain-specific query operators*

Our first example revolved around a standard query operator. The default set of operators that comes with LINQ to Objects is useful and can be applied to a wide range of situations. This is possible especially since these operators are generic: they can be used with any type of objects. However, when you are dealing with business objects, specific operations may be required.

Imagine you are working on `Book` and `Publisher` objects. How do you determine whether a book is expensive in a LINQ query? How do you retrieve a publisher's books? The standard query operators may not be adapted to satisfy such needs because as we mentioned earlier, they're generic! While being generic is a big advantage, it doesn't help when business-specific processing or concepts are required, because more specialized assistance is needed. In situations like this, you would want to use custom utility query operators.

When writing code, developers often create utility or helper methods. Utility methods are commonly used to simplify code and keep frequently used code in one place. In order to remove complexity from your LINQ queries, it may be useful to create utility methods. Imagine you want to create a method that deals with a collection of `Book` objects. You could simply create a traditional method to do this, but the best way to proceed is to create a query operator. Since a query is made of calls to query operators, utility methods integrate nicely within LINQ queries if they're written as query operators.

In order to get a feel for utility query operators, we are going to go through some samples. Each of the operators we'll introduce works on one or a collection of the business objects from our `LinqBooks` running example. This is why we could say that these operators are "domain-specific query operators."

Let's start with an operator that works on a sequence of books.

IEnumerable<Book>.TotalPrice

The code in listing 12.3 shows how you can create an operator that works on a sequence of Book objects to compute a total price.

Listing 12.3 `TotalPrice` **custom query operator (CustomQueryOperators.cs)**

```
using System;
using System.Collections.Generic;
using System.Linq;

using LinqInAction.LinqBooks.Common;

namespace LinqInAction.Extensibility
{
  public static class CustomQueryOperators
  {
    ...

    public static Decimal TotalPrice(this IEnumerable<Book> books)
    {
      if (books == null)
        throw new ArgumentNullException("books");

      Decimal result = 0;
      foreach (Book book in books)
        if (book != null)
          result += book.Price;
      return result;
    }

    ...
  }
}
```

Our new TotalPrice operator can then be nicely used in query expressions, like in the following:

```
from publisher in SampleData.Publishers
join book in SampleData.Books
  on publisher equals book.Publisher into pubBooks
select new { Publisher = publisher.Name,
             TotalPrice = pubBooks.TotalPrice() };
```

The same could be done without much difficulty by using only standard operators, but you get the idea. Creating your own operators helps write shorter and clearer code. In general, it can be useful to create utility methods that you can use in your queries.

Let's consider another utility operator that also works on a sequence of books.

IEnumerable<Book>.Min

Let's say we'd like to implement `Min` for `Book` objects. The `Min` operator provided by the standard query operators only works on numeric values. The extension method in listing 12.4 provides an implementation of `Min` that works on a sequence of `Book` objects and returns the book that has the lowest number of pages as the result.

Listing 12.4 `Min` custom query operator (CustomQueryOperators.cs)

```
public static Book Min(this IEnumerable<Book> source)
{
  if (source == null)
    throw new ArgumentNullException("source");

  Book result = null;
  foreach (Book book in source)
  {
    if ((result == null) || (book.PageCount < result.PageCount))
      result = book;
  }
  return result;
}
```

With this custom query operator, you can write the following code, for instance:

```
Book minBook = SampleData.Books.Min();
Console.WriteLine(
  "Book with the lowest number of pages = {0} ({1} pages)",
  minBook.Title, minBook.PageCount);
```

This example shows how you can adapt a concept like `Min` introduced by the standard query operators to deal with domain-specific objects.

For a change, let's now see a utility operator that works on a `Publisher` object.

Publisher.Books

You can resort to any extension method that helps you simplify your code and hide complexity. For example, in the following query, we use a `join` clause to get access to each publisher's books:

```
from publisher in SampleData.Publishers
join book in SampleData.Books
  on publisher equals book.Publisher into books
```

```
select new {
  Publisher = publisher.Name,
  TotalPrice = books.TotalPrice()
};
```

We're likely to use the same kind of `join` clause in every query each time we want to access a publisher's books. It could be useful to create a utility query operator to perform this operation. The operator in listing 12.5 selects a publisher's books from a sequence of books.

Listing 12.5   Books custom query operator (CustomQueryOperators.cs)

```
static public IEnumerable<Book> Books(this Publisher publisher,
  IEnumerable<Book> books)
{
  return books.Where(book => book.Publisher == publisher);
}
```

This new `Books` operator can be used to simplify our previous query expression as follows:

```
from publisher in SampleData.Publishers
select new {
  Publisher = publisher.Name,
  TotalPrice = publisher.Books(SampleData.Books).TotalPrice()
};
```

Of course this operator can be reused in other queries as well, which makes it easy to filter books by publisher.

> **WARNING**   This is also an interesting example of what should be avoided! The code that uses the `join` clause and not our `Books` operator will be more efficient in most cases because it uses the `GroupJoin` operator behind the scenes. `GroupJoin` is optimized to join sequences, and in our case it will loop on books only once to find their publisher. The version of the code that uses our `Books` operator will loop on the collection of books for each publisher.
>
>   This example should help you to understand that while it's easy to create new query operators, it's not always the most efficient option. The choice is yours. Always consider the implications.

Before we move on to other kinds of extensibility, let's consider one more example of a domain-specific query operator.

Book.IsExpensive

The last operator in this section will show you how query operators can be used to code a specific concept only once.

The sample operator in listing 12.6 takes a book as a parameter and returns whether or not it is expensive.

Listing 12.6   IsExpensive custom query operator (CustomQueryOperators.cs)

```
public static Boolean IsExpensive(this Book book)
{
  if (book == null)
    throw new ArgumentNullException("book");


  return (book.Price > 50) ||
         ((book.Price / book.PageCount) > 0.10M);
}
```

> A book is expensive if its price is high or its number of pages is low for the price

The `IsExpensive` operator defined in the listing can be used in LINQ queries each time we need to know whether a book is expensive. Here is a sample query that uses this operator:

```
var books =
   from book in SampleData.Books
   group book.Title by book.IsExpensive() into bookGroup
   select new { Expensive = bookGroup.Key, Books = bookGroup };
ObjectDumper.Write(books, 1);
```

The results of this query's execution looks like this:

```
Expensive=True    Books=...
  Books: Funny Stories
  Books: C# on Rails
  Books: Bonjour mon Amour
Expensive=False   Books=...
  Books: LINQ rules
  Books: All your base are belong to us
```

The advantage of creating operators like `IsExpensive` is that they abstract away some notions that need to be expressed in queries. For example, `IsExpensive` can be reused in multiple queries without having to think each time about what "expensive" means. (Whether something is expensive is subjective, so good luck writing an actual algorithm for this!) Also, if this notion needs to be changed, it can be done in only one place: the operator's code.

We've seen how you can use LINQ's extensibility to create utility operators that help you deal with business objects. The operators we've demonstrated are additional operators that can be used in LINQ queries, but only through the dot notation. Only a small set of query operators can be used implicitly with the *query expression* syntax. This is the case for basic operators like `Where`, `Select`, or `OrderBy`, for example, which are transparently invoked when `where`, `select`, or `orderby` clauses are used in a query expression. We'll now demonstrate another kind of extensibility supported by LINQ that allows you to reimplement the operators behind `from`, `where`, `join`, `orderby`, `select`, and the other keywords in a query expression.

12.3 Custom implementations of the basic query operators

In the previous section, when we demonstrated how to use our additional query operators, we used the explicit dot notation (method syntax). For example, here is a query that uses two of the operators we created, `Books` and `TotalPrice`:

```
from publisher in SampleData.Publishers
where publisher.Name.StartsWith("A")
select new {
  Publisher = publisher.Name,
  TotalPrice = publisher.Books(SampleData.Books).TotalPrice()
};
```

This query implicitly involves more operators than just ours. Namely, the `Where` and `Select` operators are also part of the query through the `where` and `select` clauses. By default, the clauses of this kind of query expression are translated into calls to standard query operators. You may wish to change how a query like this one behaves. We'll show how you can easily provide and use your own implementations of `Where` and `Select` even if they're used through the query expression notation. Thanks to the way the compiler resolves query operators when it translates a query expression, we can define what implementation of the basic query operators is used.

We'll first review how query expressions are translated into method calls. This implies that we get to know the query expression pattern. Once we know the basics of the query translation mechanism, we'll go through some sample implementations of the query expression pattern.

12.3.1 *Refresh on the query translation mechanism*

Let's review how the compiler translates query expressions into method calls. This is the starting point of the extensibility option that will allow you to create custom implementation of the basic query operators.

Imagine that we write the following query:

```
using System.Linq;
using LinqInAction.LinqBooks.Common;

static class TestCustomImplementation
{
  static void Main()
  {
    var books =
      from book in SampleData.Books
      where book.Price < 30
      select book.Title;

    ObjectDumper.Write(books);
  }
}
```

The code that actually gets executed for this query depends on one thing: the namespaces you import. Because query operators are extension methods, they're referenced through namespaces. When the compiler sees a query expression, it converts it into calls to extension methods.

One task that the compiler achieves is resolving where the Where and Select methods come from. If you import System.Linq, the compiler will find the Where and Select extension methods that the System.Linq.Enumerable class provides. The result is that the code that actually gets executed is the following:

```
var query =
  System.Linq.Enumerable.Select(
    System.Linq.Enumerable.Where(
      SampleData.Books,
      book => book.Price < 30),
    book => book.Title);
```

If you don't import System.Linq, but instead a namespace of your own that also provides implementations of the Where and Select operators, the code is translated differently.

The idea here is that the same query expression can become translated into something like this:

```
var query =
  MyNamespace.MyExtensions.Select(
    MyNamespace.MyExtensions.Where(
```

```
    SampleData.Books,
      book => book.Price < 30),
    book => book.Title);
```

The kind of extensibility we're discussing in this section relies on this mechanism. Let's now examine more precisely how the mapping between a query expression and query operators works.

12.3.2 Query expression pattern specification

We've just seen how we can provide our own implementation for a query expression's where and select clauses. The same mechanism applies to all the clauses. The C# 3.0 specification details which operators should be implemented to fully support query expressions and how they must be implemented. This document introduces the pattern of methods that types can implement to support query expressions as the query expression pattern.

The recommended shape of a generic class C<T> that supports the query expression pattern is shown in listing 12.7.

Listing 12.7 The query expression pattern

```
delegate R Func<T1,R>(T1 arg1);
delegate R Func<T1,T2,R>(T1 arg1, T2 arg2);

class C
{
  public C<T> Cast<T>();
}

class C<T>
{
  public C<T> Where(Func<T,bool> predicate);
  public C<U> Select<U>(Func<T,U> selector);
  public C<U> SelectMany<U,V>(Func<T,C<U>> selector,
                             Func<T,U,V> resultSelector);
  public C<V> Join<U,K,V>(C<U> inner,
                         Func<T,K> outerKeySelector,
                         Func<U,K> innerKeySelector,
                         Func<T,U,V> resultSelector);
  public C<V> GroupJoin<U,K,V>(C<U> inner,
                             Func<T,K> outerKeySelector,
                             Func<U,K> innerKeySelector,
                             Func<T,C<U>,V> resultSelector);
  public O<T> OrderBy<K>(Func<T,K> keySelector);
  public O<T> OrderByDescending<K>(Func<T,K> keySelector);
  public C<G<K,T>> GroupBy<K>(Func<T,K> keySelector);
  public C<G<K,E>> GroupBy<K,E>(Func<T,K> keySelector,
                             Func<T,E> elementSelector);
```

```
}

class O<T> : C<T>
{
  public O<T> ThenBy<K>(Func<T,K> keySelector);
  public O<T> ThenByDescending<K>(Func<T,K> keySelector);
}

class G<K,T> : C<T>
{
  public K Key { get; }
}
```

NOTE   The query expression pattern for VB has not been provided by Microsoft at the time of this writing.

You should refer to the C# 3.0 specification to learn about the details of this pattern. Because query expressions are translated into method invocations by means of a syntactic mapping, types have considerable flexibility in how they implement the query expression pattern. In the context of this book, there are a few things you need to know to understand the examples we're about to work out:

- A generic type is used in the query expression pattern to illustrate the proper relationships between parameter and result types, but it is possible to implement the pattern for nongeneric types as well.

- The standard query operators we described in chapters 3 and 4 provide an implementation of the query operator pattern for any type that implements the IEnumerable<T> interface. Although we're used to working on collections with the standard query operators in the context of LINQ to Objects and LINQ to XML, you can see that IEnumerable<T> is not part of the pattern. This means we can use LINQ with any object and not just enumerations/sequences.

- The standard query operators are implemented as extension methods, but the patterns' methods can be implemented as extension methods or as instance methods, because the two have the same invocation syntax.

- The methods can request delegates or expression trees as their parameters because lambda expressions are convertible to both.

- Although recommended for completeness, providing an implementation of all the previously listed methods is not required.

Everything we covered in the first part of this section is the foundation we needed to start creating custom implementations of the basic query operators. We are now ready to see some examples.

To give you a good overview of how it's possible to implement the LINQ query expression pattern, here's what we're going to demonstrate next:

- We'll show you examples of generic implementation as well as nongeneric.

- We'll build operators that work on `IEnumerable<T>` as well as operators that work on other kinds of objects.

- We'll build operators that receive delegates as well as operators that receive expression trees.

- Some of our operators will be defined as extension methods, some as instance methods.

- To keep things simple, we'll provide implementations of `Where` and `Select` only.

Let's jump right into our examples.

12.3.3 Example 1: tracing standard query operators' execution

In our first example, we'll create custom implementations of the `Where` and `Select` operators. Our methods will just delegate the processing to the standard `Enumerable.Where` and `Enumerable.Select` implementations.

Listing 12.8 shows two operators implemented in a class named `CustomImplementation` inside the `LinqInAction.Extensibility` namespace.

> **Listing 12.8 Custom implementations of `Where` and `Select` with the standard generic signatures (CustomImplementation.csproj)**

```
using System;
using System.Collections.Generic;
using System.Linq;

namespace LinqInAction.Extensibility
{
  public static class CustomImplementation
  {
    public static IEnumerable<TSource> Where<TSource>(
      this IEnumerable<TSource> source,
      Func<TSource, Boolean> predicate)
    {
      Console.WriteLine("in CustomImplementation.Where<TSource>");
```

```
      return Enumerable.Where(source, predicate);
    }

    public static IEnumerable<TResult> Select<TSource, TResult>(
      this IEnumerable<TSource> source,
      Func<TSource, TResult> selector)
    {
      Console.WriteLine(
        "in CustomImplementation.Select<TSource, TResult>");
      return Enumerable.Select(source, selector);
    }
  }
}
```

In order to use these new implementations of the two operators, all we need to do is import the `LinqInAction.Extensibility` namespace instead of the `System.Linq` namespace:

```
//using System.Linq;
using LinqInAction.Extensibility;
using LinqInAction.LinqBooks.Common;

class TestCustomImplementation
{
  static void Main()
  {
    var books =
      from book in SampleData.Books
      where book.Price < 30
      select book.Title;

    ObjectDumper.Write(books);
  }
}
```

Of course, executing this program will display our trace information:

```
in CustomImplementation.Where<TSource>
in CustomImplementation.Select<TSource, TResult>
Funny Stories
LINQ rules
Bonjour mon Amour
```

That's it for our first example. You've just seen how to provide your own implementation of the `Where` and `Select` operators. Here, we've simply added some trace information, which can be useful if you want to better understand how queries work. Of course, you could do something completely different and more useful. Maybe you could rewrite the basic query operators to improve their performance? Let's make that a challenge for you. Please let us know if you can imagine ways to do that!

Before moving on to our next example that shows another custom implementation of the basic query operators, we'd like to point out that the mechanism we've just demonstrated comes with a limitation that we'll explain in the next section.

12.3.4 *Limitation: query expression collision*

There is an important limitation you need to keep in mind when implementing the query expression pattern: You cannot implement one or two operators and mix them with the default ones if the signatures of your implementations and the default ones are the same. This is due to the way extension methods are resolved.

Let's say we change our query expression to sort the results:

```
var query =
   from Book book in SampleData.Books
   where book.Price < 30
   orderby book.Title
   select book.Title;
```

As you can see, a new query operator gets involved: OrderBy. The problem is that since we provide implementations only for Where and Select, the compiler complains that it can't find an implementation for OrderBy:

```
'System.Collections.Generic.IEnumerable<LinqInAction.LinqBooks.Com-
mon.Book>' does not contain a definition for 'OrderBy' and no extension
method 'OrderBy' accepting a first argument of type 'System.Collec-
tions.Generic.IEnumerable<LinqInAction.LinqBooks.Common.Book>' could be
found (are you missing a using directive or an assembly reference?)
```

While we wanted to put in place new implementations of Where and Select, we may not be interested in providing a custom implementation for OrderBy and the other operators at this time. The default reflex would be to reuse the standard implementation to stick with the default behavior. In order to do this, you need to import the System.Linq namespace in your code file in addition to our own namespace. You can try to do that, but you'll notice that the compiler reports a conflict because it doesn't know how to choose between the implementations of the Where and Select operators from our namespace and the ones from the System.Linq namespace. Here is what the compiler errors say:

```
error CS1940: Multiple implementations of the query pattern were found for
source type 'LinqInAction.LinqBooks.Common.Book[]'. Ambiguous call to
'Where'.

error CS1940: Multiple implementations of the query pattern were found for
source type 'System.Collections.Generic.IEnumerable<LinqInAction.Linq-
Books.Common.Book>'. Ambiguous call to 'Select'.
```

We could call this a *namespace collision.* The way extension methods are resolved makes handling multiple extension methods with the same signature in the same scope difficult.

There is unfortunately no easy way to remove the ambiguity in this case. This means that in a given file, either you use only the operators you've implemented or you use only those from System.Linq. One option would be to change our versions of the operators to work with more precise types such as IEnumerable<Book> instead of IEnumerable<T>, but obviously this would require creating an implementation for each type we want to deal with—Publisher, Author, and so on—which would make things a bit difficult.

> **NOTE** Sometimes, the compiler chooses silently between the available operators. For example, if the replacement operators are in the same namespace as the calling code, they're chosen silently. In this case, there is no conflict with the implementation from System.Linq.Enumerable either. The problem is that this situation does not happen often, because most of the time the namespaces are different.

In fact, as soon as you import the System.Linq namespace—just to get access to the Func delegate types, for example—you simply cannot use your own reimplementations of the standard query operators because of the conflict with the implementations provided by the System.Linq.Enumerable class.

> **TRICK** One way to get access to the Func delegate types and other types declared in the System.Linq namespace is to use complete type names (types prefixed by their namespace). For example, if you don't add using System.Linq; at the top of your C# file, you can use System.Linq.Func<...> to get access to the Func delegate types without creating a namespace collision.
>
> You can also use a namespace alias for long namespaces. For example, if you add using SysLinq = System.Linq; at the top of your C# file, instead of using System.Linq;, you can use SysLinq.Func<...> to reference the Func delegate types.

Let's now move on to a second example.

12.3.5 Example 2: nongeneric, domain-specific operators

In this new example, we'll create another custom implementation of the basic query operators that will show you how the query expression pattern can be implemented by domain-specific query operators.

You've just seen in the previous example that you can provide your own implementations of the basic query operators by creating extension methods for the IEnumerable<T> type. It's interesting to note that you may also create query operators that work on an enumeration of a specific type and not just on a generic enumeration.

Instead of creating an extension method for IEnumerable<T>, you can create an extension method for IEnumerable<Book>. This allows you to transparently use a custom implementation of the query operators for Book objects while using the standard implementation of the query operators for objects of other types. This can be used as a workaround for the limitation we presented in the previous section. However, doing this can make sense in itself.

Here, we'll create implementations of the Where and Select operators that work on Book objects. We'll adapt the generic implementations we provided in listing 12.8 as our first example and use the fact that we work with Book objects to display the title of each book that the operators process.

Listing 12.9 shows our domain-specific implementations.

Listing 12.9 Domain-specific implementations of Where and Select (DomainSpecificOperators.cs)

```
using System;
using System.Collections.Generic;
using System.Linq;

using LinqInAction.LinqBooks.Common;

namespace LinqInAction.Extensibility
{
  static class DomainSpecificOperators
  {
    public static IEnumerable<Book> Where(
      this IEnumerable<Book> source,
      Func<Book, Boolean> predicate)
    {
      foreach (Book book in source)
      {
        Console.WriteLine(
          "processing book \"{0}\" in "+
          "DomainSpecificOperators.Where",
```

```
            Book.Title);
          if (predicate(book))
            yield return book;
      }
    }

    public static IEnumerable<TResult> Select<TResult>(
      this IEnumerable<Book> source, Func<Book, TResult> selector)
    {
      foreach (Book book in source)
      {
        Console.WriteLine(
          "processing book \"{0}\" in "+
          "DomainSpecificOperators.Select<TResult>",
          book.Title);
        yield return selector(book);
      }
    }
  }
}
```

Let's reuse the same query as in our first example:

```
using LinqInAction.Extensibility;
using LinqInAction.LinqBooks.Common;

static class TestDomainSpecificOperators
{
  static void Main()
  {
    var books =
      from book in SampleData.Books
      where book.Price < 30
      select book.Title;

    ObjectDumper.Write(books);
  }
}
```

When executed, this program outputs the following kind of results:

```
processing book "Funny Stories" in DomainSpecificOperators.Where
processing book "Funny Stories" in DomainSpecificOperators.Select<TResult>
Funny Stories
processing book "Linq rules" in DomainSpecificOperators.Where
processing book "Linq rules" in DomainSpecificOperators.Select<TResult>
LINQ rules
processing book "C# on Rails" in DomainSpecificOperators.Where
processing book "All your base are belong to us" in
➡DomainSpecificOperators.Where
```

```
processing book "Bonjour mon Amour" in DomainSpecificOperators.Where
processing book "Bonjour mon Amour" in
⇒DomainSpecificOperators.Select<TResult>
Bonjour mon Amour
```

The trace information in these results shows which books are processed by each operator.

In comparison to generic operators, domain-specific operators know the types they're working on. This allows us to access specific members, like the `Title` property in our example.

Also, the limitation we presented in the previous section does not exist with this kind of operator. Domain-specific operators can be used in combination with the default implementation of the other operators.

This time, we can use an `orderby` clause in our query, although we didn't provide a custom implementation for the `OrderBy` operator:

```
var query =
   from Book book in SampleData.Books
   where book.Price < 30
   orderby book.Title
   select book.Title;
```

The only thing you need to do for this to work is to import both our operator's namespace (`LinqInAction.Extensibility`) and the `System.Linq` namespace.

> **WARNING** As you can see, changing or adding a namespace import can make a serious difference in the behavior of your code. A given query can behave differently if you use `System.Linq`, `LinqInAction.Extensibility`, or another namespace!
>
> The design decision of relying on namespace imports to reference extension methods (and query operators) is questionable. Anyway, be careful about this and double-check the namespaces you import when in doubt.

After demonstrating that the implementation you provide for the basic query operators doesn't have to work on generic types, we'll show you in a third example that your implementation doesn't necessarily have to work on sequences either.

12.3.6 *Example 3: non-sequence operator*

This last example of how to provide custom implementations of the operators used in query expressions demonstrates how you can integrate single objects in queries.

The standard query operators provide an implementation of the query operator pattern for `IEnumerable<T>`. This allows you to work with collections like the array of `Book` objects provided by our `SampleData.Books` property. Let's suppose we want to work with a single object and not a sequence of objects. What can we do?

In the following query, we work on a specific `Publisher` instance and use it in a way similar to how we'd use a sequence of `Publisher` objects:

```
from publisher in SampleData.Publishers[0]
join book in SampleData.Books
  on publisher equals book.Publisher into books
select new { Publisher = publisher.Name, Books = books};
```

This query seems to make sense, but the problem is that it doesn't work as is with the standard query operators. This is because the standard query operators are designed to work only with `IEnumerable<T>`. The particular problem in our case is that the compiler complains that it cannot find `GroupJoin` for the `Publisher` type:

```
error CS1936: Could not find an implementation of the query pattern for
source type 'LinqInAction.LinqBooks.Common.Publisher'.  'GroupJoin' not
found.
```

The `GroupJoin` operator—used because we are performing a join operation—is defined the following way:

```
public static IEnumerable<TResult>
  GroupJoin<TOuter, TInner, TKey, TResult>(
    this IEnumerable<TOuter> outer,
    IEnumerable<TInner> inner,
    Func<TOuter, TKey> outerKeySelector,
    Func<TInner, TKey> innerKeySelector,
    Func<TOuter, IEnumerable<TInner>, TResult> resultSelector)
```

You can clearly see that the `outer` argument is defined as a sequence (`IEnumerable<TOuter>`). All we need to do to make the compiler happy is provide a new implementation of `GroupJoin` that accepts a single element as the outer object instead of a sequence.

Listing 12.10 shows how to write this additional version of `GroupJoin`.

Listing 12.10   Implementation of `GroupJoin` for a single element (NonSequenceOperator.cs)

```
using System;
using System.Collections.Generic;
using System.Linq;

using LinqInAction.LinqBooks.Common;

namespace LinqInAction.Extensibility
{
  static class NonSequenceOperator
  {
    public static IEnumerable<TResult>
```

```
GroupJoin<TOuter, TInner, TKey, TResult>(
    this TOuter outer,          ◁───────────
    IEnumerable<TInner> inner,                  Outer argument as
    Func<TOuter, TKey> outerKeySelector,        a single element
    Func<TInner, TKey> innerKeySelector,
    Func<TOuter, IEnumerable<TInner>, TResult> resultSelector)
{
                                ◁───────────
    ILookup<TKey, TInner> lookup =              Validation of arguments
      inner.ToLookup(innerKeySelector);         ignored for simplicity
    yield return resultSelector(outer,
                              lookup[outerKeySelector(outer)]);
  }
 }
}
```

All we've done here is change the type of the first argument and adapt the code to deal with a single object.

Until now, we've used only simple examples, but you should now be able to code your own query operators. We are now going to introduce a richer example. It will have methods request expression trees as their parameters instead of delegates.

12.4   Querying a web service: LINQ to Amazon

In the previous section, we learned how to create custom query operators or implement the standard ones differently. This is a solution that works well for objects in memory, just like what LINQ to Objects offers. In this section, we'll consider a different scenario: We'll query a web service. More precisely, we'll query Amazon to get information about books.

In this section, now that you know a lot about LINQ and how it works, we're going to create our own LINQ provider: LINQ to Amazon! In the next section, we are going to further refine our implementation.

This example will allow us to address the case of query translation to another query language and remote evaluation. The query we'll write here will be translated into web queries and run on a remote web server. This requires a different extensibility mechanism than what we've seen previously.

12.4.1 Introducing LINQ to Amazon

The example we'll introduce in this section will use LINQ's extensibility to allow for language-integrated queries against a book catalog. LINQ queries will be converted to REST URLs, which are supported by Amazon's web services. These services return XML data, which we'll be able to convert from XML to .NET objects using LINQ to XML.

A use case for this example could be the following:

1 Search for books on Amazon using a LINQ query

2 Display the results in XHTML using LINQ to XML

3 Import the selected books into a database using LINQ to SQL

The goal here is not to create a complete solution, so we won't demonstrate all of this at this point. We'll focus on the first part of the scenario. We already performed this kind of operation in the prior chapters, but this time we'll create a LINQ provider that can be used to write queries without worrying about the details of the dialog with Amazon.

We won't support the complete set of operators that could be used in a LINQ query. This would be too complex to present in the context of this book. Anyway, since we are calling an underlying web service, we need to restrict the query possibilities to what the service supports.

For the moment, let's look at the client code we would like to be able to write:

```
var query =
  from book in new LinqToAmazon.AmazonBookSearch()
  where
    book.Title.Contains("ajax") &&
    (book.Publisher == "Manning") &&
    (book.Price <= 25) &&
    (book.Condition == BookCondition.New)
  select book;
```

This piece of code is nearly self-explanatory. This is LINQ to Amazon code. It expresses a query against Amazon, but does not execute it. The query variable contains...a query. The query will be executed when we start enumerating the results.

The following piece of code makes the transition from the LINQ to Amazon world to the familiar LINQ to Objects world:

```
var sequence = query.AsEnumerable();
```

The query gets executed when `AsEnumerable` is called and an enumeration of the resulting books is created. The next steps could be to use LINQ to Objects to perform grouping operations on the results:

```
var groups =
  from book in query.AsEnumerable()
  group book by book.Year into years
```

```
orderby years.Key descending
select new {
  Year = years.Key,
  Books =
    from book in years
    select new { book.Title, book.Authors }
};
```

This query can be used for displaying the results like this:

```
Published in 2006
  Title=Ruby for Rails : Ruby Techniques for Rails Developers   Authors=...
  Title=Wxpython in Action    Authors=...

Published in 2005
  Title=Ajax in Action      Authors=...
  Title=Spring in Action (In Action series)     Authors=...

Published in 2004
  Title=Hibernate in Action (In Action series)     Authors=...
  Title=Lucene in Action (In Action series)     Authors=...
```

Here is the code that produces this kind of results:

```
foreach (var group in groups)
{
  Console.WriteLine("Published in " + group.Year);
  foreach (var book in group.Books)
  {
    Console.Write("  ");
    ObjectDumper.Write(book);
  }
  Console.WriteLine();
}
```

What a great way to query a catalog of books! Don't you think that this code is comprehensible and clearly expresses the intention? It's certainly better than having to construct a web request and having to know all the details of the Amazon API.

Let's see what's needed to implement LINQ to Amazon.

12.4.2 Requirements

This time, the data we'll query will not be in memory. When the data is in memory, we can query it continuously and retrieve the results one by one.

In our now-classic LINQ to Objects example, each time we perform an iteration in `foreach`, a new result is pulled from the original list down through our query processing:

```
using System.Linq;
using LinqInAction.LinqBooks.Common;

static class LinqInAction
{
  static void Main()
  {
    var books =
      from book in SampleData.Books
      where book.Price < 30
      select book.Title;

    foreach (String book in books)
    {

    }
  }
}
```

Some processing on the book

Here is the detail of what can happen when the program is executed:

4 First iteration of the `foreach` loop

a. Is the first book cheaper than $30? No.

b. Is the second book cheaper than $30? Yes.

c. Process the second book.

5 Second iteration

a. Is the third book cheaper than $30? Yes.

b. Process the third book.

6 Third iteration

a. Is the third book cheaper than $30? No.

b. Etc.

As you can see, deferred query execution implies that we work continuously on the original data source. In our new example, we'll call a web service, so we can't rely on the same kind of processing. We want to make a query over the web only once, and we don't want to retrieve a complete list we would filter locally. Instead, we want the web service to return only those results we are interested in.

This requires the following steps:

1 As a developer, we express a query using LINQ.

2 At run-time, the query is translated into something the web service can understand.

3 The web service is called and returns the results.

The key point here is that we need the web query to be completely defined before we can make the call.

12.4.3 *Implementation*

We'll now start to write the code for creating LINQ to Amazon. Before getting to the details of the implementation code, let's describe what we need to do in order to be able to use LINQ with Amazon.

First, we'll work with books, just like in our other examples. The difference though is that a book described by Amazon is not the same as what the Book class models. For the sake of simplicity, we'll define an AmazonBook class that represents a book as returned by Amazon's web services:

```
public class AmazonBook
{
    public IList<String> Authors { get; set; }
    public BookCondition Condition { get; set; }
    public String       Isbn { get; set; }
    public UInt32       PageCount { get; set; }
    public String       Publisher { get; set; }
    public Decimal      Price { get; set; }
    public String       Title { get; set; }
    public UInt32       Year { get; set; }
}
```

> **NOTE** Here we use auto-implemented properties, a new feature of C#. We used this feature in chapters 2 and 6.

You can see that this class defines the members we use in our query (Title, Publisher, Price, and Condition), as well as others we'll use later for display. Condition is of type BookCondition, which is just an enumeration defined like this:

```
public enum BookCondition {All, New, Used, Refurbished, Collectible}
```

The next and main thing we have to do is define the AmazonBookSearch class we'll use to perform the query.

An instance of this class will represent a given query. This is why it should contain the criteria we specify in the where clause of our query. For clarity and reusability, we created the AmazonBookQueryCriteria class, which looks like this:

```
class AmazonBookQueryCriteria
{
    public BookCondition? Condition { get; set; }
    public Decimal? MaximumPrice { get; set; }
    public String Publisher { get; set; }
    public String Title { get; set; }
}
```

AmazonBookSearch contains an instance of AmazonBookQueryCriteria. Here is the first version of the AmazonBookSearch class:

```
public class AmazonBookSearch
{
   private AmazonBookQueryCriteria _Criteria;
}
```

As it stands, this class is useless. To be able to use an instance of `AmazonBook-Search` in a query expression, we need to provide the accompanying `Where` and `Select` query operators. For a change, we won't create these operators as extension methods, but instead as instance methods (we used extension methods for all the examples in sections 12.2 and 12.3). This is also supported by the query expression pattern.

Here is how we'll write the `Where` and `Select` operators:

```
public class AmazonBookSearch
{
   ...

   public AmazonBookSearch Where(
      Expression<Func<AmazonBook, Boolean>> predicate)           ◁
   {
      var visitor = new AmazonBookExpressionVisitor();                 ❸
      _Criteria = visitor.ProcessExpression(predicate);
      return this;                                   ◁                              ❷
   }

   public AmazonBookSearch Select<TResult>(                      ❶
      Expression<Func<AmazonBook, TResult>> selector)           ◁
   {
      return this;                               ◁
   }

   ...
}
```

In both methods, we just return the current `AmazonBookSearch` instance ❶ because we are still working on the same query.

You should notice an important thing here: Our operators are not receiving delegates as with our previous examples, but instances of the `Expression<TDele-gate>` class ❷. As you saw in chapter 3, the `System.Linq.Expressions.Expression<TDelegate>` class can be used to retrieve an expression tree. In operators that receive a delegate as a parameter, we can't really do much more than execute the code the delegate points to. In comparison, the expression tree we receive in `Where` describes what is written in the `where` clause of a query as data instead of code. The point is that we'll be able to analyze the *predicate* expression tree received as a parameter by the `Where` method to extract the criteria specified in the query.

The next logical step is to code the `AmazonBookExpressionVisitor` class used in `Where` ❸. This class is used to process an expression tree and extract the query criteria it contains. Before doing so, it's important to get an idea of what the expression tree contains. An expression tree is a hierarchy of expressions. Listing 12.11 shows the complete hierarchy received by the `Where` method.

Listing 12.11 Sample expression tree generated for a LINQ to Amazon query

```
var book = Expression.Parameter(typeof(AmazonBook), "book");
var expressionTree =
Expression.Lambda<Func<AmazonBook, Boolean>>(
  Expression.AndAlso(
    Expression.AndAlso(
      Expression.AndAlso(
        Expression.Call(
          Expression.Property(book,
            typeof(AmazonBook).GetProperty("Title")),
          typeof(String).GetMethod("Contains"),                    ❶
          new Expression[] {
            Expression.Constant("ajax", typeof(String)) }
        ),
        Expression.Equal(
          Expression.Property(book,
            typeof(AmazonBook).GetProperty("Publisher")),
          Expression.Constant("Manning", typeof(String)),          ❷
          false,
          typeof(String).GetMethod("op_Equality")
        )
      ),
      Expression.LessThanOrEqual(
        Expression.Property(book,
          typeof(AmazonBook).GetProperty("Price")),                ❸
        Expression.Constant(25M, typeof(Decimal))
      )
    ),
    Expression.Equal(
      Expression.Convert(
        Expression.Property(book,
          typeof(AmazonBook).GetProperty("Condition")),            ❹
        typeof(int)),
        Expression.Constant(1, typeof(int)
      )
    )
  ),
  new ParameterExpression[] { book }
);
```

If you look closely at this tree, you should be able to locate the criteria we've specified in our query: the restriction on the title ❶, the filter on the publisher ❷, the price limit ❸, and the book condition ❹. As a reminder, here is the query for which this expression tree is generated:

```
from book in new LinqToAmazon.AmazonBookSearch()
where
  book.Title.Contains("ajax") &&
  (book.Publisher == "Manning") &&
  (book.Price <= 25) &&
  (book.Condition == BookCondition.New)
select book;
```

The `ProcessExpression` method of the `AmazonBookExpressionVisitor` class should basically walk through the expression tree to extract information. Here we'll implement the Visitor design pattern to find all the criteria the expression tree contains.

Here is the main method of the `AmazonBookExpressionVisitor` class, `VisitExpression`:

```
private void VisitExpression(Expression expression)
{
  if (expression.NodeType == ExpressionType.AndAlso)
  {
    ProcessAndAlso((BinaryExpression)expression);
  }
  else if (expression.NodeType == ExpressionType.Equal)
  {
    ProcessEqual((BinaryExpression)expression);
  }
  else if (expression.NodeType == ExpressionType.LessThanOrEqual)
  {
    ProcessLessThanOrEqual((BinaryExpression)expression);
  }
  else if (expression is MethodCallExpression)
  {
    ProcessMethodCall((MethodCallExpression)expression);
  }
  else if (expression is LambdaExpression)
  {
    ProcessExpression(((LambdaExpression)expression).Body);
  }
}
```

We won't detail every method here. You can refer to the complete source code accompanying this book to see how all these methods are implemented. Just to give you an idea, here is the `VisitAndAlso` method:

```
private void VisitAndAlso(BinaryExpression andAlso)
{
  VisitExpression(andAlso.Left);
  VisitExpression(andAlso.Right);
}
```

Here is the `VisitEqual` method, which handles the `book.Publisher == "xxx"` and `book.Condition == BookCondition.*` criteria:

```
private void VisitEqual(BinaryExpression expression)
{
  if ((expression.Left.NodeType == ExpressionType.MemberAccess) &&
    (((MemberExpression)expression.Left).Member.Name ==
        "Publisher"))
  {
    if (expression.Right.NodeType == ExpressionType.Constant)
    {
      _Criteria.Publisher =
      (String)((ConstantExpression)expression.Right).Value;
    }
    else if (expression.Right.NodeType ==                    Handle
            ExpressionType.MemberAccess)          book.Publisher == "xxx"
    {
      _Criteria.Publisher =
        (String)GetMemberValue((MemberExpression)expression.Right);
    }
    else
    {
      throw new NotSupportedException(
        "Expression type not supported for publisher: " +
        expression.Right.NodeType.ToString());
    }
  }
  else if ((expression.Left is UnaryExpression) &&
    (((UnaryExpression)expression.Left).Operand.Type ==
            typeof(BookCondition)))
  {
    if (expression.Right.NodeType == ExpressionType.Constant)
    {
      _Criteria.Condition =
        (BookCondition)((ConstantExpression)expression.Right).Value;
    }
    else if (expression.Right.NodeType ==
            ExpressionType.MemberAccess)
    {                                                        Handle
      _Criteria.Condition =                        book.Condition ==
        (BookCondition)GetMemberValue(              BookCondition.*
                (MemberExpression)expression.Right);
    }
    else
    {
```

```
throw new NotSupportedException(
    "Expression type not supported for book condition: " +
    expression.Right.NodeType.ToString());
        }
    }
}
```

Handle
book.Condition == BookCondition.*

After the execution of `AmazonBookExpressionVisitor.ProcessExpression`, our `AmazonBookSearch` instance has collected all the criteria provided in the LINQ query. At this point, the query has been parsed, but hasn't been executed. No call has been made to Amazon.

As usual, we want the execution to happen when we start enumerating the results of the query. This is why we'll make `AmazonBookSearch` implement `IEnumerable<AmazonBook>`. Here is how to code the two necessary methods:

```
public class AmazonBookSearch : IEnumerable<AmazonBook>
{
    ...

    IEnumerator<AmazonBook> IEnumerable<AmazonBook>.GetEnumerator()
    {
        Var enumerable = (IEnumerable)this;
        return (IEnumerator<AmazonBook>)enumerable.GetEnumerator();
    }

    IEnumerator IEnumerable.GetEnumerator()
    {
        String url = AmazonHelper.BuildUrl(_Criteria);          Execute
        IEnumerable<AmazonBook> books =                          query
            AmazonHelper.PerformWebQuery(url);

        return books.GetEnumerator();
    }

    ...
}
```

As you can see, all the processing is delegated to a helper class, `AmazonHelper`, which knows how to build an Amazon URL and how to call Amazon and convert the results into a sequence of `AmazonBook` objects.

Here is the `AmazonHelper.BuildUrl` method, which takes the criteria and returns an URL that uses them:

```
static internal String BuildUrl(AmazonBookQueryCriteria criteria)
{
    if (criteria == null)
        throw new ArgumentNullException("criteria");

    String url = URL_AWSECommerceService;
```

```
  if (!String.IsNullOrEmpty(criteria.Title))
    url += "&Title=" + HttpUtility.UrlEncode(criteria.Title);
  if (!String.IsNullOrEmpty(criteria.Publisher))
    url += "&Publisher=" + HttpUtility.UrlEncode(criteria.Publisher);
  if (criteria.Condition.HasValue)
    url += "&Condition=" +
             HttpUtility.UrlEncode(criteria.Condition.ToString());
  if (criteria.MaximumPrice.HasValue)
    url += "&MaximumPrice=" +
             HttpUtility.UrlEncode(
               (criteria.MaximumPrice * 100)
                 .Value.ToString(CultureInfo.InvariantCulture)
             );

  return url;
}
```

The second method of the `AmazonHelper` class is `PerformWebQuery`. This method performs the actual call to Amazon and builds the results by parsing the web response using LINQ to XML:

```
static internal IEnumerable<AmazonBook> PerformWebQuery(String url)
{
  XElement booksDoc = XElement.Load(url);     ◁──── Execute query

  XNamespace ns = NAMESPACE_AWSECommerceService;
  IEnumerable<AmazonBook> books = #2
    from book in booksDoc.Descendants(ns + "Item")
    let attributes = book.Element(ns + "ItemAttributes")
    let price = attributes.Element(ns + "ListPrice")
                  .Element(ns + "Amount").Value
    select new AmazonBook
      {
        Title = attributes.Element(ns + "Title").Value,
        Isbn = attributes.Element(ns + "ISBN").Value,
        PageCount = UInt32.Parse(
          attributes.Element(ns + "NumberOfPages").Value),
        Price = price != null ? Decimal.Parse(price) / 100 : 0,
        Publisher = attributes.Element(ns + "Publisher").Value,
        Year = UInt32.Parse(
          ((String)attributes.Element(ns + "PublicationDate").Value)
            .Substring(0, 4)),
        Authors = (
          from author in book.Descendants(ns + "Author")
          select (String)author.Value
        ).ToList()
      };

  return books;
}
```

Parse
results

That's all there is to it. You should now be able to use LINQ to Amazon queries! Keep in mind that this is a straightforward implementation. This implementation supports only simple queries and is likely to fail if you try to use it with different queries. Feel free to build on this example and improve it!

You can take a look at the complete source code for the details of the implementation (look for the LinqToAmazon project).

NOTE   In order to use the Amazon.com web services and test this example fully, you need to register with the Amazon Web Services program. After registering with Amazon, you'll be assigned an access key. Edit the AmazonHelper.cs file and replace INSERT YOUR AWS ACCESS KEY HERE with your access key.

In some cases, creating additional query operators or reimplementing the standard ones is not enough. In these cases, you may resort to another extensibility mechanism offered by LINQ. We'll show you an example in the next section.

12.5 *IQueryable and IQueryProvider: LINQ to Amazon advanced edition*

In the previous version of our LINQ to Amazon example, we implemented the Where operator in such a way that it receives the criteria expressed in our query as an expression tree. All the processing happens in this operator by analyzing the expression tree.

Our first LINQ to Amazon implementation is far from being complete. We created it to take into account only one call to the Where operator. If we were to write a complete implementation of LINQ to Amazon, we'd have to resort to an advanced technique. This technique relies on the System.Linq.IQueryable<T> interface. This is the technique used for LINQ to SQL to query data from a relational database. The use of expression trees and the IQueryable<T> interface enables rich queries, obtained by numerous calls to query operators, to be converted into a single SQL query that gets sent to the database.

In this section, we'll create a new implementation of LINQ to Amazon that relies on IQueryable<T>. Before doing so, let's spend some time learning more about IQueryable<T>.

12.5.1 *The IQueryable and IQueryProvider interfaces*

Let's look at the query we used with the first implementation of LINQ to Amazon:

```
var query =
  from book in new LinqToAmazon.AmazonBookSearch()
  where
    book.Title.Contains("ajax") &&
    (book.Publisher == "Manning") &&
    (book.Price <= 25) &&
    (book.Condition == BookCondition.New)
  select book;
```

As usual, the key thing the compiler looks at when it's about to convert such a query expression into calls to query operators is the type of object the query operates on. In our case, this is an instance of `LinqToAmazon.AmazonBookSearch`. The compiler notices that `AmazonBookSearch` provides an implementation of the `Where` operator and so this is what will be invoked when the query is evaluated. Of course, the real execution only happens when the query is enumerated through a call to `GetEnumerator`.

To be able to support richer queries using the same technique, we would have to implement more operators than just `Where`. For example, with our first implementation, we get the results in an unspecified order. If we want to sort the results, we can do it locally using LINQ to Objects. If we want to be able to perform the sort operation on the server, we would have to implement the `OrderBy` operator in addition to `Where`. We would then be able to retrieve the sort information expressed in the query and transmit it as part of the web query. If the server supports sorting, the results we retrieve would be sorted without having to use LINQ to Objects afterward on the client.

Another thing that our first implementation doesn't support is retrieving partial information. If you look at our query's `select` clause, you'll notice that we return complete information on books. What if we wanted to retrieve only the titles? It would be more efficient to ask the web server to return only the title of each book instead of the complete information about it. In order to do this, we would have to implement the `Select` operator.

You should start to understand that if we do it this way, the analysis of the query is scattered in several places: in each operator's implementation. This tends to complicate the analysis of the query and makes optimization more difficult.

The `IQueryable` interface has been designed to help in situations like this. It allows us to receive all the information contained in a query as one big expression tree instead of having each operator receive partial information. Once the expression tree is ready, it can be analyzed to do whatever we want in response to the query. `IQueryable` defines the pattern for you to gather up a user's query and present it to your processing engine as a single expression tree that you can either transform or interpret.

When a query works on an object that implements `IQueryable`, the query operators that are used are not coming from the `System.Linq.Enumerable` class, but from the `System.Linq.Queryable` class. This class provides all the query operators required by the LINQ query expression pattern implemented using expression trees.

The query operators in the `Queryable` static class do not actually perform any querying. Instead, their functionality is to build an expression tree as an instance of the `System.Linq.Expressions.Expression` object representing the query to be performed and then pass that `Expression` object to the source `IQueryable` for further processing.

All the implementations of the query operators provided by the `Queryable` class return a new `IQueryable` that augments that expression tree with a representation of a call to that query operator. Thus, when it comes time to evaluate the query, typically because the `IQueryable` is enumerated, the data source can process the expression tree representing the whole query in one batch.

The actual query execution is performed by classes that implement the `IQueryable` interface, as well as the additional `IQueryProvider` interface. We'll now see how these two types work together and how to implement them.

Getting ready for the implementation

With our first implementation, the queries were applied to an instance of the `LinqToAmazon.AmazonBookSearch` type. This type implements `IEnumerable<AmazonBook>`. Here is a sample query using the first implementation:

```
var query =
  from book in new LinqToAmazon.AmazonBookSearch()
  where
    book.Title.Contains("ajax") &&
    (book.Publisher == "Manning") &&
    (book.Price <= 25) &&
    (book.Condition == BookCondition.New)
  select book;
```

In the second implementation, we're going to create new types that implement `IQueryable` and `IQueryProvider`. The entry point type will be named `AmazonBookQueryProvider`. This is the class that will implement `IQueryProvider`. A second class will provide a generic implementation of `IQueryable<T>`: the `Query<T>` class.

Here is how these two classes will allow us to write the same query as earlier using the second implementation:

```
var provider = new AmazonBookQueryProvider();
var queryable = new Query<AmazonBook>(provider);
var query =
```

```
from book in queryable
where
  book.Title.Contains("ajax") &&
  (book.Publisher == "Manning") &&
  (book.Price <= 25) &&
  (book.Condition == BookCondition.New)
select book;
```

Notice how the query is unchanged. Only the object on which we are performing the query is different. The use of an implicitly typed local variable through the var keyword abstracts away the type of the query's result, but it is different for each implementation. With the first implementation, the type of the result is IEnumerable<AmazonBook>. With the second implementation, the type of the result is IQueryable<AmazonBook>.

As we already explained, the difference is that IEnumerable<T> represents an enumeration, while IQueryable<T> represents a query. An instance of a type that implements IQueryable<T> contains all the information needed to execute a query. Think of it as a description of what you want done when the query is enumerated.

Overview of IQueryable and IQueryProvider
Before we move on to the implementation, let's look at how the IQueryable<T> and IQueryProvider interfaces are defined.

Here is the declaration of IQueryable<T>:

```
interface IQueryable<T> : IEnumerable<T>, IQueryable
{
}
```

This means that we have to implement the members of the following interfaces:

```
interface IEnumerable<T> : IEnumerable
{
  IEnumerator<T> GetEnumerator();
}

interface IEnumerable
{
  IEnumerator GetEnumerator();
}

interface IQueryable : IEnumerable
{
  Type ElementType { get; }
  Expression Expression { get; }
  IQueryProvider Provider { get; }
}
```

The main element you should pay attention to in the interfaces is the `Expression` property of the `IQueryable` interface. It gives you the expression that corresponds to the query. The actual query underneath the hood of an `IQueryable` is an expression tree of LINQ query operators/method calls. This is the part of the `IQueryable` that your provider must comprehend in order to do anything useful.

Note that the `IQueryable<T>` interface implements `IEnumerable<T>` so that the results of the query it encompasses can be enumerated. Enumeration should force the execution of the expression tree associated with an `IQueryable` object. At this time, we'll translate the expression tree into an Amazon web query and make the call to Amazon's web services. This is what the `IQueryProvider` referenced by an `IQueryable` instance will do.

We have to implement the members of the `IQueryProvider` interface in order to handle the execution of the queries. Here is how it is declared:

```
public interface IQueryProvider
{
  IQueryable CreateQuery(Expression expr);
  IQueryable<TElement> CreateQuery<TElement>(Expression expr);
  object Execute(Expression expr);
  TResult Execute<TResult>(Expression expr);
}
```

As you can see, the `IQueryProvider` interface contains two groups of methods, one for the creation of queries and another of the execution of queries. Each group contains both generic and nongeneric overloads. Implementing `IQueryProvider` may look like a lot of work. Don't worry. You only really need to worry about the `Execute` method. It is the entry point into your provider for executing query expressions. This is the quintessence of your LINQ provider implementation.

Now that you've seen what needs to be implemented to create a complete LINQ provider, you may start to wonder if it's not something difficult. Well, it is! You should never consider the creation of a LINQ provider to be an easy task. However, things should be a bit easier after you've taken a look at our sample implementation and you've been able to see how the mechanics work. The LINQ to Amazon sample is here to help you make your first steps with `IQueryable<T>` without too much difficulty. It contains the bases required for every implementation of a LINQ provider.

Let's now see how the LINQ to Amazon provider implements `IQueryable` and `IQueryProvider`.

12.5.2 *Implementation*

To implement LINQ to Amazon's query provider, we reused code provided by Matt Warren from Microsoft on his blog.[2] The code we reuse consists of a generic implementation of IQueryable<T> (the Query<T> class in the Query.cs file) and a base implementation of IQueryProvider (the QueryProvider class in the Query-Provider.cs file).

Once you have these classes at hand, what's left is to create a class that inherits from QueryProvider and provides an implementation for the Execute method, and optionally one for the GetQueryText method. Of course, implementing Execute is the most difficult part, precisely because what a LINQ provider does is execute queries!

In our case, this is not so difficult, as you can see. Here is how we implemented the AmazonBookQueryProvider class:

```
public class AmazonBookQueryProvider : QueryProvider
{
  public override String GetQueryText(Expression expr)
  {
    AmazonBookQueryCriteria criteria;

    var visitor = new AmazonBookExpressionVisitor();       Retrieve
    criteria = visitor.ProcessExpression(expr);            criteria


    String url = AmazonHelper.BuildUrl(criteria);       ◁──  Generate
                                                             URL
    return url;
  }

  public override object Execute(Expression expr)
  {
    String url = GetQueryText(expr);
    IEnumerable<AmazonBook> results =
      AmazonHelper.PerformWebQuery(url);
    return results;
  }
}
```

You can see that the work is greatly simplified because we'd already created the useful helper classes, AmazonBookExpressionVisitor and AmazonHelper, in the previous section.

---

[2] Matt Warren provides an introduction to the implementation of an IQueryable provider, as well as sample source code in his blog. The series of posts is available at the following address: http://blogs.msdn.com/mattwar/archive/2007/08/09/linq-building-an-iqueryable-provider-part-i.aspx

If we were to rewrite LINQ to SQL, the `Execute` method would convert the entire expression tree it receives as an argument into an equivalent SQL query and send that query to a database for execution. The LINQ to Amazon implementation instead needs to convert the expression tree into a web request and execute that request.

We won't give more details about the implementation here because it would be too long. You should look at the source code accompanying this book to learn more. We recommend that you also refer to Matt Warren's blog posts to fully understand how to implement a complete LINQ provider.

Before closing this chapter, we think it may be useful to review the execution of a sample query step by step to help you better understand how an implementation of `IQueryable<T>` works.

12.5.3 *What happens exactly*

You may wonder how the mechanism enabled by `IQueryable<T>` works. We'll now quickly depict this mechanism to satisfy your curiosity.

Let's consider the following sample query that works with an `AmazonBookQueryProvider`:

```
var provider = new AmazonBookQueryProvider();
var queryable = new Query<AmazonBook>(provider);
var query =
  from book in queryable
  where
    book.Title.Contains("ajax") &&
    (book.Publisher == "Manning") &&
    (book.Price <= 25) &&
    (book.Condition == BookCondition.New)
  select book;
```

Each time a query such as this one is written, the compiler generates the following kind of code:

```
var provider = new AmazonBookQueryProvider();
var queryable = new Query<AmazonBook>(provider);
IQueryable<AmazonBook> query =
  Queryable.Where<AmazonBook>(queryable, <expression tree>);
```

`Queryable.Where` is a static method that takes as arguments an `IQueryable<T>` followed by an expression tree. The `Queryable.Where` method returns the result of a call to the provider's `CreateQuery` method.

In our case, the source `IQueryable<T>` is an instance of the `Query<AmazonBook>` class. The implementation of `CreateQuery` provided by the base `QueryProvider` class creates a new Query<AmazonBook> instance that keeps track of the expression tree. We don't support complex queries, so CreateQuery is called only once in our case, but in richer implementations CreateQuery could be invoked several times in cascade to create a deep expression tree.

The next operation is the enumeration of the query. Typically, this happens in a foreach loop in which you process the results. Enumerating the query invokes the GetEnumerator method of the Query<AmazonBook> object.

In response to a call to the GetEnumerator method, the Execute method of the provider is invoked. This is where we parse the expression tree, generate the corresponding web query, call Amazon, and build a list of AmazonBook objects based on the response we get. Finally, we return the list of books as the result of the Execute method, and that becomes the result of the GetEnumerator method. The query execution is then complete and the list of books is now ready to be processed.

That's all for our LINQ to Amazon example. Implementing IQueryable<T> enables powerful scenarios that integrate LINQ with a lot of different data sources. This powerful extensibility option is not easy to implement, which is why we recommend you take a look at other implementations to make sure you fully understand how IQueryable works if you plan on creating your own implementation.

12.6 Summary

In this chapter, we presented options available to extend LINQ and adapt it to your needs. The sample extensions we demonstrated here are simple. It will be interesting to see how many real-life alternate implementations and extensions are released as people find flaws or shortcomings in the default set.

LINQ's extensibility is what allows it to offer support for several data sources. It's also what will allow wide adoption of LINQ by developers in all layers of applications. As LINQ gets adopted, we are likely to see more and more framework providers adding LINQ support to their products to offer their users the benefits of strongly typed and standard querying capabilities.

LINQ in every layer

13

This chapter covers:

- The LinqBooks application
- N-tier architecture
- Third-party LINQ providers
- The future of LINQ

Congratulations! You've reached the last chapter of this book. You should now have a good grasp of LINQ's capabilities and should now be able to put the skills you've acquired into practice in your projects. There is still one last subject we'd like to cover: the place of LINQ in your applications.

As you know, LINQ is not only a generic querying technology but a complete set of tools you can use to deal with relational databases, XML, DataSets, in-memory object collections, and many more data sources thanks to LINQ's extensibility. This means that from now on, LINQ is likely to become pervasive in your code.

In this chapter, we will look at a sample application we've created using LINQ. This application is the LinqBooks running example that we introduced in chapter 4 and that we used over this book's chapters as the base for the code samples. You'll be able to find the complete source code in the downloadable package that accompanies this book. By looking at the LinqBooks sample, you'll be able to identify where and how each LINQ flavor is used. Our goal is to help you decide whether you need to use LINQ in your application layers, as well as see what impact it can have on your applications' architecture.

We'll start by describing the LinqBooks application. We'll then focus on the place LINQ to SQL has in this application. LINQ to SQL is likely to influence your application's architecture, so it's important to spend time thinking about how to use it. Once we're done with LINQ to SQL, we'll analyze where LINQ to XML and LINQ to DataSet can be useful. Finally, we'll use LINQ's extensibility through custom query operators as well as our LINQ to Amazon implementation.

13.1 Overview of the LinqBooks application

We already introduced our sample application in chapter 4. Let's present it again, but with an accent on the architecture and the use of LINQ. The LinqBooks application allows its users to manage a personal book catalog.

13.1.1 Features

Here are the main features of the LinqBooks application:

- Tracking books users own
- Storing what users think about them
- Retrieving more information about books from external sources
- Publishing the list of books and review information to make it available to others

The technical features implemented include

- Adding books, publishers, and authors to the catalog
- Attaching books to publishers and authors
- Adding reviews to books
- Querying/inserting/updating data in a local SQL Server database
- Searching over the local catalog
- Searching over Amazon's catalog
- Importing data about books from Amazon
- Importing and persisting some data from/as XML documents
- Creating RSS feeds for the books you recommend

Let's now get an idea of the UI that exposes these features.

13.1.2 *Overview of the UI*

We decided to implement LinqBooks as a web application. It also comes with a utility for importing data from Amazon that is implemented as a Windows Forms application.

Let's see some screenshots of the application. Figure 13.1 shows the page that displays the list of books from the database.

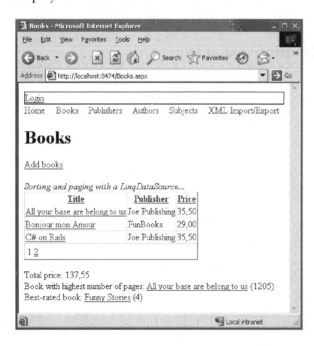

Figure 13.1
Web page that displays the list of books in a grid as well as some statistics

The page that displays the details for a book can be seen in figure 13.2.

Figure 13.3 shows the page that displays the list of publishers.

There are more pages in the LinqBooks application, of course. You'll discover some in the rest of this chapter, and all of them if you look at the source code and run the application.

Let's now give you an overview of the data model used by the sample application.

Figure 13.2
Web page that displays the details about a book and allows us to add authors and reviews

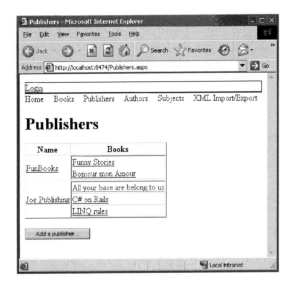

Figure 13.3
Web page that displays the list of publishers and their books in a grid

13.1.3 *The data model*

The LinqBooks application relies on a SQL Server database. The database schema we use is shown in figure 13.4.

Now that you have a good idea of what the LinqBooks application does, we can focus on the use of all the LINQ flavors in all of the application's layers. We'll start with LINQ to SQL and we'll analyze how it influences the architecture of applications that employ it.

13.2 *LINQ to SQL and the data access layer*

The flavor of LINQ that may have the biggest impact on application architecture is probably LINQ to SQL. This is why it's worth spending time thinking about the traditional three-tier architecture and how LINQ to SQL fits in the picture.

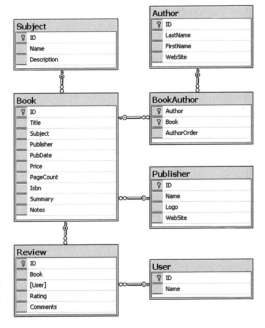

Figure 13.4   Database schema for the running example

The impact of the use of LINQ to SQL may be so profound that we may have to reconsider the very nature of a data access layer.

Let's start with a refresher on the traditional three-tier architecture and data access layer. We'll then throw LINQ to SQL in and analyze the impacts on such architectures. Finally, we'll depict the way we use LINQ to SQL in LinqBooks through some code samples.

13.2.1 *Refresher on the traditional three-tier architecture*

You probably already know how a multitier architecture is structured, but it's good to quickly go over the basic principles to ensure that we're speaking about the same things. While you can use several tiers in a multitier architecture, we'll focus here on the three-tier architecture because it's sufficient for discussing the impact of LINQ to SQL on such an architecture.

A three-tier architecture is any system that enforces a general separation between the following three parts:

- The presentation tier
- The logic tier or business logic tier
- The data access tier

NOTE   In this discussion, the words *tier* and *layer* are used to refer to the same thing.

Figure 13.5 shows the elements parts of a traditional three-tier architecture.

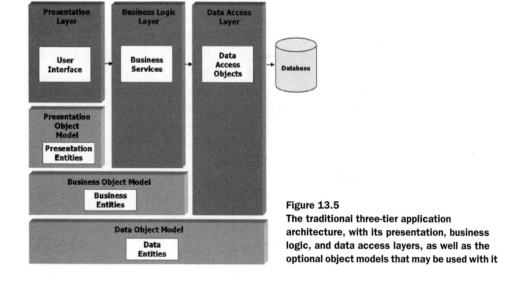

Figure 13.5
The traditional three-tier application architecture, with its presentation, business logic, and data access layers, as well as the optional object models that may be used with it

Dividing an application into several tiers or layers as described in the figure is all about *separation of concerns.* The goals of separation of concerns are to design systems so that functions can be optimized independently of other functions, so that failure of one function does not cause other functions to fail, and in general to make it easier to understand, design, and manage complex interdependent systems. This is why a common practice is to break a program into distinct layers that overlap as little as possible.

Let's review the role of each of the layers in the three-tier architecture:

- The *data-access layer* stores and retrieves information from a database, file system, or any other storage. The information is passed back to the business logic layer for processing and eventually back to the user.

- The *business logic layer* coordinates the application, processes commands, makes logical decisions and evaluations, and performs calculations. It also moves and processes data between the two surrounding layers.

- The *presentation layer* handles the topmost level of the application: the user interface. The main function of the interface is to translate tasks and results into something the user can understand. The presentation layer contains components needed to interact with the user of the application. Examples of such components are web pages and rich-client forms.

The object models shown in the figure are optional. They represent the data structures that can be used to exchange data between layers.

Obviously, we should focus on the data access layer, *DAL* for short. The purpose of a DAL is to isolate the data store from other application layers. The components in this layer abstract the semantics of the underlying data access technology, thus allowing the business layer to focus on business logic. Each component typically provides methods to perform CRUD operations for a specific business entity.

Now that we've given an overview of a traditional data access layer, it's time to get back to LINQ and see if LINQ to SQL can be used within a three-tier architecture.

13.2.2 *Do we need a separate data access layer or is LINQ to SQL enough?*

After reading about LINQ to SQL in chapters 6, 7, and 8, you're ready to use it in your applications. But the way we've used LINQ to SQL so far in this book gives no hint about how to use LINQ to SQL in a multitier architecture. This is because until now we've used LINQ to SQL in a RAD[1] way.

When you develop applications with LINQ to SQL, you can decide to follow one of two directions: Either you use LINQ to SQL transparently all through your application—this is the RAD way we've followed until now—or you stick to the traditional three-tier architecture with data access that is built using LINQ to SQL.

With the first option, you get all the benefit of LINQ to SQL. With the second option, you get the benefits of having a clearly defined data access layer. Let's describe each option separately.

Using LINQ to SQL as your DAL

When LINQ to SQL is used in a RAD way, it acts as a kind of a minimal data-access layer. The classes generated from the LINQ to SQL Designer document (the .dbml file) or the SqlMetal tool are the data entities that form the data object model. There is no data access code in these entities. The SQL code that performs the calls to the database to load or save data from the data entities is generated by a LINQ to SQL `DataContext` based on queries you write in C# or VB. To actually interact with the database, you need to write LINQ queries that LINQ to SQL will convert into SQL queries.

> **NOTE** It's true that by default the data entities generated by the LINQ to SQL designer or the SqlMetal tool are decorated with LINQ to SQL attributes. If you want attribute-free POCOs[2] for your data entity classes, you can use the SqlMetal command-line tool to generate a VB or C# source file and a mapping file, as was described in chapter 7.

We've stated that when you use LINQ without creating a real data access layer, you can get all the benefits of LINQ to SQL. Let's review these benefits.

It allows us to avoid limitations of the data access layer's API.

When you're writing an application, you may often realize that each page requires a custom database query.

For instance, if on one page you need to display the books that have a long title (for some obscure reason we won't discuss here), then you'll need a specific method in your data access layer that provides this kind of data. Chances are high that this

---

[1] RAD (rapid application development) is a software development methodology that involves iterative development and the construction of prototypes. Traditionally the RAD approach involves compromises in usability, features, and/or execution speed.

[2] POCO means Plain-Old CLR Objects. This term is used to contrast a class or an object with one that is designed to be used with a specific framework such as an object-relational mapper.

method won't be used elsewhere in your application. There is no one-size-fits-all DAL. More precisely, if there is any DAL that has code generic enough to satisfy the needs of every page, it may be at the cost of performance.

If you use LINQ to SQL directly on your page, you can write rich queries that precisely match your needs for that page. Here is an example of such a query:

```
IEnumerable<Book> booksWithLongTitles =
   from book in dataContext.Books
   where book.Title.Length > 25
   select book;
```

It can reduce the database workload and network traffic.

When you retrieve data from the database, you can easily select only the fields you need and avoid having too much data loaded for nothing. For example, in the following LINQ to SQL code, only the `Title` field of the `Books` table will be retrieved from the database:

```
IEnumerable<String> longTitles =
   from book in dataContext.Books
   where book.Title.Length > 25
   select book.Title;
```

If you instead use a standard method proposed by your DAL to retrieve a list of books, several fields can be loaded from the database even if you don't need them. Typically, such a method would return a full `Book` object, not just titles. Of course, you can always design your DAL to be able to specify which fields you want to be loaded, but this complicates the code.

More operations can be performed directly by the server.

Often, when you retrieve data from a database, you'd like to perform operations on it so it's formatted to satisfy your needs. As we've just seen, you can define the shape of the data you retrieve. But there are other operations you can do. For example, you can ask the database server to sort, group, or join the data. If you use a generic DAL method, you're likely to always return data sorted, grouped, or joined in the same way. In contrast, if you use the following query in your presentation layer, the grouping and sorting specified through the `orderby` and `group..by` clauses will be performed by the database server and returned to you as you wish them to be:

```
var longTitles =
   from book in dataContext.Books
   where book.Title.Length > 25
   orderby book.Title
   group book.Title by book.PublisherObject.Name into publisherBooks
   select new { Publisher = publisherBooks.Key,
               BookTitles = publisherBooks };
```

To sum up the benefits we've just listed, we could say that genericity has a cost. What using LINQ to SQL in a RAD way allows is fine-grained customization.

We've just identified using LINQ to SQL directly as an interesting solution for data access, but we said previously that we'd consider another option: creating a real data access layer written using LINQ to SQL. Why consider this second option? Are there problems if we use LINQ to SQL directly?

Here are some limitations you should keep in mind if you decide to go the LINQ to SQL RAD route:

- Writing database queries in your presentation layer is not as bad as using SQL code in it (think about ASP.NET's SqlDataSource web control for example), but it's still a questionable practice. If you do it, you're mixing data access code with business logic and presentation code. This means that you've decided to abandon the benefits of the separation of concerns.

- There is no single place to look when you want to find all that's related to data access. If all your LINQ to SQL queries are scattered around in your business logic or presentation code, it becomes difficult to review or update all the data access code.

- Code reuse is not central in such a design. If you want to share LINQ to SQL queries between business objects or screens, where do you put them? You can enrich the `DataContext` class with predefined queries or validation code, but this makes it look like a big bag of tricks without much structure compared to a real data access layer.

- If you don't create a concrete data access layer, where will you put all the data processing that can't be done with LINQ to SQL? This is close to the previous point. Again you can enrich the `DataContext` class if this is okay with you.

- Mapping is limited to the table-per-class model. If you want to have entities that span over several tables, as is often the case, it may be better to either use something other than LINQ to SQL or create an application layer that abstracts this limitation and returns richer entities.

If there were no way to address these concerns then LINQ to SQL would be doomed to be used only in prototypes. If you use LINQ to SQL as is without being careful, it's easy to unknowingly commit the reprehensible architectural sin of mixing the UI, business logic, and data access layers, for example.

To avoid this kind of quick-and-dirty use, let's now see how you can create a real data access layer instead of using LINQ to SQL directly in all the layers of your applications.

Using LINQ to SQL to create a real DAL

If you don't use LINQ to SQL directly in your presentation or business logic layer, you can still use it to create your DAL. This way you can get the benefits of having a true DAL, while still keeping some benefits of LINQ to SQL.

Before going further, it may be good to restate the basic goals for a DAL.[3]

- The DAL should completely hide the underlying data storage and the data access technology used, whether it's an object-relational mapping tool, hand-generated inline SQL, calls to stored procedures, or anything else. This allows the client or upper-level layers to be created with a higher level of abstraction.

- The DAL should not place any significant constraints on the design of the business object model (also called the *domain model*).

- The entire DAL should be replaceable with minimal impact.

All of the aforementioned goals can be summarized with one word: *decoupling*. When LINQ to SQL is used in a RAD way, this is not really achieved. This is why you may consider creating a real DAL instead of spreading LINQ to SQL queries all over in your applications.

When you create a concrete DAL with LINQ to SQL, there a few points to keep in mind. Here are three of them:

- The ratio of plumbing code to real code can be high compared to direct LINQ to SQL code.

- If you return LINQ to SQL entities or queries from your DAL, these objects support deferred execution and lazy fetching, weakening your division.

- Your DAL should return objects that can be passed between components at different tiers.

We won't address the first point here. It's true that the source code of a DAL that uses LINQ to SQL may look useless because it can be simple and could be used directly in other parts of your applications. However, this is what we want to avoid and one reason for creating a DAL, so this is something you should accept. The fact that the code in your DAL is simpler than equivalent code with literal SQL queries does not mean that it's useless. It's better, in fact!

Let's look at the second point. When you write your first DAL method, you may be tempted to write something like listing 13.1.

---

[3] Source: Howard Dierking at http://blogs.msdn.com/howard_dierking/archive/2007/04/23/designing-a-domain-driven-data-access-layer.aspx

Listing 13.1 Data access object with a method that returns a query (IQueryable<T>)

```
public class BookDataAccessObject
{
  LinqBooksDataContext _dataContext = new LinqBooksDataContext();

  public IQueryable<Book> GetBooksBySubjectName(String subjectName)
  {
    return
      from book in _dataContext.Books
      where book.SubjectObject.Name == subjectName
      select book;
  }
}
```

In the listing, you can see a method named GetBooksBySubjectName that returns an object of type IQueryable<Book>. The result is a simple LINQ to SQL query, hence the result type.

If you create a DAL with LINQ to SQL and have your methods return something like IQueryable<T>, as in our sample, you don't return data but you do return queries. This makes a big difference compared to a method that would return a collection of Book objects.

In this situation, the calls to the database aren't performed inside the DAL methods, but outside at a later time. Remember that due to deferred execution, LINQ queries are executed only when they are enumerated.

It may be better to return a list of entities instead of a query. In listing 13.2, the query is executed inside the DAL method, thanks to the call to ToList, and the results are returned in the form of a list of entities.

Listing 13.2 Data access object with a method that returns a collection of objects (List<T>)

```
public class BookDataAccessObject
{
  LinqBooksDataContext _dataContext = new LinqBooksDataContext();

  public List<Book> GetBooksBySubjectName(String subjectName)
  {
    var query =
      from book in _dataContext.Books
      where book.SubjectObject.Name == subjectName
      select book;
    return query.ToList();
  }
}
```

If you use lazy loading, more calls to the database happen through transparent calls to LINQ to SQL. For example, by default, if your DAL returns a `Subject` object and you access its `Books` property in your business logic or presentation layers, an implicit call to the database is done without your always being aware of it. A solution to avoid this is to return only detached objects (value objects), with lazy loading deactivated.

> **NOTE**   Some would argue that we shouldn't care when database calls get made, but this is a debate we can't address in this book.

In listing 13.3, `Book` objects are loaded in advance for each `Subject` object before the list of subjects is returned. In addition, the `DataContext.DeferredLoading-Enabled` property is set to false to ensure that no additional calls to the database are made through lazy loading.

Listing 13.3   DAL method returning subjects ordered by name, with lazy loading disabled

```
public List<Subject> GetSubjectsWithBooksLoaded()            Disable lazy
{                                                              loading
  LinqBooksDataContext dataContext = new LinqBooksDataContext();
  dataContext.DeferredLoadingEnabled = false;       ◁

  DataLoadOptions loadOptions = new DataLoadOptions();        Specify that the
  loadOptions.LoadWith<Subject>(subject => subject.Books);    books should
  dataContext.LoadOptions = loadOptions;                      be loaded with
                                                              each subject
  var query =
    dataContext.Subjects.OrderBy(subject => subject.Name);   ◁

  return query.ToList();                              Query all subjects
}                                                     ordered by name
```

Returning value objects is important also when you need to pass objects between remote tiers. This is the third concern we included in our list earlier. If you return a `Subject` object to a client remote tier, using WCF for example, and this client tier needs data that isn't loaded with the object, then a call to the database will be attempted if lazy loading is enabled, something that we don't want and that's likely to fail anyway.

The problem is that it's not always easy to know what callers of the DAL methods will need. If your DAL returns a `Book` object, some callers will access the data about the publishers while others will need to access more information, such as the data about the authors. In any case, it should be made clear which data is loaded by each DAL method, in one way or another.

We've just seen that there are a couple of ways you can use LINQ to SQL. One is to use it to replace your DAL; the other is to use it inside your DAL. In your own applications, you're free to decide what's better. It depends on whether you want to invest in long-term development or you're just creating lightweight applications or prototypes.

One of the nice things about LINQ to SQL is that it's flexible enough to allow you to easily build an object-oriented layer for your data and business logic. Specifically, it provides a way to add validation rules and some business logic in your data entity classes. The entity classes for LINQ to SQL also support persistence ignorance and flexible inheritance (no base class required). In a lot of projects, these features may be used to merge the data and business layers, while in others the traditional separation of concerns will remain the rule.

Before moving on to the other LINQ flavors, let's see how we use LINQ to SQL in the LinqBooks sample application.

13.2.3 *Sample uses of LINQ to SQL in LinqBooks*

In the LinqBooks sample, we've decided to use LINQ to SQL directly in the presentation layer in most parts of the application to demonstrate how easy it is to write flexible and robust data querying. Still, to demonstrate the second approach we described earlier, we created a sample DAL with a few data access objects. As you'll see, there are still benefits to using LINQ to SQL inside of your DAL, such as code conciseness, readability, and reliability.

Summary of the options

When LINQ to SQL is used directly in the presentation layer, the architecture of the application is simple. The `DataContext` class generated using SqlMetal or the LINQ to SQL Designer contains the entity classes that are used directly in the user interface classes. All the data access is performed by the `DataContext`. If you enrich the `DataContext` and its entity classes with business logic, the `Data-Context` replaces both the data access layer and the business logic layer.

Figure 13.6 depicts this.

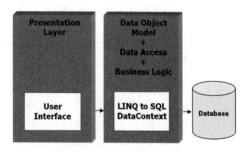

Figure 13.6 An application architecture where the data object model, the data access code and the business logic are all represented by a LINQ to SQL `DataContext`

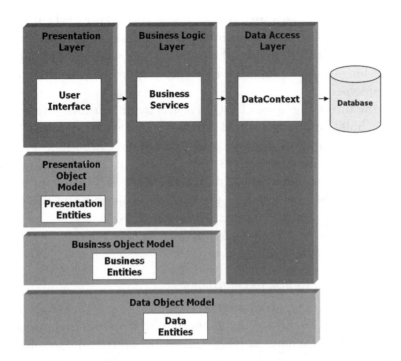

Figure 13.7 A three-tier application architecture, with its presentation, business logic, and LINQ to SQL data access layers

When you follow the traditional three-tier architecture, LINQ to SQL is used in a clearly separated data access layer. This is where the DataContext is created and used. In addition, the business logic is coded outside of the DataContext and the data access layer altogether.

Figure 13.7 shows the schema of the complete three-tier architecture, similar to the one we presented in section 13.2.1, but with a LINQ to SQL DataContext as the data access object.

Sample code

Let's now focus on some code samples to give you an idea of how LINQ to SQL can be used in an application like LinqBooks.

Let's start with the Publishers.aspx page. Figure 13.8 shows what it looks like.

In Publishers.aspx.cs, a simple LINQ to SQL query is used to retrieve the list of publishers available in the database. See listing 13.4.

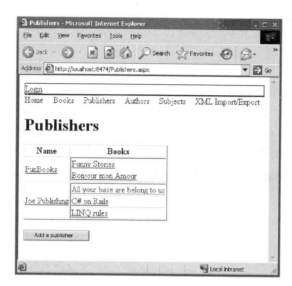

**Figure 13.8
Publishers.aspx page used to display
the list of the publishers contained in
the LinqBooks database**

Listing 13.4   Retrieving a list of publishers from a database and binding it to a `GridView`

```
var query =
  from publisher in _DataContext.Publishers
  orderby publisher.Name
  select publisher;
GridViewPublishers.DataSource = query;
GridViewPublishers.DataBind();
```

This is a straightforward way of retrieving and displaying data. The `GridView` that
is used to display the data is declared as shown in listing 13.5.

Listing 13.5   ASP.NET markup to display a list of publishers in a `GridView`

```
<asp:GridView ID="GridViewPublishers" runat="server"
  AutoGenerateColumns="False"
  OnRowDatabound="GridViewPublishers_RowDataBound">
  <columns>
    <asp:hyperlinkfield DataNavigateUrlFields="ID"
      DataNavigateUrlFormatString="~/Publisher.aspx?ID={0}"
      DataTextField="Name" HeaderText="Name">
    </asp:hyperlinkfield>
    <asp:TemplateField HeaderText="Books">
      <ItemTemplate>
        <linqBooks:BookList ID="BookList" runat="server" />
      </ItemTemplate>
```

```
      </asp:TemplateField>
    </columns>
  </asp:GridView>
```

The `BookList` tag is used to reference a custom control that displays a list of books. The `RowDataBound` event is used to provide the list of books to display to the `BookList` user control. This technique is used to ensure compile-time validation of the code. Listing 13.6 shows the code of the event handler for `RowDataBound`.

Listing 13.6   Handler for the `GridView.RowDataBound` event used to display a child collection (`Publisher.Books`)

```
protected void GridViewPublishers_RowDataBound(object sender,
  GridViewRowEventArgs e)
{
  if (e.Row.DataItem == null)
    return;

  Publisher publisher = (Publisher)e.Row.DataItem;
  BookList bookList = (BookList)e.Row.FindControl("BookList");
  bookList.Books = publisher.Books;
  bookList.DataBind();
}
```

On this first page, we display the data in a simple grid. If we want to allow the user to sort the data and activate paging, we can use a new component provided by .NET 3.5: `LinqData-Source`. The `LinqDataSource` component can work with a `DataContext`, or you can provide it a LINQ query and it'll automatically perform paging and sorting operations. This is what we use on the Books.aspx page.

Figure 13.9 shows a screenshot of the Books.aspx page.

As you can see, you can click the headers of the columns to sort them, and a pager is available at the bottom of the grid.

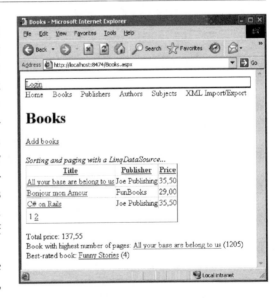

Figure 13.9   Books.aspx page used to display the list of the books contained in the LinqBooks database

A standard `GridView` control is used to obtain this display, but its `DataSource` is a `LinqDataSource`:

```
<asp:LinqDataSource ID="LinqDataSource1" runat="server"
  OnSelecting="LinqDataSource1_Selecting">
</asp:LinqDataSource>
...
<asp:GridView ID="GridViewBooks" runat="server"
   AllowSorting="True" AllowPaging="True" PageSize="3"
   AutoGenerateColumns="False" DataSourceID="LinqDataSource1">
...
```

Note that sorting and paging are activated on the `GridView` control, and `PageSize` is set to 3.

In Books.aspx.cs, the `Selecting` event of the `LinqDataSource` is handled to provide the query used by the `DataSource`, as shown in listing 13.7.

Listing 13.7 Handler for `LinqDataSource.Selecting` to provide the query used by the `DataSource`

```
protected void LinqDataSource1_Selecting(object sender,
  LinqDataSourceSelectEventArgs e)
{
  e.Result =
    from book in new LinqBooksDataContext().Books
    orderby book.Title
    select new
      {
        Id = book.ID,
        Title = book.Title,
        Publisher = book.PublisherObject.Name,
        Price = book.Price
      };
}
```

As you can see, the query doesn't return `Book` objects but uses anonymous types to return only the data we need. There is no need to load more information from the database than what we really need. Here we display only the titles of the books, the names of their publishers, and their prices, and we use the ID to create and hyperlink to the book details page (Book.aspx).

Listing 13.8 shows the markup for the `GridView`.

Listing 13.8 Markup to display a list of books in a `GridView`

```
<asp:GridView ID="GridViewBooks" runat="server"
   AllowSorting="True" AllowPaging="True" PageSize="3"
   AutoGenerateColumns="False" DataSourceID="LinqDataSource1">
```

```
<Columns>
  <asp:HyperLinkField
    DataNavigateUrlFields="Id"
    DataNavigateUrlFormatString="~/Book.aspx?ID={0}"
    DataTextField="Title" HeaderText="Title"
    SortExpression="Title">
  </asp:HyperLinkField>
  <asp:BoundField DataField="Publisher" HeaderText="Publisher"
    ReadOnly="True" SortExpression="Publisher" />
  <asp:BoundField DataField="Price" HeaderText="Price"
    DataFormatString="{0:F2}" HtmlEncode="false"
    ReadOnly="True" SortExpression="Price" />
</Columns>
</asp:GridView>
```

This example shows that a LINQ to SQL query can be used to load only the data needed in a given context. Let's now take another example: Book.aspx. This page is used to display details about a book. Figure 13.10 shows a sample display.

Again, in this page, we use a LINQ to SQL query to select the data we want to display. This example is interesting because it shows how the query and an anonymous type are used to shape the results, with subselections on authors and reviews. See listing 13.9.

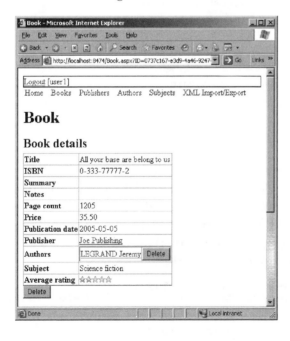

**Figure 13.10
Book.aspx page used to
display details about a book**

> **Listing 13.9 Using an anonymous type and query operators to shape a list of books for display**

```
var books =
  from book in _DataContext.Books
  where book.ID == _BookId
  select new
    {
      Title = book.Title,
      Isbn = book.Isbn,
      Summary = book.Summary,
      Notes = book.Notes,
      PageCount = book.PageCount,
      Price = book.Price,
      PubDate = book.PubDate,
      PublisherId = book.Publisher,
      PublisherName = book.PublisherObject.Name,
      Authors = book.BookAuthors.Select(
                     bookAuthor => bookAuthor.AuthorObject),
      Subject = book.SubjectObject.Name,
      AverageRating =
        book.Reviews.Average(review => (double?)review.Rating)
    };
```

We won't review all the pages of the sample application, but we'd like to point out some specifics so you know what to look at in the source code. Here are some pages you can analyze more precisely:

- In Author.aspx.cs, you can see how a parameter provided on the query string (in the URL) is used to filter data. See in the Page_Load method how the ID of the author to display is used.

- In Authors.aspx.cs, you can see how a class named AuthorPresentation-Model is used to contain the data we need about an author. As the name indicates, the code of the Authors page demonstrates how to work with a presentation model.[4] This class is then used in the GridViewAuthors_Row DataBound method to work with the retrieved data.

- The btnAddAuthor_Click method in Authors.aspx.cs shows how to add a record into the database.

---

[4] See http://www.martinfowler.com/eaaDev/PresentationModel.html for more information about the Presentation Model design pattern.

- The `btnDelete_Click` method in Author.aspx.cs demonstrates how to delete a record. The `btnDelete_Click` method in Book.aspx.cs performs the same kind of operation, but with the additional deletion of linked records.

- Open the Subjects.aspx.cs file to see how to use a method from the application's DAL. In the `DisplaySubjects` method, the DAL is invoked to get the list of all subjects in the database ordered by name, with associated books loaded and lazy loading disabled.

After our focus on LINQ to SQL, it's time to consider another flavor of LINQ. It was important to address the use of LINQ to SQL in an application, but we should not forget that LINQ is useful for dealing with other kinds of data sources than just relational databases. Let's now see how we use another major LINQ flavor in Linq-Books: LINQ to XML.

13.3   Use of LINQ to XML

LINQ to XML can be used to read or create XML. Given the wide use of XML nowadays, you can expect to find LINQ to XML employed in every layer of applications. As you saw in chapter 11, where several common LINQ to XML scenarios are covered, it can be used in combination with data from a database, to import XML data, create RSS feeds, and more.

13.3.1   Importing data from Amazon

The first usage of LINQ to XML in LinqBooks comes in the form of a standalone utility.

We covered this scenario, reading XML and updating a database, in chapter 11. In LinqBooks, we reuse the sample Windows Forms application for importing books and details about them from Amazon. See figure 13.11.

This utility allows us to search for books with keywords and select books to import in the LinqBooks database. This sample Windows Forms application demonstrates how to use LINQ to XML to parse the XML data returned by Amazon's web services. LINQ to SQL is used to insert the imported data into the database.

Here is the LINQ to XML query used to display the list of books:

```
var books =
  from result in amazonXml.Descendants(ns + "Item")
  let attributes = result.Element(ns + "ItemAttributes")
  select new Book {
    Isbn = (string)attributes.Element(ns + "ISBN"),
    Title = (string)attributes.Element(ns + "Title"),
  };

bookBindingSource.DataSource = books;
```

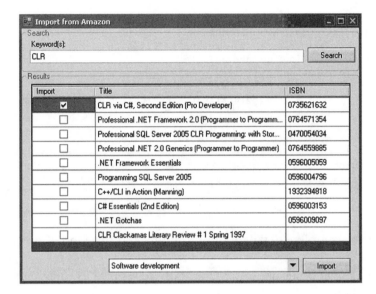

Figure 13.11
Windows Forms user
interface for importing
books from Amazon

The list of books selected using the Import check box is built using LINQ to Objects:

```
var selectedBooks =
  from row in bookDataGridView.Rows.OfType<DataGridViewRow>()
  where (bool)row.Cells[0].EditedFormattedValue
  select (Book)row.DataBoundItem;
```

The actual data to import in the database is prepared thanks to LINQ to XML again, as in listing 13.10.

Listing 13.10   LINQ to XML query used to prepare data to be inserted into a database

```
var booksToImport =
  from amazonItem in amazonXml.Descendants(ns + "Item")
  join selectedBook in selectedBooks
    on (string)amazonItem
                .Element(ns + "ItemAttributes")
                .Element(ns + "ISBN")
    equals selectedBook.Isbn
  join p in ctx.Publishers
    on (string)amazonItem
                .Element(ns + "ItemAttributes")
                .Element(ns + "Publisher")
    equals p.Name into publishers
  from existingPublisher in publishers.DefaultIfEmpty()
  let attributes = amazonItem.Element(ns + "ItemAttributes")
  select new Book {
```

```
      ID = Guid.NewGuid(),
      Isbn = (string)attributes.Element(ns + "ISBN"),
      Title = (string)attributes.Element(ns + "Title"),
      Publisher = (existingPublisher ??
                  new Publisher {
                     ID = Guid.NewGuid(),
                     Name = (string)attributes.Element(ns + "Publisher")
                  }
      ),
      Subject = (Subject)categoryComboBox.SelectedItem,
      PubDate = (DateTime)attributes.Element(ns + "PublicationDate"),
      Price = ParsePrice(attributes.Element(ns + "ListPrice")),
      BookAuthors = GetAuthors(attributes.Elements(ns + "Author"))
   };
```

See chapter 11 for complete details about this utility and this kind of use of LINQ to XML.

Let's now look at another use of LINQ to XML, relying on its capability to generate XML documents.

13.3.2 *Generating RSS feeds*

LINQ to XML can be used to generate XML documents, such as RSS feeds. This scenario was covered in chapter 11. In LinqBooks, we also create RSS feeds, based on data coming from a database through LINQ to SQL.

A sample RSS feed published by the LinqBooks web site returns the list of reviews contained in the database. This RSS feed is generated and returned by a web method as an XmlDocument. Listing 13.11 shows the complete code of the web method.

> **Listing 13.11   Web method that creates an RSS feed and returns it as an XmlDocument (RSS.asmx.cs)**

```
[WebMethod]
public XmlDocument GetReviews()
{
   var dataContext = new LinqBooksDataContext();

   var xml =
     new XElement("rss",
       new XAttribute("version", "2.0"),
       new XElement("channel",
         new XElement("title", "LinqBooks reviews"),
         from review in dataContext.Reviews
         select new XElement("item",
           new XElement("title",
             "Review of \""+review.BookObject.Title+"\" by "+
```

```
                review.UserObject.Name),
            new XElement("description", review.Comments),
            new XElement("link",
                "http://example.com/Book.aspx?ID="+
                review.BookObject.ID.ToString())
          )
      )
    );

    XmlDocument result = new XmlDocument();
    result.Load(xml.CreateReader());
    return result;
}
```

You can see how LINQ to XML streamlines the creation of simple XML documents such as RSS feeds. This is why you're likely to use LINQ to XML everywhere XML is required.

We'd demonstrate other uses of LINQ to XML, but we have other LINQ flavors to cover. Let's see how LINQ to DataSet can be useful in an application like LinqBooks.

13.4 *Use of LINQ to DataSet*

One feature of the LinqBooks application is to let you export the complete set of data contained in your book catalog as an XML document. This can be useful to create backups of your data. It can also be used to share data with your friends. To that effect, we also implemented an import feature in the application.

These import and export features are implemented through the use of DataSets. For simplicity, the export is performed using the TableAdapters generated with the typed DataSet class, so LINQ is not used in this operation. The source code, shown in listing 13.12, is pretty straightforward.

> **Listing 13.12 Loading the complete data from the database into a typed DataSet (GetXML.ashx.cs)**

```
LinqBooksDataSet dataSet = new LinqBooksDataSet();
new SubjectTableAdapter().Fill(dataSet.Subject);
new PublisherTableAdapter().Fill(dataSet.Publisher);
new BookTableAdapter().Fill(dataSet.Book);
new AuthorTableAdapter().Fill(dataSet.Author);
new BookAuthorTableAdapter().Fill(dataSet.BookAuthor);
new UserTableAdapter().Fill(dataSet.User);
new ReviewTableAdapter().Fill(dataSet.Review);
```

The import operation is more advanced. The goal is to allow you to load an existing XML document, provided by a friend for example, and select which books to import into your catalog. In the implementation, we use LINQ to DataSet to allow this.

> **NOTE**   To discover LINQ to DataSet, please read our online chapter, which is available on the web. See http://LinqInAction.net.

Figure 13.12 shows what the web page looks like once an XML document has been uploaded.

Figure 13.12   The XML import/export page displaying data from an uploaded XML document

The first step during an import operation is to load the selected XML document into a `DataSet`. Here is how it's done:

```
var dataSet = new LinqBooksDataSet();
dataSet.ReadXml(uploadXml.FileContent);
Session["DataSet"] = dataSet;
```

Note that we store the `DataSet` in the ASP.NET session so it's easily available.

Once the data is loaded, we can query the `DataSet` to display the list of the books that are already in your catalog. First, we need to prepare a list of the books in your database:

```
var dataContext = new LinqBooksDataContext();
IEnumerable<String> knownTitles =
  dataContext.Books.Select(book => book.Title);
```

Then, we can use this list to filter the list of books that are in the `DataSet`, as in listing 13.13.

**Listing 13.13   Filtering and displaying data from a `DataSet`
(XMLImportExport.aspx.cs)**

```
var dataSet = (LinqBooksDataSet)Session["DataSet"];
var queryExisting =
  from book in dataSet.Book
  where knownTitles.Contains(book.Title)
  orderby book.Title
  select new {
          Title = book.Title,
          Publisher = book.PublisherRow.Name,
          ISBN = book.Field<String>("Isbn"),
          Subject = book.SubjectRow.Name
        };
GridViewDataSetExisting.DataSource = queryExisting;
GridViewDataSetExisting.DataBind();
```

We can also display the list of the books that are not yet in your catalog, which is a similar operation, except that the condition used for filtering is reversed. Listing 13.14 shows the source code.

**Listing 13.14   Filtering and displaying data from a `DataSet`
(XMLImportExport.aspx.cs)**

```
var queryNew =
  from book in dataSet.Book
  where !knownTitles.Contains(book.Title)
  orderby book.Title
```

```
select new {
        Id = book.ID,
        Title = book.Title,
        Publisher = book.PublisherRow.Name,
        ISBN = book.Field<String>("Isbn"),
        Subject = book.SubjectRow.Name
    };
GridViewDataSetNew.DataSource = queryNew;
GridViewDataSetNew.DataBind();
```

Finally, the books you select are imported using a mix of `DataSet` and LINQ to SQL queries, as shown in listing 13.15.

Listing 13.15 Inserting books from a `DataSet` into a database (XMLImportExport.aspx.cs)

```
foreach (GridViewRow gridRow in GridViewDataSetNew.Rows)
{
  CheckBox chkImport = (CheckBox)gridRow.FindControl("chkImport");
  if (!chkImport.Checked)
    continue;

  Guid bookId =                                                    Retrieve
    (Guid)GridViewDataSetNew.DataKeys[gridRow.RowIndex].Value;     data

  LinqBooksDataSet.BookRow bookRow = dataSet.Book.FindByID(bookId);  ◁─┐
                                                                 Find book
  #region Find or create publisher

  Guid publisherId =
    dataContext.Publishers
      .Where(p => p.Name == bookRow.PublisherRow.Name)
      .Select(p => p.ID)
      .SingleOrDefault();
  if (publisherId == Guid.Empty)
  {
    publisherId = bookRow.Publisher;
    Publisher publisher = new Publisher();
    publisher.ID = publisherId;
    publisher.Name = bookRow.PublisherRow.Name;
    dataContext.Publishers.InsertOnSubmit(publisher);
  }

  #endregion Find or create publisher

  #region Find or create authors
  ...
```

Some developers depict `DataSets` as outdated or harmful and advise against using them, but they're a useful tool for features like the one we've just presented. As we demonstrate in our online chapter, LINQ to DataSet makes it easier to query `DataSets`. It's one more companion tool on your belt wherever you need to deal with `DataSets`.

13.5 Using LINQ to Objects

We don't really use LINQ to Objects separately in the LinqBooks application. It's used in combination with LINQ to XML or LINQ to SQL. However, in some places, we use small LINQ to Objects queries to simplify some code. Here is an example you already saw in the section Importing data from Amazon:

```
var selectedBooks =
    from row in bookDataGridView.Rows.OfType<DataGridViewRow>()
    where (bool)row.Cells[0].EditedFormattedValue
    select (Book)row.DataBoundItem;
```

Depending on the type of your applications, you may find LINQ to Objects useful by itself. In fact, as soon as you need to query collections, such as arrays, lists or dictionaries, you're likely to find LINQ to Objects a useful tool. The fact that it works with in-memory collections makes it suitable for any layer of your applications. We already demonstrated this extensively in other chapters, especially in part 1. This is why there's no reason to spend more time on LINQ to Objects at this point.

13.6 Extensibility

In chapter 12, we covered LINQ's extensibility and provided sample custom query operators. In the same chapter, we also introduced a new LINQ flavor named LINQ to Amazon. In LinqBooks, we reuse some of the custom query operators from previous chapters. We also use LINQ to Amazon to provide a light data import facility.

13.6.1 Custom query operators

The first custom query operator that is used in LinqBooks is `TotalPrice`. We created this query operator in chapter 12. It iterates over an enumeration of books and returns the sum of the books' prices. This operator demonstrates how you can create custom query operators to simplify your code. For example, once you've created the `TotalPrice` operator, getting the total price of all books in your LinqBooks catalog can be achieved with the following simple code:

```
var dataContext = new LinqBooksDataContext();
lblTotalPrice.Text = dataContext.Books.TotalPrice().ToString("F2");
```

Another custom query operator used in LinqBooks comes from chapter 5: `Max-Element`. The goal of this operator is to retrieve an object from a collection.

```
Book biggestBook =
  dataContext.Books.Where(book => book.Title.Length > 0)
                   .MaxElement(book => book.PageCount);
lnkBiggestBook.Text = biggestBook.Title;
lnkBiggestBook.NavigateUrl = "~/Book.aspx?ID=" + biggestBook.ID;
lblPageCount.Text = biggestBook.PageCount.ToString();
```

> **NOTE** The queries in this section retrieve all the data from the database before working in memory.
>
> The uniform syntax between the various LINQ flavors allows us to mix them together in queries. In these examples, LINQ to SQL and LINQ to Objects codes are combined in each query. This is elegant and useful, but you should be aware that the query executes in two stages. Each flavor executes separately. For example, in the case of the following query, a SQL query is first executed to fetch books that match the condition in `Where`, and then the `MaxElement` operator is executed in memory over the results:

Sample uses of both `TotalPrice` and `MaxElement` are provided in the Books. aspx.cs file.

13.6.2 *Creating and using a custom LINQ provider*

Our LinqBooks sample application offers the ability to import books from Amazon through a Windows Forms application. In order to show how a custom LINQ provider can be useful in a real-life application, we've added another import facility on the Add Books page. This time, we reuse the `AmazonBookSearch` class from LINQ to Amazon, which we introduced in the previous chapter.

Listing 13.16 shows the LINQ to Amazon query that is used.

> **Listing 13.16 Querying Amazon using LINQ to Amazon with dynamic criteria
> (AddBooks.aspx.cs)**

```
var query =
  from book in new AmazonBookSearch()
  where
    book.Title.Contains(txtSearchKeywords.Text) &&
```

```
     (book.Publisher == txtSearchPublisher.Text) &&
     (book.Price <= 25) &&
     (book.Condition == BookCondition.New)
   orderby book.Title
   select book;
```

The query is used directly to display the results:

```
GridViewAmazonBooks.DataSource = query;
GridViewAmazonBooks.DataBind();
```

A custom LINQ implementation such as LINQ to Amazon allows us to write simple and declarative code. Here we don't need to worry about how the call to Amazon is made and how to retrieve and parse the data it returns.

If you need to deal with a service or an API in your application, inquire whether a LINQ version is available. It can simplify your work. If no LINQ API is available, you may consider creating one by yourself. Be warned that this can be a difficult enterprise if you don't fully master the implementation details of a LINQ provider.

13.7 A look into the future

In this book, we presented LINQ as it stands today. A good thing about LINQ is that it's extensible and can easily evolve to support new scenarios and new data sources.

Custom LINQ flavors have already started to appear, and we'll give you a quick list of them now. We'll also spend some time describing what Microsoft has announced for the future of LINQ.

13.7.1 Custom LINQ flavors

Additional LINQ implementations have started to appear. Most of them don't come from Microsoft. They're possible thanks to the extensibility features built into LINQ.

Here are LINQ flavors:

- *WmiLinq*, WMI LINQ provider
  http://bloggingabout.net/blogs/emile/archive/2005/12/12/10514.aspx

- *DB_Linq*, LINQ provider for MySql, Oracle, and PostgreSQL
  http://code2code.net/DB_Linq/

- *A LINQ provider for CiteSeer*
  http://blogs.msdn.com/hartmutm/archive/2006/06/12/628382.aspx

- *A LINQ provider for RDF files*
  http://blogs.msdn.com/hartmutm/archive/2006/07/10/661512.aspx

- *LINQ to NHibernate*, object-relational mapping
  http://www.ayende.com/Blog/archive/2007/03/16/Linq-for-NHibernate.aspx

- *LINQ to Active Directory*
  http://community.bartdesmet.net/blogs/bart/archive/2007/11/25/linq-to-active-directory-formerly-known-as-linq-to-ldap-is-here.aspx

- *LINQ to SharePoint*
  http://www.codeplex.com/LINQtoSharePoint

- *LINQ to Google Desktop*
  http://langexplr.blogspot.com/2007/05/linq-to-google-desktop.html

- *LINQ to Google Image and Google Groups*
  http://www.codeproject.com/csharp/Linq_To_Google_Image.asp

- *LINQ to Flickr*
  http://spellcoder.com/blogs/bashmohandes/archive/2007/04/08/6552.aspx

- *LINQ.Flickr*
  http://www.codeplex.com/LINQFlickr

- *Slinq (Streaming LINQ)*, an implementation of LINQ focused on streaming data
  http://www.codeplex.com/Slinq

- *SyncLINQ*, set of extensions to LINQ that enable data binding over LINQ queries, with changes to source collections reflected in the user interface
  http://trac.paulstovell.com/wiki/SyncLINQ

- *MetaLinq*, LINQ to Expressions
  http://www.codeplex.com/metalinq

- *LINQ to Amazon* of course!
  http://linqinaction.net/blogs/main/archive/2006/06/26/introducing_linq_to_amazon.aspx

Here are products that offer support for LINQ:

- *Genome*, object-relational mapper
  http://www.genom-e.com

- *Vanatec OpenAccess*, object-relational mapper
  http://www.vanatec.com

- *EntitySpaces*, persistence layer and business objects
  http://www.entityspaces.net

- *LLBLGen Pro*, object-relational mapper
  http://llblgen.com

As far as Microsoft is concerned, the future of LINQ consists at least of LINQ to XSD, PLINQ, and LINQ to Entities. Let's review them quickly one by one.

13.7.2 *LINQ to XSD, the typed LINQ to XML*

LINQ to XSD, which is available at the time of this writing only as an alpha version, is designed to allow strongly typed XML queries. It provides developers with support for typed XML programming on top of LINQ to XML. While LINQ to XML programmers operate on generic XML trees, LINQ to XSD programmers operate on typed XML trees. A typed XML tree consists of instances of .NET types that model the XML types of a specific XML schema (XSD).

A LINQ query is worth a thousand words, so let's compare a LINQ to XML query to a LINQ to XSD query, and you'll quickly understand the difference between the two technologies.

Consider the following C# fragment for a LINQ to XML query that computes the total over the items in a XML tree for a purchase order:

```
from item in purchaseOrder.Elements("Item")
select (double)item.Element("Price") * (int)item.Element("Quantity")
```

Using LINQ to XSD, the same query is written in a much clearer and type-safe way:

```
from item in purchaseOrder.Item
select item.Price * item.Quantity
```

As you can see, there's no need for the dangerous strings and type casting with LINQ to XSD. Everything is strongly typed and structured.

Unfortunately, no release data has been announced for LINQ to XSD, and it has not been updated to the RTM of .NET 3.5. Will Microsoft pursue the work on this approach?

13.7.3 *PLINQ: LINQ meets parallel computing*

PLINQ, as we told you in chapter 2, means Parallel LINQ. It's a key component of Parallel FX *(PFX)*, the next generation of concurrency support in the .NET Framework. The goal is to take advantage of LINQ queries to distribute processing over multiple CPUs or cores. The idea is that you can write LINQ queries in the same way you do today, but they get split up and run in parallel. The advantage is that with PLINQ, LINQ queries become a source of performance gains.

The key element in PLINQ is the `AsParallel` query operator. It integrates with your LINQ queries to have them run in parallel:

```
IEnumerable<T> leftData = ..., rightData = ...;
var query =
  from x in leftData.AsParallel()
  join y in rightData on x.A == y.B
  select f(x, y);
```

A first preview of PLINQ was released November 28, 2007. Microsoft hasn't further revealed plans in terms of release schedule.

An overview of PLINQ was published in *MSDN Magazine* in October 2007 ("Running queries on multi-core processors" at http://msdn.microsoft.com/msdn-mag/issues/07/10/PLINQ/).

Another project from Microsoft related to distributed computing is DryadLINQ. DryadLINQ is a research project that combines the Dryad distributed execution engine and LINQ. Dryad enables reliable, distributed computing on thousands of servers for large-scale data parallel applications. You can learn more about Dryad and DryadLINQ at http://research.microsoft.com/research/sv/DryadLINQ/.

13.7.4 LINQ to Entities, a LINQ interface for the ADO.NET Entity Framework

We already wrote briefly about LINQ to Entities at the end of chapter 8 when we presented the ADO.NET Entity Framework. Like LINQ to SQL, the Entity Framework and LINQ to Entities can be used to perform object-relational mapping. Unlike LINQ to SQL, the Entity Framework will support more database engines than just SQL Server. The fact that LINQ to SQL works only with SQL Server is a big limitation. Will more database engines be supported? When? Microsoft has not announced anything about this lately.

Also, the Entity Framework allows a richer mapping. It works with a true abstraction layer between the application and the database. While LINQ to SQL supports only a direct one-to-one mapping between classes and tables, the Entity Framework allows creating higher-level entity models.

Several previews of the ADO.NET Entity Framework have been made available, but no precise date has been announced for the final release. Microsoft declared that it has targeted the first half of 2008 to ship the ADO.NET Entity Framework as an update to the .NET Framework 3.5 and to Visual Studio 2008.

13.8 Summary

We hope you've found everything you needed to get started with LINQ. You can now use it as a powerful tool to write your own production applications. We've told you a lot in this book, but because LINQ is a rich subject, we're sure you'll still discover a lot about it as you use it.

Happy LINQing!

Filtering

Operator name	Description
OfType	Selects values, depending on their ability to be cast to a specified type.
Where	Selects values, depending on a predicate function.

Projection

Operator name	Description
Select	Selects values, depending on a selector function.
SelectMany	Selects values, depending on a selector function, and combines resulting sequences into one sequence. SelectMany performs a one-to-many element projection over a sequence. It differs from Select in that the selector function is expected to return a sequence that is then expanded.

Partitioning

Operator name	Description
Skip	Skips *n* elements from a sequence.
SkipWhile	Skips elements based on a predicate function until an element does not satisfy the condition.
Take	Takes *n* elements from a sequence.
TakeWhile	Takes elements based on a predicate function until an element does not satisfy the condition.

Join

Operator name	Description
GroupJoin	Joins two sequences based on key selector functions and groups the resulting matches for each element.
Join	Joins two sequences based on key selector functions and extracts pairs of values.

Concatenation

Operator name	Description
Concat	Concatenates two sequences to form one sequence.

Sorting

Operator name	Description
OrderBy	Sorts values in ascending order.
OrderByDescending	Sorts values in descending order.
ThenBy	Performs a secondary sort in ascending order.
ThenByDescending	Performs a secondary sort in descending order.
Reverse	Reverses the order of the elements in a sequence.

Grouping

Operator name	Description
GroupBy	Groups elements that share a common attribute. Each group is represented by an IGrouping<TKey, TElement> object.
ToLookup	Inserts elements into a Lookup<TKey, TElement> (a one-to-many dictionary) based on a key selector function.

Set

Operator name	Description
Distinct	Removes duplicate values from a collection.
Except	Returns the set difference, which means the elements of one sequence that do not appear in a second sequence.
Intersect	Returns the set intersection, which means elements that appear in each of two sequences.
Union	Returns the set union, which means unique elements that appear in either of two sequences.

Conversion

Operator name	Description
AsEnumerable	Returns the input typed as IEnumerable<T>.
AsQueryable	Converts a (generic) IEnumerable to a (generic) IQueryable.
Cast	Casts the elements of a sequence to a specified type.
OfType	Selects values, depending on their ability to be cast to a specified type.
ToArray	Converts a collection to an array. This method forces query execution.
ToDictionary	Puts elements into a (one-to-one) Dictionary<TKey, TValue> based on a key selector function.
ToList	Converts a collection to a List<T>.
ToLookup	Inserts elements into a Lookup<TKey, TElement> (a one-to-many dictionary) based on a key selector function.

> **NOTE** By convention, the "ToXXX" operators cause the queries to execute. The "AsXXX" operators do not. This applies to the conversion operators, but should be respected for clarity for other operators as well, including custom ones.

Equality

Operator name	Description
SequenceEqual	Determines whether two sequences are equal by comparing elements in a pair-wise manner.

Element

Operator name	Description
ElementAt	Returns the element at a specified index in a sequence.
ElementAtOrDefault	Returns the element at a specified index in a sequence or default(T) if the index is out of range.
First	Returns the first element of a sequence, or the first element that satisfies a condition.
FirstOrDefault	Returns the first element of a sequence, or the first element that satisfies a condition. Returns default(T) if no such element exists.

Element *(continued)*

Operator name	Description
Last	Returns the last element of a sequence, or the last element that satisfies a condition.
LastOrDefault	Returns the last element of a sequence, or the last element that satisfies a condition. Returns default(T) if no such element exists.
Single	Returns the only element of a sequence, or the only element that satisfies a condition. Raises an InvalidOperationException if the sequence does not contain exactly one element.
SingleOrDefault	Returns the only element of a sequence, or the only element that satisfies a condition. Returns default(T) if no such element exists. Raises an InvalidOperationException if the sequence contains more than one element.

Generation

Operator name	Description
DefaultIfEmpty	Replaces an empty sequence with a default valued singleton sequence.
Empty	Returns an empty sequence.
Range	Generates a sequence of integral numbers within a specified range.
Repeat	Generates a sequence that contains one repeated value.

Quantifiers

Operator name	Description
All	Determines whether all the elements in a sequence satisfy a condition.
Any	Determines whether any elements in a sequence satisfy a condition.
Contains	Determines whether a sequence contains a specified element.

Aggregation

Operator name	Description
Aggregate	Performs a custom aggregation operation on the values of a sequence.
Average	Calculates the average value of a sequence of values.

Aggregation (continued)

Operator name	Description
Count	Counts the elements in a sequence, optionally only those elements that satisfy a predicate function.
LongCount	Counts the elements in a large sequence, optionally only those elements that satisfy a predicate function.
Max	Determines the maximum value in a sequence.
Min	Determines the minimum value in a sequence.
Sum	Calculates the sum of the values in a sequence.

NOTE In general, operators that return something other than an IEnumerable<T> will cause immediate query execution.

resources

LINQ in Action resources

LINQ in Action official site and blog
http://LinqInAction.net

Manning's home page for *LINQ in Action*
http://www.manning.com/marguerie

Microsoft resources

LINQ official web site
http://msdn2.microsoft.com/en-us/netframework/aa904594.aspx

MSDN Library LINQ documentation
http://msdn2.microsoft.com/en-us/library/bb397926(VS.90).aspx

101 LINQ samples
C#: http://msdn2.microsoft.com/en-us/vcsharp/aa336746.aspx
VB.NET: http://msdn2.microsoft.com/en-us/vbasic/bb688088.aspx
Visual Studio 2008 samples: http://msdn2.microsoft.com/en-us/bb330936.aspx

"LINQ to SQL: .NET Language-Integrated Query for Relational Data." By Dinesh Kulkarni,
Luca Bolognese, Matt Warren, Anders Hejlsberg, Kit George.
http://msdn2.microsoft.com/en-us/library/bb425822.aspx

C# 3.0 language specification
http://download.microsoft.com/download/3/8/8/388e7205-bc10-4226-b2a8-
75351c669b09/csharp%20language%20specification.doc
Also at <Program Files>\Microsoft Visual Studio 9.0\VC#\Specifications\1033 if you have
Visual Studio installed

MSDN C# Developer Center
http://msdn2.microsoft.com/en-us/vcsharp/

Visual Basic 9.0 language specification
http://www.microsoft.com/downloads/details.aspx?FamilyID=39de1dd0-f775-40bf-a191-
09f5a95ef500&displaylang=en

MSDN Visual Basic Developer Center
http://msdn2.microsoft.com/en-us/vbasic/

.NET 3.5 Runtime bootstrapper
http://go.microsoft.com/?linkid=7755937

Scott Guthrie
http://weblogs.asp.net/scottgu/archive/tags/LINQ/default.aspx

Matt Warren
LINQ (first in a series): http://blogs.msdn.com/mattwar/archive/tags/LINQ/default.aspx
IQueryable: http://blogs.msdn.com/mattwar/archive/2007/07/30/linq-building-an-iqueryable-provider-part-i.aspx

Rico Mariani
LINQ to SQL performance posts:
http://blogs.msdn.com/ricom/archive/2007/06/22/dlinq-linq-to-sql-performance-part-1.aspx

LINQ to SQL Debug Visualizer
http://weblogs.asp.net/scottgu/archive/2007/07/31/linq-to-sql-debug-visualizer.aspx

ADO.NET 3.5 Development Center (covers the ADO.NET Entity Framework)
http://msdn2.microsoft.com/en-us/data/aa937723.aspx

"Parallel LINQ: Running Queries On Multi-Core Processors." By Joe Duffy and Ed Essey.
http://msdn.microsoft.com/msdnmag/issues/07/10/PLINQ/

DryadLINQ web site
http://research.microsoft.com/research/sv/DryadLINQ/

Community resources

Official LINQ forum
http://forums.microsoft.com/MSDN/ShowForum.aspx?ForumID=123&SiteID=1

Hooked on LINQ
http://www.hookedonlinq.com

Charlie Calvert's links to LINQ wiki
http://blogs.msdn.com/charlie/archive/2006/10/05/Links-to-LINQ.aspx

Blogs

Roger Jennings
LINQ: http://oakleafblog.blogspot.com/search/label/LINQ
LINQ to SQL: http://oakleafblog.blogspot.com/search/label/DLinq
C# 3.0: http://oakleafblog.blogspot.com/search/label/C%23%203.0
VB 9.0: http://oakleafblog.blogspot.com/search/label/VB%209.0

David Hayden
LINQ: http://davidhayden.com/blog/dave/category/52.aspx
LINQ to SQL: http://davidhayden.com/blog/dave/category/59.aspx
C# 3.0: http://davidhayden.com/blog/dave/category/58.aspx

Bart de Smet
 LINQ: http://community.bartdesmet.net/blogs/bart/archive/tags/LINQ/default.aspx
 C# 3.0: http://community.bartdesmet.net/blogs/bart/archive/tags/C_2300_+3.0/
 default.aspx
 VB 9.0: http://community.bartdesmet.net/blogs/bart/archive/tags/VB+9.0/default.aspx

Others

"The entity-relationship model—toward a unified view of data." By Peter Chen.
 http://portal.acm.org/citation.cfm?id=320440

Tomas Petricek's articles about LINQ
 http://tomasp.net/blog/linq-expand.aspx
 http://tomasp.net/articles/linq-expand-update.aspx
 http://tomasp.net/blog/dynamic-linq-queries.aspx
 http://tomasp.net/articles/clinq-project.aspx
 http://tomasp.net/articles/dynamic-flinq.aspx

PredicateBuilder, dynamically building LINQ expression predicates
 http://www.albahari.com/expressions/

LINQPad, a LINQ tool that you can use to quickly try out LINQ expressions.
 http://www.albahari.com/linqpad.html

Community-driven LINQ providers
 See the resources at the end of chapter 13.

index

Symbols

=> token 59
?? 420
@ 366

A

abstract syntax tree 107
Access Key 367, 407
  ID 408
Action delegate types 61
Add 324, 331, 341–342
  content to XML 341
  See also InsertOnSubmit
Add method 53
AddAfterSelf 324, 342–343
AddBeforeSelf 324, 343
AddBooks.aspx.cs 510
AddFirst 324, 342–343
ADO.NET 10, 18
ADO.NET Entity Framework
    7, 440, 514
  See also LINQ to Entities
aggregate query operators 145
aggregating 398
Aggregation
  Average 222
  Count 221
  Max 222
  Min 222
  operators 97, 189
  Sum 222
All 227–228
  operator 101

alternate data formats 392
Amazon 351, 502–504
  importing from 502–504
Amazon e-commerce web
    services 406
Amazon web services 367
Amazon. *See* LINQ to Amazon
AncestorNodes 360
Ancestors 324, 354, 360
AncestorsAndSelf 324, 360
Annotation 324
anonymous
  iterators 45
  methods 45, 58
  structs 22
anonymous types 46, 73–78,
    165, 215, 316
  for grouping data 74
  keyed 78
  limitations 76–78
  parsing with 182
AnonymousTypes.csproj 76, 78
Any 227
  operator 101
APIs
  System.Diagnostics.Process.
    GetProcesses 46
  XmlDocument 30
  XmlReader 30
  XPathNavigator 30
  XslTransform 30
applying projections 372
architectures
  three-tier 487–488
ArrayList 162
  querying 162

Arrays 121
ascending order 372
ASP.NET 127–133
  creating web sites 127
ASP.NET pages 127–133
  creating with LINQ 128–129
AsParallel operators 514
assemblies
  System.Core.dll 67, 105, 109
  System.Data.Linq.dll 109
  System.Xml.Linq.dll 109
Association 227
  attribute 239, 243–244
  tool 304
AssociationAttribute
  DeleteOnNull 243
  DeleteRule 243
  IsForeignKey 243
  IsUnique 243
  Name 243
  OtherKey 226, 243
  Storage 243
  ThisKey 243
AST. *See* abstract syntax tree
Attach 264
Attribute 324, 354–355
  axis method 366
  axis property 366
attributes 347, 353
  mapping 239–244
  removing 347
Author 241
  class 117
  mapping 241
  property 183
AuthorUpdate 287

AuthorUser 302
auto-implemented
    properties 32, 51, 209, 226
AutoSync 240
    Always 240
    Default 240
    Never 240
    OnInsert 240
    OnUpdate 240
Average 222
    function 29
    operator 101
AWSAccessKeyId 408
AWSECommerceService 408
axis methods 351–366, 377, 389
    Ancestors 360
    Attribute 355
    Descendants 357–360
    Element 354, 356
    ElementsAfterSelf 362
    NodesAfterSelf 362
    NodesBeforeSelf 362

B

backward compatibility 20
Base Class
    code 304
    discriminator 303
BeginTransaction 277
benchmark 194
Bierman, Gavin 22
BinaryExpression 255–256
binding source 416
BindingSource 135
blank values 174
Book 208
    class 32, 117
    mapping 208
BookAuthor 244
BookCountForPublisher 284
Books
    operator 448
    Querying As Object 206
Boolean 13
bridge classes 376
building objects from
    XML 386–392
business logic
    custom 296–299

business logic layer 487–488
business logic tier. *See* logic layer
business object model 492
business tier
    improving 294–306

C

C precursors 21
C#
    extension methods in 65–67
    language extensions 5, 83–84
    new language features. *See*
        language enhancements
    query expression syntax 98
C# 3.0 389
CanBeNull 211, 240
Cartesian product 154
cast 372
Cast operator 101, 162
    query operator 162
change tracking 249, 259
ChangeConflictException
    271–272, 287
ChangeConflicts 275
    MemberConflicts 275
ChangeConflicts.ResolveAll 274
changes
    handling 268–278
    simultaneous 268–278
    submitting 260
    tracking 259
CheckRules 298
child axis property 363
child elements 389
child nodes 332, 390
children
    direct 357
    immediate 364
CiteSeer 511
class diagram 403
classes
    Author 117
    Book 32, 117
    bridge 376
    Contact 38
    DataSet 10, 109
    DataTable 10
    entity 38–39

Expression 176
    generic 162
ObjectDumper 47, 166
ProcessData 48
Publisher 117
Review 117
SampleData 393
SqlCommand 10
SqlConnection 10
SqlReader 10
Subject 117
System.Linq.Enumerable 68,
    86, 93, 109
TElement 170
TKey 170
XDocument 320
XElement 389
XmlReader 31
XmlWriter 31
code quality, impact on
    performance 10
code reuse 491
collection
    initializers 52–55
    iterating through 195
collections 125
    ArrayList 162
    in-memory 121–126
    nongeneric 162–164
    querying 162–164
    using 129–133, 135–136
collisions 457
    avoiding 458
    namespace collisions 458
Column 210
    mapping 240–243
column 401
Column attribute 239–243
    AutoSync 240
    CanBeNull 240, 242
    DbType 241
    Expression 241
    IsDbGenerated 241
    IsDiscriminator 241, 304
    IsPrimaryKey 210, 241–242
    IsVersion 241
    Name 210, 241
    Storage 241
    UpdateCheck 241, 243, 271
ColumnAttribute 110

combining
  extension methods 70
  relational and XML data 399
C-Omega. *See* C
comma-separated lists 380
comma-separated values. *See* CSV
common scenarios
  161–180, 386
compiled queries 294
CompiledQuery
  Compile 295
compile-time
  checking queries 21
  validation 15, 51
CompleteCode.csproj 80
compositional constructors 320
concatenation operator 97
Conceptual Schema Definition
  Language 308
conciseness versus
  performance 198
Concurrency 243
concurrency 234
  exceptions 272–276
  optimistic 269–272
  pessimistic 268
conditional queries 172–176
ConditionalQuery method 174
Configure Behavior 289
ConflictMode
  ContinueOnConflict 273–274
connection string 40
ConstantExpression 256
construction models
  imperative 318
constructors
  compositional 320
Contains 218
content parameter 342
context 353
context free XML creation 320
Context, GetTable 212
ContinueOnConflict 274
conversion operators 97
  query operators 143
Converter delegate type 61
converting
  text files into XML 428
  values 390

coroutines 88
  versus subroutines 88
Count operator 101, 168
  query operator 145
coupling, tight 386
coversion operators 191
CreateMethodCallQuery 293
CreateNavigator method 376
CreateReader 382
CreateWriter 382
creating
  custom query operators
    442–451
  extension methods 64–68
  XML 330–335, 381
  XML documents 338–341
  XML from databases 398–406
  XML from object
    graphs 392–398
criteria, grouping by 164–167
cross join 154, 224
CRUD 235–236, 278, 280–281,
    285, 289, 306, 488
  defined 241
CSDL. *See* Conceptual Schema
    Definition Language
CSV 178, 182
  file 430
  parsing 182
current element 364
CurrentValue 275
cursors. *See* iterators
custom business logic 296–299
custom operators 451–463
  Books 448
  IsExpensive 450
  LongSum 443
  Min 448
  Select 468
  TotalPrice 447
  Where 468
custom query operators 193,
    442–451, 509
custom sort 169–172
CustomImplementation.csproj
    455
CustomQueryOperators.cs
    447–450
CustomSort method 170

D

DAL. *See* data access layer
data
  disconnected 263–266
  grouping with anonymous
    types 74
  updating 233–236
data access layer 486–502
  creating with LINQ to
    SQL 492–495
  limitations 489
  LINQ to SQL as 489–491
  versus LINQ to SQL 488–495
  when to use 488–495
data access tier. *See* data access
    layer
data binding
  ASP.NET 127–133
  Windows Forms 133
data format 386
data integrity 419
data source 401
data sources
  dealing with multiple 20
  integrating within
    programs 15
data structures 389
.Data.Linq.Mapping. *See*
  mapping
database 398, 420
  accessing in .NET 10
  advanced capabilities
    278–294
  creating XML from 398–406
  extracting XML from 8
  normalization 13
  object-oriented 4
  reducing workload 490
  relational 4, 10, 13
  schema 401
  tables 400
  updating 386, 411–428
Database attribute 239
DatabaseValue 275
DataContext 39–42, 212, 257,
    424, 495
  Connection 277
  CreateDatabase 241
  ExecuteMethodCall 283
  ExecuteQuery 279

DataContext *(continued)*
  GetCommand 214
  Log 213
  setting up 212
  SubmitChanges 260
  using external XML
    mapping 245
DataContext.GetTable 40
DataGridView 135
DataGridViewCell 417
DataGridViewRow 417
DataGridViewRowCollection
  417
DataLoadOptions 232
  LoadWith 232
DataReader 11, 41
DataSet 109, 125, 440
  querying 164
DataSet class 10
DataTable class 10
DataTable, querying 164
DB_Linq 511
dbml 250–251
DbType 241
debugging 20
declarative 13, 29–30, 52
decoupling 492
default
  keyword 154
  namespace 369, 416
DefaultIfEmpty 224, 420, 422
  operator 420
  query operator 154
deferred evaluation. *See* deferred
  query execution
Deferred Execution 215
deferred execution
  229, 492–493
deferred query execution 89–93
DeferredLoadingEnabled 494
DeferredQueryExecution.csproj
  90
del.icio.us 351
delayed execution. *See* deferred
  query execution
delegate 56–58, 61, 454
  Action types 61
  Converter types 61
  MethodInvoker types 61
  Predicate types 61

delegates, Predicate types 61
Delete 235
DELETE FROM 235
DeleteOnNull 243
DeleteOnSubmit 235, 258
DeleteRule 243
DeleteT 288
Derived Class
  Code 303
  Discriminator 303
DescedantNodes 358
DescendantAndSelf 324
Descendants 324, 354, 357,
  359–360, 369, 416
  axis method 358, 374
  axis property 364
  query axis method 390
DescendantsAndSelf 358–359
descending 220, 373
  keyword 146
design patterns 180–186
  ForEach 184–186
  Functional Construction
    36, 181–184
  Gang of Four 180
  Visitor 470
design principles
  LINQ to XML 317–323
dictionaries 124
Dim keyword 50
  See also implicitly typed
    variable
direct children 357
DisableFormatting 348
disconnected 263–266
Discriminator Property 303
Distinct operator 101
  query operator 142
Distinct.csproj 142
Distinct.vbproj 143
distributed computing 514
DLinq 21
DLLs and LINQ 109
Document Object Model. *See*
  DOM
DOM 315–317
  See also XML Document
    Object Model
Domain Driven Design 361

domain model 492
domain-specific query
  operators 446–451
  nongeneric 459–461
DomainSpecificOperators.cs
  459
DotNet2.csproj 46
DotNet2Improved.csproj 48
Dryad 514
DryadLINQ 514
DTD 338
dynamic queries 167–178
  LINQ to SQL 177

E

ECS 408
EditedFormattedValue 417
EDM. *See* Entity Data Model
EF. *See* Entity Framework
Element 354
ElementAt 365
Elements 324, 354,
  356, 364, 389
  query axis method 389
elements 353
  current 364
  operators 97
  removing 343
ElementsAfterSelf 324, 362
ElementsBeforeSelf 324, 362
embedded expressions 396
embedding
  queries 403
  query expressions 401
  XML in code 393
encapsulating 386
encapsulation 14
EndsWith 218
entity 38–39
  life cycle 257–266
Entity Data Model 307
Entity Framework 308
  See also ADO.NET Entity
    Framework
EntitySet 226, 422
  Assign 244
EntitySpaces 513
equality operator 97

ErrorProvider 298
events, Selecting 499
exceptions
    InvalidCastException 163
    OverflowException 443
ExecuteMethodCall 282, 287
ExecuteQuery 279
executing standard query
        operators 455
execution
    deferred 89–93, 493
    immediate 92, 189–191
expanded name 320, 416
ExpensiveBooks 295
explicit
    cast operators 390
    dot notation 403, 451
    operator overloads 372
exporting XML 399
Expression 105, 176, 241
expression
    body 59
    hole 336, 396
    lambda 60
expression trees 6, 59, 104–109,
        177, 254–257, 454
    definition 105
    graphical representation 106
Expression.Constant 255
Expression.GreaterThan 255
Expression.Lambda 255
Expression.Parameter 255
Expression.Property 255
extensibility 6, 12, 20,
        438, 509–511
    LinqBooks 509–511
    mechanisms 438–442
    use cases 442
    what can be done with it 441
extension indexer 365
extension methods 46, 64, 73,
        86, 175, 316, 376, 383, 454
    in C# 65–67
    combining 70
    creating 64–68
    discoverability 71
    in VB.NET 67–68
    warnings 71–73
ExtensionMethods.csproj 65, 70
ExtensionMethods.vbproj 67

F

F# 8
factory 96
FCL 10
fetching, lazy 492
File class 430
filter 418
Filter. See Where
filtering 196, 370, 406–411
    with for loops 196
    with foreach loops 196
    operators 96
    with Where 370–372
Find method 58
First 361
    operator 192
first item 365
flat files 428
Flickr 351, 512
fnBookCountForPublisher 291
fnGetPublishersBooks 293
for loops, filtering with 196
ForEach design pattern
        184–186
foreach loops 87, 192
    filtering with 196
ForEach operator 184
    multiple statements 185
    and VB.NET 186
    with method syntax 185
    with query expressions 185
FormattedName 297
FormStrings.cs 134
from keyword 8
full expanded name 416
fully expanded XML name 333
Func delegate types 62
Function
    attribute 239
    keyword 60
functional construction 319,
        378, 396, 401, 403
Functional Construction design
        pattern 36, 181–184
functional language 8
FunctionAttribute 282
    IsComposable 291
functions
    Average 29
    Max 29

Min 29
Sum 29
user-defined 290–294
functor 58

G

Gang of Four 180
generate 401
generating RSS feeds 504
generation operators 97
generators. See iterators
generic
    classes 162
    interfaces 162
    types 45
GenericDictionary.csproj 124
GenericList.csproj 123
Genome 512
GetBook, stored procedure 281
GetCommand 214
GetEnumerator method 87
GetExpensiveBooks 296
GetHashCode 78
GetStringValue 345
GetTable 212
    See also DataContext.
        GetTable
GetXML.ashx.cs 505
Google
    Groups 512
    Image 512
GoogleDesktop 512
GridView 128, 134–135, 147,
        155, 497
group 220
    clause 165
    joins 151
    keyword 152
group…by query
        expression 374
GroupBy 372
GroupBy operator 101, 373
GroupBy standard query
        operator 373
grouping 27, 150, 199,
        219–221, 372–375
    join 420, 422
    by multiple criteria 164–167
    operators 97
    titles 166

Grouping.aspx.cs 150
GroupJoin 410
GroupJoin operator 101, 449, 462

H

hash code 78
Hejlsberg, Anders 22
HelloLinq.csproj 25
HelloLinq.vbproj 26
HelloLinqToSql.csproj 40
HelloLinqToXml.csproj 33
HelloLinqToXml.vbproj 34
HelloLinqWithGrouping-AndSorting.csproj 27
HelloLinqWithGrouping-AndSorting.vbproj 28
HelloLinqWithLiterals.vbproj 36
hierarchical XML document 428

I

IDataErrorInfo 297
Identity 241
identity management 258
IdType parameter 408
IEnumerable 86, 252, 366
IEnumerable of XElement 356
IEquatable 142
IExecuteResult 282
    ReturnValue 284
IFunctionResult 284
IGrouping 150, 374
immediate
    children 364
    execution 189–191
    query execution 92
immutability 77
impedance mismatch 13
imperative 5, 13, 30, 419
    construction 330
    construction model 318, 330
implementing
    IQueryable 479
    LINQ 439–441
    LINQ to Amazon 467–474

implicit
    conversion 332
    operator overloads 354
    overloads 325
implicitly typed variables 45, 49–51
    syntax 49–50
    versus traditional syntax 50
Import 413
importing 423, 428
    from Amazon 502–504
    namespaces 461
improving business tier 294–306
IMultipleResult 283
IMultipleResults
    GetResult 284
inheritance 14, 301–306
    and databases 13
Inheritance Default 303–304
Inheritance tool 303
InheritanceMapping 303–304
    attribute 239
initialization declarative 52
initializing objects 52
inline object initializer 416
in-memory collections 121–126
in-memory objects 389, 392
in-memory programming API 316
inner join 152, 224
innerKeySelector 223
Insert 235
INSERT INTO 235
InsertAllOnSubmit 424
InsertOnSubmit 235, 258, 264
InsertT 288
int 443
    limitations 443
    performance versus string 198
integrate data 428
integrating XML and relational data 406
integration 406
IntelliSense 18, 20, 30, 51, 66
    within Visual Studio 21
interchange 398
interfaces
    generic 162
    IQueryable 474–478

System.Collections.Generic.IEnumerable 162
System.Collections.Generic.List 162
into keyword 152, 166
InvalidCastException 163
IQueryable 108–109, 212, 252–254, 293, 366, 474–478, 493
    CreateQuery 253
    ElementType 252
    Execute 253
    Expression 252–253
    how it works 480
    implementation 479
    and LINQ to Amazon 474–481
    overview 477
    Provider 252
IQueryProvider 252, 478
    and LINQ to Amazon 474–481
    See also IQueryable
is Inheritance filtering 305
IsComposable 291
IsDbGenerated 241–242
IsDiscriminator 241
IsExpensive operator 450
IsForeignKey 243
ISingleResult 283
IsPrimaryKey 210, 241
IsUnique 243
IsVersion 241–242
<Item> 371
ItemAttributes 415
ItemId 408
ItemLookup service 406
iteration collections 195
Iterator.csproj 88
iterators 87–89
    anonymous 45

J

Join 223, 410
    Cross 224
    Inner 224
    operator 101, 410, 413, 419
    operators 96
    Outer 224

Join *(continued)*
    query operator 152
    in the where clause 222
join keyword 153, 167
joining 222–225, 407
    two sequences 410
    XML and relational data 411
    XML data 406
joins 151–155
    cross joins 154
    group joins 151
    inner joins 152
    left outer joins 153
Joins.aspx.cs 151, 153–155

K

key concepts, LINQ to XML 319
Key keyword 78
keyed anonymous types 78
keys 166
    composite 165
keywords 414
    descending 146
    Dim 10, 50
    from 8
    Function 60
    group 152
    into 153, 166
    join 167
    Key 78
    let 179
    orderby 8, 167, 169
    select 8
    this 65
    var 49
    where 8

L

lambda expressions 46, 55–64,
        316, 454
    compared to anonymous
        method 59
    expression body 59
    and expression trees 105
    parameters 60
    statement body 59
    syntax 59, 64

lambda operator 60
LambdaExpressions.csproj
        58, 62
LambdaExpressions.vbproj 63
language enhancements 45–49
language extensions 7–9, 83–84
    See also language
        enhancements
Language-INtegrated Query. *See*
        LINQ
large files 432
layers
    business logic layer 487
    data-access layer 487
    presentation layer 487
layout 251
lazy evaluation. *See* deferred
        query execution
lazy loading 226, 229–231, 492
    disabling 494
LDAP 512
left outer join 153, 420
let clause 416, 430
let keyword 179
lightweight XML programming
        API 317
LIKE 218
Lines operator 188
LINQ
    with ASP.NET 126–136
    classes 250
    consistency of syntax 6
    design goals 20–21
    DLLs and namespaces 109
    expressiveness 29
    extensibility 6, 12
        See also extensibility
    as extension of .NET 83–85
    flavors. *See* LINQ, providers
    foundation 85
    history 21–23
    implementing 439–441
    with in-memory
        collections 121–126
    integration with C# and
        VB.NET 8
    introduction 3
    as language extensions 7, 9
    language extensions 5
    motivation behind 5, 12

and .NET 2.0 runtime 24
    origins 19–23
    overview 5–6
    providers 6–7, 439–441, 511
    query expression pattern 439
    query expression syntax
        369, 375
    query expressions 401
    and Silverlight runtime 24
    the future 511–514
    as a toolset 6–7
    what is 4–9
    why 9–19
    with Windows Forms 126–136
LINQ to Amazon 463–474, 510
    implementation 467–474
    introduction 463
    requirements 465
    with IQueryable 474–481
LINQ to DataSet 6,
        440, 505–509
    LinqBooks 505–509
LINQ to Entities 6, 306, 309,
        440, 514
    See also ADO.NET Entity
        Framework
LINQ to LDAP 512
LINQ to NHibernate 512
LINQ to Objects 23–29, 116,
        314, 440, 509
    getting started 23–29
    Hello project 25–29
    LinqBooks 509
    overhead 195–198
    performance 186–200
    speed comparison 197
    supported operations 126
LINQ to SQL 19, 37–42,
        207–212, 398, 440, 495–502
    Association 250
    creating data-access layer
        with 492–495
    data-access layer 486, 489–502
    dynamic queries 177
    features 37
    getting started 37–42
    Hello example 38–42
    in multi-tier architecture 489
    LinqBooks 495–502
    mapping 491

LINQ to SQL *(continued)*
  Projecting with Select 214
  reading data 212–217
LINQ to SQL Designer
    42, 249–252
  Inheritance 251
LINQ to Text Files 178–180,
    189, 429
LINQ to XML 19, 29–37,
    313–314, 440, 502–505
  axis methods 352, 367
  class hierarchy 323
  design principles 317–323
  getting started 29–37
  Hello example 32–37
  key concepts 319
  LinqBooks 502–505
  queries 380
  Scenarios 385
  transformation 380
  versus LINQ to XSD 513
  why 30–32
LINQ to XSD 513
  versus LINQ to XML 513
LinqBooks 32, 103, 483–486
  data model 118, 486
  features 117, 483
  goals 116
  introduction 116–121
  object model 117
  overview 483–486
  sample data 118–121
  sample uses of LINQ to
    DataSet 505–509
  sample uses of LINQ to
    Objects 509
  sample uses of LINQ to
    SQL 495–502
  sample uses of LINQ to
    XML 502–505
  samples uses of LINQ's
    extensibility 509–511
  user interface 484–485
LinqBooks project
  Author class 117
  LinqBooks.CommonSample-
    Data.cs 119
  Publisher class 117
  Review class 117
  Subject class 117

LinqBooks.CommonSample-
    Data.cs 119
LinqDataSource 129, 498
LinqInAction.Extensibility 455
LinqInAction.LinqBooks.
    Common.dll 121, 130, 135
LinqInActionDataContext 410
Lisp 55
List 493
List type 47
List.FindAll method 197
lists 123
  comma-separated 380
  filtering 84
  generic 123
  sorting 84
ListView 129
literals. *See* XML literals
LLBLGen Pro 513
Load 324, 327, 354,
    389, 409, 414
loading
  immediate 231–233
  lazy 229–231
  when 229–233
loading XML 327
  data from a web service 407
LoadOptions 327
LoadOptions.Preserve-
    Whitespace 329
LoadWith 232
local names 320, 323, 416
local variables 168
Log 213
logic layer 487
logic tier. *See* logic layer
LongCount operator 101
LongSum operator 443
LongSum query operator 443
looping 184
loops 184
  foreach 192

M

Magennis, Troy 443
mapping 238–252, 418
  Association attribute 239
    See also Association attribute
  attributes 239–244

Column attribute. *See* Column
    attribute
ColumnAttribute 210
Database attribute 239
Function attribute 239
FunctionAttribute 282
InheritanceMapping
    attribute 239
InheritanceMappingAttribute
    304
Parameter attribute 239
ParameterAttribute 282–283
Provider attribute 239
ResultType attribute 239
stored procedures 251
Table attribute 239
TableAttribute. *See* Table-
    Attribute
  table-defined functions 251
  with LINQ to SQL 491
  XML 245–247
Mapping Schema Language 308
Mariani, Rico 201
matching keys 410
Max 222
  function 29
  operator 101, 191
  query operator 145, 191
MaxElement operator 193
Meijer, Erik 22
MemberConflicts 275
MetaLinq 512
method call syntax 370
MethodCallExpression 256
MethodInfo 283
MethodInfo.GetCurrentMethod
    283
MethodInvoker delegate
    types 61
methods
  Add 53, 324
  AddFirst 324
  Ancestors 360
  AncestorsAndSelf 324
  Annotation 324
  anonymous 45, 58
  Attributes 324, 355
  ConditionalQuery 174
  CustomSort 170

methods *(continued)*
  Descendants 324,
    357–360, 390
  DescendantsAndSelf 324
  Elements 324, 354,
    356, 389
  extension methods 46, 64–73,
    86, 175, 454
  Find 58
  GetEnumerator 87
  LINQ to XML axis
    methods 352–366
  List.FindAll 197
  Load 324, 389
  Nodes 324
  Parse 326
  ReadAllLines 179, 187
  Remove 324
  RemoveAll 324
  RemoveAttributes 324
  RemoveNodes 324
  ReplaceNodes 324
  Save 324
  Select 91
  SetAttributeValue 324
  SetElementValue 324
  Split 179
  Square 92
  TotalMemory 64
  utility methods 446
  WriteTo 324
Microsoft Research 8
Min 222
  function 29
Min operator 101
  custom implementation 448
  query operator 145
minPageCount variable 168
mismatch. *See* impedance mis-
    match; paradigm mismatch
mix and match data 432
mixing
  XML and databases 406–411
  XML and relational data 407
models
  business object model 492
  domain model 492
MSBuild 249
multiple data sources 411
MySql 511

N

Name 240–241, 243
names
  expanded 320
  local 320, 323
  qualified 320
  simplified 320–323
namespace 369, 416
  collisions 458
  imports 461
  prefixes 320–321, 333–334
namespaces 320, 333
  importing 461
  and LINQ 109
  System.Data.Linq.Mapping
    39
  System.Linq 24, 109
  System.Linq.Expressions
    105, 109
  System.Xml 16, 29
  System.Xml.Linq 24
native .NET types 372
nested queries 147, 183, 390
Nested.aspx 149
Nested.aspx.cs 148
.NET 2.0 24
.NET 2.0 CLR 20
.NET 2.0 runtime
  and LINQ 24
.NET 3.5 24
.NET Framework Class Library.
    See FCL
.NET Reflector 75, 89
.NET, as extended by LINQ
    83–85
.NET Framework 314
new keyword
  See anonymous types;
    collection, initializers;
    object initializers
NHibernate 16, 442, 512
Nodes 324
NodesAfterSelf 324, 362
NodesBeforeSelf 324, 362
NodeType 327
non-sequence query
  operators 461
NonSequenceOperator.cs 462
normalization 13
Northwind 38

n-tier architecture. *See* three-tier
    architecture
null coalescing operator 420

O

object graphs 146–159
  creating XML from 392–398
  translating 13
object hierarchies 226
object identity 258
object initializer syntax 389
object initializers 45, 52–55, 420
  need for 52–53
  syntax 54
object mapping 209–211
object models
  conceptual versus
    relational 15
object trees 226–229
ObjectDumper 47, 122, 391
  class 47, 166
ObjectDumper.Write 230
ObjectInitializer.csproj 55
object-oriented code
  overhead 10
object-oriented
  programming 17
object-relational mapping
    13–16
  custom LINQ providers 512
object-relational mapping tools
  limitations 11
  NHibernate 16
  support for compile-time
    validation 15
  using efficiently 15
objects 386
  building from XML 386–392
  initializing 52
  int 443
  mapping 209–211
  mapping to data 238–252
  StreamReader 187
  transforming with XSLT 382
ObjectSpaces 22
ObjectTrackingEnabled
    263, 266
OfType 305, 417
  extension method 417
  operator 164

OldSchoolHello.csproj 27
OldSchoolXml.csproj 35
OnChanged 299
OnChanging 299
OnCreated 299–300
one-to-many relationships 421
OOP. *See* object-oriented
        programming
OPath 22
OpenAccess 512
opening the file 430
Operation 408
operations supported 126
operator
    LongCount 101
    Min 101
    OrderBy 101
    OrderByDescending 101
operators
    aggregate operators 145
    aggregation 97, 189
    All 101
    Any 101
    AsParallel 514
    Average 101
    Books 448
    Cast 101
    concatenation 97
    conversion 97
    conversion operators 143
    Count 101, 168
    coversion 191
    custom 442–463, 509
    Distinct 101, 142
    domain-specific 459–461
    element 97
    equality 97
    explicit cast operators 390
    filtering 96
    First 192
    ForEach 184
    generation 97
    GroupBy 101
    grouping 97
    GroupJoin 101, 449, 462
    IsExpensive 450
    Join 96, 101
    lambda 60
    Lines 188
    LongSum 443
    Max 101, 191

MaxElement 193
Min 448
nongeneric 459–461
non-sequence 461
OfType 164
OrderBy 169, 372, 461
OrderByDescending 68–69
ordering 97
partitioning 96
projection 96
projection operators 139–142
quantifiers 97
restriction 370
Reverse 189–190
Select 101, 139, 190, 369
SelectMany 101, 140
set 97
Skip 101, 157
SkipWhile 101
standard query operators
        68–69, 366–375
Sum 69, 102, 443
Take 69, 102, 157
TakeWhile 102
ThenBy 102
ThenByDescending 102
ToList 66, 93
ToLookup 66
TotalPrice 447
tracing execution 455
utility operators 446–451
Where 94, 102, 138, 175, 190
See also query operators;
        standard query operators
optimistic concurrency 269–272
Oracle 511
Orcas 22, 24
orderby 219
    keyword 8, 146, 167, 169
    operator 373
OrderBy operator 101, 169,
        372, 461
    Descending 219
OrderByDescending 372
    operator 86, 101
    query operator 68–69, 171
ordering and grouping 372–375
ordering operators 97
OriginalValue 275
ORM. *See* object-relational
        mapping

OtherKey 227, 243–244
outer join 224
outerKeySelector 223
output format 380
OverflowException 443
overhead
    LINQ to Objects 195–198
    reducing 10
OverwriteCurrentValues 274

P

PageCount property 176
paging 155
Paging data 215
Paging.aspx.cs 156
paradigm mismatch 12–18
parallel computing 513
Parallel FX 513
Parallel LINQ. *See* PLINQ
Parameter attribute 239
parameterized queries
        168, 217, 280
parameters, loosely defined 11
params 332
Parent axis property 324
parse 326, 329, 429
parsing
    CSV 182
    imperative approach 183
    with anonymous types 182
    with existing types 182
    with Lines operator 188
    XML 329
partial classes 296
Partial methods 248
partial methods 248, 299–301
partitioning 155–159
    operators 96
Partitioning.aspx.cs 157
paste XML as LINQ 379–380,
        399, 402
PDC 22–23
performance 411
    and code quality 10
    and collections 195
    improving 490
    int versus string 198
    versus conciseness 198
    See also LINQ to Objects,
        performance

pessimistic concurrency 268
PFX. *See* Parallel FX
pipeline 71, 94
PLINQ 78, 201, 513
plumbing 10, 17
    code 492
POCO 489
Polyphonic C# 21
populating 389
PostgreSQL 511
predicate 372
Predicate delegate types 61
presentation layer 487–488
    database queries 491
presentation tier. *See* presenta-
    tion layer
preserve whitespace 327
PreserveWhitespace 327
ProcessData class 48
processes variable 47
processing 398
    instruction 338–339
programming API 393
programming languages
    general-purpose 5
    imperative 5, 13
programming models
    declarative 13, 30
    imperative 13, 30
programming styles
    declarative 52, 184
    imperative 318
    rapid application develop-
        ment (RAD) 489
programs, integrating data
    sources 15
projection 369
    operators 96
    query operators 139–142
projects 507
    AddBooks.aspx.cs 510
    AnonymousTypes.csproj
        76, 78
    CompleteCode.csproj 80
    CustomImplementation.
        csproj 455
    CustomQueryOperators.cs
        447–450
    DeferredQueryExecution.
        csproj 90
    Distinct.csproj 142

Distinct.vbproj 143
DomainSpecificOperators.cs
    459
DotNet2.csproj 46
DotNet2Improved.csproj 48
ExtensionMethods.csproj
    65, 70
ExtensionMethods.vbproj 67
FormStrings.cs 134
GenericDictionary.csproj 124
GenericList.csproj 123
GetXML.ashx.cs 505
Grouping.aspx.cs 150
HelloLinq.csproj 25
HelloLinq.vbproj 26
HelloLinqToSql.csproj 40
HelloLinqToXml.csproj 33
HelloLinqToXml.vbproj 34
HelloLinqWithGrouping-
    AndSorting.csproj 27
HelloLinqWithGrouping-
    AndSorting.vbproj 28
HelloLinqWithLiterals.vbproj
    36
Iterator.csproj 88
Joins.aspx.cs 151, 153–155
LambdaExpressions.csproj
    58, 62
LambdaExpressions.vbproj
    63
LinqBooks.CommonSample-
    Data.cs 119
Nested.aspx 149
Nested.aspx.cs 148
NonSequenceOperator.cs
    462
ObjectInitializer.csproj 55
OldSchoolHello.csproj 27
OldSchoolXml.csproj 35
Paging.aspx.cs 156
Partitioning.aspx.cs 157
QueryExpressionWith-
    Operators.csproj 103
SelectIndex.csproj 141
Sorting.aspx 146
Step1.aspx 128
Step1.aspx.cs 128
Step2a.aspx 130
Step2a.aspx.cs 131
Step2b.aspx 132
Step2b.aspx.cs 131

String.csproj 125
SumExtensions.cs 445
TypedArray.csproj 122
UntypedArray.csproj 121
UsingVar.csproj 50
XMLImportExport.aspx.cs
    507–508
properties
    Attribute axis property 366
    Authors 183
    auto-implemented 51, 209
    child axis property 363
    DeferredLoadingEnabled
        494
    Descendants axis
        property 364
    PageCount 176
    Title 176
Provider 252
    attribute 239
providers 439–441
    LINQ to DataSet 440
    LINQ to Entities 440
    LINQ to Objects 440
    LINQ to SQL 440
    LINQ to XML 440
providers. *See* LINQ, providers
Publisher 301
    class 117
Publisher.Books 498
PublisherUser 302

Q

qualified names 320
quantifier operators 97
queries 13
    compiled 294
    compile-time checking 21
    conditional 172, 176
    creating at run-time 176
    deferred execution 89–93
    dynamic 167–178
    immediate execution 92
    nested 147, 183
    parameterized 168
    presentation layer 491
    query expression
        pattern 453–455
    refining 217–225
    reusing 91

queries *(continued)*
  second-level 395
  translating 452
  what can be queried 121–126
query a web service 412
query expression 12, 390, 403,
    415, 419
  clause 370
  syntax 370, 451
query expression pattern
    451, 453–455
  and VB.NET 454
query expressions 6, 97–104,
    360, 389, 401, 403, 429
  collision 457
  definition 98
  limitations 102–104
  LINQ query expression
    pattern 439
  mapping to the standard
    query operators 100
  query expression pattern
    451, 453–455
  syntax 98–100, 451
  translating to SQL 252–257
  with ForEach operator 185
query languages, text-based 376
query operations with LINQ 5
query operators 6, 93–97,
    137–145
  Cast 162
  creating custom operators. *See*
    custom query operators
  custom 193, 509
  definition 93
  domain specific. *See* domain-
    specific query operators
  domain-specific 459–461
  GroupJoin 449
  LongSum 443
  nongeneric 459–461
  non-sequence 461
  OrderByDescending 86
  Select 86
  standard query operators 86
  Sum 443
  TotalPrice. *See* TotalPrice
    operator
  Where 86, 138
  See also standard query
    operators

query plan caching 218
query reuse 91
query syntax 98
  C# 98
  VB.NET 99
query translation 452
query variable 177
Query Visualizer 213
query XML data 375
QueryExpressionWithOperators
    .csproj 103
querying
  based on user input 173
  at compile-time 176
  custom data sources 442
  DataSet 164
  DataTable 164
  LINQ to XML 376
  nongeneric collections
    162–164
  objects 367
  presentation layer 491
  relational databases 401
  at run-time 176
  web services 442, 463–474
  what can be queried 121–126
  XML 377

R

RAD. *See* rapid application devel-
    opment
rapid application
    development 489
  limitations 491
RDF 512
ReadAllLines 179, 430
  method 187
reading data, LINQ to
    SQL 212–217
reducing
  database workloads 490
  network traffic 490
Refactoring 362
refining queries 217–225
Reflector. *See* .NET Reflector
RefreshMode 273
  KeepCurrentValues 273
  OverwriteCurrentValues 273
related data 403
relational algebra 17

relational data 398
relational databases 4, 10, 13,
    206, 398, 406
relationships 401, 403
Remove 324
  See also DeleteOnSubmit
RemoveAll 324
RemoveAttributes 324
RemoveNodes 324
removing attributes 347–348
removing content from
    XML 343
removing elements 343
replace an entire node 346
ReplaceNodes 324, 345
ReplaceWith 346
replacing XML 345
Request Parameters 408
request URL 409, 414
requirements 23–25
  software 24
ResponseGroup 408
REST 367, 407–408
  web service API 407
restriction operator 370
ResultType attribute 239
retrieve XML data from
    Amazon 407
ReturnValue 285
reusing code 491
Reverse 361
  operator 189–190
  query operator 189
Review class 117
routines 88
ROW_NUMBER 216
RowCount to test
    concurrency 270
RowVersion 271
rowversion 242
RSS 19, 117, 392, 484, 504
RSS feed 363, 392
  generating 504
running example. *See* LinqBooks
run-time, creating queries
    at 176

S

SampleData 393
Save 324, 348

SaveOptions 348
saving XML 348
SAX 316
Scalar functions 290
scenarios, common 161–180
schema 400
Schulte, Wolfram 22
second-level queries 395
Select 369
  all elements 389
  method 91
  operator 86, 101, 190,
    369, 468
  standard query operator 368
select clause 166, 389, 407
select keyword 8
Select query operator 139, 155
  with index 141
SelectIndex.csproj 141
selecting 411
Selecting event 499
SelectMany operator 101
SelectMany query operator
    140, 154–155
  with index 141
SendPropertyChanged 300
SendPropertyChanging 300
separation of concerns 488, 491
sequences 85–93, 352, 369
  sorting 372
servers, improving
    performance 490
Service 408
set operations with LINQ 5
set operators 97
SetAttributeValue 324, 347
SetBaseUri 327
SetElementValue 324, 343–344
SetLineInfo 327
SharePoint 512
Silverlight runtime and
    LINQ 24
simplified names 320–323
single dot 365
Skeet, Jon 191
Skip 215
  operator 101
  query operator 157
SkipWhile operator 101
Slinq 512

SOAP 367, 407–408
software requirements 24
sort 372
sorting 27, 146, 219–221
  ascending order 372
  custom sort 169–172
  descending order 373
  keys 165
  sequences 372
Sorting.aspx 146
Split 430
  method 179
SQL
  dialects 11
  pass-through 278–280
  queries 13
  translating to query
    expressions 252–257
SQL injection 279
SQL injection attack
  avoiding 218
SQL pass-through 278–280
SQL Server 206
  with LINQ to SQL 206
SQL. See LINQ to SQL
SqlCommand class 10
SqlConnection class 10
SqlExpress 247
SqlMetal 247–249, 401, 403
  code 247
  language 247
  mapping stored
    procedures 248
  Namespace 247
SqlMethods 218
  Like 218
SqlReader class 10
SQLXML 4.0 18
Square method 92
SSDL. See Store Schema Defini-
    tion Language
standard query operators
    68–69, 86, 96–97, 137–145,
    314, 352, 360, 366–375, 377
  aggregate. See aggregate query
    operators
  Cast. See Cast operator
  compared to query
    expressions 100

conversion. See conversion
    operators
  Count. See Count operator
  custom
    implementations 451–463
  DefaultIfEmpty. See Default-
    IfEmpty, query operator
  Distinct. See Distinct operator
  ForEach. See ForEach
    operator
  improvements 443
  Join. See Join, query operator
  Lines. See Lines operator
  Max. See Max, operator; Max,
    query operator
  MaxElement. See Max-
    Element operator
  Min. See Min, query operator
  OfType. See OfType, operator
  OrderBy. See OrderBy
    operator
  OrderByDescending. See
    OrderByDescending,
    query operator
  projection. See projection,
    query operators
  Reverse. See Reverse, operator
  Select. See Select
  SelectMany. See SelectMany
    operator
  Skip. See Skip, query operator
  Sum. See Sum, query operator
  Take. See Take, query operator
  ToArray. See ToArray, query
    operator
  ToDictionary. See ToDic-
    tionary, query operator
  ToList. See ToList, query
    operator
  tracing execution 455
  Where. See Where operator
StartsWith 218
statement body 59
statement lambda 60
  and VB.NET 186
statements, yield return 87
Step1.aspx 128
Step1.aspx.cs 128
Step2a.aspx 130
Step2a.aspx.cs 131

Step2b.aspx 132
Step2b.aspx.cs 131
Storage 241–243
Store Schema Definition
  Language 308
stored procedures 280–290
  reading data 281–285
  updating data 285–290
storing 398
stream type 22
streaming 187–189, 432, 512
  API 315
StreamReader object 187
String.csproj 125
String.Format 279
String.Join 361
strings 125
  length in databases 13
strongly typed 6, 18, 20–21,
  38, 40
stub code 403
Subject 222
  class 117
SubmitChanges 234, 260,
  270, 424
  ChangeConflictException
  273
  Updating 234
submitting changes 260
subroutines 88
  versus coroutines 88
SubscriptionId 408
Sum 222
  function 29
  operator 102, 443
  query operator 69, 145
SumExtensions.cs 445
SyncLINQ 512
syntactic sugar 7
syntax
  consistency 6
  explicit dot notation 451
  method syntax 451
  query expression syntax 451
System.Collections.Generic.IEn
  umerable 162
System.Collections.Generic.List
  162
System.Core.dll 62, 67–68,
  105, 109

System.Data.DataSetExtensions.
  dll 109
System.Data.Linq 39, 209
System.Data.Linq.Compiled-
  Query 295
System.Data.Linq.DataLoad-
  Options 232
System.Data.Linq.dll 109
System.Data.Linq.EntitySet 226
System.Data.Linq.Mapping 39
  See also Mapping
System.Data.Linq.Table. *See*
  Table
System.Diagnostics.Process.Get-
  Processes 46
System.Linq 24, 109, 129, 452
System.Linq.Enumerable 68,
  86, 93–94, 109, 126
System.Linq.Expressions
  105, 109
System.Linq.IQueryable 212
System.Runtime.Compiler-
  Services.Extension 67
System.Transactions 277
System.Xml 16, 18, 29–30
System.Xml.Linq 24
System.Xml.Linq.dll 109
System.Xml.XmlReader 414
System.Xml.XPath 376
System.Xml.Xsl 382

T

Table 210, 212
  attribute 239
  mapping 240
TableAttribute 240
  Name 240
Table-valued functions 290
<Tag> 368
Tag Lookup service 367, 369
<TaggedItems> 368
Take 215
  operator 102
  query operator 69, 157
TakeWhile operator 102
TElement class 170
template 380
text files, transforming into
  XML 428–432

text-based query language 376
ThenBy operator 102
ThenByDescending
  operator 102
this keyword 65
ThisKey 243–244
three-tier architecture 487–488
  and LINQ to SQL 489
tiers. *See* layers
tight coupling 386
TimeStamp 264, 271
timestamp 241–242
<Title> 369
Title property 176
TKey class 170
ToArray 231
  query operator 143
ToDictionary 231
  query operator 144
tokens => 59
ToList 231
  operator 66, 93
  query operator 143, 156
ToLookup 231
  operator 66
tools
  NHibernate 16
  object-relational mapping 15
  SqlMetal 247–249
TotalMemory sample helper
  method 64
TotalPrice operator 447
tracking changes 259
traditional code
  drawbacks 10
transactions 276–278
TransactionScope 277
  Complete 278
transformation 387
  technology 381
transforming
  LINQ to XML objects with
    XSLT 382
  text files into XML 428–432
  with XSLT 382
  XML 377–378, 380–383,
    387, 389
translating 13
  queries 452
  SQL to query
    expressions 252–257

traverse 357
triple-dot notation 365
tuple 22
type safety. *See* strongly typed
type, List 47
TypedArray.csproj 122
types
    anonymous 46, 73–78, 165
    generic 45, 454
    without names 74
typing, strong 6, 18

U

UnaryExpression 256
unit of work 234, 263
Unix pipes 71
UntypedArray.csproj 121
Update 234
UpdateAuthor 288
UpdateCheck 241, 243, 265
    Always 241, 271
    Never 241, 243, 271
    WhenChanged 241, 271
UpdateT 288
updating
    data 233–236
    databases 386, 411–428
updating XML content 344
Use Runtime 290
User 301
user friendly XML API 406
user input, querying 173
user interfaces
    LinqBooks 484–485
UserBase 302
user-defined functions 290–294
UserType 301
UsingVar.csproj 50
utility methods 446
utility query operators 446–451

V

validation, compile-time 15
Value extension 365
Value property 343
values
    blank 174
    converting 390
Vanatec 512

var keyword 49
    See also implicitly typed
        variables
variables
    grouping 166
    implicitly typed 45, 49–51
    local 168
    minPageCount 168
    processes 47
    query 177
VB.NET
    extension methods in 67–68
    and ForEach operator 186
    language extensions 5, 83–84
    new language features. *See*
    language enhancements
    query syntax 99
    and statement lambdas 186
view 307
views, creating on object
        graphs 146–159
Visitor design pattern 470
Visual Basic 335, 363, 392
Visual Basic XML axis
        properties 363
Visual Studio 24, 126
    and IntelliSense 21
Visual Studio .NET Add-in 379
Visual Studio 2008 399
Visual Studio Add-In 399

W

W3C Information Set 317
Warren, Matt 479
web applications. *See* ASP.NET
web request 414
web services 367
    querying 442, 463–474
    See also LINQ to Amazon
Where 361, 370
    filtering with LINQ to
        SQL 217–219
where clause 168
    predicate 372
where keyword 8
Where operator 86, 94, 102,
        175, 190, 468
    filtering with 370–372
where query expression
    clause 371

Where query operator 138
White, Eric 178, 187
Windows applications. *See*
        Windows Forms
Windows Forms 133, 413
    creating 133
    creating with LINQ 134–135
Windows Presentation
        Foundation 370
WinFS 22
WMI 511
WmiLinq 511
WriteTo 324

X

X# 21
XAttribute 324, 347, 366, 372
XCData 326
XComment 325, 341, 358
XContainer 324, 345
XDeclaration 325, 339
XDocument 320, 325, 328,
        338, 382
XDocumentType 325, 340
XElement 324, 330, 354, 372,
        389, 414
Xen 21
XHTML 378, 381
XLinq 21
XML
    adding content to 341
    alternate formats 389
    building objects from
        386–392
    context-free creation 320
    creating 330, 335, 381
    creating from databases
        398–406
    creating from object
        graphs 392–398
    documents 319
    DOM. *See* XML DOM
    embedding in code 393
    extracting from databases 8
    loading 327
    mapping 245–247
    mapping to objects 16–18
    mixing with databases
        406–411
    names. *See* XML names

XML *(continued)*
  namespaces. *See* XML
    namespaces
  parsing 329
  pervasiveness 17
  programming APIs 316
  querying 377, 386
  reading 411–428
  removing content from 343
  saving 348
  transforming 377–383,
    386–387, 389
  transforming text files
    into 428–432
  ubiquity 30
  updating content 344
XML API 314, 316
  user-friendly 406
XML comments 328
XML declaration 338–339
XML declarations 328
XML Document Object
  Model 30
XML document type
  definition 328, 340
XML documents 319
  creating 338–341
XML DOM 316, 319
  See XML Document Object
    Model
XML element 354, 430

XML feed 395
XML formats 389
XML literals 36, 335, 363, 393
XML names 320
XML namespace 320–321, 334
XML processing
  instructions 328, 339
XML programming APIs
  316, 386
  lightweight 317
XML query axis methods 342
XML representation 398
XML syntax 392, 396
XML trees 401
XML web services 351
XML. *See* LINQ to XML
XmlDocument API 30
XMLImportExport.aspx.cs
  507–508
XmlMapping 245
  Association 246
  Column 246
  Database 246
  Member 245
  Table 246
  Type 245
XmlMappingSource 246
XMLNamespaceManager 322
XmlNode 315
XmlReader 31, 315, 327, 382
XmlReader API 30

XmlTextReader 315
XmlTextWriter 348
XmlWriter 31, 348, 382
XName 320, 322–323, 325,
  332, 354
XNamespace 323, 325, 333,
  369, 416
XNamespace.Xmlns 334
XNode 324, 358, 376
XObject 324
XPath 5, 12, 29, 316, 373, 376
  expressions 376
  queries 376–377
XPathEvaluate 376
XPathNavigator 315, 376
  API 30
XPathSelectElement 376
XProcessingInstruction 326,
  339, 358
XQuery 20, 22, 316
XSD. *See* LINQ to XSD
XSL 382
XslCompiledTransform 382
XSLT 29, 316, 381–382
XslTransform API 30
XStreamingElement 326
XText 326

Y

yield return 87

C# in Depth
  by Jon Skeet
  ISBN: 1-933988-36-3
  500 pages
  $44.99
  April 2008

C##/CLI in Practice
  by Nishant Sivakumar
  ISBN: 1-932394-81-8
  416 pages
  $49.99
  April 2007

For ordering information go to www.manning.com

MORE TITLES FROM MANNING

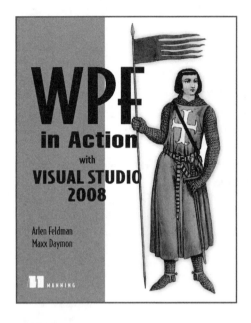

WPF in Action
with Visual Studio 2008

> by Alan Feldman
>   and Maxx Daymon
> ISBN: 1-933988-22-3
> 525 pages
> $44.99
> May 2008

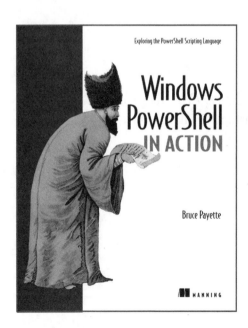

Windows PowerShell in Action
>   by Bruce Payette
> ISBN: 1-932394-90-7
> 576 pages
> $44.99
> February 2007

For ordering information go to www.manning.com

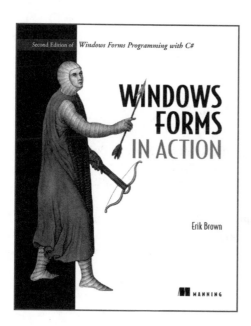